AFRICAN HISTORICAL DICTIONARIES
Edited by Jon Woronoff

1. *Cameroon,* by Victor T. LeVine and Roger P. Nye. 1974. *Out of print. See No. 48.*
2. *The Congo,* 2nd ed., by Virginia Thompson and Richard Adloff. 1984. *Out of print. See No. 69.*
3. *Swaziland,* by John J. Grotpeter. 1975.
4. *The Gambia,* 2nd ed., by Harry A. Gailey. 1987.
5. *Botswana,* by Richard P. Stevens. 1975. *Out of print. See No. 70.*
6. *Somalia,* by Margaret F. Castagno. 1975.
7. *Benin [Dahomey],* 2nd ed., by Samuel Decalo. 1987. *Out of print. See No. 61.*
8. *Burundi,* by Warren Weinstein. 1976.
9. *Togo,* 3rd ed., by Samuel Decalo. 1996.
10. *Lesotho,* by Gordon Haliburton. 1977.
11. *Mali,* 3rd ed., by Pascal James Imperato. 1996.
12. *Sierra Leone,* by Cyril Patrick Foray. 1977.
13. *Chad,* 2nd ed., by Samuel Decalo. 1987.
14. *Upper Volta,* by Daniel Miles McFarland. 1978.
15. *Tanzania,* by Laura S. Kurtz. 1978.
16. *Guinea,* 3rd ed., by Thomas O'Toole with Ibrahima Bah-Lalya. 1995.
17. *Sudan,* by John Voll. 1978. *Out of print. See No. 53.*
18. *Rhodesia/Zimbabwe,* by R. Kent Rasmussen. 1979. *Out of print. See No. 46.*
19. *Zambia,* by John J. Grotpeter. 1979.
20. *Niger,* 3rd ed., by Samuel Decalo. 1996.
21. *Equatorial Guinea,* 2nd ed., by Max Liniger-Goumaz. 1988.
22. *Guinea-Bissau,* 2nd ed., by Richard Lobban and Joshua Forrest. 1988.
23. *Senegal,* by Lucie G. Colvin. 1981. *Out of print. See No. 65.*
24. *Morocco,* by William Spencer. 1980. *Out of print. See No. 71.*
25. *Malawi,* by Cynthia A. Crosby. 1980. *Out of print. See No. 54.*
26. *Angola,* by Phyllis Martin. 1980. *Out of print. See No. 52.*
27. *The Central African Republic,* by Pierre Kalck. 1980. *Out of print. See No. 51.*
28. *Algeria,* by Alf Andrew Heggoy. 1981. *Out of print. See No. 66.*
29. *Kenya,* by Bethwell A. Ogot. 1981.
30. *Gabon,* by David E. Gardinier. 1981. *Out of print. See No. 58.*
31. *Mauritania,* by Alfred G. Gerteiny. 1981. *Out of print. See No. 68.*

63. *Ghana,* 2nd ed., by David Owusu-Ansah and Daniel Miles McFarland. 1995.
64. *Uganda,* by M. Louise Pirouet. 1995.
65. *Senegal,* 2nd ed., by Andrew F. Clark and Lucie Colvin Phillips. 1994.
66. *Algeria,* 2nd ed., by Phillip Chiviges Naylor and Alf Andrew Heggoy. 1994.
67. *Egypt,* 2nd ed., by Arthur Goldschmidt, Jr. 1994.
68. *Mauritania,* 2nd ed., by Anthony G. Pazzanita. 1996.
69. *Congo,* 3rd ed., by Samuel Decalo, Virginia Thompson, and Richard Adloff. 1996.
70. *Botswana,* 3rd ed., by Jeff Ramsay, Barry Morton, and Fred Morton. 1996.
71. *Morocco,* 2nd ed., by Thomas K. Park. 1996.

Historical Dictionary of Mauritania

Second Edition

by
Anthony G. Pazzanita

African Historical Dictionaries, No. 68

The Scarecrow Press, Inc.
Lanham, Md., & London

SCARECROW PRESS, INC.

Published in the United States of America
by Scarecrow Press, Inc.
4720 Boston Way
Lanham, Maryland 20706

4 Pleydell Gardens, Folkestone
Kent CT20 2DN, England

Copyright © 1996 by Anthony G. Pazzanita

British Cataloguing-in-Publication Information Available

Library of Congress Cataloging-in-Publication Data

Pazzanita, Anthony G., 1959–   .
Historical dictionary of Mauritania, second edition / by Anthony G. Pazzanita.
p.   cm. — (African historical dictionaries ; no. 68)
Includes bibliographical references.
1. Mauritania — History — Dictionaries.   I. Title.   II. Series.
DT554.15.P39   1996   96601'003 — dc20   95-40674   CIP

ISBN 0-8108-3095-7 (cloth : alk. paper)

♾ ™The paper used in this publication meets the minimum requirements of
American National Standard for Information Sciences — Permanence
of Paper for Printed Library Materials, ANSI Z39.48–1984.
Manufactured in the United States of America.

To my mother and father

Contents

Maps

Editor's Foreword

With its many straight-line borders, it is fairly obvious that Mauritania was carved out of Africa by the colonial powers with little concern for any geographic, historic, ethnic, economic, or other logic. Thus, it is not surprising that it should be difficult to govern and develop the new state, let alone to create a sense of nationhood. These difficulties have been shown by periodic bouts of political instability, recurrent friction among ethnic groups, and an economy that has gone from bad to worse as the poorer portion of the country—the Sahel—encroaches upon the richer areas of the southwest. The best that can be said (yet this is not little) is that Mauritania has managed to hold together and largely avoid the temptation of external adventures.

Still, as a country twice the size of France, even with a small population of some two million, Mauritania cannot be ignored in the overall African context, for it is one of the crucial links between North and sub-Saharan Africa and what happens in Mauritania could be reflected elsewhere. To understand its position and its somewhat less than enviable role, it is necessary to look back to earlier, occasionally more glorious times of kingdom and empire. From there its history can better be traced through the colonial period and into the era of independence. This is done, carefully and comprehensibly, with a multitude of entries on significant persons, places, and events and others explaining the ethnic, social, and economic situation in Mauritania. The trends are broadly reflected in the chronology and analyzed in an introduction. Further information can be sought by turning to the bibliography.

What makes this *Historical Dictionary of Mauritania* particularly important is not only that it is a completely new edition but also that it is one of terribly few books on the country to appear of late. It is written by Anthony G. Pazzanita, one of the rare specialists on this corner of Africa, which he has been studying and writing on for well over a decade. Aside from articles in learned journals, he has recently expanded and updated the *Historical Dictionary of Western Sahara* in this series. Both of these volumes are essential sources on a region that is too little known to the general public.

Jon Woronoff
Series Editor

Preface

Sparsely populated and occupying a position at the extreme western edge of the Arab world where the North African civilization of the Maghreb gives way to black West African culture, Mauritania's characteristics, history, and present situation are often only dimly perceived in Western countries, as media coverage in English is scarce and wide-ranging published books and articles almost equally so. The present book is an attempt to fill part of that gap and provide a survey of several centuries of Mauritanian history, with a strong emphasis on events since the end of the Second World War. During the last half century, Mauritania peacefully achieved independence from France, slowly began to build an identity as a separate and autonomous nation, and underwent numerous hardships and a period of governance by its armed forces before embarking in 1991 on a process of democratization, of which only the broad contours can as yet be fully appreciated by outsiders.

Although the primary focus on this dictionary is on the history and politics of modern Mauritania, I have endeavored to provide enough geographical, economic, cultural, and other data to place recent events in some sort of long-term perspective, difficult as that may be in the case of an ancient society with a lengthy oral, as opposed to written, tradition.

I would like to thank Dr. Mohamed Fall Ould Ainina, the former Mauritanian ambassador to the United States, for his time, insights, and receptivity to my questions as I wrote this book. In addition, thanks are due to Mohamed Said Ould Hamody, scholar and former ambassador of Mauritania to the United Nations, for his helpfulness and efficiency in illuminating many of the personalities and other aspects of his country. I also wish to express my deep gratitude to the Rector of the University of Nouakchott, Dr. Mohamed El-Hacen Ould Lebatt, the secretary-general of the University, Dr. Mohamed Yehdih Ould Tolba, and the head of the University's English Department, Professor Ahmed Said Ould Bah, for making my visit to Mauritania in May 1995 possible and for their hospitality and generosity. I alone, of course, bear full responsibility for any errors of fact or interpretation contained in this volume.

Anthony G. Pazzanita
April 1996

User's Notes

In this dictionary, Mauritanians are listed under their first names rather than under their last, or family names, as this is the normal practice in Mauritania itself. Thus, for example, Mohammed Khouna Ould Heydallah appears under the letter "M," not under the letter "H." Also, the words *ould* and *mint* in Mauritanian names denote son and daughter, respectively.

The transliteration of personal and place names from the Arabic (and sometimes from the French) to English presents certain problems, particularly since there are no universally accepted standards for transliteration from Arabic. Overall, the present writer has attempted to find a consensus of usages and spellings in the English language literature for the purposes of this book, although a few variations and anglicized spellings are apparent. In addition, Arabic definite articles ("al-," "el-") are included as part of the title of a particular entry in relation to their place in the alphabet. When alternative names for persons, places, or things are found, the most common alternate usages are set forth, followed by instructions to refer to the current or most common name or word. Thus, Port-Etienne is listed with directions to see the entry for Nouadhibou, the name given to the city after Mauritania's independence.

Distances and measurements in this book are given in the metric system, as this is the customary usage in the Islamic Republic of Mauritania. To aid readers in the conversion of metric units to English ones, the following equivalents are given:

  1 kilometer equals 0.6214 miles (3,280 feet, 10 inches);
  1 meter equals 39.37 inches (1.1 yards);
  1 centimeter (10 millimeters) equals 0.3937 inches;
  1 hectare equals 2.471 acres.

In order to facilitate the location of information, extensive cross-references have been provided. Within individual entries, the names of other entries, where first mentioned, are followed by the signal "q.v." (plural, qq.v.).

Abbreviations and Acronyms

AAU	Arab African Union
ABSP	Arab Baath Socialist Party
ADB	African Development Bank
AJM	Association de la Jeunesse Mauritanienne
ALMAP	Société Algéro-Mauritanienne des Pêches
AMD	Alliance pour une Mauritanie Démocratique
AOF	Afrique Occidentale Française
ARABSAT	Arab Satellite Telecommunications Organization
BALM	Banque Arabe Libyenne-Mauritanienne pour le Commerce Extérieur et le Développement
BAMIS	Banque al-Baraka Mauritanienne Islamique
BCM	Banque Centrale de Mauritanie
BDG	Bloc Démocratique du Gorgol
BED	Bureau d'Etudes et de la Documentation
BIMA	Banque Internationale pour la Mauritanie
BMCI	Banque Mauritanienne pour le Commerce International
BMD	Banque Mauritanienne de Développement
BNM	Banque Nationale de Mauritanie
BPN	Bureau Politique National
BRGM	Bureau des Recherches Géologiques et Minières
c.	*circa* (about)
CFA	Communauté Financière Africaine
CGEM	Confédération Générale des Employeurs de Mauritanie
CGTM	Confédération Générale des Travailleurs de Mauritanie
CMRN	Comité Militaire de Redressement National
CMSN	Comité Militaire de Salut National
CNAN	Compagnie Nationale Algérienne de Navigation
COMACOP	Compagnie Mauritano-Coréenne de Pêche
COMAUNAM	Compagnie Mauritanienne de Navigation Maritime
COMINOR	Comptoir Minier du Nord
CSA	Commissariat à la Sécurité Alimentaire

DED	Direction d'Etudes et de la Documentation
DNE	Direction Nationale d'Elevage
ECOWAS	Economic Community of West African States
EEZ	Exclusive Economic Zone
EMIA	Ecole Militaire Interarmes d'Atar
ENA	Ecole Nationale d'Administration
ENFVR	Ecole Nationale de Formation et Vulgarisation Rurale
FAR	Forces Armées Royales
FDUC	Front Démocratique Uni des Forces du Changement
FLAM	Forces de Libération Africaine de Mauritanie
FNLM	Front National de Libération Mauritanien
FRUIDEM	Front de la Résistance pour l'Unité, l'Independance et la Démocratie en Mauritanie
FURAM	Front Uni pour la Résistance Armée en Mauritanie
GDP	Gross Domestic Product
ICJ	International Court of Justice
IMF	International Monetary Fund
INTELSAT	International Telecommunications Satellite Organization
MAUSOV	Mauritanienne-Soviétique des Ressources Maritimes
MDI	Mouvement des Démocrates Indépendants
MICUMA	Société des Mines de Cuivre de Mauritanie
MIFERMA	Société Anonyme des Mines de Fer de Mauritanie
MND	Mouvement National Démocratique
MNF	Mouvement National Féminin
MORAK	Mines d'Or d'Akjoujt
NADHA	An-Nadha al-Wataniyya al-Mauritaniya
NAFTAL	Entreprise Nationale de Raffinage et de Distribution des Produits Pétroliers
OAU	Organization of African Unity
OMVS	Organisation pour la Mise en Valeur du Fleuve Sénégal
ONM	Organisation des Nationalistes Mauritaniens
ORTM	Office de Radiodiffusion et Télévision de Mauritanie
PAGN	Patri de l'Avant Garde Nationale
PKM	Parti des Khadihines de Mauritanie
pl.	plural
PMR	Parti Mauritanien pour Renouveau
Polisario Front	Frente Popular para la Liberación de Saguia el-Hamra y Río de Oro
PPM	Parti du Peuple Mauritanien

PRDS	Parti Républicain, Démocratique et Social
PRM	Parti de Regroupement Mauritanien
q.v.	*quod vide* (which see)
RDU	Rassemblement pour la Démocratie et l'Unité
RENAM	Rassemblement pour la Renaissance des Négro-Africains de Mauritanie
SADR	Saharan/Saharawi Arab Democratic Republic
SALIMAUREM	Société Arabe Libyenne-Mauritanienne des Ressources Maritimes
SAMIA	Société Arabe des Industries Métallurgiques Mauritano-Koweitienne
SAMIN	Société Arabe des Mines d'Inchiri
SAMIP	Société Arabe Mauritano-Irakienne de Pêche
SEM	Structures pour l'Education des Masses
SFIO	Section Française de l'Internationale le Ouvrière
SIMAR	Société Industrielle Mauritano-Roumaine de Pêche
sing.	singular
SMAR	Société Mauritanienne d'Assurances et de Réassurances
SMB	Société Mauritanienne de Banque
SMCP	Société Mauritanienne de Commercialisation du Poisson
SMCPP	Société Mauritanienne de Commercialisation des Produits Pétroliers
SNIM-SEM	Société Nationale Industrielle et Minière et Société d'Economie Mixte
SOCOGIM	Société de Construction et de Gestion Immobilière de Mauritanie
SOCUMA	Société de Cuivre de la Mauritanie
SOFRIMA	Société des Frigorifiques Mauritaniens
SOMECOB	Société Mauritanienne de la Commercialisation de Bétail
SOMIMA	Société Minière de Mauritanie
SONADER	Société Nationale pour le Développement Rural
SONELEC	Société Nationale d'Eau et d'Electricité
SONIMEX	Société Nationale d'Importation et d'Exportation
UBD	Union des Banques de Développement
UFD–Ere Nouvelle	Union des Forces Démocratiques—Ere Nouvelle
UM	Mauritanian ouguiya
UMA	Union du Maghreb Arabe
UMOA	Union Monétaire Ouest-Africaine
UN	United Nations
UNESCO	United Nations Educational, Scientific, and Cultural Organization

UNFM	Union Nationale des Femmes Mauritaniennes
UNHCR	United Nations High Commission for Refugees
UNM	Union Nationale Mauritanienne
UOVF	Union des Originaires de la Vallée du Fleuve
UPD	Union pour le Progrès et la Démocratie
UPM	Union Progressiste Mauritanienne
UPSD	Union Populaire Socialiste et Démocratique
USMM	Union Socialiste des Musulmans Mauritaniens
UTM	Union des Travailleurs Mauritaniens
VCT	Vivres Contre Travail

Chronology

Headings of dictionary entries are set forth in capital letters the first time they appear.

c. 5000 B.C.	Neolithic period; Bafour people believed to be predominant
c. 2500 B.C.	Initial onset of DESERTIFICATION in Mauritania; savannas and grasslands give way to desert in the north
c. 500 B.C.	Founding of AOUDAGHOST
c. 300 A.D.	Start of BERBER influence and dominance
c. 800	Final defeat of the Bafour by Berbers
c. 900–1000	Zenith of the SANHADJA CONFEDERATION
c. 990	Berbers lose Aoudaghost to the Empire of Ghana led by the SONINKE
1039	Arrival of Abdallah Ibn Yacin in Mauritania
c. 1041–42	Ibn Yacin gathers his followers at a *ribat* (religious retreat); he organizes the ALMORAVIDS
1054	Capture of Aoudaghost and Sijilmasa by Almoravid forces
1056	Berbers revolt against Ibn Yacin
1059	Abdallah Ibn Yacin killed in battle
1076	Capture of KOUMBI SALEH by the Almoravids and submission of the Soninké to ISLAM
c. 1150	Collapse of the northern Almoravid Empire in Spain and Morocco
c. 1218–80	Arrival of the BENI HASSAN to northwest Africa and diffusion into Mauritania
1644–74	CHAR BOBHA, or Thirty Years' War, fought between the Beni Hassan and the Berbers; Berbers are defeated
1814	Treaty of Paris recognizes French sovereignty over Senegal and present-day Mauritania
1854–61; 1863–65	LOUIS FAIDHERBE governor of Senegal; expresses interest in Mauritania
1899	France announces its intention to "pacify" Mauritania
1902	XAVIER COPPOLANI persuades the rulers of TRARZA to accept French control (December 15)

1904   Coppolani brings BRAKNA under the control of France (February)

1905   TAGANT conquered by the French (April); supporters of resistance leader Cheikh MA EL-AININ assassinate Coppolani in TIDJIKJA (May 12); French decree outlaws SLAVERY

1909   ADRAR CAMPAIGN launched by General HENRI GOURAUD (January 9); Ma el-Ainin defeated by Gouraud in the ADRAR (July 28)

1920   AFRIQUE OCCIDENTALE FRANÇAISE (AOF), in existence since 1895, includes Mauritania as a constituent part (December 12)

1925   GRAND CONSEIL D'AOF established

1934   Last major GHAZZI (April 16)

1946   Mauritania separated administratively from Senegal (October 26); CONSEIL GENERAL set up; HORMA OULD BABANA wins election to the French National Assembly as Mauritania's delegate (November)

1948   Formation of the UNION PROGRESSISTE MAURITANIENNE (UPM) (February)

1951   Sidi el-Mokhtar N'Diaye narrowly wins seat in French National Assembly over Horma Ould Babana

1952   The UPM, headed by MOKHTAR OULD DADDAH, wins twenty-two of twenty-four seats in the Conseil Général elections (November)

1956   N'Diaye overwhelmingly reelected to the French National Assembly; LOI CADRE promulgated (June)

1957   Mokhtar Ould Daddah's UPM wins thirty-three of the thirty-four seats in the new ASSEMBLEE TERRITORIALE (March 31); the interim body convenes on May 21

1958   OPERATION OURAGON, a French-Spanish campaign against the ARMY OF LIBERATION, begins (February 10); and ends (February 24); construction of Mauritania's new capital, NOUAKCHOTT, begins (March); Ould Daddah holds CONGRESS OF ALEG (May); Horma Ould Babana expelled from the ENTENTE MAURITANIENNE (June 28); NADHA Party founded (September 26); Mauritanians vote to join the French Community (September 28); the Islamic Republic of Mauritania formally established (November 28)

1959   First Mauritanian CONSTITUTION approved (March 22); Elections to the ASSEMBLEE NATIONALE are won by Mokhtar Ould Daddah's PARTI DE REGROUPEMENT MAURITANIEN (PRM) (May 17)

1960	Formal transfer of governmental authority from France to Mauritania (October 19); Mauritania achieves full independence (November 28)
1961	Replacement Mauritanian CONSTITUTION approved (May 20); Mokhtar Ould Daddah elected president without opposition (August 20); he holds the CONGRESS OF UNITY (October 4); Mauritania is admitted to the UNITED NATIONS (October 27); the new PARTI DU PEUPLE MAURITANIEN (PPM) is formed as the sole legal political party (December 25)
1963	TREATY OF KAYES with Mali (February 16); start of IRON ORE mining near ZOUERATE (April)
1964	KAEDI CONFERENCE (January 28–29)
1966	Beginning of ARABIZATION POLICY in EDUCATION (January)
1968	Iron ore miner's strike at Zouerate put down by force (May); Mauritanian local government reorganized (July 30)
1970	King HASSAN II of Morocco formally abandons his claim to Mauritania (April)
1972	ORGANISATION POUR LA MISE EN VALEUR DU FLEUVE SENEGAL (OMVS) founded (October 29)
1973	Formation of the POLISARIO FRONT (May 10); the CFA franc is replaced by the OUGUIYA (June 30); Mauritania admitted to the ARAB LEAGUE (October)
1974	EL-HOR Movement founded; MIFERMA iron ore mining company nationalized (November 28)
1975	Spain, Morocco, and Mauritania sign the MADRID AGREEMENT partitioning WESTERN SAHARA (November 14)
1976	Final Spanish withdrawal from Western Sahara (February 26); the Polisario Front proclaims the SAHARAN ARAB DEMOCRATIC REPUBLIC (SADR) (February 27); signing of the MOROCCAN-MAURITANIAN CONVENTIONS (April 14); Polisario stages the first NOUAKCHOTT RAID (June 8)
1977	Polisario forces raid and occupy Zouerate (May 1); President Ould Daddah signs the MOROCCAN-MAURITANIAN DEFENSE COMMITTEE agreement (May 13); Polisario raids Nouakchott for the second time (July 3)
1978	President Mokhtar Ould Daddah is overthrown by a bloodless military coup led by Colonel MUSTAPHA OULD MOHAMMED SALEK; Colonel Ould Salek sets

up the COMITE MILITAIRE DE REDRESSEMENT NATIONAL (CMRN) (July 10)

1979   Colonel Ould Salek is stripped of power; the CMRN is abolished and replaced with the COMITE MILITAIRE DE SALUT NATIONAL (CMSN) headed by Lieutenant Colonel AHMED OULD BOUCEIF as prime minister (April 6); Ould Bouceif is killed in a plane crash near Dakar, Senegal (May 27); a power struggle within the CMSN ensues, with Lieutenant Colonel MOHAMMED KHOUNA OULD HEYDALLAH assuming the premiership (May 31); he ousts Colonel Ould Salek as head of state and replaces him with Lieutenant Colonel MO-HAMMED MAHMOUD OULD LOULY (June 3); the Polisario Front resumes attacks on Mauritania (July 12); Ould Heydallah's regime then signs the ALGIERS AGREEMENT with Polisario, giving up its claim to Western Sahara (August 5)

1980   Ould Heydallah formally assumes the Mauritanian presidency, displacing Ould Louly (January 4); the new president promulgates a PROVISIONAL CONSTITUTION to prepare for a return to civilian rule (December)

1981   A violent coup attempt led by the exiled ALLIANCE POUR UNE MAURITANIE DEMOCRATIQUE (AMD) fails (March 16); the leaders of the attempt, two ex-CMSN members and two junior officers, are executed by a firing squad (March 26); the Provisional Constitution is shelved by Ould Heydallah and direct military rule is re-instituted (April); Ordinance 81.234 is issued, reabolishing slavery (November 9)

1982   An attempted coup led by Colonel Ould Salek is suppressed (February 6); he is later sentenced to ten years' imprisonment

1983   LAND REFORM ACT promulgated (June 5); Mauritania adheres to the Algerian-Tunisian TREATY OF FRA-TERNITY AND CONCORD (December 12);

1984   President Ould Heydallah formally recognizes the SADR (February 27); Colonel MAAOUIYA OULD SID' AHMED TAYA and others are demoted for reportedly raising objections to this move (March 8); Ould Heydallah is overthrown in a nonviolent "restructuring" of the CMSN and is replaced as head of state by Colonel Ould Taya (December 12)

1985   The reorganized CMSN issues a new CONSTITU-TIONAL CHARTER (February 5); President Ould Taya

	resumes diplomatic relations with Morocco, which had been broken since 1981 (April 13)
1986	The FORCES DE LIBERATION AFRICAINE DE MAU-RITANIE (FLAM) issues LE MANIFESTO DU NEGRO-MAURITANIEN OPPRIME (April); partially in response, Lieutenant Colonel DJIBRIL OULD ABDELLAHI is reappointed minister of the interior, replacing a prominent HALPULAAR officer, Lieutenant Colonel ANNE AH-MADOU BABALY (August 31); President Ould Taya holds municipal elections (December)
1987	Ethnic tension increases; coup plot against the CMSN, allegedly by FLAM supporters, is uncovered (October); three Halpulaar junior officers are executed after trial for allegedly masterminding the conspiracy (December 6)
1988	A controversial series of deaths takes place at the OUA-LATA prison; those imprisoned there include ex-ministers and army officers (September)
1989	Mauritania joins the UNION DU MAGHREB ARABE (UMA) (February 17); an incident between Mauritania and Senegal takes place between LIVESTOCK herdsmen (March 30); Senegalese allegedly attack Sunko, Mauritania, killing two people and taking thirteen others captive (April 8–9); prisoners are released (April 10); André Sonko, Senegal's minister of the interior, goes to Nouakchott to meet with Mauritanian Interior Minister Djibril Ould Abdellahi (April 12); Ould Abdellahi pays a reciprocal visit to Dakar (April 18–19); riots against MOORISH Mauritanians break out in Dakar (April 21–23); disturbances then erupt in Nouakchott and NOUADHIBOU against Senegalese (April 24–25); Djibril Ould Abdellahi broadcasts a strong warning to Mauritanian rioters (April 25); an estimated 300 Mauritanian Moors are killed in Dakar (April 27–29); over the next two weeks, a massive airlift sends tens of thousands of Mauritanians and Senegalese back to their home countries; a Senegal-Mauritania conciliation meeting in Bamako, Mali, fails (May 17–18); the Mauritanian ambassador to Senegal, Mohamed el-Mokhtar Ould Zamel, is recalled by his government from Dakar (May 23); a second Senegal-Mauritania settlement effort, also in Bamako, meets with failure (June 3–5); a third meeting in ROSSO also leads nowhere (June 28); Senegal's ambassador to Mauritania is expelled and Dakar announces the

	severance of diplomatic relations with Nouakchott (August 21)
1990	Djibril Ould Abdellahi is removed from his post as minister of the interior (February 4); he is also dropped from the CMSN and placed in detention in KIFFA, his birthplace (February 8); Iraq invades Kuwait, touching off the GULF CRISIS (August 2); the Ould Taya regime announces it has foiled a coup attempt allegedly backed by Senegal (December 4)
1991	Iraq is attacked by air and ground forces from the United States and several other nations (January and February); Iraq's forces formally surrender to the coalition (March 3); rallying from the influence in Mauritania of the ARAB BAATH SOCIALIST PARTY (ABSP), President Ould Taya announces a plan for the country's democratization (April 15); the FRONT DEMOCRATIQUE UNI DES FORCES DU CHANGEMENT (FDUC), an illegal group, is formed (June 5); its leaders are arrested and jailed the next day; a new constitution is approved by Mauritanian voters (July 12); it is formally ratified (July 20); the first legal political party, the RASSEMBLEMENT POUR LA DEMOCRATIE ET L'UNITE (RDU) is founded (August 22); President Ould Taya's PARTI REPUBLICAIN, DEMOCRATIQUE ET SOCIAL (PRDS) is formed (August 29)
1992	Mauritania's first contested election for president is won by Ould Taya (January 17); a losing candidate, AHMED OULD DADDAH, announces that his UNION DES FORCES DEMOCRATIQUES (UFD) will boycott further elections (January 28); consequently, the PRDS wins most seats in the new National Assembly (March 6 and 13) and in the SENATE (April 3 and 10); President Ould Taya inaugurates the Mauritanian SECOND REPUBLIC (April 18); diplomatic relations with Senegal are restored (April 24)
1993	In a sign of dissent from Ahmed Ould Daddah's political strategies, the UNION POUR LE PROGRES ET LA DEMOCRATIE (UPD), with ex–Foreign Minister HAMDI OULD MOUKNASS as one of its leaders, is chartered (June 15); the PRDS-dominated parliament passes a wide-ranging amnesty law relative to alleged human rights violations from 1989 to 1991 (June)
1994	Municipal elections are held: PRDS wins all but thirty-six of the country's 208 ARRONDISSEMENTS (Janu-

ary 28); elections for seventeen Senate seats result in a PRDS victory in sixteen, with the UFD capturing one seat (April); the EL-HOR movement leaves the UFD (June 6); Ahmed Ould Daddah formally assumes the secretary-generalship of the UFD as the party continues to suffer defections and splits (September 11); the government announces the arrest of sixty Islamic leaders allegedly "in contact with certain parties abroad" for engaging in unauthorized political activity (September 30); the opposition UFD and UPD parties denounce the arrests, saying that no Islamic fundamentalist movements exist in Mauritania (October 4); the Mauritanian minister of the interior charges the arrested individuals with plotting to overthrow the government and with using religious organizations for antiregime activity (October 9); ten of the sixty defendants confess their membership in Islamist groups on national television (October 10); President Ould Taya announces he is pardoning all sixty suspected Islamic activists (October 11); the government accuses Sudanese and Algerian groups of assisting like-minded Mauritanians (November 9); Prime Minister SIDI MOHAMED OULD BOUBACAR, delivering his annual report to the National Assembly (early December), states that the Mauritanian economy grew at a rate of 4.4 percent during 1994, somewhat above expectations

1995   Riots protesting bread price increases take place in Nouakchott and other cities (January 21); the police and army restore order (January 23), but UFD leader Ahmed Ould Daddah, UPD head Hamdi Ould Mouknass, and six other opposition leaders are arrested and detained in Ouadane and Tichit in connection with the disturbances, but they are soon released (February 3); meanwhile, breaking a seventeen-year silence, exiled former President Mokhtar Ould Daddah speaks by radio to Mauritanians and gives newspaper interviews critical of the Ould Taya government (January 25); he continues his critical statements into late February; a significant portion of the membership of an opposition party, the *Mouvement des Démocrates Indépendants* (MDI) headed by Béchir El-Hassen, announce their adherence to the PRDS-led regime (March 10); El-Hassen states that "the opposition is at an advanced state of implosion" and that a new approach was necessary, including working from within the government; an official visit to Mauritania by the Inter-

national Monetary Fund (IMF), during which it pronounced itself satisfied with the country's fiscal affairs,
results in the partial annulment and rescheduling of
many of Mauritania's external debts for the 1995–98 period (mid-May); foreign minister Mohamed Salem Ould
Lekhal meets in Madrid with Israeli foreign minister Shi-
mon Peres (mid-June); their hour of talks constituted the
first official contacts between Israel and Mauritania;
President Ould Taya visits Brakna (June 15–30) and conducts a 1000-kilometer tour of the critical région, reportedly encountering much popular support and winning
additional converts to the PRDS; the leaders of six prominent opposition parties, including the UFD, UPD, UPSD,
and the Baathist-oriented *Parti de l'Avant Garde Nationale* (PAGN) agree to coordinate their efforts to formulate a "common platform" of action (late July); a new
opposition political party, Action for Change, announces
its formation (August 22); one of its members is El-Hor,
the movement of ex-slaves led by Messaoud Ould
Boukheir which left the UFD in September 1994; police
arrest over one hundred suspected pro-Iraq Baathists and
accuse them of activities on behalf of Baghdad (October
23); the same day, the Iraqi ambassador to Mauritania,
Anwar Molad Phibiane, is expelled from the country;
most of the accused are released (end October) and have
the charges against them commuted to lesser offenses
(November 8); on the other hand, seven Mauritanian
army officers are detained for pro-Baathist activity (November 10)

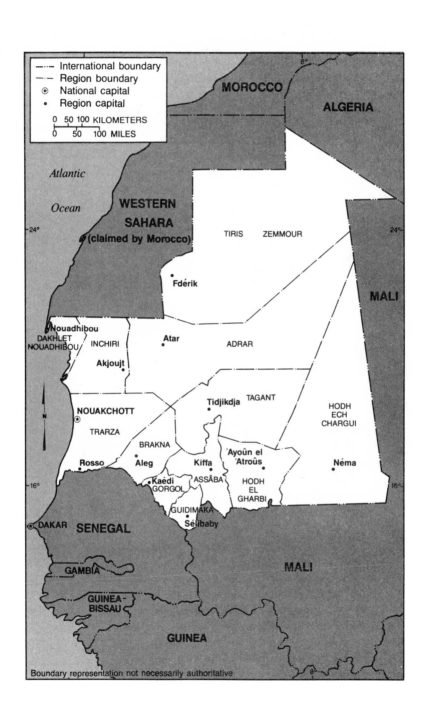

International boundary
Region boundary
National capital
Region capital

0 50 100 KILOMETERS
0   50   100 MILES

Atlantic

Ocean

MOROCCO

ALGERIA

WESTERN

SAHARA

(claimed by Morocco)

TIRIS   ZEMMOUR

MALI

Fdérik

Nouadhibou
DAKHLET
NOUADHIBOU   INCHIRI   Atar   ADRAR

Akjoujt

Tidjikdja   TAGANT   HODH
ECH
CHARGUI

NOUAKCHOTT

TRARZA

BRAKNA

Rosso   Aleg   Kiffa   'Ayoûn el
'Atroûs   Néma

Kaédi   ASSÂBA
GORGOL   HODH
EL
GHARBI

GUIDIMAKA
Sélibaby

DAKAR   SENEGAL

GAMBIA   MALI

GUINEA-
BISSAU

GUINEA

Boundary representation not necessarily authoritative

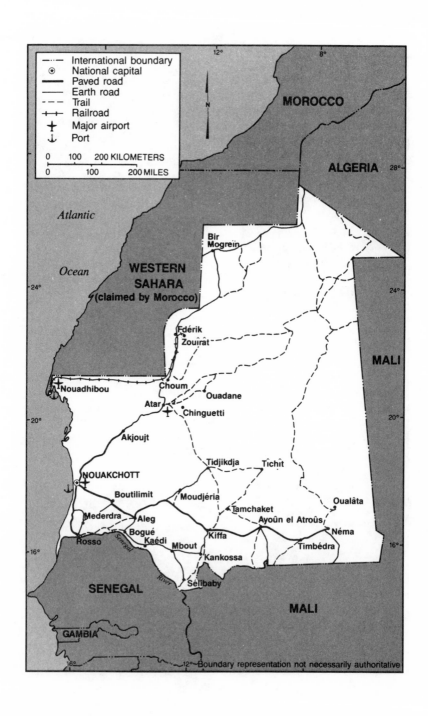

Introduction

Occupying an area of 1,030,700 square kilometers in northwest Africa and bordered by Senegal and Mali in the south and east respectively, Algeria in the far northeast, and the disputed territory of Western Sahara to the north, the Islamic Republic of Mauritania remains one of the least-studied and least-remarked countries of Africa in the 1990s. While this state of affairs may have been due to its sparse population (about 2.1 million people in 1995) and the fact that the young nation is mostly made up of vast stretches of desert, the truth is that Mauritania, with few exceptions, has notably escaped the ravages of the violent interstate and civil conflicts that have so bedeviled Africa and catapulted the affected countries into the popular media. Also, Mauritanian society possesses quite ancient antecedents and a universal religious faith that has been practiced over centuries. More than any other factors, perhaps, these twin characteristics have given the country a sometimes fragile but relatively resilient sense of separate identity which has proven its worth as it confronted powerful tribal, regional, ethnic, and political rivalries and economic difficulties since its independence in 1960.

In Neolithic times, when what is now Mauritania was predominantly grassland, it is believed that the Bafour, a nomadic grouping of hunter-gatherers, held sway over most of the land until the encroachment of the Sahara, caused by climatic shifts as well as by increased human activity. This resulted in the Bafour's gradual displacement to the south, leaving behind a fairly extensive archeological record, possibly along with the unique Imraguen fishing tribe, an independent, black-skinned people who continued to inhabit the remote, unspoiled Atlantic coastline of Mauritania into the late twentieth century. The Bafour, though, were eclipsed not only by the insidious forces of desertification, but also by the arrival of Berbers from North Africa around the beginning of the Christian era. Over the next several hundred years, Berbers not only pushed the Bafour aside (in roughly 300 A.D.) but also began a thriving commerce among themselves and the Black African kingdoms of Ghana and Mali to the south and east. As inveterate traders, the Berbers soon formed a geographically sprawling and administratively loose confederation, with the Sanhadja subgroup taking a dominant role and largely relegating the Djodala, Lemtuna, and Messufa to the sidelines. From 900

1

to 1000 A.D., the Sanhadja Confederation was at its height, drawing its strength from its commercial contacts both in the Maghreb and with the cities of Aoudaghost, Koumbi Saleh, and Oualata (among others), and from the growing sense of unity afforded by Islam.

This stable situation came to an end in about 990 A.D. In that year, the Sanhadja Confederation lost control of Aoudaghost to the ascendant Ghana Empire, led by the Soninké. Thus weakened, the Berbers were additionally subjected, beginning in 1039, to the influence of Abdallah Ibn Yacin, who traveled to Mauritania. Despite being initially ostracized by many Sanhadja who wanted little to do with Yacin's austere, puritanical teachings, Yacin organized his followers at a *ribat* (religious retreat) over the next few years and then succeeded in short order in not only winning back Aoudaghost from the Soninké (in 1054), but also capturing Sijilmasa, an important trading city in the Maghreb which had been coveted by the Sanhadja. After these events, the Almoravid Empire (as it became known) expanded explosively, eventually encompassing much of the Maghreb, southern Spain, and all of present-day Mauritania nearly down to the Senegal River. This process put to flight many Black Africans and led in 1076 to the capture of the city of Koumbi Saleh by Ibn Yacin's successors and by the submission of the Soninké to Islam for the first time. Even as all these conquests were being made, however, strains were starting to show: the often fanatical ways of the Almoravids often drove some independent-minded Berbers to revolt. The Almoravids were unable to resist the dismemberment of their empire by Christian Spain, which vanquished Muslim rule there by about 1150, leaving Mauritania as practically the only location where Almoravid rule survived due almost entirely to the territory's isolation.

In 1218 or so, a new invader appeared on the Mauritanian horizon. The Maqil Arabs, a group of warriors and devout Muslims from the east soon to be known as the Beni Hassan, penetrated into northern Mauritania and disrupted the Berbers' lucrative caravan trade by their exactions and rapacity. For reasons of commercial expediency, apparently, some Sanhadja Berbers formed alliances with the Beni Hassan, but they never lasted long, as the Arabs relentlessly pushed onward to the Atlantic coast of Mauritania, Morocco, Western Sahara, and then south toward Mali and the Senegal River. Sporadic revolts against the Maqil accomplished little except to heighten the Arabs' already strong martial inclinations, and by the mid-1600s, the situation exploded into open warfare, as the Berbers made what turned out to be a final attempt to preserve their cultural and political identity. This period is termed the Char Bobha, or Thirty Years' War, and although records of it are almost entirely based on oral history and the progress of the various battles is often only dimly recalled, there is no doubt as to its outcome—a crushing, humiliating defeat for the Berbers. By the severe terms of the Peace of Tin Yedfad, the vanquished Berbers placed themselves in a permanently subordinate position to the *hassan,* or warrior tribes, and pledged forever to "abandon the sword for the book." Some successfully sought to retain some of their status through religious practice and scholarship and became *zawiya* (roughly "people of the book," or scholars), eventually renowned for their learning and non-warlike disposition. The rest of the defeated Berbers became *znaga,* or vassals, nearly completely dependent on the hassan tribes. In an even less advantaged position were the black slaves of the hassan, pressed into servitude after having been captured by Maqil warriors. The upshot of this violent and decisive period (1644–74) was the creation of the outlines of modern Mauritanian society, characterized by pronounced divisions between the Arabo-Berbers ("Moors," as they came to be known) and Black Africans, and by a rigidly hierarchical social order amongst the Moorish population, with the hassan occupying the top position, the zawiya slightly below them, and the znaga in a decidedly underprivileged status, a station shared by assorted other occupational groups such as bards, musicians, storytellers, and the like, who helped to give Mauritanian Moorish society its complex, multivariate character.

An exceedingly independent, religiously inclined, and self-conscious group such as the Moors were naturally suspicious of outside influences in the form of Europeans. Indeed, for much of the seventeenth and eighteenth centuries, Spanish, French, Portuguese, and English commercial interests traded with the Moors regularly, but their own rivalries caused the Beni Hassan to refuse to grant substantial favors to any of them. Of course, with minimal contacts such as these, the period of early European exploration and penetration did nothing to alter Mauritanian society as it had developed after the end of the Char Bobha. Although France acquired exclusive "rights" to Mauritania by the Treaty of Paris in 1814, it was slow to exercise them, with the governor of adjacent Senegal, Louis Faidherbe, being the only colonial administrator of consequence to show any real interest in the lands north of the Senegal River, mainly in the 1860s. Mauritania continued to be spoken of by the Paris authorities dismissively as "*le vide*" (the vacuum), although its formal name, "land of the Moors," meant that France, even at this time, took careful note that the peoples who inhabited the territory north of the Senegal River were distinct from the Black Africans in and near the Senegal River Valley itself.

December 1899 marked a turning point in Mauritanian history. In that month, France took a firm decision to penetrate and "pacify" the hitherto untamed interior of the colony, but its proposed method for doing so was unusual for its time. From 1900 to 1905 the Algerian-born French administrator of Corsican extraction, Xavier Coppolani, attempted to secure French domination peaceably, making alliances with the monastic zawiya against the dominant hassan and following a skillful policy of setting tribe against tribe and region against region. In rapid succession, Coppolani managed to get the leaders of Trarza, Brakna, and Tagant provinces to agree to French "protection," all the while keeping his eye toward the conquest of the crucial Adrar region farther north. Before he could do this, however, Coppolani was assassinated in his home in Tagant's main town, Tidjikja, on May 12, 1905, at the hands of followers of Cheikh Ma el-Ainin, a noted anticolonial campaigner throughout northwest Africa who had become alarmed at Coppolani's designs on Mauritania. The death of Xavier Coppolani threw French policy into disarray for a few years, but a new French official, General Henri Gouraud, adopted a much more aggressive strategy early in 1909, when he launched a sharp military assault against Ma el-Ainin's forces in the Adrar, eventually defeating them by July of that year. Thereafter (except for a few desultory revolts by the Moors), Mauritania was taken into the French sphere, but Paris did not follow up its military successes in the territory with any development programs or investments in material and personnel. Until the Second World War, Mauritania remained much as it had been since medieval times and was easily one of the most neglected constituent parts of *Afrique Occidentale Française* (AOF), the vast French West African Federation formed in 1895. The colonial regime, based in St. Louis, Senegal, did try to discourage slavery, however, and ended the widespread, destructive, and self-perpetuating practice of raids (*ghazzis*) by one tribe against another by 1934.

Facing widespread domestic and international opposition to the continued maintenance of its extensive overseas holdings after World War II, and itself weakened by the war, France began as early as 1946 to contemplate giving some form of autonomy to its African colonies. At first, Paris held elections in each AOF territory for seats in its National Assembly, balloting which was won in Mauritania by Horma Ould Babana, a rising young politician who was dedicated to working closely with the colonial regime. But Ould Babana chose to absent himself from the country for much of his term as parliamentary deputy, a passivity that, in addition to damaging his political party, the *Entente Mauritanienne*, left the way clear for rival interests in the country to form their own group, the *Union Progressiste Mauritanienne* (UPM) in February 1948. The UPM succeeded in defeating Ould Babana for reelection to the French National Assembly in 1951. But regional, clan, and tribe based divisions in the territory were already glaringly apparent, not to mention a more basic split—that between the majority Moorish population and the Black Africans in the Senegal River Valley who feared being overshadowed by their Arab neighbors. The person who could best deal with these differences and still retain France's backing in the preliminary steps toward what was to become full independence turned out to be

Mokhtar Ould Daddah, a young, soft-spoken lawyer (the only lawyer in Mauritania) who belonged to an eminent zawiya tribe, the Oulad Berri from the historic religious center of Boutilimit. Assuming the leadership of the UPM a year after Ould Babana's defeat, Ould Daddah was able to lead the party to a convincing victory over the Entente and other groups, gaining fully twenty-two of the twenty-four seats in the *Conseil Général,* a French-sponsored interim advisory body. Five years later, in March 1957, Ould Daddah's fortunes remained ascendant, as the UPM succeeded in capturing all but one of the thirty-four seats in a newly formed Territorial Assembly, an event which came on the heels of French Premier Guy Mollet's *loi cadre* in June 1956, which conceded the principle of independence within the French Community for Paris's African possessions.

Political divisions kept reappearing, however, based not only on tribal and ethnic factors but also on ideological grounds, partially a symptom of the varying attitudes Mauritanians harbored toward the newly independent Kingdom of Morocco, which served as a point of attraction for some in the old Entente and for the pan-Arab nationalist party, *An-Nadha al-Wataniyya al-Mauritaniya* (Mauritanian National Renaissance) founded by Ahmed Baba Miské in June 1958. Nevertheless, Mokhtar Ould Daddah eventually co-opted all of these discordant elements in time, ensuring that on November 28, 1960, he led a relatively unified country to independence from France as the world's first Islamic Republic. The ruling political party of Mauritania, the *Parti de Regroupement Mauritanien* (PRM), the UPM's successor from 1958, was fused into still another group, the *Parti du Peuple Mauritanien* (PPM), with Ould Daddah as its head. Gradually, Mauritania took the path traveled by many other African states in the 1960s—the enshrinement of one-party rule behind a powerful presidential office. This began to transpire in the aftermath of the Congress of Unity of October 1961, which declared the PPM the sole legal political organization in the country, and reflected President Ould Daddah's considered opinion that only he could keep his young, fragile nation together to face the challenges he knew were in the offing.

The Mauritanian state began its existence with (relatively) bright economic prospects, fortified by the vast fisheries off its Atlantic shoreline and by enormous iron ore reserves in the north that were discovered by French geologists. Though these two sectors remained largely under foreign control into the 1970s, they soon came to comprise nearly all of Mauritania's foreign exchange earnings. Politically, too, the early 1960s were largely an "era of good feelings" in domestic affairs, with pre-independence differences mostly submerged and with Ould Daddah and his advisers concentrating on making the best of a sometimes difficult foreign relations situation, given that Morocco did not relent on its refusal to recognize Mauritanian independence until 1970, forcing the country to rely heavily on France (and Black Africa) for diplomatic and military support. Beginning in 1966, President Ould Daddah felt sufficiently secure at home and abroad to institute a controversial policy of "Arabization," stressing Hassaniya Arabic as the national *lingua franca* and alienating some Halpulaaren and other blacks who wanted the educational system and other aspects of the society to remain oriented toward African languages and French. Arabization's initial steps, however, did not alter Ould Daddah's political strategies, although mass-scale nationalist protests in the late 1960s and early 1970s, spearheaded by those who resented continued PPM rule and who chafed at Mauritania's continuing close links with France, did result in a series of "radical" domestic and external relations policy shifts, among which were the nationalization of the iron ore mines and the introduction of a new, purely Mauritanian currency, the *ouguiya*. These steps, as well as others, were made possible by the country's increasing good fortunes among the states of the Arab League, who had finally abandoned their reluctance to recognize Mauritania and who proved to be a critical source of economic aid. Consequently, President Ould Daddah's administration reached 1975 in a fairly optimistic mood.

In that year, however, Ould Daddah embarked on a risky, high stakes venture which was to prove his own downfall and nearly that of his country. In November 1975, Mauritania and Morocco jointly and formally agreed to divide the contested Spanish colony of Western Sahara between them, with President Ould Daddah receiving the southern one-third of the desert territory that he had long coveted as Mauritania's own. Agreeing to partition, on the other hand, meant ignoring demands for an independent Western Saharan state articulated by the nascent liberation movement in the territory, the Polisario Front.

Starting in earnest in early 1976, Polisario's motivated, Algerian-equipped guerrilla forces, indignant at the so-called Madrid Agreement, singled out Mauritania for especially harsh treatment. Polisario forces ranged far and wide over the country, disabling the iron ore mines and driving the economy virtually to ruin, even attacking the capital, Nouakchott, twice in 1976 and 1977. Increasingly desperate, President Ould Daddah increased the size of his army from 3,000 to 17,000 men, signed a defense treaty with Morocco, and embraced France as a source of direct military support and aerial intervention. None of these measures sufficed to turn the military tide or to secure Mauritanian cities and towns from the Polisario Front. Moreover, in exposing his army to a costly, seemingly unwinnable war, he created heightened frustrations and feelings of wounded pride on the part of his small, largely French-educated officer corps, prompting them to rise up and overthrow his government on July 10, 1978, arresting him and establishing a military council, the

Comité Militaire de Redressement National (CMRN), headed by the army's chief of staff, Colonel Mustapha Ould Mohammed Salek. Mauritania's new rulers had no real common ideology or political strategy beyond an overriding desire to extricate their country from embroilment in the Western Sahara conflict. But for a variety of reasons, and only after a complicated series of maneuvers within the highest echelons of the regime, peace with the Polisario Front and the abandonment of Mauritania's claims to Western Sahara was not consummated until August 5, 1979, when the Saharan nationalist group and the representatives of the CMRN's successor, the *Comité Militaire de Salut National* (CMSN), signed the Algiers Agreement in the capital of Polisario's staunchest backer.

After the Algiers peace treaty, Mauritania's involvement in Western Sahara was for the most part ended, but the problems of peace proved almost as vexing as those of war. The country's head of state, Colonel Mohammed Khouna Ould Heydallah, a skilled army commander and a product of the renowned French military academies at St. Cyr and St. Maxen, found himself confronted not only with a complex interstate relations structure in the Maghreb (partly a result of the Western Sahara dispute) but also with a declining economy, advancing desertification, poor agricultural yields caused by persistent droughts, and emerging ethnic tensions. Government corruption also reached pandemic levels by the early 1980s. Ould Heydallah dealt with these problems imaginatively but often repressively, imprisoning dissenters and instituting some of the harsher provisions of the Islamic legal code (the *sharia*) to increase social discipline and cohesion. But a reputation for inconstancy, inordinate independence from his CMSN colleagues, and Ould Heydallah's evident closeness to the Polisario Front spelled the end of the Mauritanian president's tenure in office after four years. On December 12, 1984, Ould Heydallah was bloodlessly sacked as CMSN chairman by a fellow officer, Colonel Maaouiya Ould Sid'Ahmed Taya.

In Ould Taya's early years as President of Mauritania, he instituted sweeping reforms. Corruption was suppressed, collegiality became the watchword once again on the governing council, ties with Polisario were loosened, the strictures of the sharia were relaxed, and links with France and the West were reinforced. Most political prisoners were freed, and the new regime made strenuous efforts to overcome the disastrous economic legacy of the Western Sahara war, in particular rescheduling and restructuring the country's crushing debt burden. All told, Ould Taya's diligence, professional outlook, and lack of rigid ideology served critically to decompress the Mauritanian social and political scene in the 1985–86 period. This favorable situation, however, was not destined to continue. In April 1986 a group of black Mauritanians calling themselves the *Forces de Libération Africaine de Mauritanie* (FLAM) issued a forceful and controversial tract, "The Manifesto of the Oppressed Black Mauritanian," detailing what the organization considered to be a pattern of systematic discrimination and hostile acts directed against them by their Moorish counterparts. While the actual degree of support for FLAM was uncertain, the government responded strongly, dismissing many in the army and civil service who were believed to sympathize with FLAM's aim of deposing Ould Taya and the CMSN. Also an irritant during the late 1980s was the increasing level of activity by the pro-Iraq Baath Party in Mauritania, a phenomenon which was suppressed in the same manner as FLAM activity, but which was later relaxed, allowing the Baathists a virtually free rein throughout the government. Successive alleged coup attempts and a still parlous economic situation clouded the waters further. About the only bright spot in Mauritanian civil life at this time were the municipal elections held by President Ould Taya in December 1986 as a prelude to eventual democratization, an exercise which drew praise from Mauritanians and international observers alike and which produced some surprising results, even though the formation of independent political parties was still not permitted.

Any hopes of a further opening of the political system were dashed in April 1989. In that month, a series of incidents between Senegalese and Mauritanian livestock herders in the Senegal River Valley exploded into open intercommunal violence directed against Mauritanian Moors resident in Senegal and, to a lesser extent, against Senegalese in Mauritania's two largest cities, Nouakchott and Nouadhibou. Both expatriate groups, of whom hundreds were to perish in arson and rioting, made significant contributions to each country's economic life, and the losses suffered by Senegal and Mauritania were all the greater, therefore, when it was agreed by the two governments that an exchange of populations, by land and air, would be the most effective way of preventing continued strife. Hundreds of thousands of often destitute refugees were thus evacuated. Disagreements over the causes and motivation for the rioting, and the extent of governmental sponsorship of the violence, quickly soured relations between Senegal and Mauritania. Diplomatic ties were severed in August 1989 in the midst of an escalating round of recriminations over border questions, the alleged expulsion of black Mauritanians to Senegal by the Ould Taya regime, and an array of other factors. For the following year, the two states often verged on all-out warfare.

The Senegal-Mauritania crisis also had a negative domestic effect well beyond its immediate ramifications. Relations between black and Moorish Mauritanians suffered a setback, FLAM activity in the Senegal River Valley area increased, and stories of government repression drew severe international condemnation. In addition, interethnic tensions served as an additional opening to the Mauritanian Baathists, whose followers used their privileged position in the bureaucracy to move the state ever closer to Saddam Hussein's Iraq and to accelerate the Arabization program. Mauritania became so closely identified with Iraq that when Kuwait was invaded by Saddam Hussein's forces on August 2, 1990, it suffered heavily as a result, with economic aid and political support being withdrawn for a time by the conservative oil-rich Gulf monarchies who demanded unconditional opposition to the Kuwaiti takeover and support for the United States–led military effort to expel Iraq from its new acquisition. The Mauritanian political scene became still more uncertain, especially given that the rupture with Senegal was only slowly beginning to heal and the long-running Western Sahara dispute continued to elude a settlement despite a major United Nations peacekeeping endeavor.

After the end of the Gulf War in early 1991, President Ould Taya realized that direct military rule was quickly showing its limits, and that at least the beginnings of a new civil society ought to be allowed to take root. In short order, the Mauritanian head of state announced plans to promulgate a new, liberal democratic constitution (duly approved by voters on July 12, 1991) and to hold contested presidential and parliamentary elections for the first time in the country's thirty-year history. These measures were accompanied by a loosening of controls in many walks of life, a freer press, and few limits on the nature and number of independent political parties that might be formed. In January 1992, Ould Taya was elected president in the face of credible opposition from Ahmed Ould Daddah, the brother of the first Mauritanian head of state. Although the conduct and results of the balloting were disputed by some, elections to a new National Assembly and Senate were held over the next two months, albeit marred by an opposition boycott, which resulted in the preponderance of seats going to President Ould Taya's *Parti Républicain, Démocratique et Social* (PRDS). Thus, Ould Taya emerged from the first phase of the democratization process with almost as much influence as he had entering it, though a relative lack of restrictions on speech, press, and association remained.

By 1996, the dominance of President Ould Taya and his PRDS organization seemed firmly established. Despite this, questions of tribe, race, and religion, as well as sharp disputes over the persistence of slavery in the countryside, persisted, and problems of urban overcrowding, desertification, and indebtedness showed no sign of relenting. But there were positive signs, too: a stabilized economic situation, improving livestock and fisheries sectors, huge new iron ore reserves in the north of the country, and a rising sense of civic consciousness and identification with the Mauritanian national entity among at least some segments of the population. All this stands in contradiction to the prognostications of some observers who only a few years before had remarked upon the fragility of the state. As the twentieth century nears an end, though, it is too early to hazard firm predictions about Mauritania's overall future, especially those which take account of the array of political, social, economic, and environmental factors facing the country. However, Mauritania, benefiting from a common, fervent Islamic faith and enjoying a degree of cultural cohesiveness not often found in Africa, seems destined to remain a significant presence on the continent for the foreseeable future.

The Dictionary

ABD. See Slavery

ABID. See Slavery

ADRAR. Mauritania's second-largest province and administrative région (215,000 square kilometers), the Adrar roughly bisects the country, starting about 250 kilometers inland from the Atlantic coast and extending eastward, bounded by the régions of Hodh ech-Chargui, Tagant, and Tiris Zemmour (qq.v.) and ending at the border with Mali. Most of the Adrar is monotonous desert with very little rainfall (q.v.) or vegetation, although several minor mountain ranges and plateaux exist, mainly around the provincial capital of Atar (q.v.). The Adrar also includes the village of Ouadane, a major caravan stop in Almoravid (q.v.) times and dating from possibly as early as the ninth century A.D. Also of great interest is the ancient Islamic (q.v.) city of Chinguetti (q.v.), reached by a road (q.v.) running east from Atar. Other roads in the province extend west from Atar toward Akjoujt (q.v.) and eventually the Mauritanian capital of Nouakchott (q.v.) and also northward to Choum and the twin towns of F'Derik and Zouerate (qq.v.). According to the Mauritanian government, the Adrar had a population (q.v.) of about 55,000 in 1977, rising slightly to a reported 61,043 in 1988, most living in the towns after having been forced by drought and desertification (q.v.) to forsake their traditional nomadic way of life.

In the tribally and regionally based politics of independent Mauritania, the Adrar has always held great significance. Until 1978, the région was noted for its resistance to the policies of the country's first president, Mokhtar Ould Daddah (q.v.), who hailed from faraway Boutilimit (q.v.). After the assumption of power by the successive CMRN and CMSN (qq.v.) military councils in 1978 and 1979, respectively, the regional factor continued to be important, as no head of state (until 1984) had been raised there. However, President Maaouiya Ould Sid'Ahmed Taya (q.v.), who assumed office on December 12, 1984, resided in the Adrar in his formative years, and his regional counterparts were reported to be influential in the higher echelons of the civil service and in the Mauritanian armed forces (q.v.).

ADRAR CAMPAIGN (Of 1909). One of the most significant military efforts made by France to conquer and "pacify" Mauritania, the *Colonne d'Adrar,* as it was called, was launched after the basically successful occupation of such areas as Brakna and Trarza (qq.v.) to the south under the direction of the governor-general of the territory, Xavier Coppolani (q.v.). The campaign was also initiated on the heels of a series of sharp military setbacks for the French at the hands of the prominent anticolonial leader Cheikh Ma el-Ainin (q.v.), who urged a holy war (*jihad*) to drive out the French invaders and force them back across the Senegal River from whence they came. After the assassination of Coppolani at Tidjikja (q.v.) on May 12, 1905, French policy went through a period of uncertainty and indecision, but in late 1907, French forces in Mauritania were placed under the command of Colonel (later General) Henri Gouraud (q.v.), who had previously proven himself as a desert campaigner farther east in the "Soudan" (present-day Mali) and who was instructed to bring the Adrar finally under French control. After making careful preparations, he launched an attack against Ma el-Ainin's forces on January 9, 1909, and quickly captured the key town of Atar (q.v.). Due to French overconfidence, overextension of supply lines in the trackless desert wilderness, and a lack of effective cooperation with sympathetic tribes, however, Gouraud's forces soon began to lose the initiative to Ma el-Ainin's motivated warriors, who counterattacked and inflicted great losses upon the colonial army. A futile series of skirmishes and small engagements followed into June 1909, with each side making gains and suffering reverses. This stalemated situation led many French administrators to doubt the wisdom of the campaign. But just as it looked as though Gouraud would be unsuccessful, he hit upon a strategy borrowed from his predecessor, Coppolani: he would occupy the palm groves in the province, which produced dates that the Moorish (q.v.) tribesmen needed to survive, and thereby provoke a frontal engagement that would divert Ma el-Ainin's attention away from the Chinguetti (q.v.) area, which would then be occupied as well. This phase of the operation worked almost precisely as planned, and by July 28, the battle that Gouraud had hoped for materialized. By this time, Ma el-Ainin's sons, el-Oueli and Hassena, were in command of the resistance, assisted by the Emir of Adrar, Ould Aida. In the "battle of the palm groves," they were routed and pursued north to Idjil, where the destruction of their forces was completed. The Adrar was now firmly in the hands of the French and would remain "pacified" for the next half century.

AFRICAN LIBERATION FORCES OF MAURITANIA. See Forces de Libération Africaine de Mauritanie (FLAM)

AFRIQUE OCCIDENTALE FRANÇAISE (AOF). The Federation
of French West Africa, organized in 1895, was the overall administrative instrument of French colonial rule in the region, with most of
its territorial components becoming independent in 1960. At first
made up of five territories, the number grew to eight on December 4,
1920, when Mauritania and two other colonies were included after the
effective completion of the "pacification" efforts in those areas. Besides Mauritania, AOF included Dahomey (since 1975 known as
Benin), Guinea, Ivory Coast, Niger, Senegal, the Soudan (Mali), and
Upper Volta (since 1983 known as Burkina Faso). AOF was not organized democratically, nor did it have any legislative bodies before
1946. Headquartered in Dakar, Senegal (from which the Mauritanian
colony was also run), the West African Federation was led by a
governor-general (*commissaire de gouvernement*) who had near-
absolute power, being responsible only to the president of the French
Republic in Paris, who appointed him for a five-year term. A lieu-
tenant-governor presided over each colony, with supervisory powers
over each *cercle* (q.v.) within the territory, the commandant of each
cercle (almost always a European) in turn overseeing the largely indigenous town and rural authorities. In 1925, a *Grand Conseil* (q.v.)
was set up in Dakar as a consultative body and was organized along
corporatist lines, with primarily European interest group representatives such as civil servants and military officers among its forty members. The Grand Council was a purely advisory panel, however, with
real power residing in the governor-general who likely acquired even
more influence than was intended due to the rapid turnover of subordinate personnel in Dakar and the frequent changes in the composition of the Second French Republic. Mauritania's place in AOF was
essentially the same as that of the other colonies in the federation, the
only significant differences being the lack of a capital for the territory
(it was governed first from Dakar and then from St. Louis, Senegal),
the high profile of the French army in the ranks of the colonial government due to the recency of the "pacification," and, finally, the innovative use by France of traditional tribal, especially *zawiya* (q.v.)
Mauritanian authorities as a means of indirect rule.

Following the end of the Second World War, during which the Federation had fallen to the Nazi-inspired Vichy regime but whose
African soldiers had contributed massively to the Free French cause,
the new Third Republic decided, as a mark of gratitude, to reorganize
AOF and give it a slightly more democratic cast. On October 25, 1946,
a decree opened the Grand Council to wider participation, although
the franchise was still restricted and the Council's role remained entirely consultative. In addition, a *Conseil de Gouvernement* (q.v.) was

set up in Dakar and resembled an actual legislature, with five members representing each of the eight colonies of the Federation (for a total of forty), who were in turn assisted by a Permanent Commission to oversee the work of the governor-general and by a variety of other administrative and conflict resolution bodies. Each AOF territory could also for the first time elect delegates to the French National Assembly in Paris. For Mauritania, the 1946 reforms were especially significant, as the territory was now separated from Senegal for the purposes of administration and was not only given representation in the Council of Government and a seat in the National Assembly, but also was awarded its own *Conseil Général* (q.v.). The General Council was at first an advisory organ that each colony possessed, but from here would emerge experienced politicians, such as Mauritania's Mokhtar Ould Daddah (q.v.), who would often play decisive roles in their countries' affairs. In practice, however, most power still lay with the governor-general.

Growing anticolonial feelings among the native populations of AOF, coupled with the outbreak of a violent independence war in Algeria in 1952, convinced Paris that at least some real autonomy would have to be granted to its West African possessions. Consequently, the General Councils were renamed Territorial Assemblies (q.v.) in 1952, suffrage for the legislative and other AOF elections was gradually made universal, and an orderly release from French control was eventually negotiated with leaders such as Ould Daddah who could be counted on to remain close to France after its departure. Beginning on August 1, 1960 (when Dahomey became independent), AOF quickly began losing the component parts that had made it one of the largest colonial governments in the world, and on November 28, 1960, when Mauritania became independent, AOF finally passed into history.

AGRICULTURE. Of Mauritania's vast land mass comprising 1,030,300 square kilometers, only about 14 percent of the total is considered suitable for agricultural purposes, and only a small part of that is actually in productive use. In addition, rainfall (q.v.) patterns often fluctuate radically from year to year, with sustained droughts a common occurrence. The process of desertification (q.v.) has also ruined large tracts of otherwise useful land. Since northern and eastern Mauritania is almost entirely desert, the growing of crops can take place only along a fairly narrow belt near the country's southern border, in the administrative régions of Assaba, Brakna, Gorgol, Guidimaka, southern Hodh ech-Chargui and Hodh el-Gharbi, and Trarza (qq.v.). In these areas, the quantity of rainfall is generally enough, and the Senegal River flooded sufficiently, that sorghum, rice, corn, barley, and millet can be harvested in amounts that make farming a viable enterprise. In other areas of Mauritania, the only agriculture is found in a limited number of oases, notably in the régions of Adrar and Tagant (qq.v.). There, dates, gum arabic from acacia trees, and some corn are raised, but since rainfall is often completely absent, the only water resources (q.v.) available come from wells.

From the time of Mauritanian independence in 1960, agriculture steadily declined in importance, falling from 50 percent of the total gross domestic product (GDP) in 1960 to an estimated 3 percent by 1985, propelled downward by a succession of droughts, poor bureaucratic performance, and the encroaching Sahara. Beginning in the mid-1970s, moreover, the Senegal River entered a period in which it seasonally rose and overflowed its banks to a degree far below what had been considered normal, aggravating the effects of poor rainy seasons which generated 40 percent less precipitation than had been expected. By 1980, only 24,000 tons of cereals could be produced, necessitating the importation of 80,000 additional tons to sustain a growing Mauritanian population (q.v.) and putting enormous strains on the national budget (q.v.) and scarce reserves of foreign exchange. The response of Mauritania's government, then headed by CMSN (q.v.) chairman Colonel Mohammed Khouna Ould Heydallah (q.v.), was twofold. First, it asked for (and received) massive food aid from outside the country; at various times Belgium, France, Canada, the United States, and Saudi Arabia, as well as the World Food Programme of the United Nations (q.v.), all pitched in to help. Secondly, the regime assumed a much more active role in the farming sector and its allied activities, with the main state agricultural agencies, the *Commissariat à la Sécurité Alimentaire* (CSA) and the *Société Nationale pour le Développement Rural* (SONADER) (qq.v.), paying subsidies and providing price supports to farmers and directly assuming control over some storage, distribution, and marketing functions. These steps could not arrest the downward spiral of crop yields, however; the rural areas of Mauritania still received only about 10 percent of total government expenditures, price subsidies tended to discourage production, and what rains came were still late in arriving. To make matters worse, the CSA and SONADER were the targets of corruption allegations, adding to a feeling of malaise among Mauritanians in the early 1980s.

The "restructuring" of the CMSN on December 12, 1984, that deposed Ould Heydallah and put in his place Colonel (later President) Maaouiya Ould Sid'Ahmed Taya (q.v.), brought about a significant reorientation of governmental resources toward agriculture. Almost overnight, infrastructural investment in rural areas more than quadrupled (to 42.1 percent of the total budget, with 36.5 percent of all the regime's money going toward agriculture), the CSA and SONADER were reorganized to shed corrupt or inefficient personnel, and subsidies were gradually phased out over the next few years. The substitution of rice for other crops was also encouraged, as it is less difficult to raise and harvest and can survive more easily in a harsh climate. President Ould Taya also increased cooperation with Mali and Senegal through Mauritania's membership in the *Organisation pour la Mise en Valeur du Fleuve Sénégal* (OMVS) (q.v.): a number of OMVS dam projects including those at Foum Gleita, Diama, and Manantali were expected to produce over 150,000 hectares of cultivable land, although some of the projects were not operational until the early 1990s due to financial constraints and the Senegal-Mauritania Crisis (q.v.) that began in April 1989. Helped by increasing rainfalls, agricultural production rebounded smartly, with cereal output reaching 165,000 tons in 1987 (and a record 183,600 tons in 1989–90)—still below the country's overall requirements but impressive for a sector that many observers had virtually written off a few years before. The mainly Halpulaar and *haratine* (qq.v.) farmers in the Senegal River Valley soon were selling their produce at market rates, ignoring the official quotas and subsidies put into place by the Ould Heydallah government, a state of affairs which allowed the CMSN to eliminate its agriculture-related practices, including the widely circumvented food export monopoly of the *Société Nationale d'Importation et d'Exportation* (SONIMEX) (q.v.).

A few discordant notes were present on this greatly improving agricultural scene, though. The application of the provisions of the Land Reform Act of June 5, 1983 (q.v.), which appropriated to government ownership "dead" or fallow lands, also altered land tenure regulations to the disadvantage—some observers believed—of black Mauritanians and to the benefit of Beydane Moors (qq.v.) who, along with their haratine counterparts, urgently sought additional farmland. And good crop yields always remained dependent upon adequate precipitation, a fact brought into high relief in 1992 when three abundant harvests were followed by poor rainfall resulting in a yield of only 84,000 tons of cereals. These results were a particular disappointment for President Ould Taya, for he had counted on the domestic production of at least half of the country's grain needs, a pattern that had been developing since 1988.

In 1993, the rains came once again in plentiful amounts, and the year's harvest of cereals and other staples was expected to be 60 percent over that of the admittedly below par prior year. The Mauritanian livestock (q.v.) sector also showed improvement, as did the harvest of millet, sorghum, and corn. Importantly, the government also chose to expand an innovative program of rural development, founded in 1985, known as *Vivres Contre Travail* (VCT). This "food for work" project utilized money from the internal sale of foreign-supplied food-stuffs to finance development and antidesertification measures such as reforestation and dune control. The building of roads (q.v.) in the country's southern régions was also undertaken under VCT. Managed by the CSA food agency, over 700 small projects were finished in the 1991–93 period, with an additional 200 or so scheduled to be completed by the end of 1994. VCT, which earned high marks from international donor countries, also advanced certain political objectives for the Mauritanian regime, including fostering a better work ethic, promoting national unity by the targeted allocation of resources to outlying areas, and enhancing employment opportunities. By 1995, the outlook for Mauritanian agriculture appeared much more favorable than it had a decade earlier, even taking into account the continuing need for outside assistance and the susceptibility of the sector to the vagaries of the area's climatic conditions.

AHMED BABA MISKE. A prominent Mauritanian political personality in the country's pre-independence period and a somewhat unpredictable figure in later years, Ahmed Baba Miské was born in 1932 or 1933 in northern Adrar (q.v.) province and was a member of the Ahel Berikallah, a Moorish (q.v.) tribe found in both Mauritania and adjacent Western Sahara (q.v.). He attended both primary and secondary schools in Mauritania, but then traveled to the University of Dakar and also studied in France for a time. Upon his return to Mauritania, he became an early opponent of the country's rising leader, Mokhtar Ould Daddah (q.v.), whom Baba Miské considered inordinately traditionalist, too pro-French, and out of touch with the "radical" nationalist currents then prevalent in developing countries. He was one of a core group of youthful Mauritanians who felt excluded from influence within the *Parti de Regroupement Mauritanien* (PRM) (q.v.), an organization created through a fusion of several other political groups at the Congress of Aleg (q.v.) in May 1958, an event which further solidified Ould Daddah's position as Mauritania's foremost politician and the one most trusted by France. Two months after the Aleg congress, a PRM meeting in Nouakchott (q.v.) expelled Baba Miské and other youth leaders from the party because of their vocal opposition to Mokhtar Ould Daddah. On September 25 and 26, 1958, at Kaédi (q.v.), Baba Miské founded *An-Nadha al-Wataniyya al-Mauritania* (q.v.), in which he held the post of secretary-general. Nadha called upon the citizens of Mauritania to reject membership in the French community after independence, urged rapprochement with Morocco, and seemed to favor Moorish Mauritanians at the expense of the Black Africans in the Senegal River Valley, an attitude that cost it considerable support. Under the pretext of discovering corruption in Nadha's ranks, Ould Daddah banned the party's activities on the eve of the 1959 elections to the *Assemblée Territoriale* (q.v.). A limited campaign of Nadha-inspired bombings and other acts of violence followed, and Baba Miské was arrested and imprisoned from May 1960 to February 1961 in the remote eastern province of Hodh ech-Chargui (q.v.). After his release, he became reconciled with President Ould Daddah, and took an active role in the Congress of Unity (q.v.) of October 1964, which merged Nadha, two other groups, and the PRM into a new *Parti du Peuple Mauritanien* (PPM) (q.v.), in which Baba Miské became secretary. Although allied with Ould Daddah at this point, Baba Miské built up a separate power base within the PPM that the head of state believed might make him a threat. Ould Daddah's response, then, was in effect to banish Baba Miské to the United States to serve as Mauritania's ambassador to the U.S. and permanent representative to the United Nations (q.v.) between 1964 and 1966. After being recalled home that year, he was arrested on corruption charges and after one month in prison was found not guilty. Soon Baba Miské went into exile, mainly in Paris, for the next twelve years and founded the magazine *Africasia*.

Ahmed Baba Miské's sympathies took another turn in the period of 1974–75, when, while still in exile, he publicly opposed President Ould Daddah's plan to annex Western Sahara in cooperation with Morocco's King Hassan II (q.v.). In an open letter to the PPM's Fourth Congress held in August 1975 (which, as expected, endorsed Ould Daddah's Saharan policy without demur), he warned the delegates of the dangers posed by Moroccan "expansionism," fearing that Mauritania itself would be next in line for conquest after King Hassan had digested Western Sahara. Around the time of the Madrid Agreement (q.v.) of November 14, 1975, he moved to Algiers and promptly joined the Polisario Front (q.v.), a nationalist group which advocated the creation of an independent Saharan Arab Democratic Republic (SADR) (q.v.) on Western Saharan soil. Grateful to have such a respected figure on its side, the front made him a spokesperson and elected him to its political bureau, a group of high-ranking personalities, at Polisario's Third Congress, held in the Tindouf region of southwestern Algeria on August 26–30, 1976. However, after his old adversary, Mokhtar Ould Daddah, was overthrown by the Mauritanian armed forces (q.v.) on July 10, 1978, Baba Miské found the lure of reentry into Mauritania's politics irresistible. Having evidently fallen out with the Polisario Front (he was not reelected to its political bureau at the Front's Fourth Congress in September 1978), he journeyed to Mauritania for the first time since 1966 and tried to reestablish his political credentials. It was a difficult process: in December 1980 he was arrested by the CMSN (q.v.) government headed by

Colonel Mohammed Khouna Ould Heydallah (q.v.) and charged with complicity in an alleged plot by Libya's leader, Colonel Muammar el-Qadaffi, to unseat the Mauritanian leader. Baba Miské was released on March 3, 1981, and quit politics for a short time, attending to various business interests. But in February 1984, he dissented from Ould Heydallah's decision, on behalf of Mauritania, to confer diplomatic recognition on the SADR, and probably for this reason he was again arrested (on April 24) and imprisoned. He remained jailed until December 16, 1984, when he was amnestied (along with dozens of other political prisoners) by Colonel Maaouiya Ould Sid'Ahmed Taya (q.v.), who had bloodlessly displaced Ould Heydallah a few days before. Once freed, Baba Miské praised Ould Taya's more neutral stance on the Western Sahara conflict, then bowed out of the political spotlight. In 1995, he resided in Paris, where he was an official of the United Nations Educational, Scientific, and Cultural Organization (UNESCO).

AHMED OULD BOUCEIF. The second military leader of Mauritania and the one with the shortest tenure in office, Ahmed Ould Bouceif was born in 1934 in Kiffa (q.v.) and joined the fledgling Mauritanian armed forces (q.v.) in 1962 as an infantryman. Later on, he attended the officer training academy at Saumur, France. Thereafter, he held increasingly responsible positions within the army, and was drawn along with his colleagues into military operations against the Polisario Front (q.v.) in the early stages of the Western Sahara conflict (q.v.) in late 1975. Mauritania was already feeling the severe effects of Polisario attacks by June 24, 1976, when Ould Bouceif was appointed army chief of staff by the civilian president, Mokhtar Ould Daddah (q.v.). Several months later, he was given command of all Mauritanian forces in the vast northeast of the country, with his responsibilities centered on the critical mining center of Zouerate (q.v.) and at the garrison further north at Bir Moghrein (q.v.). His appointment as commander, however, did not result in the abatement of Polisario's destructive activities, which by this time had devastated Zouerate and crippled Mauritania's railway carrying iron ore (qq.v.) to the Atlantic coast for export. In common with many in the army and elsewhere, he began to see the Saharan war as a pointless and harmful exercise.

Ould Bouceif therefore fully supported—though he apparently did not directly participate in—the military *coup d'état* of July 10, 1978, that displaced Mokhtar Ould Daddah and placed Colonel Mustapha Ould Mohammed Salek (q.v.) at the head of the ruling officers' council, the *Comité Militaire de Redressement National* (CMRN) (q.v.). In the new CMRN-appointed Council of Ministers (q.v.), Ould Bouceif became minister of fisheries and industry, a post which he held until

April 6, 1979. On that date, Ould Salek was forced to cede most of his powers to Ould Bouceif, who became prime minister of a new governing group, the *Comité Militaire de Salut National* (CMSN) (q.v.), though Ould Salek remained the titular head of state. Although the rationale for this bloodless palace revolution was military frustration with Ould Salek's Western Sahara policy, which had still not extricated Mauritania from its war with the Polisario Front, Ould Bouceif, during April and May 1979, followed basically the same course as his predecessor—attempting to conclude a "global" peace treaty among all the parties involved, directly or indirectly, in Western Sahara.

Less than two months after assuming power, on May 27, 1979, Ould Bouceif, along with several other members of the Mauritanian delegation to a West African summit conference, was killed in a plane crash near the international airport at Dakar, Senegal. It was reported that the plane carrying Ould Bouceif to the conference was attempting to land in a severe sandstorm against the advice of the control tower. Ould Bouceif's death touched off a short, intense power struggle within the CMSN, with another Western Saharan war veteran, Lieutenant Colonel Mohammed Khouna Ould Heydallah (q.v.) assuming most power on June 3, 1979.

AHMED OULD DADDAH. Mauritania's best-known opposition politician was born in 1942 in Boutilimit (q.v.) as the younger brother of the country's future first president, Mokhtar Ould Daddah (q.v.). After primary schooling in Boutilimit, he resided in Dakar, Senegal, while pursuing his secondary education, attending the *Lycée Van Vollennoven*. After graduation, he traveled to Paris to attend university, receiving a degree in economics from the *Faculté de Droit et Sciences Economiques de Paris* in the mid-1960s. Once back in Mauritania, he began work as an economic and financial counselor to President Ould Daddah from 1967 to 1968, then became executive secretary to the *Organisation des Etats Riverains du Sénégal* from August 1968 through March 1971, laying the groundwork for what later became the *Organisation pour la Mise en Valeur du Fleuve Sénégal* (OMVS) (q.v.). For the next two years (from March 1971 to March 1973), Ahmed Ould Daddah served as director-general of the Mauritanian state trading agency, the *Société Nationale d'Importation et d'Exportation* (SONIMEX) (q.v.), and between June 1973 and May 1978 occupied the crucial post as governor of the *Banque Centrale de Mauritanie* (BCM) (q.v.). In one of Mokhtar Ould Daddah's last cabinet reshuffles before he was deposed by the armed forces (q.v.) on July 10, 1978, he named his brother minister of finance, effective May 30. But after the July 10 coup, Ahmed Ould Daddah was arrested by the new military council, the *Comité Militaire de Redressement National* (CMRN) (q.v.) and placed in detention for two years. In 1982 he was permitted to leave Mauritania, and for the next decade he lived in exile and became a prominent figure in international banking circles, serving in the 1980s as the representative of the World Bank in Bangui, Central African Republic. After Mauritania's head of state, President Maaouiya Ould Sid'Ahmed Taya (q.v.) announced in April 1991 that the country's political affairs were to be henceforth liberalized and multiple political parties would be allowed to function, Ould Daddah decided to return to Mauritania and oppose Ould Taya in the country's first-ever contested presidential election scheduled for January 1992. Upon taking up residence in Nouakchott (q.v.) in late 1991 it became apparent to most observers that he was the only real challenge to the president's *Parti Républicain, Démocratique et Social* (PRDS) (q.v.), although two other candidates had announced their intention to seek the Mauritanian leadership. On the campaign trail in December 1991 and January 1992, Ould Daddah attacked President Ould Taya's administrative and human rights record and called for the legalization of Islamic (q.v.) political groups, something Ould Taya refused to contemplate. The PRDS, for its part, characterized Ould Daddah as "the West's whipping boy," a reference, presumably, to his employment by Western-dominated financial institutions unpopular with many Mauritanians. The PRDS also had superior organization compared to the party backing Ould Daddah, the *Union des Forces Démocratiques* (UFD) (q.v.). On January 17, 1992, Ahmed Ould Daddah garnered about 33 percent of the total presidential votes cast, a respectable figure but one that did not come close to the 62 percent favoring Ould Taya.

Smarting from his rebuff in the election, which he claimed was marred by extensive fraud and other irregularities, Ould Daddah announced that the UFD would boycott the elections to the *Assemblée Nationale* and the Senate (qq.v.), the two chambers of the new bicameral Mauritanian legislature. Other opposition parties followed suit, and as a result, in February and March 1992, the PRDS swept both houses, leaving the UFD with no seats in either branch and ensuring that Ould Taya would face little official opposition to PRDS political and economic policies. Casting about for a new strategy in the aftermath of this severe setback, the UFD appointed Ahmed Ould Daddah its "coordinator" in August 1992. Frustrations at the UFD's low fortunes, however, did not abate, and on February 20, 1993, a group of disgruntled members, led by former Foreign Minister Hamdi Ould Mouknass (q.v.), defected from the party to form a new "centrist" group, the *Union pour le Progrès et la Démocratie* (UPD) (q.v.). Ould Daddah, facing an implied challenge to his party leadership, agreed in July 1993 to abandon his boycotting strategy, but the UFD-Ere Nouvelle, as it was now known, performed poorly in municipal and senatorial elections held in January and April 1994, respectively, winning only a few local council seats and a single place in the Senate. Moreover, an important component of the UFD, the El-Hor (q.v.) movement made up of ex-slaves or *haratines* (q.v.), decided to leave the party along with other supporters in June 1994, calling Ould Daddah "too passive" in his political approach. In spite of being formally elevated to the post of secretary-general of the Union of Democratic Forces-New Era on September 11, 1994, Ahmed Ould Daddah's fortunes, like those of his party, continued their steady decline. Although he was not believed by most observers to have had any role in the largely spontaneous outbreak of violence in Mauritania over increases in the price of bread and other staples on January 21–23, 1995, Ould Daddah, along with UPD chairman Hamdi Ould Mouknass and six other opposition leaders, was arrested and briefly placed into internal exile in connection with the riots. After being released on February 3, he returned to a political scene that was, if anything, even less favorable than before, with more opposition leaders and rank-and-file aligning themselves with the Ould Taya regime and with Ould Daddah's authority increasingly called into question in light of statements made from exile by his brother and ex-president, Mokhtar Ould Daddah.

AHMED OULD MINNIH. One of Mauritana's most versatile and highest ranking armed forces (q.v.) officers, Ahmed Ould Minnih was born in 1944 in Boutilimit (q.v.) and received a primary education there before going on to secondary schools in Rosso and Nouakchott (qq.v.). Electing to become an officer in the recently founded Mauritanian army, he was seconded to two of France's most well-regarded military academies, the *Ecole Militaire de Cavalérie* at Saumur, and the military school at St. Maxen. Upon graduation, he returned to Mauritania newly commissioned and was successively given field command of several units. Around 1970, he achieved distinction as chief of the *deuxième bureau* (intelligence corps) under Mauritania's army chief of staff, holding that position until 1972. In that year, he traveled to Algeria, where he was Mauritanian military attaché at his country's embassy until 1975. In 1975, about the time Mauritania's involvement in the Western Sahara conflict (q.v.) was beginning, Ould Minnih returned home and was assigned to various military regions of the country, including the critical sector headquartered at Bir Moghrein (q.v.). As the Western Sahara war was winding down as a result of the accession to power of the *Comité Militaire de Redressement National* (CMRN) (q.v.) on July 10, 1978, Ould Minnih was appointed governor of the administrative région of Tagant (qq.v.). In April 1979, at the time of intense factional infighting within the CMRN's ranks, he was told to leave Tagant and take up the leadership of the Army Engineering Corps. After the CMRN was replaced by a new military council, the *Comité Militaire de Salut National* (CMSN) (q.v.) on April 6, 1979, Ould Minnih, though still holding the rank of captain, became a member of the ruling body while continuing with his field and administrative duties. Then, in August 1981, he was appointed foreign minister by the CMSN chairman, Colonel Mohammed Khouna Ould Heydallah (q.v.), a considerable promotion through which he put to use all of his administrative and interpersonal skills. By now holding the rank of major, he remained as head of the Foreign Ministry after Ould Heydallah was displaced by a CMSN colleague, Colonel Maaouiya Ould Sid'Ahmed Taya (q.v.), on December 12, 1984. Under Ould Taya, Ould Minnih played a major role in subtly reorienting the pattern of Mauritanian foreign relations (q.v.) away from what some observers considered an inordinate closeness to the Polisario Front (q.v.) in Western Sahara, and toward a more evenhanded relationship with all the countries of the Maghreb, including Morocco's King Hassan II (q.v.), Polisario's opponent.

Ould Minnih held the foreign ministership until December 1986, when he was chosen army chief of staff after severe difficulties had arisen with regard to the armed forces' stability and loyalty, concerns heightened by the apparent discovery within the Mauritanian officer corps of supporters of the black opposition group, the *Forces de Libération Africaine de Mauritanie* (FLAM) (q.v.) as well as backers of the Arab Baath Socialist Party (ABSP) (q.v.). Because Ould Minnih was not identified with any of the country's major tribal, political, or regional cliques (a characteristic he shared with Ould Taya), his move to the army's top position was interpreted by some analysts as an attempt to strengthen army professionalism and cohesion. His transfer out of the Foreign Ministry carried with it an advancement to the rank of lieutenant colonel, and he remained chief of staff through the worst phases of the Senegal-Mauritania Crisis (q.v.) of 1989 and 1990, in which the eruption of outright warfare between the two countries was a distinct possibility. After the crisis with Senegal had abated, and the Gulf Crisis (q.v.) of 1990 and 1991 concluded, Ould Minnih was appointed (effective July 27, 1991) minister of the interior, occupying that key post as Mauritania took the first steps towards democratization and free elections, which were held in early 1992. On April 18 of that year, concurrent with President Ould Taya's inauguration of the Mauritanian Second Republic (q.v.) and the selection of a new, broadly based Council of Ministers (q.v.), Ould Minnih was appointed minister of defense, the only serving military officer in the cabinet. His selection also marked the first time in several years that the defense portfolio had been separated from the presidency. Ahmed Ould Minnih continued to head the Defense Ministry until February 21, 1995, when he relinquished the post to a civilian, Abdellahi Ould Abdi, and took up another important position, that of secretary-general of the office of the President of the Republic.

AHMED SALEM OULD SIDI. After choosing a career with Mauritania's armed forces (q.v.) in his youth, Ahmed Salem Ould Sidi rose to the rank of major in time to participate actively in the country's involvement in the Western Sahara conflict (q.v.) as commander of the garrison at Dakhla (q.v.) from January 1976. Soon afterwards, Ould Sidi became head of Mauritania's new military academy, the *Ecole Militaire Interarmes d'Atar* (EMIA) (q.v.). After the July 10, 1978, *coup d'état* against President Mokhtar Ould Daddah (q.v.), he became a member of the new military government, the *Comité Militaire de Redressement National* (CMRN) (q.v.) under the leadership of Colonel Mustapha Ould Mohammed Salek (q.v.). During late 1978 and early 1979 he also held the post of minister of supply and transport. On June 3, 1979, he left his cabinet post but, in a sign of continued favor, was chosen as second vice-president of the reorganized ruling group, the *Comité Militaire de Salut National* (CMSN) (q.v.), after having had the distinction of presiding over a short but fierce power struggle after the death of Prime Minister Ahmed Ould Bouceif (q.v.) on May 27. The new leader of the CMSN, Colonel Mohammed Khouna Ould Heydallah (q.v.) soon detailed Ould Sidi to negotiate, and on August 5, 1979, to sign, the Algiers Agreement (q.v.) with the representatives of the Polisario Front (q.v.), formally ending Mauritania's involvement in the Western Sahara dispute and leaving Morocco and Polisario to continue their struggle alone.

Ould Sidi soon became disaffected with the CMSN and its policies, and he left the government in the spring of 1980 and moved to Morocco, where he joined an umbrella grouping of various opposition tendencies, the *Alliance pour une Mauritanie Démocratique* (AMD) (q.v.). He publicly criticized Mauritania's exit from Western Sahara, and alongside his fellow officer in exile, Lieutenant Colonel Mohammed Ould Bah Ould Abdel Kader (q.v.), urged a continuing close Mauritanian relationship with Morocco's King Hassan II (q.v.). In early 1981, he clandestinely moved back into Mauritania as one of the AMD's key figures in a plot to overthrow the CMSN and Ould Heydallah. On March 16, 1981, a violent coup attempt was staged in downtown Nouakchott (q.v.), but was put down by loyal army units. Ould Sidi was captured, and on March 26 he and three others, including Ould Abdel Kader, were executed by a firing squad.

AIR FORCE. Always the smallest component of Mauritania's armed forces (q.v.), the air force in 1996 has only about 150 men assigned to it, and its combat capabilities are minimal. Utilized in a ground attack and counterinsurgency role were five Britten-Norman BN-2 Defenders, a twin-turboprop aircraft with a top speed of 170 miles per hour and armed with a variety of underwing rockets and bombs. By around 1991 these planes were supplemented with two United States–built Cessna FTB-337 Skymaster Milirole craft, also outfitted for close air support missions. In the important area of maritime reconnaissance, two Piper Cheyenne II planes are present to assist the Mauritanian navy (q.v.); these have a range of over 1500 nautical miles and could stay aloft for about seven hours at a time. The transport arm's strength was highly variable, but by the mid-1990s had dwindled to two Cessna Skymasters, an uncertain number of Shorts Skyvans, and two De Havilland DHC-5D Buffalo cargo carriers. There was also a single U.S.-built Grumman Gulfstream II jet for VIP use, but it and another aircraft set aside for use by high government officials, a Sud-Aviation Caravelle jet airliner, had been either sold or retired by 1989.

The Mauritanian air force played only a very minor role during the Western Sahara conflict (q.v.), as its planes were either out of service due to maintenance problems or vulnerable to surface-to-air missiles used by the Polisario Front (q.v.); indeed, two Defenders may have been lost during the Saharan war. After the end of Mauritania's involvement in the conflict, the air arm underwent little change either in staffing or equipment, and most personnel continued to receive training in France and Algeria. The air force has airfields available to it in the form of the country's improving network of civilian airports (q.v.), and is often commanded by a colonel who has been a member of what was until 1992 the country's ruling body, the CMSN (q.v.).

AIRLINES. Since independence in 1960, Mauritania's airline services have been limited, constrained by a lack of finance, a shortage of potential passengers in many of the country's outlying areas, and undeveloped airports (q.v.) at several locations. The Mauritanian capital, Nouakchott (q.v.), with an airport located about four kilometers from the city center, has served as the hub for nearly all domestic and international services, with runways capable of accommodating widebodied jet aircraft. The most frequent connections outside the country have been between Nouakchott and Dakar, served five times per week, though this service was suspended during the Senegal-Mauritania Crisis (q.v.) that began in April 1989. The West African airline consortium Air Afrique (of which Mauritania is a shareholder) has handled most of this service, with some being provided by the Senegalese national carrier, Air Sénégal. Air Afrique has conducted two flights per week between Nouakchott and Paris, with two more being run by Air France. The Spanish airline Iberia has also served Nouadhibou (q.v.)

from Las Palmas in the Canary Islands. Air Afrique has also operated a weekly flight from Nouakchott to Jeddah, Saudi Arabia, for pilgrims making the *hajj* to Mecca. Other airlines serving Mauritania have included Air Algérie (to Algiers), Royal Air Maroc (to Casablanca), and Libyan Arab Airlines (to Tripoli), although the latter was discontinued in 1992 after Libya was subjected to an aircraft embargo by the United Nations (q.v.).

Domestic air travel within Mauritania has been provided by the national carrier, Air Mauritanie, organized in 1962 and owned jointly by the Mauritanian government and Air Afrique. Its flights have often been a low-cost alternative to overland travel, especially given the general lack of good roads (q.v.). Air Mauritanie owned two Fokker F-28 twin-jet aircraft, acquired in the early 1980s, each with a seating capacity of 110 persons. One of these planes was lost in a disastrous crash in a sandstorm at Tidjikja (q.v.) on July 1, 1994, in which about 95 people were killed. The most frequent domestic services have been daily from Nouakchott to Nouadhibou, three times per week to Atar (q.v.) with two of those runs being extended to Zouerate (q.v.). Kaédi, Kiffa, Sélibaby, and Tidjikja (qq.v.) have been served twice a week, with one flight weekly to the remoter towns of Ayoun el-Atrouss and Néma (qq.v.). Air Mauritanie's only international services have been to Dakar and Las Palmas. In 1988, Air Mauritanie boarded 124,000 domestic and 92,000 international passengers.

AIRPORTS. In the mid-1990s Mauritania possesses an improving system of airports, although only three—at Nouakchott, Nouadhibou, and Néma (qq.v.)—are suitable for international traffic using modern widebodied aircraft. Nouakchott's airport, built around the time of the country's independence, was cramped and inconvenient to travelers, despite the several scheduled airlines (q.v.) which utilized it. A new terminal opened, after some delays, in June 1993, and included improved runways and better air traffic control equipment. The airport at Nouadhibou was also built to an international standard. To tie the remote administrative région of Hodh ech-Chargui (q.v.) more closely to the rest of Mauritania, the airport at Néma, the provincial capital, was upgraded mainly with West German assistance and reopened in 1981. The country's other cities and towns have airports as well, including Akjoujt, Aleg, Atar, Ayoun el-Atrouss, Bir Moghrein, Boutilimit, Chinguetti, F'Derik, Kaédi, Kiffa, Rosso, Sélibaby, Tidjikja, and Zouerate (qq.v.). In addition, the towns of M'bout and Maghama in the région of Gorgol (q.v.), as well as a few other locations, have usable airports, and there are several other airstrips, of doubtful reliability, scattered elsewhere in Mauritania. The airport system has also been available for use by the country's small air force (q.v.).

AKJOUJT. Virtually the only population (q.v.) center of consequence in Mauritania's administrative région of Inchiri (qq.v.), of which it is the capital, Akjoujt is situated roughly halfway between the country's capital, Nouakchott (q.v.), and the city of Atar (q.v.) farther to the northeast. Akjoujt was also the site of Mauritania's only copper (q.v.) mining operation, which was conducted between 1970 and 1978 by the SOMIMA (q.v.) parastatal. From 1991, the town has also been the site of a successful gold (q.v.) mining endeavor, using the tailings from the old copper mine.

ALEG, CONGRESS OF (May 1958). Following the promulgation of the *loi cadre* (q.v.) by France in April 1957, and even before, several political parties were formed in what was to become independent Mauritania. Sharp differences, partly but not exclusively based on tribal and racial factors, quickly made themselves apparent, much to the anxiety of both Paris and the territory's rising political figure, Mokhtar Ould Daddah (q.v.), who led the *Union Progressiste Mauritanienne* (UPM) (q.v.), a grouping that attempted to accommodate all Mauritanians. In May 1958, at Ould Daddah's instigation, a meeting of all political groups was held at Aleg, the provincial capital of Brakna (q.v.). At the congress, it was agreed that in order to preserve national unity during the independence process, the UPM, a section of the country's first party, the *Entente Mauritanienne* (q.v.), and the *Bloc Démocratique du Gorgol* (BDG) (q.v.) would all merge and form the *Parti de Regroupement Mauritanien* (PRM) (q.v.), with Mokhtar Ould Daddah as the party's secretary-general. This move greatly increased Ould Daddah's credibility both at home and in France as seemingly the only person who could keep Mauritania unified and govern it after independence. The outcome of the Congress of Aleg was a blow, however, to those who desired closer association or outright integration with Morocco, and indeed, within a few months, the pro–Moroccans, joined by militant nationalists and youth leaders, formed a new opposition party, Nadha (q.v.).

ALGIERS AGREEMENT (Of August 5, 1979). A bilateral agreement signed in the Algerian capital between Mauritania's governing *Comité Militaire de Salut National* (CMSN) and the Polisario Front (qq.v.), this treaty finally extracted Mauritania from its calamitous involvement in the Western Sahara conflict (q.v.), which had begun in late 1975 with the partition of the former Spanish colony between the government of President Mokhtar Ould Daddah (q.v.) and Morocco. The period leading up to the signing ceremony was marked by a great deal of temporizing at the highest levels of the Mauritanian military regime, causing frequent changes in personnel and intense power struggles.

Widespread dissatisfaction with the conduct and effects of the Western Saharan war within Mauritanian society and within the country's armed forces (q.v.) culminated in the July 10, 1978, overthrow of President Ould Daddah by a group of army officers who formed a new ruling body, the *Comité Militaire de Redressement National* (CMRN) (q.v.). The new regime, however, was far from sure of how to bring the war to an end with the country's dignity and security reasonably intact. The first military leader, Colonel Mustapha Ould Mohammed Salek (q.v.) held that only a strategy of devising a "global" peace agreement among all of northwest Africa's states as well as France would suffice. The reasons for this were simple: despite a unilateral Polisario cease-fire on Mauritanian territory proclaimed shortly after the coup, Mauritania was still host to 9000 Moroccan troops stationed there pursuant to the arrangements of the May 1977 Moroccan-Mauritanian Defense Committee (q.v.). This was a very delicate situation, and the CMRN (and later the CMSN) feared Moroccan retaliation for any gesture it might make that King Hassan II (q.v.) could perceive as favoring Polisario.

For a time, Colonel Ould Salek doggedly pursued his comprehensive peace idea, but in April 1979, with Mauritania's economy still a shambles and Polisario's patience wearing thin, he found himself divested of all real power by Lieutenant Colonel Ahmed Ould Bouceif (q.v.). After Ould Bouceif's death in a plane crash a few weeks later (on May 27), Lieutenant Colonel Mohammed Khouna Ould Heydallah (q.v.) rose to the fore, and after some hesitation—and a renewal of armed actions by the Polisario Front—negotiations were begun, resulting after only a few days in the Algiers Agreement. In relevant part, the treaty read:

> The Islamic Republic of Mauritania solemnly declares that it does not have, nor will ever have any territorial or other claims on Western Sahara.
> The Islamic Republic of Mauritania has decided definitely to abandon the unjust war of Western Sahara according to the modalities agreed in common accord with the representative of the Saharan people, the Polisario Front.
> The Polisario Front solemnly declares in the name of the Saharan people, that it has no, and will never have any, territorial or other claims on Mauritania. . . .

There was more, however. Ould Heydallah secretly agreed to convey the Mauritanian share of Western Sahara, which it called Tiris el-Gharbia (q.v.), directly to the Polisario Front within seven months of the agreement. But as soon as the pact was signed and Mauritania began to withdraw, King Hassan took no chances: his troops at once occupied Tiris el-Gharbia, including its main settlement of Dakhla (q.v.), and Morocco formally annexed it a few days later. In spite of this, Morocco did remove its soldiers from Mauritania proper by early 1980, and did not challenge the continuing Mauritanian control of the small Western Saharan outpost of La Guera (q.v.), strategically located opposite the country's economic center of Nouadhibou (q.v.).

AL-ITTAFAQ. The first newspaper (q.v.) to be published in Mauritania, it was founded in the summer of 1948. Printed in a mimeographed bilingual Arabic/French format (it was also known as *La Concorde*), it played a major role in publicizing Mokhtar Ould Daddah's *Union Progressiste Mauritanienne* (UPM) (qq.v.), contributing to the UPM's victory over the more established *Entente Mauritanienne* (q.v.) in elections held in November 1952 for the French Territorial Assembly (q.v.).

ALLAL EL-FASSI. As a prominent Moroccan politician in the 1950s and 1960s and the leader of the *Istiqlal* (Independence) Party, he originated the concept of a "Greater Morocco," based upon the alleged historical ties between the Alawite monarchy and areas lying to the south of present-day Morocco. In practice, this meant that el-Fassi advocated the absorption into the Moroccan state of not only all of Mauritania, but also the adjacent Spanish colony of Western Sahara (q.v.), large tracts of the Algerian Sahara including the important town of Tindouf, the Spanish presidios of Ceuta and Melilla on Morocco's Mediterranean coast, and even parts of Mali far to the southeast. El-Fassi's views did not at first find great acceptance among the Moroccan public, but since the Istiqlal was an important competitor to the fledgling regime of King Mohammed V, the monarch felt that he could not be outmaneuvered on such obviously nationalistic grounds, and so embraced many of el-Fassi's positions.

The specter of a possible Moroccan move against Mauritania was a source of constant anxiety to President Mokhtar Ould Daddah (q.v.) following his country's independence in November 1960, and greatly affected his foreign relations (q.v.) posture for a decade. In the late 1960s, Mohammed V's successor, Hassan II (q.v.), who had also adopted the "Greater Morocco" cause, gradually softened his opposition to Mauritania's existence once he saw international and Arab League (q.v.) support for his territorial designs crumbling. As a result, King Hassan established diplomatic relations with Mauritania in April 1970. Allal el-Fassi, along with the rest of the Istiqlal ultranationalists, vehemently opposed this rapprochement, but King Hassan's political position within Morocco by that time was such that he could afford to disregard them. Allal el-Fassi died in 1974.

ALLIANCE POUR UNE MAURITANIE DEMOCRATIQUE
(AMD). The July 10, 1978, *coup d'état* in Mauritania which over-threw the civilian government of President Mokhtar Ould Daddah (q.v.) was not welcomed by all segments of the country's elite. Some were in favor of a continued alignment with Morocco's King Hassan II (q.v.) and opposed any attempt by Mauritania to relinquish its share of Western Sahara, Tiris el-Gharbia (qq.v.). Others found themselves disenchanted with the governing CMRN and CMSN (qq.v.) military councils as time went on, seeing the country's foreign relations (q.v.) as inordinately sympathetic to Algeria and the other "radical" states of the Arab League (q.v.). Furthermore, the consolidation of power by Colonel Mohammed Khouna Ould Heydallah (q.v.) in January 1980 meant that pro-Moroccan and other dissenting elements found themselves in relative eclipse. Various opposition groups soon formed, and in May 1980 in Paris, they agreed to form the Alliance for a Democratic Mauritania. It advocated multiparty government after the removal of the CMSN, although the rest of the AMD's agenda was ambiguous.

From the beginning, the AMD was an unwieldy organization. It included smaller groups all the way from an Islamic (q.v.)–oriented party led by ex–CMSN member Lieutenant Colonel Mohammed Ould Bah Ould Abdel Kader (q.v.) to the Marxist-inclined *Parti des Khadihines de Mauritanie* (PKM) (q.v.). Later, another demoted and self-exiled CMSN member, Lieutenant Colonel Ahmed Salem Ould Sidi (q.v.), threw in his lot with the AMD from his new home in Morocco. Some backing also came from the exiled president himself, Mokhtar Ould Daddah, although he reportedly became disillusioned by the presence of factional infighting within the AMD's ranks. The AMD was soon established in Dakar, Paris, and Rabat, and received some funding from the conservative Gulf monarchies who shared the AMD's suspicions of the Ould Heydallah regime. Rounding out the Alliance's disparate membership were a small number of *haratines* (q.v.) as well as some supporters of the pro-Iraq Arab Baath Socialist Party (ABSP) (q.v.).

Fairly rapidly adjusting their thoughts to action, elements of the AMD, led by the dissident army officers Ould Sidi and Ould Abdel Kader, infiltrated Mauritania from Senegal and mounted a coup attempt against Ould Heydallah on March 16, 1981. Considerable violence ensued around many government buildings in Nouakchott (q.v.) and about eight people were killed. Loyalist troops soon crushed the rebellion, and put Ould Sidi and Ould Abdel Kader before a firing squad a few days after their capture. Ould Heydallah publicly accused King Hassan of being behind this attempt to unseat him, and soon ended diplomatic relations with Rabat in retaliation. The CMSN chairman also did not hesitate to pressure the governments of France and Senegal to restrict the AMD's activities, an effort which met with some success and had the effect of crippling an already shaky patchwork of quarreling groups.

Many AMD members, including its leader, the former PKM militant Mustapha Ould Obeidrahmane, and the prominent Mauritanian civil servant Mohammed Abderrahmane Ould Moine, remained in exile until Ould Heydallah's successor, Colonel Maaouiya Ould Sid' Ahmed Taya (q.v.) amnestied them and invited them to return to Mauritania if they wished to join his government. At the investiture of President Ould Taya's new Council of Ministers (q.v.) in April 1992, Ould Moine was awarded the key post of foreign minister, a move seen by many observers as an attempt to restore good relations with the oil-rich Gulf monarchies (with whom Ould Moine had always been close) after those ties were badly frayed during the Gulf Crisis (q.v.) of 1990 and 1991. In addition, Ould Obeidrahmane became secretary-general at the Presidency in the first cabinet of Mauritania's Second Republic (q.v.), having previously served as minister of energy in 1991.

ALMORAVIDS. A powerful yet relatively short-lived religious movement in the eleventh century A.D., the Almoravids (also called *murabitun*) united the Sanhadja Berber (qq.v.) populace of modern-day Mauritania and converted them to the strict Malekite Sunni Islam (q.v.) that characterizes the country today. After their successes in Mauritania, the Almoravids went on to conquer vast stretches of North Africa and southern Spain, converting their inhabitants (often forcibly) to the Muslim faith. Disunity and outside pressures soon forced the northern Almoravid Empire out of existence, but in Mauritania its imprint went considerably deeper.

Around 1035 A.D., the leaders of the Gadala, one of the three component groups of the Sanhadja Confederation, returned from the pilgrimage (*hajj*) to the holy city of Mecca accompanied by Abdallah Ibn Yacin, a Muslim theologian who agreed to travel to Mauritania after Gadala leaders had argued to him that the superficial attachment of the Sanhadja to Islam needed rectification. Back home, however, many Gadala resented Ibn Yacin's authoritarianism and austere faith, and requested that he leave. Consequently, Ibn Yacin and his followers, by around 1041, constructed a *ribat,* or religious retreat, the location of which is unknown but which is believed by some historians to have been on the island of Tidra on Mauritania's Atlantic coast. A year or two later, having recruited many disciples from the nomadic tribes of the area (and gathering a good supply of weapons), the Muslims under Abdallah Ibn Yacin rapidly forced the Gadala, Lemtuna, and Messufa tribes to embrace Islam and abandon their "heretical" and animist ways. A decade later (in 1054) Almoravid power was enhanced immeasurably by the capture of the Maghrebi trading city of Sijilmasa and by the conquest of Aoudaghost (q.v.), the most important commercial outpost of the Soninké (q.v.), a key component group of the Kingdom of Ghana. With this pair of successes, Ibn Yacin gained control of both ends of the lucrative north-south caravan trade routes, but the social implications of Almoravid ascendancy were less clear, as only two years later (in 1056), both the residents of Sijilmasa and the Gadala Berbers rose in revolt against Ibn Yacin, who was killed in battle near Rabat, Morocco, in 1059 despite the crushing of the uprisings by Ibn Yacin's successor, Abu Bakr Ibn Omar, and his cousin, Yousuf Ibn Tasfin.

These revolts, coming just a short time after Almoravid rule had been instituted, illustrate the lack of cohesion in ancient Mauritanian society and the intense resentments of those (especially the Gadala) who perceived that fanatical outsiders were intent on destroying their independent way of life. But Ibn Omar and Ibn Tasfin carried their campaign to Morocco, invading it and founding Marrakesh in 1062 and sacking Fez and northern Morocco a few years later (1059). Meanwhile, the Almoravid Empire was threatened from another quarter—the Lemtuna and the Messufa, hitherto some of the most reliable followers of Islam, began fighting amongst themselves, dismaying Ibn Omar. While Ibn Tasfin was busy in Morocco, Ibn Omar decided to distract the attention of the two warring tribes by launching a *jihad* (holy struggle) against the still-powerful Kingdom of Ghana and the Soninké. For the next fourteen years (until 1076), the war raged on, finally ending with the defeat of Ghana and the capture by the Almoravids of the great Soninké trading city of Koumbi Saleh (q.v.). The Soninké, for their part, submitted to Islam for the first time. Ibn Omar's strategy of unifying his subjects by rallying them against a traditional external foe was, on the surface, successful, but events in Morocco and beyond belied any claims to unity. Owing to the long distances and poor communications between Mauritania and Morocco, Ibn Tasfin went his own way while Ibn Omar was engaged against Ghana, following up his conquest of Morocco with the occupation of western Algeria in 1082 and crossing into Muslim Spain in 1086, where he seized Andalucía by 1091 (Ibn Omar having been killed in Tagant [q.v.] in 1087 while quelling another insurrection). These actions had the effect of dividing the already loosely organized Almoravid Empire into two parts, northern and southern. While Mauritania in the south remained relatively peaceful in the early part of the twelfth century, the opposite was true in Morocco and Spain. After Ibn Tasfin's death in 1106, things went from bad to worse for the

Almoravids. Spain rebelled against Islam in 1144 as part of the Christian *reconquista,* and in 1147 Marrakesh was abandoned. By 1150, the northern Almoravid Empire was in a state of collapse. However, Almoravid rule lasted a while longer in Mauritania due to its geographical isolation. It would not be until over a century later that a group of Arab invaders from the east, the forerunners of the Beni Hassan (q.v.), would enter the country and eventually (by 1674) wipe out most remnants of Berber and Almoravid civilization in the Char Bobha (q.v.) or Thirty Years' War. The main historical contribution of the Almoravid period was its importation of Malekite Sunni Islam to the entire population, producing a remarkable degree of religious unity and enabling Mauritania, centuries later in 1960, to achieve independence as the world's first Islamic Republic.

AN-NADHA AL-WATANIYYA AL-MAURITANIYA (NADHA).
The Mauritanian National Renaissance (or Awakening) Party was founded in the politically unsettled aftermath of the Congress of Aleg (q.v.), which was held in May 1958 under the sponsorship of the country's foremost politician and future president, Mokhtar Ould Daddah (q.v.). The congress, which fused two previously existing groups, Ould Daddah's *Union Progressiste Mauritanienne* (UPM) and the smaller *Entente Mauritanienne* (qq.v.), resulted in the formation of a new organization, the *Parti de Regroupement Mauritanien* (PRM) (q.v.). The outcome of the Aleg meeting did not please everyone, particularly the younger, more radical members of the PRM who were upset by some of Ould Daddah's conservative policy stances. In July 1958 the PRM held its own congress at Nouakchott (q.v.) and the split became formal, as the younger rank and file were expelled from the party after having their policy proposals soundly rejected by the rest of the membership. The PRM outcasts then met at Kaédi (q.v.) on September 25 and 26, 1958, and officially formed Nadha; it was Mauritania's first opposition party specifically conceived as such. The secretary-general of the party was Ahmed Baba Miské (q.v.). Nadha's platform was, in the view of some commentators, closer in content and style to the nationalistic currents then sweeping the African continent than that of the more cautious PRM—it rejected Mauritanian participation in the French Community, insisted on immediate and total independence from France, and called for rapprochement with Morocco, which many took to be a sign that the party was in effect endorsing the "Greater Morocco" concept enunciated by Allal el-Fassi (q.v.) which favored federation, if not outright integration, with Rabat.

Although the formation of Nadha was intended to unify various strands of opposition to the PRM and its leader, Mokhtar Ould Daddah, the pan-Arab views of its leadership frightened many

Mauritanians, particularly Black Africans in the Senegal River Valley, who saw Nadha as solely oriented towards the country's Moorish (q.v.) element. As a consequence, the ethnic divide in the country widened rather than narrowed. Despite this, Nadha did score impressive gains in popularity, with substantial money for its activities coming from Morocco as well as from business interests in Mauritania. By May 1959, though, the fortunes of Nadha were in steep and, as it transpired, irreversible decline, as factional infighting within the party as well as allegations of corruption gave the PRM-dominated government the pretext to ban all political activity (except for the PRM itself) on the eve of the May 17 elections to Mauritania's first *Assemblée Nationale* (q.v.). In the polling, the PRM won all forty seats, leaving Nadha in the wilderness and outlawed. For a brief time, extremists in the now fragmented party mounted a campaign of violence and civil disobedience in Atar (q.v.) as well as in Nouakchott during May 1960, which resulted in Ould Daddah placing five Nadha leaders, (including Ahmed Baba Miské) in detention in the remote eastern province of Hodh ech-Chargui (q.v.). They were held there until February 1961, three months after Mauritania achieved full independence.

Despite the rough treatment that Nadha had received at the hands of President Ould Daddah, the remnants of the party responded favorably to calls from the head of state to put aside old differences and work together to strengthen the institutions of the infant state. Ahmed Baba Miské and his colleagues actively campaigned on Ould Daddah's behalf before the country's first presidential election, and were rewarded when Ould Daddah emerged victorious by being included in the first post-independence Council of Ministers (q.v.). In October 1961 Nadha, along with the dominant PRM and several other groups, agreed to merge at the Congress of Unity (q.v.) and form the *Parti du Peuple Mauritanien* (PPM) (q.v.), which soon established itself as Mauritania's only legal political organization.

ANNE AHMADOU BABALY. A Halpulaar (q.v.) from the Senegal River Valley, Anne Ahmadou Babaly was born in 1942, entered the Mauritanian armed forces (q.v.) in his youth, and attended a succession of French military academies, including the artillery and infantry school at Montpellier and the *Ecole Supérieure Intendance Militaire de Paris,* receiving his diploma in the early 1970s. Like most of his officer colleagues in Mauritania, he was drawn into the Western Sahara conflict (q.v.), although his duty postings were usually in the area of administration and finance. As a supporter of the military uprising that overthrew the country's civilian president, Mokhtar Ould Daddah (q.v.) on July 10, 1978, he became a member of the first army junta, the *Comité Militaire de Redressement National* (CMRN) (q.v.), serving there until the CMRN's replacement by a new council, the *Comité Militaire de Salut National* (CMSN) (q.v.). By now holding the rank of Commandant (major), he served for a short time as the CMSN's comptroller-general, but on June 3, 1979, he was named minister of supply and transport by the ascendant CMSN chairman, Lieutenant Colonel Mohammed Khouna Ould Heydallah (q.v.). He held that position until April 11, 1980, when his cabinet post was combined with the ministry of equipment, and so he emerged from this reshuffle with expanded responsibilities. In February 1983 Ould Heydallah moved him to the Ministry of Planning, where his financial talents could be better utilized. This appointment carried with it a promotion to lieutenant colonel, making him one of the highest-ranking black Mauritanian officers. A little over a year later, however, in March 1984, he was dismissed from the Council of Ministers (q.v.) by Ould Heydallah, reportedly because of his reservations about the head of state's abrupt diplomatic recognition, on February 27, of the Saharan Arab Democratic Republic (SADR) (q.v.), the government-in-exile of Western Sahara's Polisario Front (q.v.). Despite this, Babaly was restored to favor by July 1984, being appointed minister of mining and energy. At the same time, according to some observers, he conspired with his longtime friend, Colonel Maaouiya Ould Sid'Ahmed Taya (q.v.), an officer also demoted by Ould Heydallah, to depose the Mauritanian president, as he and Ould Taya were not only unhappy with Ould Heydallah's handling of the SADR issue, but were also alarmed at the corruption and mismanagement pervading the country at this time. As a result, Babaly was one of the prime movers of the peaceful palace coup that replaced Ould Heydallah with Ould Taya on December 12, 1984. At once, Babaly became minister of finance in the reorganized cabinet, occupying that post until April 1985, when he took over the key portfolio of minister of interior from its previous occupant, Lieutenant Colonel Djibril Ould Abdellahi (q.v.). The following year, however, his Interior Ministry position made him vulnerable to allegations of laxity when the militant black–led group, the *Forces de Libération Africaine de Mauritanie* (FLAM) (q.v.) became more active, in particular issuing its pamphlet, *Le Manifesto du Négro-Mauritanien Opprimé* (q.v.), in April 1986. In the atmosphere of suspicion which surrounded FLAM's emergence, Djibril Ould Abdellahi was able to win back the Interior Ministry for himself, sending Babaly into a lesser job as minister of commerce and transport on August 31, 1986. About five weeks later, on October 4, Babaly was ousted from the Council of Ministers entirely, also losing his seat on the CMSN by October 10, reportedly due to the governing council's belief that he was sympathetic to FLAM's objectives. Restored to private life, Babaly lived quietly until October 28, 1987, when he was arrested and accused of complicity in an alleged coup attempt said to have been planned for October 22 by FLAM-oriented army officers. Soon after this, he was placed on trial along with about fifty others before a special tribunal of military men at the J'reida barracks near Nouakchott (q.v.). On December 3, he was acquitted of all the charges against him, becoming one of the few officers to escape conviction. In early 1989 Babaly was partially rehabilitated by the CMSN, being made managing director of Mauritania's state insurance company, the *Société Mauritanienne d'Assurances et de Réassurances* (SMAR). He occupied that position until SMAR was liquidated in February 1994.

AOF. See Afrique Occidentale Française

AOUDAGHOST. The great trading and political capital of the Sanhadja Confederation (q.v.) and later of the Almoravid (q.v.) Empire, Aoudaghost is believed by historians and archeologists to have been first inhabited around 500 B.C. when long caravans of horses bound for Morocco passed through. Later, the increasing use of the camel as a means of transport brought the town further prosperity in the third century A.D. In the eighth century, Islam (q.v.) quickly took root in what is now Mauritania, imported from the east mainly by the Lemtuna Berbers (q.v.), who fairly rapidly gained control of the caravan routes between the Kingdom of Ghana, dominated by the Soninké (q.v.), and the city of Sijilmasa. From the eighth century to c. 990, the Sanhadja Confederation exercised unchallenged sway over Aoudaghost, but in 990 or so the town was captured by the Soninké in an attempt (which was successful for only 50 years) to cement their own political control. In 1054 the Almoravids, a fiercely Islamic movement led by Abdallah Ibn Yacin, seized Aoudaghost from the Ghanaians and began a period of about a century of Almoravid rule. The town is described during that period (the eleventh century A.D.), as having between 5000 and 6000 inhabitants, several mosques, and extensive agricultural (q.v.) activity around its perimeter supported by an impressive irrigation system. But Aoudaghost began to decline in importance after the collapse of the Almoravid Empire around the year 1200, and in the ensuing years trading patterns started to shift away from the traditional caravan routes and toward the coastal zones, where the first commercial contacts with Europeans were being made. Modern researchers have found that as the area became part of the Mauritanian Sahara, sand began to cover parts of the town, which was progressively rebuilt until its final abandonment around 1700. In the late twentieth century, its ruins are accessible by means of an unimproved road (q.v.) running about forty kilometers northeast of Tamchekket, a settlement located in the région of Hodh el-Gharbi (qq.v.).

ARAB BAATH SOCIALIST PARTY (ABSP). The Arab Baath (Renaissance) Socialist Party was founded in Damascus, Syria, in 1947 by two Arab intellectuals, Michel Aflaq and Salah al-Din Bitar and advocated, among other things, pan-Arab unity and resistance to the colonial rule then prevalent in North Africa and the Middle East. Despite the fact that branches of the Baath Party were established in many independent Arab capitals (including Amman and Cairo), the ABSP eventually came to power only in Syria (in 1963) and in Iraq (in 1963 and again in 1968), in the process undergoing a permanent schism between the Iraqi and Syrian "regional commands." After Iraq and Syria fell under Baathist domination, few if any other Arab countries had an ABSP presence, except, curiously, Mauritania, which (alone among North African states) acquired a pro-Iraq branch of the party in 1979 or 1980. The Mauritanian Baathists, drawn exclusively from the Moorish (q.v.) segment of the country's society, were not a significant political force in the beginning, as their patron, Iraqi President Saddam Hussein, was completely preoccupied with his seemingly endless war with Ayatollah Khomeini's Iran. The Mauritanian Baathists also had very little popular following; indeed, they were feared for their secretiveness and often exclusivist pan-Arab feelings, which sometimes threatened to alienate further Mauritania's substantial Black African population (q.v.) situated mainly in the Senegal River Valley.

The President of Mauritania from 1980 to 1984, Colonel Mohammed Khouna Ould Heydallah (q.v.), had little real difficulty with the Baath: he dealt with them as he did most of the other discordant elements in the country by alternately harassing, detaining, and releasing the party's members, moves which were sometimes followed by the elevation of some of the involved persons to positions of responsibility, by way of cementing their loyalty. A tougher approach could be discerned, however, in October 1982, when eleven Baathists were convicted of conspiring to overthrow Mauritania's CMSN (q.v.) regime. All were sentenced to between ten and twelve years' imprisonment, including a well-known Baath Party leader, a former journalist and minister of information, Mohammed Yehdih Ould Breideleil (q.v.). But as it turned out, the defendants served only a little more than two years behind bars, as they were amnestied by Colonel Maaouiya Ould Sid'Ahmed Taya (q.v.), a leading CMSN member who displaced Ould Heydallah on December 12, 1984, and who started his presidency by freeing many political prisoners. For a time, little more was heard of the Baath, but this situation lasted only into 1987, as the country's unsettled ethnic and economic situation worsened and gave pan-Arabists a chance to increase their influence in many spheres of Mauritanian life, including within the armed forces (q.v.) and inside (and close to) the CMSN itself.

For the moment, though, ABSP cadres had to undergo another period of repression. In September 1987 (and again in July 1988), many Baathists (including Ould Breideleil) were arrested, tried, and convicted on a variety of charges, most prominent among them what amounted to espionage on behalf of Baghdad. In the armed forces, the specter of the pro-Iraq Baath insinuating itself into Mauritania's most important institution was too much for Ould Taya and his cautious and nationalistic colleagues. Hence, virtually every Baath sympathizer in the army was dismissed by early 1988, particularly in the officer corps. But the Baath Party's cadres seemed to take these severe measures in stride, since they were trained by their Iraqi supporters to survive in exactly such an environment, and had organized all ABSP activities into tight-knit cells into which only dedicated, high-quality militants would be allowed. The Baathists, according to some observers, were a substantial force on the country's political scene more by virtue of organization and dedication than due to any support from ordinary Mauritanians.

By the middle of 1988, despite the repressive steps taken against them by the CMSN, the Baath Party managed to effect a sea change in Mauritanian domestic politics and its foreign relations (q.v.) alignments. Helped by Saddam Hussein's perceived victory over Iran in that year (conferring much added prestige upon Baghdad) and by Iraq's advertisement of itself as a dependable source of economic aid, military hardware, and technical expertise, the Mauritanian regime had come to rest by 1989 firmly within the orbit of that faraway Arab country, as the benefits of friendship with Iraq proved difficult for the CMSN to refuse. Visits by Iraqi emissaries soon became commonplace, and various governmental positions, notably those in education (q.v.), went increasingly to Baathists or their sympathizers. In a tense racial situation, moreover, the ABSP was Mauritania's most fervent supporter of Arabization (q.v.), considered by some black Mauritanians as well as by outside observers as harming the state of interethnic relations in the country. But the Baath's influence was destined to reach even greater heights after April 1989, the month which began a series of intercommunal disturbances that ignited the Senegal-Mauritania Crisis (q.v.) and which nearly brought the two states to war over their treatment of each other's nationals. The ABSP took full advantage of the crisis by exerting more pressure on the Ould Taya government to move closer to the Iraqi camp and further Arabize the country. President Ould Taya himself was increasingly isolated due to his non-Baathist proclivities, and watched uncomfortably as military deliveries from Baghdad increased exponentially. Baathists were reinstated into the armed forces and civil service at a rapid rate, and Ould Breideleil, who was released from prison in December 1989, was by the middle of 1990 promoted to executive secretary of the CMSN, becoming the highest-ranking civilian in the entire government. The ABSP also may have had some role in effecting the dismissal of the powerful (and anti-Baathist) minister of the interior, Djibril Ould Abdellahi (q.v.), in February 1990.

In the view of some, Mauritania appeared well on its way to becoming a satellite of Iraq, and the Baathists might have consolidated their presence further but for Saddam Hussein's invasion of Kuwait on August 2, 1990. Overnight, the political equations both inside Mauritania and outside the country underwent a reversal. Although Mauritanian public opinion was strongly pro-Iraq, these feelings were duplicated throughout North Africa and were not a reflection of Baathist influence. In fact Baathist influence sharply declined during the 1990–91 Gulf Crisis (q.v.), which ended in an Iraqi defeat on the battlefield and its forced ejection from Kuwait, consequently discrediting its Mauritanian backers. In addition, more neutralist figures, chief among them Ould Taya himself, were able during the period leading up to the Gulf War to garner a position of greater influence. After the end of the Gulf War in March 1991, the Arab Baath Socialist Party went into eclipse. The Baath Party did not field candidates under its banner for any of the elections that were held in Mauritania in early 1992, and suffered a telling reversal when Ould Breideleil, one of the leaders of the party for years, left the organization to become a leading member of the *Parti Républicain, Démocratique et Social* (PRDS) (q.v.). In the 1991–95 period, thus, the Baath Party appeared to have only a very minor presence on the Mauritanian political stage, although an officially-registered, Baath-oriented political party, known variously by its Arabic name, *Attali'a,* Vanguard or its French appellation, the *Parti de l'Avant Garde Nationale* (PAGN), existed with little apparent popular support.

This somnolent period for Mauritania's Baathists ended abruptly on October 23, 1995, when, in a massive police sweep, anywhere from 50 to 150 suspected Baathists, including Mohammed Yehdih Ould Breideleil, were arrested and detained for allegedly working on behalf of foreign (i.e., Iraqi) interests and for accepting funds for political activity from Baghdad. The arrests had foreign policy implications, too, as evidenced by the government's demand that Iraq's ambassador to Mauritania, Anwar Molad Dhibiane, leave the country immediately, bringing the already cloudy relations between the two countries to a new low. The Mauritanian interior minister, Mohamed Lamine Salem Ould Dah, hinted darkly at a coup attempt masterminded by Saddam Hussein, but as it had done a year earlier with a group of suspected Islamic fundamentalists, President Ould Taya's regime either released the ABSP militants outright or commuted the most serious charges against them to lesser offenses. However, seven supposedly pro-Baath Mauritanian army officers were arrested in early November, and it was not immediately clear whether the government would show the same leniency towards them as with the accused civilian Baathists.

ARABIZATION POLICY. As the term used to describe the Mauritanian government's gradual shift away from its alignment with Black Africa and toward the states of the Arab League (q.v.), Arabization was a largely unofficial policy in that no single law expressly provided for its application in all areas of Mauritanian life. However, the preference that successive regimes showed for Arabic culture and language could be seen primarily in the field of education (q.v.) and—according to critics—in the effects of otherwise neutrally drafted legislation such as the Land Reform Act of June 5, 1983 (q.v.), which allegedly discriminated against black Mauritanians who did not belong to Arab civilization.

Arabization's beginning could be traced not only to the numerical preponderance of Moorish (q.v.) Mauritanians, but also to the greater diplomatic recognition that the country began to receive in the mid-1960s from Arab states, which eased its isolation. This improving foreign relations (q.v.) climate was accompanied by domestic change: in January 1966, President Mokhtar Ould Daddah (q.v.) decreed the exclusive use of Hassaniya (q.v.) Arabic as the medium of instruction beyond the primary level. Although this move was protested by blacks, who preferred to be taught either in their own native tongues or in French, the policy was continued by later Mauritanian governments, albeit at a slower pace during the 1980–84 tenure of CMSN (q.v.) chairman Colonel Mohammed Khouna Ould Heydallah (q.v.). In other areas of Mauritanian life, such as land reform and the institution of the Islamic *sharia* (qq.v.), there was still a decided preference for the Arab point of view. On another level, blacks complained that Moors were given preference out of proportion to their numbers in employment by state enterprises, the civil service, and the armed forces (q.v.), and that this amounted to a conscious policy of "marginalization." Discriminatory enforcement of otherwise neutral laws and regulations was also alleged throughout the 1980s.

In foreign affairs, the admission of Mauritania to the Arab League in 1973 was a milestone along the road to orienting the country towards the Maghreb and with the Arab Middle East, a trend which was reinforced by Mauritania's need for financial and development aid from the wealthier Arab countries. The seal on this Arabist proclivity was set in February 1989, when Mauritania, along with Algeria, Libya, Morocco, and Tunisia, became a member of the *Union du Maghreb Arabe* (UMA) (q.v.). Still, Mauritania continued to earmark substantial financial aid to the black-dominated southern régions (q.v.) of the country for the purpose of promoting agriculture (q.v.), and always played a very active role in the affairs of the *Organisation pour la Mise en Valeur du Fleuve Sénégal* (OMVS) (q.v.).

The Arabization process in Mauritania reached a high point during the late 1980s. Due to the increasingly dominant role played in political life by the Arab Baath Socialist Party (ABSP) (q.v.), an Arab nationalist group with close ties to Saddam Hussein's Iraq, more key government ministries and civil service positions went to Baathists or their sympathizers. This was especially true in the sensitive areas of education and culture, and came at a time when aggressive Arab nationalism was on the rise due to increasing activism among some black Mauritanians, manifested by the high profile assumed by the *Forces de Libération Africaine de Mauritanie* (FLAM) (q.v.). After the Baathists' patron, Iraq, was defeated in the closing stages of the Gulf Crisis (q.v.) in January and February 1991, Arabization slowed considerably as the government of President Maaouiya Ould Sid'Ahmed Taya (q.v.) struggled to stabilize Mauritania's troubled internal situation and to mend fences with neighboring Senegal, with which relations had been extremely tense since the start of the Senegal-Mauritania Crisis (q.v.) in April 1989. But it was clear that the basic thrust of the Arabization policy would continue for the foreseeable future.

ARAB LEAGUE. After more than a decade of ostracism from intra-Arab affairs caused in large part by Morocco's claim to all of Mauritania, the country finally joined the League of Arab States in October 1973, after King Hassan II (q.v.) modified his territorial ambitions and established relations with the government of President Mokhtar Ould Daddah (q.v.) in April 1970. Arab League membership was also the culmination of Ould Daddah's realignment of Mauritania's foreign relations (q.v.) away from Black Africa and toward the Maghreb and the Middle East. Ould Daddah's decision to join the Arab League, however, was not universally well received at home: some black Mauritanian citizens protested the move, seeing it as potentially short-changing their interests relative to the country's Moors (q.v.). Despite these feelings, subsequent Mauritanian governments maintained a fundamental orientation toward the Arab world, due not only to ethnic affinity but also in an effort to attract much-needed financial assistance. Ties to the Gulf emirates, though, suffered a severe setback starting in August 1990, when Mauritania's perceived pro-Iraq stance during the Gulf Crisis (q.v.) cost it much goodwill and backing from the wealthy, oil-producing Arab League members who felt most threatened by Saddam Hussein's invasion of Kuwait.

ARAB MAGHREB UNION. See Union du Maghreb Arabe (UMA)

ARMED FORCES. When Mauritania became independent in November 1960 the country had no army of its own. For a variety of reasons, not least of which were a lack of finance and a paucity of trained officers from the politically dominant Moors (q.v.), the formation of a purely indigenous force (aside from paramilitary and police units) had to be deferred for a year. In October 1961 Mauritania began to field a 1000-man army known as the First Infantry Batallion. The personnel of this unit were spread thinly throughout the country's vast territory and served as little more than an internal security force with almost no capability against an external foe. The former colonial power, France, continued to station its own troops on Mauritanian soil until 1966 to take care of any outside threat, although President Mokhtar Ould Daddah (q.v.) ended their presence that year as part of a gradual reorientation of the country's foreign relations (q.v.) alignments. Between 1961 and 1976 the size of the armed forces never exceeded 3000 troops, a minuscule number even by African standards. This number included, in fact, several hundred men assigned to the air force and navy (qq.v.), the latter founded in January 1966 and based mainly in Nouadhibou (q.v.). Although the army was patterned after its French counterpart and officers received training at France's military academies (notably those at St. Cyr and St. Maxen), it remained internally oriented through the mid-1970s, and saw action on very few occasions, mostly to disperse demonstrations and put down strikes in the late 1960s and early 1970s in the economically vital iron ore (q.v.) industry. These tasks were undertaken in conjunction with Mauritania's other security forces, the National Guard and the *Gendarmerie Nationale* (qq.v.), and often involved considerable violence and some loss of life. President Ould Daddah, it was widely believed, kept the size of the army small in order to ward off any possibility of a *coup d'état*.

The Mauritanian national security outlook was completely transformed beginning in November 1975, when Ould Daddah joined with Morocco's King Hassan II (q.v.) and the Spanish government in the Madrid Agreement (q.v.), which partitioned the Spanish colony of Western Sahara (q.v.) between Mauritania and Morocco. The treaty gave Mauritania control over Tiris el-Gharbia (q.v.), an arid slice of desert adjacent to its northern administrative régions (q.v.). President Ould Daddah believed that his Saharan takeover would engender little opposition from the native Saharawi (q.v.) inhabitants of the territory, but he was soon proven to be quite mistaken. Beginning in late 1975, the forces of the pro-independence Polisario Front (q.v.) mounted sustained military attacks on Mauritanian targets, in particular its iron ore facilities and the railway (q.v.) connecting the mines to the port city of Nouadhibou. The armed forces were completely unprepared and outgunned from the beginning, and soon few areas of Mauritania were safe from Polisario's depredations. To hold onto Tiris el-Gharbia and to defend Mauritania proper Ould Daddah was compelled to massively increase the army's size: its personnel grew from 3,000 in early 1976 to 12,000 a year later, climbing again to 17,000 by the start of 1978. An unpopular conscription law was passed by an obedient *Assemblée Nationale* (q.v.) and recruiting drives in the countryside were stepped up, with many *haratines,* Halpulaaren (qq.v.), and other black Mauritanians being inducted into the enlisted ranks, a phenomenon which exacerbated the country's latent racial tensions, since the new troops were usually officered by Moors. Moreover, the Western Saharan war was widely disliked by most Mauritanians: many Moors felt ties of kinship with the Saharawis, and the blacks living in the Senegal River Valley saw the conflict as a faraway "Arab war" that could only affect their own interests negatively. As a consequence, morale in the army plummeted rapidly from 1976 to the middle of 1978.

The combat performance of the Mauritanian armed forces during their involvement in Western Sahara was mixed. Individual units often fought well in situations where they confronted Polisario units directly, and there were some excellent officers, such as Commandant Major Mohammed Khouna Ould Heydallah (q.v.), who distinguished himself during the first Nouakchott raid (q.v.) by Polisario in June 1976 by reacting quickly to intelligence on Saharawi guerrilla movements (partly supplied by the air force) and inflicting a severe defeat on the Polisario Front in the région of Inchiri (q.v.), in the process killing the Front's charismatic leader, El-Ouali Mustapha Sayed. The Mauritanian army also acted imaginatively in attempting to protect the critical mining town of Zouerate (q.v.): a wide, deep trench was dug around the entire settlement, a step which shielded it from capture until May 1, 1977, when the moat was circumvented by Polisario, who occupied Zouerate for several hours. The Zouerate raid placed into high relief the great dependence of enlisted men and noncommissioned officers on their superiors, as Ould Heydallah, the commander of the Zouerate area forces, was away on business in Nouakchott (q.v.) at the time and the entire garrison surrendered without firing a shot. Some observers ascribed this and other disasters to a lack of training and a defective command structure, but the real problem for Mauritania was one of numbers, mobility, and motivation. The small number of men in the armed forces were simply at a loss to defend a vast area with widely spaced population centers against an extremely mobile adversary whose morale only increased as Mauritania's declined. Air support was nearly nonexistent, and logistical backup in the Saharan wilderness, never an easy matter even in peacetime, was stretched beyond the breaking point. Constant reshuffles of commanders and Defense Ministry personnel by Mokhtar Ould Daddah did nothing for morale, and immediately after the debacle at Zouerate, he moved even closer to his former adversary, King Hassan, by agreeing to form a Moroccan-Mauritanian Defense Committee (q.v.) on April 13, 1977, a pact that gave Morocco the authority to station its *Forces Armées Royales* (FAR) in almost every significant northern Mauritanian town except the capital. This move upset many Mauritanians, not least the more nationalistically inclined army officers such as the chief of staff, Colonel Mustapha Ould Mohammed Salek (q.v.), whose relations with Ould Daddah were already strained and who resented being placed in a subordinate position to King Hassan's larger army. Around the same time, a new training facility for Mauritania's officer candidates, the *Ecole Militaire Interarmes d'Atar* (EMIA) (q.v.) was set up with French assistance in its namesake city. The country was soon obliged to call upon Paris for military help of a far more significant kind: in December 1977, Operation Lamantin (q.v.), a series of French air strikes against Polisario forces near the Zouerate-Nouadhibou railway, was carried out, inflicting great losses on the Saharawi nationalists but without altering the parlous state of Mauritania's own defenses.

On July 10, 1978, the Mauritanian armed forces ceased to be merely a defensive force and became the country's governing institution. A bloodless coup, led by Colonel Ould Salek, deposed the Ould Daddah regime and instituted direct army rule in the form of the *Comité Militaire de Redressement National* (CMRN) (q.v.), a group of high-ranking officers who had little in common with one another politically but who all shared an overwhelming desire to extract the nation from its ruinous entanglement in Western Sahara. A definitive peace with the Polisario Front, however, was to take a year to achieve, as there were 9000 Moroccan troops in Mauritania in 1978. The attitudes of France, which opposed a separate agreement with Polisario, also had to be considered. But while Colonel Ould Salek and his CMRN colleagues temporized over the following nine months, the quality of the army in the field deteriorated practically to vanishing point, as there was a great deal of anticipation in the ranks that no further fighting would take place and that demobilization was around the corner. Also, the officer corps' newfound preoccupation with politics and state administration left no time for leadership activity in the field, and so readiness hit bottom by early 1979. After several reorganizations of the military government in April and June 1979 (which involved establishing a new *Comité Militaire de Salut National* [CMSN] [q.v.] to replace the CMRN), and spurred on by a resumption of military attacks by Polisario in July 1979, the *de facto* CMSN leader, Lieutenant Colonel Ould Heydallah, signed a treaty with the front on August 5: the Algiers Agreement (q.v.) called for the abandonment of Mauritania's claim to Tiris el-Gharbia and was swiftly consummated, to the immense relief of virtually all the country's citizens.

Even before the Algiers peace treaty, roughly half of the army began to be disbanded, with the number of soldiers falling from 17,000 to about 7,500 in July 1980. A limited reequipment endeavor was begun, and a civic action program was inaugurated by Ould Heydallah under which soldiers would assist civilian farmers and workers in an attempt to integrate the army into national life. Military officers continued to govern Mauritania until April 1992, though, and the political nature of the army command, coupled with a pressing need to allocate scarce funds elsewhere, caused the force to remain underequipped and ill-prepared for combat throughout the 1980s. The life of a Mauritanian officer was not a tranquil one as the decade progressed, even without the stresses of war: coup plots and other alleged conspiracies were a constant reality and often resulted in the arrest, detention, and even execution of those thought by the CMSN to be allied with either France, Libya, Morocco, or, as the Senegal-Mauritania Crisis (q.v.) heated up in 1989 and 1990, with the Dakar government of Abdou Diouf (q.v.). In 1986 there was also a wholesale purge of black army personnel suspected of being sympathetic to the nascent armed opposition movement, the *Forces de Libération Africaine de Mauritanie* (FLAM) (q.v.), and about a year later, another batch of officers was cashiered for their supposed affiliation with the pro-Iraq Arab Baath Socialist Party (ABSP) (q.v.), although many of these were rehabilitated beginning in 1988 as the country's relationship with Saddam Hussein deepened.

Despite these events, the army did what it could to defend Mauritanian territory, extensively patrolling the Western Saharan border area from its base at Inal to prevent either Moroccan or Polisario forces from trespassing and possibly drawing the country into renewed involvement in the still unsettled dispute. In the Senegal River Valley, the army's role was far more controversial, as it was charged with preventing Senegalese forces, FLAM militants, or other non-Mauritanians from attempting to cross the border. To fulfill its mandate, army units, some reportedly made up of haratines and augmented by thousands of reservists called up during the crisis with Senegal, operated from bases at Aleg, Kaédi, and Rosso (qq.v.), maintaining, in the opinion of some international observers, a repressive atmosphere and holding certain towns, such as Bogué in the région of Brakna (q.v.), in the grip of martial law. Additional tasks for the army included guarding Zouerate's iron ore extraction facilities, ensuring the free passage of traffic along the *Route de l'Espoir* (q.v.) connecting Nouakchott with Néma (q.v.), and providing internal security in places as diverse as Akjoujt, Ayoun el-Atrouss, and Kiffa (qq.v.). There was also some reconnaissance of the sensitive Western Sahara border from a Mauritanian base at Bir Moghrein (q.v.), where soldiers undertook duties in some of the country's most forbidding terrain and climate (q.v.). In the capital, the regular army's strength was kept low due to Nouakchott's distance from any international frontier, although the Gendarmerie and the National Guard were present there along with the most elite national force, the *Bataillon de la Sécurité Présidentielle* (q.v.), which were under the authority of the Ministry of the Interior. An important army facility, the barracks at J'reida, was located about twenty-five kilometers north of Nouakchott.

The equipment and weapons possessed by the Mauritanian army in the mid-1990s mirrored its small size, limited means, and shifting mission. There were thirty-five or so Soviet-built T-54 and T-55 tanks supplied by Iraq before the Gulf Crisis (q.v.) of 1990–91, twenty AML-60 and forty AML-90 armored fighting vehicles purchased from France, and forty *Saladin* and five *Saracen* light armored vehicles from Great Britain. The artillery arm was made up mostly of 105 mm and 122 mm towed guns, numbering seventy-five to eighty all told and reportedly used in border skirmishes with Senegal. There were also a variety of mortars and recoilless guns used in an antitank role, and the French *Milan* antitank missile system was in use. The antiaircraft capability was at a rudimentary level, with twenty to thirty ZU-23-2 and M-1939 guns from the former Soviet Union, supplemented by SAM-7 hand-held rockets. A considerable number of Land Rover, Berliet, and Mercedes Benz Unimog trucks were also on the army roster, as airborne transport was not possible in most cases (for equipment levels in the AIR FORCE and NAVY, see those entries).

The roughly 14,000 men serving in Mauritania's ground forces in 1995 are divided into fifteen infantry battalions, three artillery battalions, four batteries of antiaircraft troops, and a single, well-equipped paratroop battalion along with an engineer company and an armored reconnaissance squadron. Rounding out the total are a varying number of headquarters and support personnel. Administratively, Mauritania's territory is divided into five military regions (a sixth was abolished soon after the Western Sahara war), the commanders of which are responsible to the army chief of staff (*chef d'état-major*) in Nouakchott, reporting to the minister of defense, who in turn answers to President Maaouiya Ould Sid'Ahmed Taya (q.v.), a former colonel who exercises his constitutional role as commander-in-chief of all Mauritanian forces. The headquarters staff comprises functions found in most armies, such as personnel, logistics, signals, and quartermaster. The officer rank structure, too, is fairly conventional, with the noncommissioned ranks of *sergent* to *adjudant-chef* being the equivalent of staff sergeant to sergeant-major in Western armed forces, on up to commandant (major) and lieutenant colonel and full colonel, the latter being the highest rank of any Mauritanian officer and which also made up a preponderance of CMRN/CMSN members from 1978 to 1992. Mauritania's colonels, however, have a wide variety of responsibilities beyond the superintendence of groups of fighting units. A colonel, for example, usually heads the air force and navy, and is also in charge of the EMIA military school. Other officers with colonel's rank also work in areas of finance and administration, with Anne Ahmadou Babaly and Mohammed Mahmoud Ould Louly (qq.v.), as well as CMRN leader Ould Salek showing a particular aptitude in those disciplines.

Although the two-year term of service for enlisted men is often fraught with hardship, the officer corps constitutes an elite segment at least in Moorish society, an outlook that has its roots in the martial inclinations of the *Beni Hassan* (q.v.). There is also a feeling of considerable pride, for officers and men alike, in belonging to one of the only all-Mauritanian institutions and in helping to promote national unity — and enjoying superior pay and material conditions into the bargain.

ARMY OF LIBERATION. An anticolonial guerrilla force that included various Mauritanian politicians among its supporters, the Army of Liberation (known in Arabic as the Jaich at-Tahrir), received its largest impetus from Morocco's accession to full independence from France on March 2, 1956. This event caused many Moroccans (particularly those from the south of the country), Saharawis (q.v.) from the Spanish colony of Western Sahara (q.v.), and some Mauritanians to focus their attention on those areas which were still under European rule. Although the Army of Liberation was composed for the most part of Berber (q.v.) peasants from the Rif mountains, some residents of Mauritania who were, for one reason or another, opposed to the generally conservative policies of Mokhtar Ould Daddah (q.v.) were also represented, notably one of the country's first indigenous elected officials, Horma Ould Babana (q.v.), who, after losing elections in Mauritania in 1952 and 1956, traveled in the summer of 1956 to Morocco, where he founded the Mauritanian National Liberation Front (q.v.), an element of the Jaich at-Tahrir. For the most part, Army of Liberation members espoused the "Greater Morocco" aspirations of the veteran Moroccan politician Allal el-Fassi (q.v.). In practice, this meant that the army's military campaign (which began in mid-1956) would not only be directed against the French and Spanish colonialists, but also would have the long-range goal of affiliating Western Sahara and Mauritania more closely with Morocco, with complete integration an objective held by many. One of the Army of Liberation's largest attacks took place on February 15, 1957, when a French force was ambushed in the northern Adrar (q.v.) region near the Algerian border, causing much loss of life. The attackers, significantly, fled back into Western Sahara, which was being utilized as a "safe haven" by the irregulars.

It was the Spanish who suffered the greatest number of reverses in the low-key, hit-and-run war in the desert reaches of Western Sahara—even the city of Smara in Saguia el-Hamra (q.v.) was abandoned to the guerrillas in July 1957. The French were deeply anxious too. The campaigns of the Army of Liberation had created an atmosphere of insecurity in northern Mauritania, where immense deposits of iron ore (q.v.) were awaiting extraction by the MIFERMA (q.v.) consortium, in which French capital was heavily represented. More generally, the Army of Liberation was a threat to Paris's autonomy plans for the country, to be followed by full independence under the decidedly Francophile Mokhtar Ould Daddah. Ould Daddah himself felt threatened as well, and Morocco's king, Mohammed V, who had previously supported some of the irregulars' activities, felt increasingly uncomfortable with their presence in his country, terming them "uncontrolled." The Spanish continued to suffer further military reverses all through 1957 in Western Sahara, which in turn caused the French still more consternation, since Madrid's forces were not able to defend themselves, let alone prevent attacks on Mauritanian targets. As Gaston Cusin, the high commissioner of *Afrique Occidentale Française* (AOF) (q.v.) said on February 28, 1957, "the Spanish authorities in Río de Oro (q.v.) have given us their full cooperation in the recent Mauritanian events, but they have only been able to do so to the extent of their military means which are very limited." This situation, both Paris and Madrid realized, could not continue indefinitely, and they decided at the end of 1957 to take swift and drastic military action.

After extensive planning, a massive French-Spanish joint campaign, code-named Operation Ouragon (q.v.), swung into execution on February 10, 1958. With 14,000 troops (5,000 French and 9,000 Spanish), it succeeded within two weeks by dint of concentrated firepower in clearing Western Sahara and northern Mauritania of Army of Liberation fighters, who were forced into headlong retreat. By February 24, the operation had ended with French control of its Mauritanian territory preserved and Spain enjoying similar fruits of victory next door in its "Saharan province."

Operation Ouragon was the Army of Liberation's death knell. A falling out, already in progress between the younger, more radical leaders of the organization and the older tribesmen who made up the guerrillas' rank and file, grew steadily worse following their military defeat, which left thousands destitute in southern Morocco. In addition, Mohammed V's government was steadily bringing southern Morocco under royal control, ending the Army of Liberation's freedom of movement. In return for laying down their weapons and submitting to Moroccan rule, the former irregulars were offered the chance to enlist in Morocco's developing regular army, the *Forces Armées Royales* (FAR), in addition to other financial incentives such as land and jobs with the government, offers which were nearly always accepted with alacrity.

ARRONDISSEMENT. The smallest unit of local government in Mauritania, these were known as "administrative posts" under the Constitution of May 20, 1961 (q.v.). On July 30, 1968, as part of a reorganization of the structure of the government by President Mokhtar Ould Daddah (q.v.), the administrative posts were renamed *arrondissements,* although the relatively small areas covered by each (usually a town or settlement and its environs) stayed essentially the same. A varying number of arrondissements made up a *département* (q.v.), the next highest step on the governmental ladder, which in turn were combined to form *régions* (q.v.), of which there were twelve in Mauritania, along with a special district encompassing the capital, Nouakchott (q.v.). In reality, the country had always been governed mainly from the center, and, during the 1978–1992 period of direct rule by the armed forces (q.v.), the arrondissements ceased to be anything but a formality, although the regime of President Maaouiya Ould Sid'Ahmed Taya (q.v.) held municipal elections in December 1986, which marked an end to the direct appointment of mayors and *chefs d'arrondissement* by the ruling *Comité Militaire de Salut National* (CMSN) (q.v.). In 1995, arrondissements make up the majority of the country's 208 electoral units, most of which are controlled by the dominant political party, President Ould Taya's *Parti Républicain, Démocratique et Social* (PRDS) (q.v.).

ASSABA. A Mauritanian administrative région (q.v.) covering 37,000 square kilometers in the south-central portion of the country, Assaba had a population (q.v.) in 1977 of about 129,000 people, which declined somewhat by 1988, when a government census put the figure at 107,123. Assaba has a short border with Mali in the south of the province, along the Karakoro River, and is one of the relatively few areas of Mauritania whose climate (q.v.) can support agriculture (q.v.). Assaba has been connected to the rest of the country by the Trans-Mauritanian Highway (q.v.) since the 1970s, but its only large town is Kiffa (q.v.), which has over 30,000 people.

ASSEMBLEE NATIONALE. (1) Mauritania's first National Assembly or parliament was elected by universal suffrage on May 17, 1959, replacing the former representative body, the Constituent Assembly (q.v.). All forty seats in the unicameral Mauritanian legislature were won by candidates put forward by Mokhtar Ould Daddah's *Parti de Regroupement Mauritanien* (PRM) (qq.v.). The National Assembly existed as an officially coequal branch of the government (along with the executive and the judiciary) under the Constitutions of Mauritania dated March 22, 1959 and May 20, 1961 (qq.v.). In practice, the National Assembly's powers were sharply circumscribed, with President Ould Daddah retaining nearly plenary powers over national defense and foreign relations (q.v.) as well as exercising complete authority over his Council of Ministers (q.v.). Moreover, Ould Daddah was not necessarily obliged to accept contrary votes or resolutions by parliament. He could, for example, circumvent a legislative vote against his annual budget (q.v.) by the simple expedient of promulgating an interim budget which possessed equal legal effect. In another tactic, the president deluged the assembly on more than one occasion with proposed laws, each of which was required to be voted on before parliament could put forward any bills of its own. This, more than any other factor, effectively stifled the independence of the National Assembly. On December 25, 1961, one year after Mauritania's independence and two months after the Congress of Unity (q.v.) that amalgamated the PRM and other groups into a single organization, the *Parti du Peuple Mauritanien* (PPM) (q.v.), the PPM was proclaimed the sole legal political party in the country, putting to an end a brief experiment in multiparty democracy. With all other parties outlawed, the PPM's monopoly in the National Assembly was assured, although it would be a few years before the last stirrings of independent initiative from PPM members were squelched and national policy deliberations put firmly into the hands of the *Bureau Politique National* (BPN) (q.v.), a handpicked group of Ould Daddah loyalists. Thereafter, the Mauritanian legislature became a somnolent, wholly symbolic body, serving merely as a rubber stamp for presidential decisions. From its original membership of forty, the National Assembly grew in size to fifty in 1971 and seventy-eight by 1975. The National Assembly was dissolved along with the PPM on July 10, 1978, by means of one of the first edicts issued by the *Comité Militaire de Redressement National* (CMRN) (q.v.), a group of officers from the Mauritanian armed forces (q.v.) who had overthrown the Ould Daddah regime earlier that same day.

(2) After fourteen years without a parliament, Mauritanian voters elected a new National Assembly on March 6 and 13, 1992, as part of a thoroughgoing reform of the country's political order instituted by President Maaouiya Ould Sid'Ahmed Taya (q.v.), who had decisively triumphed in Mauritania's first-ever open presidential elections on January 17. The new National Assembly, like its legislative counterpart, the Senate (q.v.), owed its existence and authority to the Constitution of Mauritania of July 20, 1991 (q.v.), approved in a referendum

held two weeks earlier. The balloting for the National Assembly was significantly marred by a boycott of the election called by opposition groups, notably the *Union des Forces Démocratiques* (UFD) (q.v.). The UFD and others alleged that the government had engaged in massive vote fraud in the presidential election and that Ould Taya's *Parti Républicain, Démocratique et Social* (PRDS) (q.v.) enjoyed an unfair advantage. As a result of the UFD-led abstention, the outcome of the National Assembly election was an unsurprising landslide for the PRDS. Of a total of seventy-nine seats at stake, Ould Taya's organization captured sixty-seven, with one seat apiece going to two political groups that had not joined the boycott, the *Rassemblement pour la Démocratie et l'Unité* (RDU) and the *Parti Mauritanien pour Renouveau* (PMR) (qq.v.). Another ten seats were awarded to independent candidates, but the composition of the National Assembly meant that President Ould Taya and his new prime minister, Sidi Mohamed Ould Boubacar (q.v.), would encounter little difficulty in instituting their political and economic agenda for the country, which required parliamentary approval. Pursuant to the 1991 constitution, all the National Assembly's deputies were elected for five-year terms and were required to be Mauritanian citizens and at least twenty-five years of age (Article 47). Parliament was to meet twice a year, in May and November, for a maximum of two months (Article 52), although the President of the Republic could convene the assembly for a specific reason (Article 53). Officially, the National Assembly enjoyed a broad scope of authority, as described in Articles 56–58, including the power to declare war and to approve treaties with other countries. In addition, detailed procedures were outlined by the constitution (Articles 61–70) for the proposal, amendment, approval, and ratification of legislative measures, especially in the area of state finances. The National Assembly could also institute a vote of no confidence in the Council of Ministers (Articles 74 and 75) and thus force the cabinet's resignation. Since President Ould Taya's PRDS dominated the assembly's affairs, it was not immediately possible to gauge the practical extent of parliamentary powers that existed on paper, a situation that has made it difficult to render an overall verdict on the workings of Mauritania's Second Republic (q.v.) in the mid-1990s.

ASSEMBLEE TERRITORIALE. The successor body to the *Conseil Général* (q.v.) under French colonial administration, the unicameral Territorial Assembly was established in 1952 and was designed as an interim legislative chamber, with circumscribed powers, that would facilitate the transition to independence in close association with Paris. In November 1952, elections to the new assembly were held, and the results marked the beginning of the rapid ascent in the political fortunes of the future president of Mauritania, Mokhtar Ould Daddah (q.v.). His *Union Progressiste Mauritanienne* (UPM) (q.v.) won twenty-two of the twenty-four seats, while the two others went to the *Entente Mauritanienne* (q.v.). After a period of several years, during which several political realignments took place, new elections to the Territorial Assembly were held on March 31, 1957, which resulted in another sweep for the UPM, which received all but one of the thirty-four seats in the chamber. Despite this overwhelming victory, Mokhtar Ould Daddah attempted to include as many political tendencies as he could in his new Mauritanian government, which was formed on May 21, and a year later, May 1958, he felt sufficiently sure of his own influence that he persuaded several smaller parties to merge with the UPM at the Congress of Aleg (q.v.) and to form the *Parti de Regroupement Mauritanien* (PRM) (q.v.). On November 28, 1958, the Islamic Republic of Mauritania was formally declared (although full autonomy was not to occur until two years later), and the Territorial Assembly was replaced by a new body, the Constituent Assembly (q.v.).

ASSOCIATION DE LA JEUNESSE DU PRM. A small yet influential political party and youth organization made up of those Mauritanians who chose not to associate themselves with the radical, pan-Arab Nadha (q.v.) party founded by Ahmed Baba Miské (q.v.) in September 1958, the group was made up of both black and Moorish (q.v.) Mauritanians who wanted a more broadly based, yet still nationalistic party to represent them. The formation of the Youth Association of the *Parti de Regroupement Mauritanien* (PRM) (q.v.) came in a rather roundabout manner: those members of the earlier *Association de la Jeunesse Mauritanienne* (AJM) (q.v.) who had chosen to join hands with Mokhtar Ould Daddah's (q.v.) PRM after that party was created at the Congress of Aleg (q.v.) in May 1958, found themselves once again in the wilderness two months later, in July 1958, when they were expelled from the PRM for their "radical" sentiments and their desire for more pluralism in Mauritanian political life. Some former AJM cadres decided to form Nadha, but that party's strongly pro-Arab, anti-French line did not attract everyone; more moderate elements decided to return to the PRM's fold and open its membership rolls to blacks and Moors alike. As such, the Youth Association of the PRM played a key role in helping to reduce racial and ethnic tensions in Mauritania at a time when the country's political situation looked cloudy and some observers were questioning its viability as a future independent state.

ASSOCIATION DE LA JEUNESSE MAURITANIENNE (AJM). The Association of Mauritanian Youth, the country's first political party specifically designed to attract young people, was formed out of a split with the older, more established leaders of the *Union Progressiste Mauritanienne* (UPM) (q.v.), which had defeated Mauritania's very first political grouping, the *Entente Mauritanienne* (q.v.), in territorial legislative elections in November 1952. Younger, more radical elements of the UPM, despairing of the pro-French, basically conservative attitudes of the party's leader, Mokhtar Ould Daddah (q.v.), broke with the party at the UPM congress held at Rosso (q.v.) in November 1955, and the AJM was formally established a few days later. Staunchly anticolonialist, the AJM lacked a clear platform and never broadened its base of support, which was confined to a few groups of sympathizers in Mauritania's northern towns, which were dominated by Moorish (q.v.) interests. Indeed, many AJM leaders were aggressively pan-Arab, limiting the group's appeal to black Mauritanians in the Senegal River Valley. In the 1956 elections to the *Conseil Général* (q.v.), the AJM lost badly, polling a mere 585 votes. Thereafter, the party's fortunes went into a steep decline and it stayed outside the main currents of the country's politics, refusing, for example, to participate in Ould Daddah's first Territorial Assembly (q.v.) convened on May 21, 1957. The formation of the *Parti de Regroupement Mauritanien* (PRM) (q.v.) by Ould Daddah at the Congress of Aleg (q.v.) in May 1958 made the AJM even less relevant, and the party soon splintered completely when tensions between Moorish and black youths resulted in the formation on September 26 of *An-Nadha al-Wataniyya al-Mauritaniya* (q.v.), led by the ardently pan-Arab politician, Ahmed Baba Miské (q.v.). Some AJM cadres joined Nadha, but other, more moderate nationalists refused to become members and instead formed their own organization, the *Association de la Jeunesse du PRM* (q.v.).

ATAR. As one of the most important and strategic population (q.v.) centers in Mauritania and the administrative capital of the Adrar région (qq.v.), Atar had a reported population of 16,326 in 1976, a number which according to some observers had at least doubled by the early 1990s, as droughts and the process of desertification (q.v.) compelled many nomadic Moorish (q.v.) inhabitants of the Adrar to settle on the city's outskirts, where they often had to subsist on imported food. Atar is a significant oasis in the midst of the country's unrelieved Saharan expanses, and supports extensive groves of date palms as well as other agricultural and livestock (qq.v.) activity. In addition, the city was a major resting point and commercial center for the caravan routes that dated to antiquity, particularly those whose destination lay in Morocco, hundreds of kilometers to the north. Atar consists of an older core area, the *ksar,* surrounded by a newer quarter with more modern buildings. In the early twentieth century, the city was a crucial objective of the

French colonial "pacification" effort; indeed, the primary goal of Xavier Coppolani (q.v.), who was assassinated in Tidjikja (q.v.) in May 1905, was the conquest of Atar as the lynchpin of the surrounding countryside. After the death of Coppolani, it was left to his successor, Colonel (later General) Henri Gouraud (q.v.), to enter the city during his *Colonne d'Adrar* (q.v.) of 1909 and claim it as a French possession. Until Mauritania's independence in November 1960, Atar continued to host a significant French military presence as well as an elaborate fort on the city's periphery. In the midst of the Western Sahara conflict (q.v.) in 1976, Mauritania established (near the old French fort) the *Ecole Militaire Interarmes d'Atar* (EMIA) (q.v.), the country's center for the training of officer candidates for its armed forces (q.v.). Atar is connected by an improved road (q.v.) to the Mauritanian capital, Nouakchott (q.v.), which is located about 500 kilometers to the southwest, and the city has an airport (q.v.) with regular service.

AYOUN EL-ATROUSS. The administrative center of Mauritania's Hodh el-Gharbi région (qq.v.), Ayoun el-Atrouss had an officially reported population (q.v.) of 12,000 in 1977, a figure which had probably at least doubled by the mid-1990s. The town is located two hundred kilometers east of Kiffa (q.v.) on the Trans-Mauritanian Highway (q.v.), a high-quality road extending from the Mauritanian capital of Nouakchott to Néma (qq.v.). The town is also an important center for commerce (q.v.) not only for the Western Hodh itself but also for Mali, whose border lies about one hundred kilometers to the south. Some agriculture and livestock (qq.v.) activity is also carried on there, as it has a Sahelian climate (q.v.).

BAATH PARTY. See Arab Baath Socialist Party (ABSP)

BAIE DU LEVRIER. (1) The name given by the French colonial regime to the present-day administrative région of Dakhlet-Nouadhibou (qq.v.), an area that encompasses about 22,000 square kilometers and whose center is the city of Nouadhibou (q.v.).

(2) Sometimes also known as Dakhlet-Nouadhibou, and occasionally called Greyhound Bay in some publications, the Baie du Lévrier is one of the largest natural harbors on the entire West African coast, and the only such harbor in Mauritania. Formed by the Cape Blanc peninsula (now known as Ras Nouadhibou) which extends about fifty kilometers and which is shared by Mauritania and a portion of Western Sahara (q.v.), including the small settlement of La Guera (q.v.), the bay is about forty-three kilometers long and thirty-two kilometers wide at its broadest point. Because of its sheltered location, it has been independent Mauritania's prime area of economic activity and commerce

(q.v.), not only supporting a major fisheries (q.v.) industry but also the place where iron ore (q.v.) shipments, carried from inland locations by the country's only railway (q.v.) line, are loaded onto ships at the *Port Minéralier* (q.v.), ten kilometers south of Nouadhibou. The Baie du Lévrier features an absence of strong currents along with favorable prevailing winds, with very few storms occurring that would adversely impact shipping. However, shallow water in much of the bay has made it necessary for the Mauritanian mining parastatal, SNIM-SEM (q.v.), to spend considerable time and money dredging the ship channel. With new iron ore deposits at M'Haoudat in Tiris Zemmour (q.v.) promising to keep the Port Minéralier busy well into the twenty-first century, SNIM-SEM undertook an extensive study of needed modifications to the loading areas and ship channels in the early 1990s. Possible projects include either building a new loading quay 430 meters south of the existing one, or building an entirely new loading facility about six kilometers south, near the tip of Ras Nouadhibou. The latter project would be connected to the ore stockpile area by a conveyor belt.

BAMBARA. One of Mauritania's smallest Black African groupings, the Bambara have been estimated to number only about 10,000, concentrated almost exclusively in the eastern régions of Hodh ech-Chargui and Hodh el-Gharbi (qq.v.). Most other Bambara live in adjacent Mali. In common with their more numerous black counterparts, notably the Halpulaaren and Soninké (qq.v.), they are mostly sedentary farmers and livestock (q.v.) herders. Like Moorish (q.v.) Mauritanians, the Bambara have historically recognized the existence of occupational castes and the institution of slavery (q.v.), although both had vastly declined by the late twentieth century.

BANKING SYSTEM. Mauritania's commercial and development banks were in a state of considerable flux in the mid-1990s after going through a difficult decade. In addition to the state-run *Banque Centrale de Mauritanie* (BCM) (q.v.), there were a varying number of other lending institutions, some of them capitalized by fellow Arab League (q.v.) members such as Kuwait, Libya, and Saudia Arabia. This seeming abundance of capital, however, did not prevent certain banks from experiencing severe trouble from about 1982, due to a rash of nonperforming loans, poor financial management, and a general downturn in the Mauritanian economy. For a time, the BCM was forced to draw down its own scarce fiscal resources to rescue the other banks, an effort that was not always successful, as when the *Union des Banques de Développement* (UBD), formed by a 1987 consolidation of two earlier banks, was obliged to close its doors on June 24, 1993, after running up losses of $30 million from unwise lending decisions.

Also, the *Banque Internationale pour la Mauritanie* (BIMA), and the *Société Mauritanienne de Banque* (SMB) were forced to merge in 1987. Together they formed a new *Banque Nationale de Mauritanie* (BNM) whose 50 percent state ownership had, by 1995, been liquidated as almost exclusive private participation in the lending sector became the rule. The country's primary commercial bank in 1996 is the *Banque Mauritanienne pour le Commerce International* (BMCI), whose capital is 90 percent derived from the Mauritanian private sector, and which maintains branches in Ayoun el-Atrouss, Néma, and Nouadhibou (qq.v.), in addition to its head office in Nouakchott (q.v.). The BMCI's reserves are estimated at 750 million *ouguiyas* (q.v.). Other commercial banks include the *Banque Arabe Libyenne-Mauritanienne pour le Commerce Extérieur et le Développement* (BALM), which is partly owned by the Libyan government, and the *Banque al-Baraka Mauritanienne Islamique* (BAMIS), which is 50 percent owned by Saudi interests and is operated according to Islamic (q.v.) banking principles. BAMIS is the wealthiest of Mauritania's banks, with a capitalization of about 1 billion ouguiyas in 1995. Since the Mauritanian government has been attempting to jettison its shares in these banks as well as others, the country seems headed for a situation, by the mid-1990s, in which it would be nearly the only African state with little or no state involvement in banking. Even with thoroughgoing reforms, though, Mauritania's banking sector faces all the difficulties that accompany an economy acutely sensitive to worldwide recession, variable prices for iron ore (q.v.) and other export commodities over which the country has little control, and the changing fortunes of the agricultural and fisheries (qq.v.) sectors. The temptation (often coupled with necessity) for the regime to borrow from European banks is always present, and there is a continuing absence of international banks from Europe and North America in Mauritania. Moreover, banking facilities for the average Mauritanian outside of Nouakchott and Nouadhibou are scarce, although the BNM does maintain branch offices in Akjoujt, Kiffa, Rosso, and Zouerate (qq.v.)

BANQUE CENTRALE DE MAURITANIE (BCM). The Central Bank of Mauritania was opened in 1973 by the government of President Mokhtar Ould Daddah (q.v.) as the country's bank of issue, charged with the distribution and pricing of the national currency, the *ouguiya* (qq.v.), which was established that same year after Ould Daddah took Mauritania out of the *Communauté Financière Africaine* (CFA) (q.v.), the French-dominated monetary consortium. The BCM was also responsible for the supervision of the lending activities of the other components of the Mauritanian banking system (q.v.) and functioned as a lender of last resort for the indigenous and Arab-supported banks in the country. Beginning in the early 1980s, concomitant with a general deterioration in the state of the Mauritanian economy, the BCM was saddled with a great number of nonperforming loans, and in addition had its capital depleted by at least 50 percent by a combination of high government demands for funds and by the need to salvage other Mauritanian banks to enable them to remain open. At the urging of the World Bank and the International Monetary Fund (IMF) in the late 1980s, the BCM's operations were reorganized and government participation was greatly reduced, coupled with stricter oversight of the other development banks and foreign-based lending institutions. The capital of the Central Bank of Mauritania in 1992 stood at approximately 200 million ouguiyas, much less than its private counterparts. Even after additional privatization of the banking sector, the BCM was still envisioned to be Mauritania's primary national bank with some continued responsibilities in the area of monetary policy. Headquartered in the Mauritanian capital, Nouakchott (q.v.), the BCM also has four branches elsewhere in the country, and is supervised by the President of the Republic through the Ministry of Finance.

BATAILLON DE LA SECURITE PRESIDENTIELLE. An elite, specially equipped unit of the National Guard (q.v.), the Presidential Security Battalion is composed of several hundred men and is operationally responsible to the minister of the interior. It is charged with the protection of Mauritania's President, his family, and his offices and residence. During the late 1980s, at the height of the Senegal-Mauritania Crisis (q.v.) and of the influence of the Arab Baath Socialist Party (ABSP) (q.v.) in the country, the unit became the object of attention when it was rumored that the regime was considering the use of Iraqi troops as staff, a move which might have placed President Maaouiya Ould Sid'Ahmed Taya (q.v.) in a compromising position relative to Iraq's leader, Saddam Hussein. However, it was decided in the end that Iraq would only train and equip the unit's Mauritanian members, who were reported to be mostly Ould Taya's tribal kinsmen, the Semassides of the région of Adrar (q.v.).

BENI HASSAN. A prominent Arab grouping of warriors, the Beni Hassan, also called Maqil Arabs, succeeded, in the period extending from the fourteenth to the seventeenth century A.D., in overcoming all resistance, passive as well as active, to their domination of present-day Mauritania. After the decline of the Almoravid (q.v.) Empire starting in the late eleventh century, a succession of other dynasties, some Berber (q.v.) but also some controlled by Black Africans, exercised their sway over the region, notably the Mali and Songhai Empires, the Songhai being defeated by a Moroccan force in the sixteenth century.

After this, the way was open for the Beni Hassan, thought to have originated in Yemen, to migrate south and west, having already caused most of the western Maghreb to submit to their rule. The Berber groups, most notably the Sanhadja, bitterly resisted the Beni Hassan invaders, who were noted for their near-fanatical adherence to Islam (q.v.) and for the destruction they left in their wake. In addition, the Beni Hassan skillfully made (and broke) a series of alliances with the Sanhadja Berbers in order to further their own ends. A century later, by about 1600, the Beni Hassan had pushed most black Mauritanians south to the Senegal River Valley, usually impressing into slavery (q.v.) those who stayed behind. The Berbers made what turned out to be one final effort to throw off the yoke of the invading Beni Hassan — the Char Bobha (q.v.), or Thirty Years' War, which lasted from 1644 to 1674 and which ended in the total defeat of the Berbers and forced them, by the terms of the Peace of Tin Yedfad, to submit permanently to the victors, "giving up the sword for the book." Some of the vanquished Berbers became *zawiya* (q.v.), or religious tribes, thereby preserving considerable social status, and many others became *znaga* (q.v.), or tributaries, forced to pay an exacting and humiliating form of "protection" known as *horma*. Soon after the end of the Char Bobha, the term *hassan* (q.v.) became the generic term for those tribes that occupied the highest position in the fast-developing Moorish (q.v.) social hierarchy, although the processes of intermarriage and fusion with Berber and other Arab tribes continued into the nineteenth century. Interestingly, it was in the Adrar (q.v.) region where some resistance to the hassan continued into the late 1800s, just before the period of French penetration and "pacification." But by then, the victory of the Beni Hassan over the Berbers was well-nigh complete, achieved as much by weight of numbers and religious piety as by skill on the battlefield. By the twentieth century most, if not all, Moors in the territory of Mauritania considered themselves Arabs, not Berbers, and nearly all spoke Hassaniya (q.v.) Arabic, the name deriving from the Beni Hassan themselves and which included some Berber elements. The rigid hierarchy established by the hassan tribes in the sixteenth century gave Mauritania much of its sociological character and remains valuable in analyzing the country in the post-independence period. Before then, though, the French, most prominently Xavier Coppolani (q.v.) and his successors, weakened the hold of the hassan tribes by using the French army to displace the Arab warriors, and simultaneously encouraged the ascendancy of the zawiya tribes (whom the French authorities called *marabouts*).

BERBERS. As the first of many outside occupiers of modern-day Mauritania whose existence and activities can be discerned from the historical record, Berber groups established domination over great portions of the territory from around 300 A.D. to around 800 A.D., when they were in turn displaced by Black Africans belonging to the Ghana, Mali, and Songhai Empires as well as by Arab groups migrating from the northern Maghreb. Like their Arab conquerors, the Berbers arrived in Mauritania from the north, where they sought pastureland, trading opportunities, and freedom from the incessant internecine strife in other Maghrebi territories. By the eighth century, they had completely displaced their predecessors, the Bafour, leaving only (it is thought) the Imraguen (q.v.) fishing tribe as a trace of that earlier period. The Berbers, however, were not a united group: they were divided into the Gadala, the Lemtuna, and the Messufa, of which the Lemtuna were politically and economically dominant, controlling a thriving commerce (q.v.) which extended from the far north of Africa to the Senegal River, where they traded with the Ghana Empire at its capital, Koumbi Saleh (q.v.). From their own cosmopolitan capital, Aoudaghost (q.v.), the Lemtuna governed Mauritania along with the Gadala and the Messufa, who together formed the loosely knit but powerful Sanhadja Confederation, whose activities were greatly facilitated by the introduction of the camel to the desertified region, and by the slow spread of Islam (q.v.), which acted as a unifying force amidst sharp tribal differences. As a political entity, the Sanhadja Confederation was highly decentralized, with the main lines of division existing between the nomadic elements who operated the lower levels of the caravan trade and who were often fiercely independent, and the ardently Muslim (and sedentary) merchants who managed the commercial sector. At its apogee around 900–1000 A.D., the Sanhadja Confederation controlled a vast network of trade routes, extending from the Maghrebi city of Sijilmasa in the north to Koumbi Saleh and Aoudaghost in the south and taking in towns such as Chinguetti and Oualata (qq.v.) as well as Ouadane and Tichit. The institution of slavery (q.v.) had its origin under Berber rule, as the pre-Islamic Bafours and other black groups who had not fled south earlier were put to work in salt mines near Sebkhet d'Idjil and in a variety of agricultural (q.v.) ventures. Salt, gold, copper, ivory, and cloth (as well as the slaves themselves) were actively bought and sold.

The relatively disorganized political nature of the Sanhadja Confederation as well as the Berbers' uneven adherence to Islam opened the way for their downfall starting around 1039. In about that year, devout Gadala tribesmen making the *hajj* to Mecca brought back with them a Berber holy man, Abdallah Ibn Yacin, who believed in an uncompromising and austere brand of the Muslim faith that attracted many followers. After suffering some initial reverses, notably when the Gadala rejected his teachings, Ibn Yacin led his adherents into battle against the Gadala in 1042, vanquished them, and forced them to submit to Islam in short order. Having defeated the Berbers, the Almoravids (q.v.) went on to capture Aoudaghost, Koumbi Saleh, and Sijilmasa and instill a greater degree of unity into Mauritanian society than had previously been the case. This rapid succession of victories, however, did not mean that Berber culture was totally eradicated, and indeed it enjoyed a renaissance beginning in the early twelfth century, when the Almoravid Empire went into decline. But in the Char Bobha (q.v.), which was fought between 1644 and 1674, the Sanhadja Berbers were finally completely routed at the hands of the fierce Arab invaders from the north, the Beni Hassan (q.v.). Despite this, some Berber place names, linguistic usages, and traditional practices survive in modern Mauritania. Some experts, moreover, describe present-day Mauritanian civilization as "Arabo-Berber," at least insofar as the country's Moorish population (qq.v.) is concerned.

BEYDANE (variant: Bidan). As a word meaning "white" in Hassaniya (q.v.) Arabic, the term was used interchangeably with the words "Moorish" (q.v.) or "Arab" to describe persons who, as a general rule, used Arabic as their *lingua franca,* possessed "Caucasian" features, and adhered to a traditionally nomadic way of life in Mauritania's Saharan zone. Many observers, however, considered this description far from comprehensive due to the frequency of intermarriage and, especially, the sense of cultural identification of the black-skinned *haratines* (q.v.) with their former "white" Moorish slavemasters. Since the mid-1980s at least, the term assumed considerable political significance as well: some black Mauritanians, particularly those sympathetic to the *Forces de Libération Africaine de Mauritanie* (FLAM) (q.v.) and who felt that the country's political arrangements discriminated against them, spoke openly of the "Beydane system" and "Beydane domination," which led in turn to protests by Moors that the word was being converted into a term of racial disparagement.

BIR MOGHREIN. Known as Fort Trinquet until Mauritania's independence from France in November 1960, Bir Moghrein was the country's northernmost town of consequence, having a population (q.v.) of several thousand and located in the administrative région of Tiris Zemmour (q.v.), about 400 kilometers from Zouerate (q.v.). Owing to its exposed location only a short distance from Western Sahara (q.v.), it was the scene of considerable military activity by the Mauritanian armed forces (q.v.) against the Polisario Front (q.v.) from late 1975 until 1979.

BLOC DEMOCRATIQUE DU GORGOL (BDG). A small, preindependence political party dominated by Halpulaaren (q.v.) from its namesake administrative *cercle* (q.v.), the Gorgol Democratic Bloc was formed in 1957. The party's platform was committed to opposing any federation or union with the Arab countries of the Maghreb, particularly with Morocco, which had already articulated a claim to all of Mauritania. The BDG also advocated close ties to Black African states such as Senegal after the attainment of Mauritanian independence. In the elections to the *Assemblée Territoriale* (q.v.) held on March 31, 1957, the party did poorly, obtaining only 5,125 votes of a reported total of 272,474, an indication that its base of support was quite narrow and regionally based. Nevertheless, when Mauritania's future president, Mokhtar Ould Daddah (q.v.), formed a new cabinet on January 13, 1958, he was careful to include one of the Bloc's representatives. This appointment did not alter the BDG's overall meager fortunes, however, and at the Congress of Aleg (q.v.) held in May 1958, the Gorgol Democratic Bloc, along with several other groupings, ceased to exist. In their place, a new *Parti de Regroupement Mauritanien* (PRM) (q.v.) was set up, with Ould Daddah as its paramount leader.

BOUMEDIENNE, HOUARI. As Algeria's president from June 1965, when he led a *coup d' état* that removed the country's first leader, Ahmed Ben Bella, until December 1978, Houari Boumedienne played a key role in the shaping of Mauritania's domestic and foreign relations (q.v.) policies. The two countries shared one common attribute—opposition to the Moroccan government's territorial claims to Mauritania, an attitude that kept King Hassan II (q.v.) from recognizing Mauritanian independence until 1970, a decade after the country's release from French colonial rule. Boumedienne, therefore, extended assistance to Mauritania almost as soon as he assumed power, taking a liking to President Mokhtar Ould Daddah's (q.v.) increasingly nationalist, nonaligned positions. He encouraged Ould Daddah to distance himself from France and provided economic aid that was instrumental to Mauritania's decision in 1973 to withdraw from the *Communauté Financière Africaine* (CFA) (q.v.) and issue its own currency, the *ouguiya* (qq.v.). Algerian investments in the fisheries and petroleum (qq.v.) sectors were increased in the early 1970s. Houari Boumedienne was also pleased by Ould Daddah's nationalization of the iron ore (q.v.) mining concern MIFERMA (q.v.) in late 1974 and with Mauritania's increasing orientation toward the Arab Maghreb and the Middle East. The strong-willed Algerian leader also had a hand in reconciling Mokhtar Ould Daddah and King Hassan starting in 1969, paving the way for the establishment of diplomatic relations between Rabat and Nouakchott (q.v.) in April 1970.

Algerian-Mauritanian relations were thus excellent by 1975, but were soon to undergo a drastic decline. Although Houari Boumedienne was content to give verbal support to Mauritania's claim to the adjacent territory of Western Sahara (q.v.), he rapidly shifted gears by the end of the year. Faced with President Ould Daddah's evident willingness to accept for his country one-third of Western Sahara while allowing Morocco to annex the remainder, Boumedienne responded by giving full support to a Saharawi (q.v.) liberation movement, the Polisario Front (q.v.), which planned to set up an independent nation in the Spanish colony. He gave Mauritania one final opportunity to disengage itself from its imminent embrace of King Hassan. On November 10, 1975, Boumedienne met for five hours with Ould Daddah at Béchar, in western Algeria, and warned his fellow head of state that if he participated in the takeover of Western Sahara, Algeria would give such strong backing to the Polisario guerrillas that Mauritania's small armed forces (q.v.) would be unable to defend its borders. Mokhtar Ould Daddah had already made up his mind, though, and went on four days later to sign the Madrid Agreement (q.v.), by which Western Sahara was partitioned.

In the following two years, Ould Daddah must have had occasion to recall Houari Boumedienne's words at Béchar. Mauritania severed diplomatic relations with Algiers after Boumedienne recognized Polisario's state-in-exile, the Saharan Arab Democratic Republic (SADR) (q.v.), on March 6, 1976, and soon found itself singled out by the Saharawis as the weaker of its two adversaries, as Polisario attacks devastated many areas of the country and brought the state close to complete ruin. Suffering from an incurable illness, Boumedienne observed with satisfaction the downfall of Mokhtar Ould Daddah on July 10, 1978, and his replacement by an armed forces council, the *Comité Militaire de Redressement National* (CMRN) (q.v.), led at first by Colonel Mustapha Ould Mohammed Salek (q.v.). Before Mauritania could definitively extricate itself from the Western Sahara conflict and make peace with Polisario, Houari Boumedienne died on December 27, 1978, leaving it to his successor, Chadli Benjedid, to reestablish ties to Mauritania after it signed the Algiers Agreement (q.v.) on August 5, 1979. Thus restored, the Algerian-Mauritanian relationship has remained close through the mid-1990s.

BOUTILIMIT. A small town of a few thousand people situated about 150 kilometers southeast of Mauritania's capital, Nouakchott (q.v.), Boutilimit has had an importance out of proportion to its size, both before and after the country's independence. Traditionally a center of higher Islamic (q.v.) learning in West Africa by virtue of the presence of a substantial *zawiya* (q.v.) or *marabout* population, the town boasts one of the largest and most comprehensive libraries of Islamic manuscripts and books in the entire region. In 1961, the Institute for Higher

Islamic Studies was founded in Boutilimit, building upon its religious heritage. The town was also the birthplace of Mokhtar Ould Daddah (q.v.), a member of the Oulad Berri marabout tribe, Mauritania's foremost pre-independence political personage and the country's first president, holding office from 1960 to 1978.

BRAKNA. Covering 33,000 square kilometers in Mauritania's southwest and roughly bisected by the Trans-Mauritanian Highway (q.v.), the administrative région (q.v.) of Brakna had a 1977 population (q.v.) of about 151,000, a figure that increased, according to government census information, to 192,157 in 1988. With the provincial capital located at Aleg, it was a stronghold of black Mauritanian farmers and livestock (q.v.) herders, including those of Halpulaar, Soninké, and Wolof (qq.v.) extraction. However, in the 1980s, there was an influx of Moorish (q.v.) Mauritanians from the north, attracted by the promise of government support in establishing agricultural (q.v.) enterprises pursuant to the controversial Land Reform Act of June 5, 1983 (q.v.). Due to its large black population, Brakna was the scene of considerable tension during the Senegal-Mauritania Crisis (q.v.) that began in April 1989, with Bogué and other towns becoming inaccessible to outsiders and under virtual martial law. Like many of Mauritania's régions, the province has suffered greatly from the seemingly inexorable process of desertification (q.v.).

BUDGETS. Scarce and uncertain sources of revenue, massive internal needs, and varying prices for Mauritania's exports have made the country's budgets problematic and generally unsatisfactory. After roughly a decade of reasonably healthy finances resulting from the extraction and export of iron ore (q.v.) and a relatively small population (q.v.), the government of President Mokhtar Ould Daddah (q.v.), because of its involvement in the Western Sahara conflict (q.v.), was forced beginning in 1975 to vastly increase expenditures on the Mauritanian armed forces (q.v.). In 1976, military spending shot up 33 percent, and by the following year, fully 60 percent of total revenues were going to the army. At the same time, the export of iron ore through the port of Nouadhibou (q.v.) dropped precipitously due to attacks on its vital facilities by the guerrillas of the Polisario Front (q.v.), throwing the financial situation into complete chaos and necessitating foreign assistance from a great variety of donors. These subventions and loans were to account for one-third of the entire Mauritanian budget in 1978. Outside help, however, could not salvage the fortunes of Mokhtar Ould Daddah, as he was overthrown on July 10, 1978, by a group of key army officers who formed a new government led by the *Comité Militaire de Redressement National* (CMRN) (q.v.). After the military takeover, expenditures were slashed by over 30 percent, assisted by the cessation of Polisario attacks against Mauritania and by the (eventual) signing of the Algiers Agreement (q.v.) with the Saharawi (q.v.) nationalist organization in August 1979. One legacy of the Western Saharan war that could not be so easily overcome, though, was the extraordinary load of indebtedness incurred by Mauritania to outside creditors. Servicing these debts (which amounted to 138 percent of the country's total gross domestic product [GDP] by 1983) required not only continued austerity measures, but the orientation of nearly 40 percent of export earnings toward repayment. The goal of a balanced budget remained elusive in the early 1980s, as deficits usually ran into the billions of *ouguiyas* (q.v.) annually. Nevertheless, the head of state at the time, *Comité Militaire de Salut National* (CMSN) (q.v.) chairman Colonel Mohammed Khouna Ould Heydallah (q.v.), made a concerted effort to cut the deficit, freezing civil service appointments and trying to restrict expensive imports. These steps yielded some positive results, but there was a continued drain on revenues due to lower prices for iron ore on the world market, difficulties in the management of the fisheries (q.v.) sector, and the perceived need to keep military spending high. The poor efficiency and high costs associated with Mauritania's industrial development (q.v.) projects were also a constant problem, as was the increasing national demand for imports of petroleum (q.v.).

The December 12, 1984, palace revolution that peacefully displaced Ould Heydallah in favor of Colonel Maaouiya Ould Sid' Ahmed Taya (q.v.) also brought with it a new approach to budgetary problems. Although a great deal more government money would subsequently be spent on the agricultural and livestock (qq.v.) sectors, the overall rate of expenditure was cut still further, and in return, external lending institutions agreed to reschedule and restructure Mauritania's heavy debt repayments. For the first time in years, the 1986 and 1987 budgets were balanced, as much of the remaining government spending was oriented to running the central administration of the country more efficiently. By 1989, 71 percent of the budget was directed towards this end. However, the twin shocks of the Senegal-Mauritania Crisis (q.v.) which began in April 1989 and the sharp temporary rise in oil prices during the Gulf Crisis (q.v.) of 1990 and 1991 ensured that Mauritania could not meet its fiscal targets or repay its obligations on time. In April 1991 President Ould Taya began a substantial liberalization of Mauritanian political life, a process which ended with contested presidential and parliamentary elections and the inauguration of the Second Republic (q.v.) of Mauritania on April 18, 1992. Ould Taya's new prime minister, Sidi Mohamed Ould Boubacar (q.v.), moreover, was highly respected in world banking circles, and his efforts, coupled with the regime's commitment to an "orthodox" economic policy, resulted in the cancellation by the International Monetary Fund (IMF) of one-half of Mauritania's interest payments on its debt, with the rest generously rescheduled. In 1993 additional concessionary loans were granted, opening the way to additional private foreign investment. Ould Boubacar also attacked the other negative influences on the Mauritanian budget by raising tax rates and partially privatizing state companies such as the *Société Mauritanienne de Commercialisation du Poisson* (SMCP) (q.v.). Other parastatals, such as the national insurance company, the *Société Mauritanienne d'Assurances et de Réassurances* (SMAR), were shut down entirely by 1994. Public investment was also reduced by 10 percent. But the sharply competing demands on very limited state resources would not go away despite these measures, and by the mid-1990s Mauritania's debt amounted to 205.6 percent of its GDP—making it one of the five most indebted countries in the world. Finally, the fiscal outlook remains clouded not only by debt, but also by the economy's great sensitivity to external events such as fluctuating prices for fish and iron ore. All these factors conspired to make Mauritanian budgetmaking a very difficult exercise.

BUREAU POLITIQUE NATIONAL (BPN). Established in 1963 as the leadership body of Mauritania's ruling *Parti du Peuple Mauritanien* (PPM) (q.v.), the bureau consisted, for the most part, of PPM members who had distinguished themselves for their loyalty to the country's president, Mokhtar Ould Daddah (q.v.), and provided the dedicated personnel he needed to execute national programs. The emergence of the National Political Bureau marked the end of any real intra-PPM democracy due to its close ties to Ould Daddah, and it was also used to bypass the Mauritanian legislature, the *Assemblée Nationale* (q.v.), whose opinions the head of state could not always take for granted. In 1964, the obedient BPN declared Mauritania a one-party state, a decision enshrined in an amendment to the country's constitution the following year.

CAMEL CORPS. See Nomad Security Guard

CERCLE. Mauritania's primary unit of regional administration under both French colonial rule and in the eight years following independence in 1960, the *cercles* were established by the AOF (q.v.) as an instrument for securing the centralized authority of the government over the Mauritanian countryside. Each cercle had a large geographic base, often covering tens of thousands of square kilometers. By 1947, there were nine such units, and eleven at the time of Mauritania's release from French control. A twelfth cercle, Tiris Zemmour (q.v.), was created by the regime of President Mokhtar Ould Daddah (q.v.) out of the northern Adrar (q.v.) area. Under the Constitution of Mauritania of May 20, 1961 (q.v.), *Conseils Locaux* (q.v.) were to be the governing bodies of these territorial divisions, but in practice they had little authority, the Nouakchott (q.v.) government of Ould Daddah holding the reins of real power. On July 30, 1968, in a sweeping reorganization, the cercles were abolished and replaced with twelve administrative *régions* (q.v.) plus one special district encompassing Nouakchott.

CFA. See Communauté Financière Africaine

CHAR BOBHA. Often referred to as Mauritania's Thirty Years' War, the Char Bobha was fought, ultimately unsuccessfully, between 1644 and 1674 by the Berber-dominated Sanhadja Confederation (qq.v.) against the invading *Beni Hassan* (q.v.) who had reached the Maghreb from their starting point in Yemen by the end of the seventeenth century A.D. Reacting to the disruption of their long-established caravan trading routes in the north, particularly in the Adrar (q.v.), the Sanhadja, led by the Lemtuna *imam* (Islamic [q.v.] holy man) Nasir ed-Din, tried to resist the Arab advance and reclaim Berber predominance in the territory, which had steadily been on the wane. The Sanhadja proved to be no match for the Beni Hassan, who possessed a more martial inclination than their adversaries, and who in any event had honed their fighting skills in prior North African campaigns renowned for their destructiveness. Defeated on the battlefield, the Sanhadja were compelled, by the peace treaty of Tin Yedfad, permanently to "abandon the sword for the book" and place themselves at a social level below that of their Arab conquerors—that is, as *znaga* (q.v.) or vassals. The most learned (and religious) Berbers over time became *marabouts,* or *zawiya* (q.v.), and so ranked below only the *hassan* (q.v.) tribes in overall status. The social structure of present-day Mauritania can in great measure be traced to the outcome of the Char Bobha, at least among the Moors (q.v.). Although resentments and rivalries among these various social strata have by no means vanished by the late twentieth century (and had been exploited by the French colonialists for their own advantage), intermarriage and the growth of Mauritania's towns and cities in the years since independence have gradually made these distinctions less important.

CHARIA. See Sharia

CHEIKH MA EL-AININ. See Ma el-Ainin, Cheikh

CHINGUETTI. One of Mauritania's oldest and best-known towns, Chinguetti (known in Arabic as *Shinqit*) was believed to have been founded in about the third century A.D. as an important caravan stop and commercial center for the Sanhadja Confederation (q.v.), which controlled large parts of Mauritania until the Almoravid (q.v.) conquest around 1076 A.D. Under Almoravid rule, Chinguetti remained a prominent trading center, and also acquired a lasting reputation as a preeminent location for Islamic (q.v.) scholarship, so much so that it came to be considered, by the sixteenth century, as the seventh holiest place in all Islam. Mauritanian Muslims seeking to make the arduous pilgrimage (*hajj*) to faraway Mecca would often use Chinguetti as their starting point for the journey eastward. Also in the sixteenth century, a large mosque was constructed of native rock, with five distinctive pinnacles atop its minaret, each pinnacle surmounted by a single ostrich egg—apparently, a symbol of fertility. With the reorientation of trade routes away from the town and toward routes that offered more convenient access to the European-controlled coastal areas of the Maghreb, Chinguetti fell into the status of a relative backwater, although as one of the main settlements of the Adrar (q.v.) and a famous religious center, it continued to host a substantial collection of Koranic manuscripts (about 1300 in all), as well as other written materials dating back to the founding of the town. During the period of French domination, a newer quarter of Chinguetti sprang up, largely concentrated around a fort that was used by the French Foreign Legion and situated across a usually dry *wadi* (q.v.) from the old town. In the late twentieth century, Chinguetti's decline accelerated, with desertification (q.v.) threatening to overwhelm not only its buildings but also its ancient manuscripts which were, in many cases, irreplaceable. Chinguetti is reached by an unimproved road (q.v.) running about eighty kilometers east from Atar (q.v.), the Adrar's provincial capital. The town also has a primitive airport (q.v.), albeit without scheduled service.

CIMPER, GABRIEL. See Djibril Ould Abdellahi

CLIMATE. Despite its territory's being two-thirds desert, Mauritania's climate shows significant regional variation, with temperature and rainfall patterns falling into distinct zones, with hot and dry conditions giving way to a relatively more humid and more temperate environment as one moves from north to south, with tropical weather predominating along the Senegal River Valley. In addition, the 754-kilometer Atlantic coastline of Mauritania has a distinct climate all its own.

The Saharan Zone is by far the most prevalent in the country, covering virtually all of the administrative régions (q.v.) of Adrar,

Dakhlet-Nouadhibou, Inchiri, northern Tagant, Tiris Zemmour, and northern and eastern Trarza (qq.v.). Here, rainfall is less than 150 mm per year, although some localities, notably F'Derik, Nouadhibou, and Zouerate (qq.v.), often go for months or even several years with no detectable rainfall. Temperatures are extremely high during the daytime and during the night in the summer months, with the only relief occurring during nighttime hours from October to March, when readings below twenty degrees Celsius are not uncommon. The *hivernage* (q.v.) or rainy season is restricted to a three-month period between July and September, making any semblance of agriculture (q.v.) an impossibility, the only exceptions being a few *wadis* (q.v.) and oases, particularly in the environs of Atar (q.v.), where dates and gum arabic are grown with some success.

The Sahelian Zone encompasses approximately the area from the southern fringe of the Saharan Zone to about thirty to fifty kilometers north of the Senegal River; that is, along the isohyet line delineating a rainfall of 150 mm annually. Mauritanian régions falling within the climatic area include southern Trarza, Assaba, Brakna (qq.v.), southern Tagant, and certain parts of Hodh ech-Chargui and Hodh el-Gharbi (qq.v.). This zone is distinguished from its Saharan counterpart primarily in its slightly lower average temperatures, as well as by its longer hivernage, which runs from June to October with rainfall often reaching 250 mm a year or more. These relatively wetter conditions are sometimes sufficient to support limited wild vegetation as well as to make possible some agriculture and livestock (q.v.) herding. Animal husbandry was especially prevalent on the Tagant plateau until droughts and the process of desertification (q.v.) destroyed the grasslands and savanna upon which the livestock herders depended. The Sahelian Zone has suffered more from desertification than the other climatic regions of Mauritania since the early 1970s, primarily due to its greater exposure to the Saharan Zone, which allows the desert to encroach unimpeded upon fertile areas. Average temperatures range between sixteen and twenty-one degrees Celsius on a typical day, lower than the stifling heat of the Sahara but still high enough to make the prevailing westerly wind, the *harmattan* (q.v.), quite uncomfortable, particularly when it throws up fine desert sand and produces the *irifi* (q.v.), a sandstorm that reduces visibility for hours at a time and disrupts most human activity.

The Senegal River Valley (Chammama) Zone is the most humid and tropical area of Mauritania, and comprises a narrow belt running from the north bank of the river to thirty to fifty kilometers north. The administrative régions of Gorgol and Guidimaka (qq.v.) and extreme south Brakna and Trarza fall within this zone. These provinces remain the country's best-watered into the mid-1990s, often boasting a rainfall of 400 to 600 mm per year, enough to support sedentary agriculture and sustain substantial animal herds. The hivernage extends for nearly half the year, from May through September, with high temperatures fluctuating between thirty-five and forty-five degrees Celsius during the day.

The Coastal (Littoral) Zone is found only in the vicinity of Mauritania's Atlantic coastline, and is the country's most temperate area, as it is affected by the moderating trade winds from the Canary Islands, which lessen the impact of the brutal harmattan. At the same time, however, the zone is quite humid, even though rainfall is minimal, amounting to only about 30 mm per year (and often much less) in Nouadhibou, and 150 mm or so annually in the capital, Nouakchott (q.v.). This sub-Canarian climate is not an unmixed blessing, though: the harmattan and its insidious cousin, the irifi, remain a constant threat, as desertification eliminates the grasslands and vegetation of the littoral belt and extends the Sahara's dunes into the heart of the capital.

COLLECTIVITES TERRITORIALES. See Region

COLONNE D'ADRAR. See Adrar Campaign (Of 1909)

COMITE MILITAIRE DE REDRESSEMENT NATIONAL (CMRN). In early July, 1978, the chief of staff of the Mauritanian armed forces (q.v.), Colonel Mustapha Ould Mohammed Salek (q.v.), asked for and received permission to move troops into the country's capital, Nouakchott (q.v.), ostensibly to guard against an attack on the city by the highly mobile guerrillas of the Polisario Front (q.v.) with whom Mauritania was embroiled in combat over possession of Western Sahara (q.v.). The request was reasonable—Polisario had already mounted two prior Nouakchott raids (q.v.) in June 1976 and July 1977—but instead, in the early dawn of July 10, 1978, Ould Salek, aided by a substantial number of his colleagues in the military high command, led a *coup d'état* which seized all governmental installations and overthrew (and arrested) President Mokhtar Ould Daddah (q.v.), Mauritania's head of state since 1960. There was no bloodshed. An eighteen-member Military Committee for National Recovery assumed supreme power over the country, with Ould Salek as chairman. The officers who made up the CMRN had little by way of common ideology or political program, but all shared one overriding objective—the extrication of Mauritania from the Western Sahara conflict, which had inflicted catastrophic damage on the economy, exposed its population (q.v.) centers to Polisario assaults, and even kindled racial tensions between Moorish (q.v.) Mauritanians and their Black African counterparts living in the Senegal River Valley. A few days after the coup, Ould Salek stated that the CMRN's priorities were to achieve a settlement to the Saharan war "which is commensurate with the supreme interests of the Mauritanian people in agreement with the sister Moroccan kingdom," to preserve Islamic (q.v.) ethics and practices, and to liberalize both the strapped economy and the exclusionary political system. The first harbingers were good—encouraged by the downfall of its nemesis, Ould Daddah, the Polisario Front declared an immediate cease-fire against all Mauritanian targets. The military takeover was also welcomed by many of Mauritania's citizens, as they believed that an expeditious peace agreement could be reached by the CMRN, followed by an economic rebound.

But a settlement was to prove very difficult to achieve. Colonel Ould Salek preferred to construct a "global," or comprehensive peace treaty that would involve Morocco's King Hassan II (q.v.), Algeria, and France as well as Mauritania and Polisario, thus sparing the new junta the prospect of signing a separate agreement with the Saharawi (q.v.) nationalists and antagonizing Morocco, which at this time still had 9000 troops in Mauritania under the auspices of the Moroccan-Mauritanian Defense Committee (q.v.). Due to a variety of factors, as well as to factional dissention in the CMRN itself, this sort of settlement proved impossible to carry out; secret contacts between the ruling council and Polisario led nowhere, and for many months the CMRN looked stricken and adrift. Domestically, the situation was even worse. The economy still needed a massive infusion of cash and confidence, the level of indebtedness to foreign countries and institutions was daunting, and disputes over the Arabization of the educational (qq.v.) system reared their head by the end of 1978. Anti-CMRN protests were also staged for the first time.

On March 17, 1979, Colonel Ould Salek, faced with persistent criticism over his stewardship of the country, set up a National Consultative Council to "reopen" the political system and facilitate eventual civilian rule. But the composition of this body, eighty-seven Moors and seventeen blacks, led some black Mauritanians to decide that they were not sufficiently represented. Around the same time, Ould Salek persuaded the rest of the CMRN to grant him plenary powers, transforming him into a virtual dictator and fracturing the junta's carefully cultivated reputation for collegiality. Soon after, on March 30, all seventeen black Mauritanians on the National Consultative Council resigned in protest over "unequal racial representation" in the government, further heightening tensions. On April 6, 1979, Ould Salek was stripped of all but his titular position as head of state in a sudden "rectification" led by a rival officer, Lieutenant Colonel Ahmed Ould Bouceif (q.v.), who became prime minister. The CMRN was abolished and replaced by a new thirteen-member *Comité Militaire de Salut National* (CMSN) (q.v.).

COMITE MILITAIRE DE SALUT NATIONAL (CMSN). The Military Committee for National Salvation was established on April 6, 1979, as the result of an intense power struggle in the ranks of the senior members of the Mauritanian armed forces (q.v.), with regard to the inability of the former junta, the *Comité Militaire de Redressement National* (CMRN) (q.v.) successfully to extract the country from the Western Sahara conflict (q.v.), which had begun in late 1975 under the civilian presidency of Mokhtar Ould Daddah (q.v.). The CMRN leader, Colonel Mustapha Ould Mohammed Salek (q.v.), faced a delicate situation, not knowing what Mauritania's ally, Morocco, would do if he unilaterally signed a peace agreement with the Polisario Front (q.v.) and assented to leave Tiris el-Gharbia (q.v.) unconditionally. Economic and social difficulties also made themselves apparent, caused in large part by Polisario attacks to the vital Mauritanian iron ore (q.v.) industry. In early 1979, opposition to Ould Salek intensified, and on April 6, he found himself suddenly deprived of all but his nominal position as head of state and replaced as prime minister by Lieutenant Colonel Ahmed Ould Bouceif (q.v.), one of the prime movers of dissent from Ould Salek's policies. The CMRN was abolished and a new ruling council, the CMSN, was set up, with thirteen members and a set of internal guidelines that reserved to itself nearly unlimited policymaking powers. Even as the CMSN established itself, however, it was evident that some of its members were more influential than others. Ould Bouceif's power, for instance, seemed constrained by his powerful minister of defense, Lieutenant Colonel Mohammed Khouna Ould Heydallah (q.v.), who was thought to be less opposed to a separate peace treaty with the Polisario Front. Indeed, Ould Bouceif reportedly found himself outmaneuvered within the CMSN by Ould Heydallah on several occasions. The CMSN's frustration grew as Mauritania's inability to exit from the Western Sahara dispute began to tell heavily on the country's economy.

The country's internal predicament received another severe shock on May 27, 1979, when Ould Bouceif was killed in a plane crash near Dakar, Senegal, as he was arriving for a West African summit conference. Within the CMSN, the scene was undoubtedly one of some drama over the next few days as the factions inside the council jostled for domination. Four days later, on May 31, Ould Heydallah succeeded in assuming the prime ministership, while keeping the defense portfolio and ousting the powerless official president, Ould Salek, and appointing another figurehead, Lieutenant Colonel Mohammed Mahmoud Ould Louly (q.v.) in his place. A new government was announced on

June 3, 1979, with fifteen members, nine of whom were military officers, and five of whom were black Mauritanians. After some continued hesitations—and a brief resumption of military attacks against Mauritania by Polisario—a peace treaty with the Saharawi (q.v.) nationalist group, the Algiers Agreement (q.v.), was signed on August 5, 1979. Under the treaty, Mauritania agreed to leave Tiris el-Gharbia.

For Mauritania, the Western Sahara conflict was over, but there was to be little respite from other problems. In the four years following January 4, 1980, when Ould Heydallah assumed full powers as head of state (sending Ould Louly into retirement), he began to act in a more dictatorial manner, consulting his CMSN colleagues less and less after some of them vocally dissented from his policies and national budgets (q.v.). He also reshuffled the Council of Ministers (q.v.) every few months, made appeals to populist sentiments by instituting some of the stricter provisions of the Islamic *sharia* (qq.v.) in 1980 (including public floggings and amputations), and reportedly allowed corruption in public life to become virtually institutionalized. On the economic front, droughts, continued desertification (q.v.), and falling commodity prices for Mauritania's exports were pushing the country's people to the point of despair. Through it all, Ould Heydallah continued to make many decisions on his own, a practice that threatened to turn the CMSN into a legal fiction.

The final indignity for the other military officers on the CMSN may have come on February 27, 1984, when, fulfilling a pledge he had often made, Ould Heydallah formally recognized the Polisario Front's government-in-exile in Western Sahara, the Saharan Arab Democratic Republic (SADR) (q.v.). Again, the head of state had acted by himself, angering many of his colleagues, who were concerned that Morocco's King Hassan II (q.v.) would initiate reprisals against Mauritania for its recognition of the Saharawi state. Ould Heydallah responded to this criticism by jailing some and demoting others, notably his influential minister of defense, Colonel Maaouiya Ould Sid'Ahmed Taya (q.v.), who was soon shifted back to his old post, army chief of staff. To the other members of the governing council, Mauritanian politics were becoming dangerously unbalanced, with their advice spurned or avoided. A group of officers, led by Ould Taya and by Lieutenant Colonel Anne Ahmadou Babaly (q.v.), ousted Ould Heydallah from the presidency on December 12, 1984, while he was away at a Franco-African summit conference in Burundi. The putsch was bloodless and efficient, and was welcomed by many Mauritanians.

Once he assumed power as the new head of state, Ould Taya moved quickly to restore the collegial, consensus-based nature of the CMSN. The exercise of arbitrary power, so common under Ould Heydallah, ended for a time as Mauritanian society and politics went through a period of decompression. But as the decade progressed, the problems inherent in military government reasserted themselves, not least of which was the rise of factions in or near the CMSN who responded to outside pressure groups and who were willing to do these groups' bidding in a manner largely closed to public scrutiny. For a narrow, parochial governing body such as the CMSN administering the affairs of an impoverished state susceptible to external shocks as well as internal conflicts, this state of affairs assumed a much greater importance than it might otherwise have had, since the council's secret proceedings and lack of democratic debate resulted in rapid shifts in Mauritania's domestic affairs and foreign relations (q.v.). One prominent example was the great sway exercised over the CMSN from 1986 to 1990 by the minister of the interior, Colonel Djibril Ould Abdellahi (q.v.), who was believed to be almost as powerful as President Ould Taya himself. Moreover, around the same time, from 1988 to 1990, the CMSN found itself vulnerable to the activities of the Arab Baath Socialist Party (ABSP) (q.v.), closely allied with Saddam Hussein's Iraq. Baath Party influence eventually led to a full-scale "tilt" by Mauritania toward Baghdad and may have temporarily overshadowed Ould Taya and his like-minded, nonideological counterparts. Mauritania's alliance with Iraq caused the country grave embarrassment and hardship during the Gulf Crisis (q.v.) of 1990 and 1991, but Iraq's defeat on the battlefield after it invaded Kuwait diminished Baathist power in Mauritania and allowed Ould Taya to reassert himself. From that time onward the CMSN's days were numbered, as Ould Taya soon decided to phase out military rule entirely in favor of a civilian government elected by universal suffrage within the framework of a new constitution approved by voters on July 12, 1991 (q.v.). In an interview with the Paris-based weekly *Jeune Afrique* (in October 1991), Ould Taya said "the army has acquitted its task. It will now return to its traditional mission." To many observers, however, it seemed likely that after having been in power for so long, the military establishment would still play an outsized role in Mauritanian politics, at least until independent centers of state authority could firmly establish themselves. Nevertheless, on April 18, 1992, when the newly elected President, Ould Taya (who had since retired from the armed forces), inaugurated the Second Republic (q.v.), the CMSN was finally disbanded.

Although the councils of the CMSN were often racked by severe disputes among its members, the ruling group of officers did display a remarkable degree of consideration for one another, even when members showed signs of disloyal behavior. For example, in February 1982, President Ould Heydallah announced that his predecessor, Colonel Ould Salek, had plotted to kidnap him and thus topple his regime. Despite the gravity of these charges, Ould Salek and his confederates, who all pleaded guilty, received relatively light prison sentences—in Ould

Salek's case, ten years' imprisonment, with lesser terms meted out to the others. But CMSN members who went into exile and affiliated them-selves with foreign countries (such as Morocco) could not expect such leniency. After masterminding a violent coup attempt against Ould Hey-dallah on March 16, 1981, two former junta members, Lieutenant Colonels Ahmed Salem Ould Sidi and Mohammed Ould Bah Ould Ab-del Kader (qq.v.) were rounded up and executed after a perfunctory trial. Similar firmness was shown to three Halpulaar (q.v.) officers outside the CMSN, who were convicted on December 3, 1987, of conspiring to un-seat the Ould Taya regime and proclaim a separate "Walo Republic" in the Senegal River Valley. All three were shot a few days later, and many others were given long prison sentences, an indication that the ruling council, however much it might tolerate internal discussion, would deal strictly with any perceived threat to the integrity of the Mauritanian state.

As an illustration of the size and composition of the CMSN, its roster in 1989 was as follows (see individual entries where indicated):

President and Minister of Defense	Colonel Maaouiya Ould Sid' Ahmed Taya (q.v.)
Permanent Secretary to the CMSN	Captain Mohamed Lamine Ould N'Diayane
Commander of the *Gendarmerie Nationale* (q.v.)	Lieutenant Colonel Ney Ould Abdel Malick
Commander of the Army	Colonel Ahmed Ould Minnih (q.v.)
Commander-Adjutant of the Army	Lieutenant Colonel Mohamed Ould Lekhal
Commander of the National Guard (q.v.)	Colonel Brahim Ould Alioune N'Diaye
Director, *Ecole Militaire Inter-armes d'Atar* (q.v.)	Commandant Cheikh Sid' Ahmed Ould Baba
Director of the Air Force (q.v.)	Commandant Hamadi Demba
Director of the Navy (q.v.)	Lieutanant Abderrahmane Ould Lekouar
Minister of the Interior	Colonel Djibril Ould Abdellahi (q.v.)
Director of the Police	Captain Ely Ould Mohamed Vall
Minister of Foreign Affairs	Lieutenant Colonel Sidina Mohamed Ould Sidiya
Minister of Health and Social Affairs	Lieutenant Colonel Dr. N'Diaye Kane
Minister of Equipment and Transport	Lieutenant Colonel Dieng Oumar Harouna

COMMERCE. Mauritanians have a long tradition of privately conducted commercial activity with neighboring territories. As early as the ninth century A.D., the Sanhadja Confederation, dominated by the Berbers (q.v.), had control of the lucrative north-south caravan trading routes connecting the Maghreb with Black Africa. After the displacement of the Sanhadja Berbers by the Almoravids (q.v.) beginning in the early eleventh century, commerce expanded further; salt, gold, carpets, and handicrafts, as well as slaves (q.v.), were actively exchanged, with the outposts of Aoudaghost, Koumbi Saleh, and Oualata (qq.v.) being especially important to the trade, as was the city of Sijilmasa in modern-day Morocco. Owing partly to a degree of isolation from the outside world until the advent of French "pacification" in the late nineteenth and early twentieth centuries, Mauritania's trade routes proved remarkably durable, with by far the greatest amount of commerce at independence in 1960 being with Mali and Senegal. France provided imports of consumer goods not manufactured in either of those countries. As an autonomous nation, however, Mauritania was almost completely dependent upon the export of iron ore and fish (qq.v.) to fuel its economy, as they were less difficult to tax and regulate than the largely informal cross-border trade with Senegal. Iron ore, extracted from the open-cast mines in the région of Tiris Zemmour (qq.v.), was mostly exported to Belgium, Italy, France, Germany, and the Netherlands from 1963, although Japan showed a rising level of interest in both iron ore and fish from the late 1970s. The fishing sector was hamstrung from the beginning by poor infrastructure, corruption, and poaching, making that sector an uneven performer until at least the mid-1980s. Despite this, a great number of countries, including those in Western Europe as well as Algeria, Iraq, Japan, Romania, South Korea, and the former Soviet Union showed interest at various times in Mauritanian fisheries. Fish overtook iron ore as the country's primary export commodity starting in 1983. Nearly two decades earlier, in 1966, President Mokhtar Ould Daddah (q.v.) formed the *Société Nationale d'Importation et d'Exportation* (SONIMEX) (q.v.) to bring commercial activity, particularly agriculture and livestock (qq.v.), under state control. But the independent ways of the country's farmers and herders frustrated any attempt at central control just as they had in antiquity, and private trade, much of it conducted by women (q.v.), helped to tide Mauritania over at difficult moments in its existence. Even if the legal SONIMEX monopoly on foreign trade was effective, it could not have altered the fact that the country was always in the position of exporting only a very few foreign exchange–earning products, while at the same time needing to import nearly all of its other necessities, including transportation equipment, the great majority of its foodstuffs, petroleum (q.v.), and construction materials. Fully one-third of all imports in the 1973–86 period were for food, correspondingly making less money available for other sectors and contributing to perennially strapped Mauritanian budgets (q.v.). Another large "export" was the country's people: remittances from Mauritanians working in France and in the states of the Arab League (q.v.) assisted the economy greatly. Expatriates in pastoral and other occupations in Mali and Senegal also served as a safety valve of sorts for a nation with chronically high unemployment, advancing desertification (q.v.), and periodic droughts.

The accession to power on December 12, 1984, of Colonel Maaouiya Ould Sid'Ahmed Taya (q.v.) as head of Mauritania's governing body, the *Comité Militaire de Salut National* (CMSN) (q.v.), resulted in many changes in the country's commercial life. The range of foreign business partners was expanded, with Japan accounting for 28 percent of exports in 1986, mainly for iron ore and fish. The People's Republic of China also became an important trading partner, and constructed a new Friendship Port (q.v.) near the Mauritanian capital of Nouakchott (q.v.) to remove transportation bottlenecks caused by a lack of adequate ports (q.v.) elsewhere and by a lack of good roads (q.v.). Trade with other African states was also kept up, with their imports comprising about 15 percent of the total by the late 1980s. The official SONIMEX monopoly was ended a few years after Ould Taya came to power, and commerce was, in general, deregulated. To reduce expensive imports of oil and other products, energy conservation measures and other austerity programs were put into effect, enabling the country to show an increasing trade surplus in all of the years from 1985 to 1989. Possibly due to the Senegal-Mauritania Crisis (q.v.) of 1989 and 1990, though, a deficit of 770 million *ouguiyas* (UM) (q.v.) was registered for 1990, aggravated by a sharp temporary rise in oil prices after Iraq's invasion of Kuwait on August 2, 1990. By 1991, Mauritania was in the black again (a surplus of UM 1,512 million), only to return to a deficit (of UM 870 million) the following year, as rainfall (q.v.) amounts were lower than expected and led to decreased crop yields and a need for costly food imports. Although better news was forecast for the mid-1990s, the fluctuating trade statistics (which, to be sure, rarely included the thriving commerce across the Senegal River) illustrate the sensitivity of the Mauritanian economy to climatic and other external factors beyond its control.

COMMISSARIAT A LA SECURITE ALIMENTAIRE (CSA). The Food Security Commission of Mauritania was formed in 1982 through the merger of two antecedent organizations by the government of Colonel Mohammed Khouna Ould Heydallah (q.v.). It was set up at a time of enormous changes in the country's social and economic life, most notably the migration of a significant part of the Mauritanian population (q.v.) from the rural areas of the country to the larger cities and towns such as the national capital, Nouakchott (q.v.). These shifts were caused by several years of droughts, coupled with the ongoing process of desertification (q.v.), which turned the already parlous state of Mauritanian agriculture (q.v.) into a full-fledged crisis by the time of Ould Heydallah's assumption of full powers in January 1980. In the early 1980s, nearly 90 percent of the country's food had to be imported from overseas, usually from Europe and North America. To administer the distribution effectively, marketing, pricing (and in some cases, processing) of Mauritania's scarce food supplies, the CSA, a wholly governmental organization, maintained a system of several dozen warehouses in most of the country's régions (q.v.) for the storage of cereals and grains, which would be released gradually, with prices being subsidized both as to payments to producers and consumer prices. The large stocks of food donated by foreign countries were also distributed by the CSA. However, overall direction of this facet of Mauritania's food network was vested with the *Société Nationale d'Importation et d'Exportation* (SONIMEX) (q.v.), and even then, a variety of private traders continued to operate outside governmental control. This combination of guaranteed minimum prices for producers and price ceilings for consumers did function remarkably well for a time—for several years, no one was reported to have starved to death in Mauritania, although the rate of malnutrition was probably high. But the CSA soon fell under the influence of less scrupulous government officials, who allegedly distributed food and other aid on the basis of tribal, regional, or political factors, unrelated to need. Relatives and friends of the head of state, Ould Heydallah, were among those implicated in the use of the CSA to line their own pockets. The atmosphere of corruption surrounding the Food Security Commission's activities played a substantial role in the removal of Ould Heydallah on December 12, 1984, and his replacement by Colonel Maaouiya Ould Sid'Ahmed Taya (q.v.). One of Ould Taya's first acts was to dismiss the director of the CSA and reorganize the agency to eliminate corruption. In 1985, moreover, the agency began paying farmers 40 percent more for the produce they sold to the Mauritanian government, in order to provide an incentive for increased production. At the same time, consumer price subsidies were drastically slashed, with prices often rising by 50 percent as a result. By 1990 further reforms were undertaken in the food sector, including the privatization of the rice and cereal mills operated by the CSA and by the *Société Nationale pour le Développement Rural* (SONADER) (q.v.) and the abandonment of the CSA's direct marketing and distribution efforts, although it still had a role in warehousing and price stabilization. By the mid-1990s, most food subsidies had been eliminated in line with Ould Taya's increasing reliance on the private sector to manage Mauritania's economy, and the CSA's role correspondingly declined further.

COMMUNAUTE FINANCIERE AFRICAINE (CFA). The African Financial Community is a French-dominated common market and currency (q.v.) zone that from 1960 to 1973 included Mauritania, and which utilized the CFA franc as its regional standard medium of exchange. CFA members in 1996 were Benin, Burkina Faso, Cameroon, Central African Republic, Chad, Comoros, Congo, Ivory Coast, Equatorial Guinea (although it was a former Spanish, not French, colony), Gabon, Mali, Niger, and Senegal. The CFA tightly linked the economies of France's former African colonies to the policies and fortunes of the Paris banking establishment, but held out the promise of a fixed exchange rate and guaranteed convertibility with other major world currencies. In the early 1970s, Mauritania's head of state, President Mokhtar Ould Daddah (q.v.), who until then had been a supporter of his country's membership in the CFA and the French Community, perceived that these monetary arrangements were unsatisfactory from his country's point of view. Therefore, as part of the nationalistic measures Ould Daddah was carrying out in his foreign relations (q.v.), an extraordinary congress of the ruling *Parti du Peuple Mauritanien* (PPM) (q.v.) in June 1972 decided that Mauritania should leave the French Community and launch its own currency. With financial assistance from a variety of sources, including from Algeria's president, Houari Boumedienne (q.v.), Mauritania was able, on June 30, 1973, to secede from the African Financial Community (and its associated body, the West African Monetary Union), abolish the use of the CFA franc, and issue its own currency, the *ouguiya* (q.v.).

COMMUNES. Established under the Constitution of Mauritania of May 20, 1961 (q.v.), the *communes* replaced the former *Conseils Locaux* (q.v.) of the French colonial period as the basic tool of local administration in the country in the immediate post-independence era. In the 1961–63 period, communes for both urban and rural areas of Mauritania were established under President Mokhtar Ould Daddah (q.v.). The urban communes had elected mayors from 1961, and were set up in the capital, Nouakchott (q.v.), as well as in Bogué in the Senegal River Valley *cercle* of Brakna (qq.v.). Other urban communes were located in Atar, Kaédi, and Rosso (qq.v.). Later on, communes were set up on an experimental basis in Ayoun el-Atrouss, F'Derik, and Nouadhibou (qq.v.). Despite the fairly elaborate nature of these locally based governing organs, they remained of little real significance, as the Mauritanian governmental system, closely patterned after that of France's, was highly centralized and the local and regional bodies served as a "transmission belt" between Nouakchott and the people of the country, and not as a mediatory mechanism between the capital and the populace. Due to a lack of resources and shortages of trained personnel, moreover, the communes soon shrank even further in importance, and were abolished in 1968, with the rural bodies going first (on March 4) and the rest following by the end of the year. Effective July 30, 1968, all local administration was revamped, with the cercles being renamed *régions* (q.v.), the *sous-préfectures* redesignated *départements* (qq.v.), and the limited functions of the former communes transferred, for the most part, to *arrondissements* (q.v.), the smallest units of local governance in a still centralized Mauritanian polity.

COMMUNES INDIGENES. One of the more interesting institutions of French colonial rule in Mauritania, the *Communes Indigènes* were the low-level, locally based advisory bodies (with no actual authority whatsoever), composed of tribal chieftains and other traditional figures who carried out French policy and who served also to communicate information concerning local conditions to the AOF (q.v.) government in Dakar, Senegal. As such, these assemblies were a departure from the usual French practice of direct colonial administration, resembling instead Great Britain's system of indirect governance. Some historians have ascribed this difference to the recognition by Paris that Mauritanians were a proud, highly independent people with a decided martial tradition who had always resisted centralized rule. The Communes Indigènes also helped to prevent coordinated opposition to the French from emerging, due to their success in harnessing the loyalties of at least some of the subject population—essentially a "divide and rule" tactic.

COMMUNICATIONS. As is the case with the country's network of roads (q.v.) and its system for the generation and distribution of electricity (q.v.), Mauritania's radio, telephone, and television facilities remain underdeveloped in the mid-1990s, with a prime obstacle to improvements to the system being a perennial shortage of money to defray the high initial costs for the installation of equipment. The Mauritanian telephone system is sparse, with only about 6700 receivers in the capital, Nouakchott (q.v.), a small number compared to the city's overall population (q.v.). There is also telephone service in Nouadhibou and some other centers, but these are far fewer in number, and some towns in remote areas, such as Oualata (q.v.), have little or no service. In an effort to improve Nouakchott's telephones, a $27 million project to add 13,000 receivers to the capital was started in early

1993, funded by a Kuwait-based consortium and carried out by the French firm Alcatel. Completion was scheduled for 1994. Although Mauritania has only one television station (founded in 1984 and firmly under the control of the government), the country is connected with both INTELSAT (International Telecommunications Satellite Organization) and ARABSAT (Arab Satellite Telecommunications Organization), the latter comprising the members of the Arab League (q.v.). By the mid-1980s, ground stations were in operation in Nouakchott and Nouadhibou, and plans were being formulated for a third. French-funded ground links to ARABSAT and INTELSAT also existed, linking Mauritania to Paris and other world capitals, and carried with them some capacity (about ninety circuits in all) for cellular telephone connections to many of the more remote administrative régions (q.v.). Equipment for television programming was also provided by Iraq during its period of friendship with Mauritania in the 1980s. But the primary means of communication remains radio, which assumes particular importance in a nation with only a relatively small proportion of literate individuals. There were roughly 225,000 radio sets in Mauritania in the early 1990s. In 1995, two AM radio stations were in service, broadcasting throughout most of the day in French and Hassaniya (q.v.) Arabic as well as the other national languages—Fulani, Sarakolé, and Wolof (qq.v.). Both radio stations, like their television counterpart, are operated by the state *Office de Radiodiffusion et Télévision de Mauritanie* (ORTM), under the overall supervision of Mauritania's minister of the interior.

COMPAGNIE MAURITANIENNE DE NAVIGATION MARITIME (COMAUNAM). The Mauritanian Maritime Navigation Company, established in 1973, operates a fleet of merchant vessels of various tonnages between the country's two ports, Nouakchott and Nouadhibou (qq.v.), and destinations primarily in Europe. The company also performs stevedore and other marine-related functions, and acts as a freight forwarding agent. In 1995, COMAUNAM was 51 percent owned by the Mauritanian government, with the Algerian shipping parastatal, the *Compagnie Nationale Algérienne de Navigation* (CNAN), holding the remainder.

COMPTOIR MINIER DU NORD (COMINOR). The Northern Mining Syndicate was established in 1972 as a wholly owned subsidiary of the Mauritanian government enterprise, the *Société Nationale Industrielle et Minière* (SNIM) (q.v.), with responsibility for extracting and transporting the country's enormous reserves of iron ore (q.v.) located primarily near the twin towns of F'Derik and Zouerate (qq.v.). For two years after its formal establishment, COMINOR remained little more than a shell, as the iron mining sector was still controlled by the French-owned MIFERMA (q.v.) consortium. But spurred on by public protests against what was seen as French neocolonialism, and in line with President Mokhtar Ould Daddah's (q.v.) wish to adopt more nationalistic and "progressive" policies both at home and in Mauritania's foreign relations (q.v.), the government nationalized MIFERMA on November 28, 1974, and placed all iron ore–related facilities under SNIM, with COMINOR handling most of the actual mining operations. The changeover from European to Mauritanian management was remarkably smooth, with most expatriate workers staying in place, although the Ould Daddah regime hired more Mauritanian workers to satisfy nationalist demands. Over time the division of responsibilities between SNIM and COMINOR became clear—SNIM was charged with the development of mining sites throughout the country, while COMINOR would concentrate on the mines in the Zouerate area, the railway (q.v.) line running from the mines to the *Port Minéralier* (q.v.), and other ancillary functions such as housing and supplying the work force and maintaining rail rolling stock and marine equipment.

CONSEIL DE GOUVERNEMENT. An institution based in Dakar, Senegal, between 1925 and 1946 with the responsibility of assisting the governor-general of *Afrique Occidentale Française* (AOF) (q.v.), the Council of Government played a major role in administering the territory of what would become Mauritania, although its influence was always firmly subordinate to the governor-general himself, as he was appointed by, and answerable only to, the President of the French Republic in Paris. The council consisted of forty members, among whom were representatives of each AOF territory (eight including Mauritania), high judicial and army officials, and selected tribal chieftains and others chosen for their loyalty to France. The Conseil de Gouvernement held only one plenary session per year, to discuss primarily budgetary and administrative matters, though it did have a Permanent Commission to oversee the regular work of AOF and recommend policies to the plenary session. By a decree of October 25, 1946, however, the council found most of its authority transferred to the *Grand Conseil d'AOF* (q.v.), which also had forty members and was also subordinate to the governor-general in Dakar, now bestowed with the additional title of High Commissioner of the Republic.

CONSEIL GENERAL. The *Conseil Général* was a bicameral legislative body of a largely consultative nature, put into place as a result of the administrative separation of Mauritania from Senegal following the 1946 promulgation of the Constitution of the Fourth French

Republic, which had the effect of decentralizing the authority of the colonial governmental structure, *Afrique Occidentale Française* (AOF) (q.v.). In Mauritania, the General Council had twenty-four members divided into two houses: one chamber had purely French nationals, while the other was composed of French subjects (whether European or Mauritanian) who were eligible for election if they were in full possession of their legal rights. Both houses were elected for five-year terms, but the body's competence to govern was sharply restricted by the fact that it could not discuss "political" issues in any of its two yearly mandatory sessions; the deputies were to concern themselves only with local administrative and budgetary (q.v.) matters. The General Council sat at St. Louis, Senegal (the "capital" of Mauritania until the founding of Nouakchott [q.v.] over a decade later), and had a Permanent Commission to facilitate its work between sessions, as well as various other adjudicatory and advisory panels which, like the council itself, had very little real power. In 1952, the General Council was renamed the *Assemblée Territoriale* (q.v.).

CONSEILS LOCAUX. Under the Constitution of March 22, 1959 (q.v.), of the soon-to-be-independent Islamic Republic of Mauritania, the *Conseils Locaux* were established to ensure the functioning of the country's administration at the level of its twelve *cercles* (q.v.), later renamed *régions* (q.v.). The Local Councils were the middle-level governing bodies in Mauritania, below the central authority in Nouakchott (q.v.) but above the *communes* (q.v.), which were smaller institutions covering both urban and rural areas. In actual practice, the Local Councils had limited influence, as the Mauritanian head of state, Mokhtar Ould Daddah (q.v.), retained the highly centralized French system of government. The Local Councils were abolished in 1968 as part of a sweeping governmental reorganization.

CONSTITUENT ASSEMBLY. As the transitional legislative chamber established after the proclamation of the Islamic Republic of Mauritania on November 28, 1958, the Constituent Assembly replaced the prior legislature, the *Assemblée Territoriale* (q.v.), although its powers and membership were almost the same. From the beginning, the Constituent Assembly was dominated by Mokhtar Ould Daddah's *Parti de Regroupement Mauritanien* (PRM) (qq.v.), which had won thirty-three of the thirty-four seats in the Territorial Assembly in elections held in March 1957. Immediately after it convened, the new assembly was put to work drafting a constitution for the soon-to-be-independent Mauritanian state, but in reality the body completely lacked the expertise needed to perform such a task, and instead simply accepted, by a unanimous vote on March 22, 1959, the Constitution of

1959 (q.v.), the country's first, which had been written by a small group of French jurists in cooperation with Ould Daddah and a few of his closest aides. Barely two months later, on May 17, 1959, elections were held for the *Assemblée Nationale* (q.v.), independent Mauritania's parliament, and the Constituent Assembly was dissolved.

CONSTITUTIONAL CHARTER (February 9, 1985). Two months after the overthrow of Colonel Mohammed Khouna Ould Heydallah (q.v.) as Mauritania's head of state, the country's ruling body, the *Comité Militaire de Salut National* (CMSN), led by Colonel Maaouiya Ould Sid'Ahmed Taya (qq.v.), promulgated, without consulting public opinion, an interim Constitutional Charter meant to serve as Mauritania's organic governing document until its eventual replacement by democratic institutions. Along with several ordinances intended to supplement its provisions, it survived until July 20, 1991, when a new democratic constitution (q.v.) was overwhelmingly approved by the Mauritanian electorate, paving the way for the formation of multiple political parties, contested presidential and parliamentary elections, and the advent of the Second Republic (q.v.) on April 18, 1992.

The Constitutional Charter amounted to a set of procedural rules for the operation of the CMSN, regularizing its affairs. By virtue of Article 3 of the Charter, the CMSN was given almost unlimited powers over national policies, foreign relations (q.v.), and oversight of the Mauritanian civil service. The only limits on its power were in those areas of the law that were outside the regular judicial system (q.v.) and fell instead under the purview of Islamic (q.v.) courts applying the *sharia* (q.v.). The CMSN, henceforth, would consist of persons nominated to it, and would include a Permanent Committee, made up of all members who were posted to the Mauritanian capital, Nouakchott (q.v.). It would meet every fifteen days, or more often if convened by the President of the Republic. The CMSN as a whole was to meet at least once every three months, thereby giving an advantage to those members who were physically present in Nouakchott over those in the outlying régions (q.v.). Other articles dealt with presidential succession in the event of his death or incapacity. Moreover (per Articles 11 and 12), the Mauritanian president was empowered to make all nominations to the governmental apparatus outside the CMSN, and could dismiss them at any time.

A supplementary ordinance, also dated February 9, 1985, left little doubt as to the allocation of real power in Mauritania: the CMSN, *de jure,* held a position higher than that of the Council of Ministers (q.v.), which headed the ordinary state bureaucracy, and the CMSN alone would decide whether criminal or civil charges could be maintained against one of its members, irrespective of whether the alleged offense was related to official duties. The ordinance also established five advisory commissions, which would deal, respectively, with matters of defense, economics, education and justice, public works, and social welfare. Finally, it provided that Mauritania's head of state would be chosen from among all the CMSN members by a secret ballot, with a two-thirds majority required for selection (indeed, some reports stated that Ould Taya himself had been subjected to such a vote). Two-thirds of the CMSN could also depose a president, a procedure that was intended to make any further presidential changes in a more orderly fashion under the institution of military rule that had begun on July 10, 1978.

CONSTITUTION OF MAURITANIA (March 22, 1959). Two years before gaining formal independence from France, Mauritania's Constituent Assembly (q.v.), a legislative body that had over the previous decade been known first as the *Conseil Général* and then as the *Assemblée Territoriale* (qq.v.) and which was completely dominated by Mokhtar Ould Daddah's *Parti de Regroupement Mauritanien* (PRM) (qq.v.), met to draft a constitution for the embryonic Mauritanian state. However, the politicians who made up the Assembly (all but one of whom were PRM loyalists) were not qualified for this task, and so the Constituent Assembly did little but discuss and approve, by a unanimous vote on March 22, 1959, a draft constitution that was the work of French legal experts, colonial advisors, and Ould Daddah's aides.

Mauritania's first constitution closely mirrored that of the French Fifth Republic. After a preambular statement in which Islam (q.v.) and basic human rights were declared to form the foundation of the new state, Article 1 provided that Mauritania would have a republican and democratic nature, and Article 2 decreed Islam as the state religion but provided that religious freedom would be guaranteed. Article 3 stated that Arabic would be the national language and French the official one—a concession to black Mauritanian interests. Article 8 provided for universal suffrage, and Article 9 allowed the formation of political parties so long as they adhered to democratic principles and did not question the unity of the state. As for the structure of the government, the most important actors were the prime minister and the *Assemblée Nationale* (q.v.): the parliament would select the prime minister by a one-third vote, and he was to be subsequently elected by a simple majority of the Assembly's members. Once elected, the prime minister would choose a Council of Ministers (q.v.) to preside over a variety of governmental functions, including foreign relations (q.v.). Overall formulation and direction of Mauritania's national policies would rest with the prime minister, but he would always be subject to a vote of no confidence by the National Assembly, in which case new elections would be conducted after the mandatory resignation of the prime minister and his cabinet. Both the executive and legislative branches shared the prerogative of initiating legislation, and the National Assembly was required to limit its sittings to two per year, with each session not to exceed two months. Each member of parliament was elected for a term of five years, and any Mauritanian who was twenty-five years or older could stand for election. The 1959 constitution also reiterated that the practice of slavery (q.v.) was forbidden, following a 1905 French decree to the same effect. The document also provided for local government in the form of *cercles* and *sous-préfectures* (qq.v.), but their actual authority, as well as their method of election, was left indeterminate. The Constitution of 1959 remained in effect for the short time Mauritania had left to it under colonial rule, and a few months after the country's accession to independence on November 28, 1960, a new constitution, similar in some respects but with important differences, was promulgated on May 20, 1961 (q.v.).

CONSTITUTION OF MAURITANIA (May 20, 1961). Following Mauritania's independence from France on November 28, 1960, the country's leader, President Mokhtar Ould Daddah (q.v.), continued his efforts not only to unite a series of disparate political tendencies, but also to consolidate his own position as head of what he evidently wished to be a strong, centralized state patterned after the institutions of the French Fifth Republic. Hence in May 1961 Ould Daddah proposed to replace the earlier constitution of March 22, 1959 (q.v.), with a new organic law that he believed would be better suited to Mauritanian realities. On May 20 the recently convened National Assembly (q.v.), Mauritania's parliament, approved the new draft constitution, an unsurprising move since that body was dominated entirely by Ould Daddah's *Parti de Regroupement Mauritanien* (PRM) (q.v.), and which merely gave its mark of assent to what had already been decided beforehand, without any popular participation. Although there were some similarities between the 1961 constitution and the one it replaced, it contained crucial differences. The President of the Islamic Republic of Mauritania, the constitution provided, was the head of state and of the government, and was the commander-in-chief of the country's armed forces (q.v.). He had the unlimited power to select and dismiss his Council of Ministers (q.v.), to name ambassadors, and to declare war and ratify treaties with other countries. Legislatively, the President's authority was immense. He had the power to propose legislation that would take precedence over those measures put forward by the National Assembly, a privilege which Ould Daddah was later to use, in 1963 and 1964, effectively to curtail parliament's initiative by proposing dozens of bills that had to be given priority, thus preventing the National Assembly from proposing its own laws. In the alternative, the head of state could bypass the Mauritanian legislature by submitting proposals directly to the people via a referendum. The President was to be elected for a five-year term, indefinitely renewable. Foreign relations (q.v.) was one area where Ould Daddah had virtually unlimited authority, with very few checks and balances within the constitutional framework.

Even the limited powers vested in the National Assembly were, in practice, steadily whittled away in the coming months and years. In October 1961 a first step towards Ould Daddah's complete domination of the Mauritanian political scene was taken at the Congress of Unity (q.v.), where the remaining political parties not under the sway of the head of state, along with Ould Daddah's own PRM, were merged into a new grouping, the *Parti du Peuple Mauritanien* (PPM) (q.v.), which quickly became a virtual "vanguard" party with limited opportunities for internal dissent. This evolution was continued at the Kaédi Conference (q.v.) of January 1964, in which the PPM's structure was made totally subservient to Mokhtar Ould Daddah's wishes, expressed through his like-minded colleagues on the PPM leadership organ, the *Bureau Politique National* (BPN) (q.v.). The 1961 constitution then lost what little real meaning it had, because the following year, in 1965, it was amended to make the PPM the sole legal political party, ignoring the detailed amendment procedures set forth in the document. In 1968, another series of amendments was undertaken, this time pertaining to local government and the designation of Hassaniya (q.v.) Arabic as the official language of Mauritania as a part of Ould Daddah's Arabization policy (q.v.). Constitutional procedures were again disregarded. Although Ould Daddah did stand for reelection as president at five-year intervals (in 1966, 1971, and 1976), the process had no substance, as non-PPM candidates were proscribed and the incumbent was in any case unopposed. By now little more than a hollow shell, the Mauritanian Constitution of May 1961 remained nominally in effect until July 10, 1978, when it was suspended by order of the *Comité Militaire de Redressement National* (CMRN) (q.v.), a committee of army officers who had overthrown President Ould Daddah in a bloodless *coup d'état*.

CONSTITUTION OF MAURITANIA (July 20, 1991). After the suspension of the Constitution of May 20, 1961 (q.v.), by Mauritania's *Comité Militaire de Redressement National* (CMRN) (q.v.) military government on July 10, 1978, the country went for the next thirteen years without a regular governing document, although in December

1980 the Mauritanian head of state, Colonel Mohammed Khouna Ould Heydallah (q.v.) did promulgate a provisional constitution (q.v.), only to retract it after a serious coup attempt against his regime in March 1981. The *Comité Militaire de Salut National* (CMSN) (q.v.), the CMRN's successor, tried to introduce some formal legality by issuing a Constitutional Charter (q.v.) in February 1985 following the ouster of Ould Heydallah by Colonel Maaouiya Ould Sid'Ahmed Taya (q.v.). But the Charter was little more than a unilateral statement of the ruling council's prerogatives and internal operating procedures, which, as might be expected, were virtually unchecked. Particularly in the destructive aftermath of a twin set of events in the 1989–1991 period, the Senegal-Mauritania Crisis and the Gulf Crisis and War (qq.v.), Mauritania's political and social affairs urgently needed the stamp of popular approval and the resultant legitimacy. Also necessary were mechanisms to ensure basic civil liberties as well as institutions that would allow policy differences to be aired openly, avoiding the concealed exercise of unlimited power not only by the CMSN itself, but also by determined groups such as the Arab Baath Socialist Party (ABSP) (q.v.), which had acquired a high degree of influence in the country by 1990.

Only a matter of weeks after the conclusion of the Gulf War, and at a time when Mauritania was still suffering the severe political and economic effects of that conflict, President Ould Taya announced, on April 15, 1991, that a draft constitution would be submitted to the country's voters for their approval, the first time this had been done in Mauritania's thirty-one-year history. Despite the fact that the 103-article document was presented to the electorate without the possibility of popular comment on its specific provisions, a referendum was held on July 12, 1991, in which the "constitutional project" was overwhelmingly endorsed. According to the government, 97.9 percent of those who voted cast "yes" ballots, with a reported turnout of 85.3 percent. After its approval and its formal ratification by Ould Taya on July 20, a period of transition went into effect, with the CMSN continuing to govern until the basic institutions of what became known as the Mauritanian Second Republic (q.v.) were established, a process that was concluded on April 18, 1992.

The new Constitution of Mauritania continued the country's tradition of investing the executive branch with substantially greater power than the legislature. The President of the Republic, pursuant to Article 25, appointed and presided over the Council of Ministers (q.v.), and thus had the direction of the general policy of the state. In foreign relations (q.v.) and defense, the powers of the head of state were almost plenary (Article 30), with some important exceptions: a declaration of war must be approved by the legislative branch (Article 58), and treaties, which the President, acting alone, may otherwise sign and ratify (Article 36), required the assent of parliament when budgetary (q.v.) matters were affected or the provisions of the treaty affected the rights and duties of Mauritanian citizens or in any manner altered the boundaries of the country (Article 78). In domestic affairs, the President's prerogatives were also great. He could dissolve the *Assemblée Nationale* (q.v.) pursuant to Article 31, although this was forbidden when the head of state declared a "state of siege and emergency" during a severe internal crisis or external threat (Articles 39 and 71). On any matter of his choosing, the President could circumvent the legislature by having recourse to a popular referendum (Article 38) and had a limited veto power on bills passed by the legislative branch (Article 70). The President of the Republic, required to be a Muslim under Article 23, was elected to a six-year term by direct and universal suffrage, with no limits on reelection (Articles 26 and 28).

The Mauritanian legislature had a structure that was practically unique in Africa and the Middle East: it was bicameral, with both a National Assembly, elected by direct vote, and a Senate (q.v.), chosen indirectly by the municipal councils in each of the country's twelve régions (q.v.) as well as for a separate district comprising the capital, Nouakchott (q.v.). The existence of a Senate was an attempt to guarantee a minimum level of representation to every part of Mauritania, irrespective of population (q.v.). The legislature had extensive authority in budgetary matters (Article 68) and in the general finances of the state, and had the use of commissions to assist its work, ensuring at least some oversight of the governmental machinery.

Aside from detailing responsibilities of the President and the National Assembly, the 1991 constitution, after declaring Islam (q.v.) to be the state religion (Article 5), guaranteed to all Mauritanians basic civil rights such as freedom of speech, travel, assembly, and association (Article 10). It also prohibited torture and other extralegal actions against the individual (Article 13), but provided, rather sweepingly, that "treason, espionage, and going over to the enemy as well as all infractions committed with prejudice to the security of the State shall be punished with all the rigor of the law (Article 18)." Private property, long a fundamental characteristic of Mauritanian society, was accorded explicit protection (Article 15). In a concession to the concerns of the Black African citizens of Mauritania, Fulani, Soninké, and Wolof (qq.v.) were declared to be, along with Arabic, national languages, although Arabic was proclaimed the official language (Article 6). Finally, a Constitutional Council, a High Court of Justice, a revamped judicial system (q.v.), an Economic and Social Council, and a High Islamic Council were also established by the constitution in Titles VI through IX. However, their precise practical roles in the government, like those of the other evolving institutions of the Second Republic, remain uncertain in the mid-1990s.

COPPER. Although commercially exploitable deposits of copper had been known to exist in Mauritania since the early 1930s, it was not until several decades later, in 1970, that mining operations could finally begin, only to cease after eight years for a variety of financial and technical reasons. Even at the height of production in the early 1970s, shipments of copper never contributed nearly as much to the Mauritanian economy as the massive iron ore (q.v.) reserves near the town of Zouerate (q.v.) in the northeastern part of the country. Overall, therefore, the impact of copper mining on Mauritania's budgetary (q.v.) situation remained fairly low.

The first attempt to marshal the necessary resources to extract copper ore, whose location had been pinpointed at a site called Guelb el-Moghrein located a few kilometers west of the town of Akjoujt in the administrative région of Inchiri (qq.v.), came in 1953 when a French-dominated consortium, the *Société des Mines de Cuivre de Mauritanie* (MICUMA) (q.v.) was organized with a total capital of $1.6 million. But MICUMA never got off the ground because of several factors: the difficulty in refining copper ore due to the level of technology then current; the distance from the Akjoujt mine to the nearest water resources (q.v.) necessary to supply the operation (the closest was at Bennichab, over one hundred kilometers distant); and finally, daunting problems of transporting the ore from Inchiri to the Atlantic coast, a problem that was not helped by the refusal of the (also French-run) MIFERMA (q.v.) iron mining company to consider extending its railway (q.v.) line to Akjoujt to handle copper shipments. The estimated amount of copper deposits involved—32 million tons—looked promising, but no progress was made in preparing to exploit them until after Mauritania's independence in November 1960, when improvements in refining techniques and the construction of a port (q.v.) facility near Nouakchott (q.v.) made it possible to consider restarting the endeavor. In April 1963, after a series of talks between the government of President Mokhtar Ould Daddah (q.v.) and MICUMA shareholders and other overseas interests, a new company, the *Société de Cuivre de la Mauritanie* (SOCUMA) was formed with a total capital of $10 million and an eighteen-month mandate to review the prospects for beginning copper extraction. SOCUMA's owners included the United States–Canadian Homestake-Southfield Group (55 percent) and the government of Mauritania itself (25 percent). The U.S.-led Lindsley Group (Northfield Mines, Inc.) also held a substantial stake in the project and had long expressed interest in the Akjoujt deposits. After SOCUMA's final report was issued, however, various disputes among the shareholders resulted in the company's dissolution in late 1965.

Mauritania's copper mining aspirations looked stricken once again, but in 1967 the *Société Minière de Mauritanie* (SOMIMA) (q.v.) was formed, again with heavy European participation and with only a minority stake (22 percent) held by the Mauritanian government. SOMIMA proved more successful in its preparations than its two predecessors; helped by the presence of a transshipment port at Nouakchott, an improved road (q.v.) from Inchiri, and a solution to the water supply problem at Bennichab, it was able to begin mining operations at Akjoujt in 1970. The mine was of the open-cast variety, centered on a "lens" approximately 300 meters by 500 meters, with an estimated depth of 100 meters, where the ore was concentrated. After the ore was loosened from the surrounding earth by a combination of explosives and heavy machinery, the deposits were loaded onto trucks for the 250-kilometer journey to Nouakchott, where ships would be waiting to transport it to market, mainly to Europe and North America. Over the next few years, production increased steadily, rising to a peak of 28,982 tons taken out in 1973. But the quality of the Akjoujt ore was low, the large deposits of gold (q.v.) thought to accompany the copper did not immediately materialize, and world prices for copper were starting to drop. Technical problems were also making themselves apparent, and in 1975 President Ould Daddah shut down SOMIMA in frustration, nationalizing the company (as he had already done to MIFERMA) and putting it under the auspices of the newly formed parastatal, the *Société Nationale Industrielle et Minière* (SNIM) (q.v.), which thus found itself responsible for both iron ore and copper mining. About a year later, SNIM resumed operations at the Inchiri mine and ran it at a loss until 1978, when it was closed for a second time.

Still another attempt to exploit Mauritania's copper deposits came in 1981, when the *Société Arabe des Mines d'Inchiri* (SAMIN) was set up, a consortium owned by the Mauritanian government (37.5 percent) and various Arab states and private investors (62.5 percent). SAMIN estimated at first that it could get 105,000 tons of ore annually from the Akjoujt area, but this figure soon declined to 65,000 tons. The projected required investment also declined (from $100 million to $40 million) but the necessary funding had not been secured in 1994, making any reentry by Mauritania into the copper extraction business problematic. Still, the mine at Akjoujt had not yet exhausted its usefulness. In 1991, a SNIM subsidiary, *Mines d'Or d'Akjoujt* (MORAK) began exploitation of the gold deposits located in the tailings of the inactive copper mine. It turned out to be a relatively successful endeavor, contributing about $15 million per year to Mauritania's treasury by 1995.

COPPOLANI, XAVIER. One of the great personalities of the period of French penetration and colonization of West Africa in the late nineteenth and early twentieth centuries, Xavier Coppolani was Corsican by birth, but was raised in Algeria, which had been under French domination beginning in 1830. By virtue of his long residence in North Africa, he became fluent in Arabic and possessed an extensive knowledge of Islam (q.v.) from a fairly early age. He first acquired diplomatic and political-military experience in the French territory of "Soudan" (present-day Mali), where he managed to bring the traditionally independent tribes of that area into cooperative agreements with France. But his most significant achievements were yet to come. In response to a 1901 request by France's prime minister to study various methods of bringing West Africa under colonial administration, Coppolani proposed a course that he felt would be most efficacious and which held out the prospect of being completed without wholesale violence. It was a policy of "peaceful pacification," followed by persuasion—as he put it, "cooperation with financial rewards, or resistance with military consequences." Although elements of a "divide and rule" strategy could be discerned, coupled with the constant threat of force if the Mauritanian tribes resisted, Coppoolani's overall plan was more subtle, and for its time, relatively enlightened. He sought to replace the domination of the *hassan* (q.v.) tribes, which had existed since the end of the Char Bobha (q.v.) in 1674, with greater influence by the *zawiya* (q.v.) or monastic religious tribes who constituted the second—but still privileged—tier of Moorish (q.v.) society, with the idea that they would find it "easier to spread the word of Allah." He strategized that once the hassan (warrior) tribes had been vanquished, peace would reign in the Sahara, the seemingly endless *ghazzis* (q.v.) and reprisals would cease, and collaboration with the French would ensue. Although French colonial rule elsewhere in Africa (and certainly in Algeria) was characterized by its directness, Coppolani felt that indirect rule would be appropriate in Mauritania, for he appreciated the fiercely independent nature of the nomadic Moors, and felt that very little should be done to disturb their traditional way of life. French military power would substitute for that of the warrior tribes, presumably invoking a grateful response on the part of the less advantaged castes, including the *znaga* (q.v.).

Upon arrival in Mauritania in 1902, Xavier Coppolani quickly set to work, assiduously courting some of the most respected zawiya tribes and reportedly winning converts to his plans among more conservative tribal leaders, who—as the contemporary accounts had it—were impressed by his low-key personality and religious erudition. He offered them peace, security from the ghazzis, and expanded commerce (q.v.) in return for submitting to French governance. It was in Trarza (q.v.)

where his efforts first bore fruit, as both of the major leaders there, Cheikh Sidiya Baba of the Oulad Berri monastic tribe and Cheikh Saad Bou, were won over by Coppolani's entreaties. In the case of Saad Bou, the results were particularly worth obtaining, for he held great spiritual sway over not only Trarza but also the Tagant (q.v.) region as well as in the Senegal River Valley, places where the French had already set their sights. Coppolani, however, was not adverse to using intertribal disputes among Tagant's inhabitants to secure a complete agreement in February 1903, after which he moved to establish French administrative centers and leave behind a contingent of seasoned French colonial troops to maintain order. It did not work: after Coppolani left to conquer more areas, notably the Adrar (q.v.), the Trarza revolted before the end of the year, and although the uprisings were put down by early 1904, they served as a warning sign to the French that "pacification," at least by nonmilitary means, was not necessarily a device to guarantee long-term control. Still, during a spell of home leave in France (May–October 1904), Coppolani managed to convince his government that his policies should be extended to Adrar, Tagant, and possibly Brakna and Gorgol (qq.v.). These plans were to prove far more difficult to realize, due to the emergence of an uncompromisingly anticolonial Saharawi (q.v.) religious leader, Cheikh Ma el-Ainin (q.v.) whose influence extended from northern Mauritania to Saguia el-Hamra (q.v.) into southern Morocco. Ma el-Ainin had already been petitioned by other tribes that felt threatened by French incursions to join with them to drive the French back across the Senegal River. In the meantime, Coppolani set out to pacify—by overt military means this time—the Tagant region, and eventually succeeded in doing so, by dint of the application of armed forces led by Colonel Fréréjean in conjunction with the deliberate implanting of suspicions among rival or even allied tribes. Thus, despite a serious reversal for the French on March 24, 1905, when the Oulad Berri forces of Cheikh Sidiya Baba were routed by troops loyal to Ma el-Ainin, the occupation force finally reached Tidjikja (q.v.), the center of Tagant's commercial and religious life, on April 1. Coppolani soon arrived in the town to plan his next campaign, into Adrar, where Ma el-Ainin's strength was even more pronounced. But before he could begin to carry out his plans, Coppolani was assassinated while sleeping in his bed at Tidjikja on May 12, 1905, by a small group of men who apparently acted on behalf of Ma el-Ainin. Coppolani's death was a significant encouragement to the anti-French resistance, and it threw Paris into a period of uncertainty regarding its objectives in Mauritania. It would be left to Coppolani's successor as governor-general of the territory, Colonel (later General) Henri Gouraud (q.v.) to complete the task of pacifying the Adrar in July 1909 (see ADRAR CAMPAIGN).

COUNCIL OF GOVERNMENT. See Conseil de Gouvernement

COUNCIL OF MINISTERS. Mauritania's first governing cabinet was invested by the country's foremost political personality, Mokhtar Ould Daddah (q.v.), on May 21, 1957, after the organization he founded, the *Union Progressiste Mauritanienne* (UPM) (q.v.), won a decisive victory over its opponents in the March 1957 elections to the *Assemblée Territoriale* (q.v.). Although this cabinet was subordinate to the French colonial authorities, the Constitutions of Mauritania adopted on March 22, 1959, and May 20, 1961 (qq.v.), accorded the Council of Ministers a substantial role in the day-to-day operation of the government. In particular, the cabinet members were always to serve exclusively at the pleasure of the head of state, and were tasked with the overall supervision of the various ministries that comprised the foundation of the regime. From the beginning, successive Mauritanian cabinets were made up of supporters either of President Ould Daddah's *Parti du Peuple Mauritanien* (PPM) (q.v.) or of the various armed forces (q.v.) governments that held office from July 1978 to April 1992. Also, the shifting of particular ministers from one portfolio to another over a relatively short period of time was a recurrent phenomenon on Mauritania's political landscape, caused, in the view of some observers, not so much by a rise or fall in a minister's political standing than by shortages of qualified personnel, necessitating frequent reshuffles to make the best use of scarce administrative talent. Therefore, careers such as that of Hamdi Ould Mouknass (q.v.), who served President Ould Daddah as foreign minister for a full decade (1968–1978) without interruption, or Hasni Ould Didi (q.v.), a long-serving minister of education, were very much the exception. Under the CMRN and CMSN (qq.v.) military councils, serving armed forces officers sometimes doubled as ministers, although a high level of civilian participation in most cabinets was maintained. However, the CMRN and CMSN were always strictly separate from, and superior in position to, the Council of Ministers.

A sea change in the composition of the cabinet was effected on April 18, 1992, when the Mauritanian Second Republic (q.v.) was inaugurated by President Maaouiya Ould Sid'Ahmed Taya (q.v.), who had emerged victorious in presidential balloting held in January. Despite the fact that Ould Taya's *Parti Républicain, Démocratique et Social* (PRDS) (q.v.) easily vanquished all its rivals, the first cabinet of the new regime was unprecedented in the breadth of its membership. There was, for example, only one serving military officer present, Colonel Ahmed Ould Minnih (q.v.), who was minister of defense, and the new foreign minister, Mohammed Abderrahmane Ould Moine, was a former CMSN opponent in exile who belonged to the influential *Alliance pour une Mauritanie Démocratique* (AMD) (q.v.) in the 1980s. Also, members of opposition political parties who did not join the boycott of the elections for the National Assembly and the Senate (qq.v.) in early 1992 were often rewarded, regardless of their electoral performance. Lastly, the all-important post of prime minister went to a respected and relatively apolitical technocrat, Sidi Mohamed Ould Boubacar (q.v.). Under Article 30 of the Constitution of Mauritania of July 20, 1991 (q.v.), the prime minister and cabinet are responsible directly to the President of the Republic, as is the case in many countries with a parliamentary system of government.

The full roster of the Mauritanian Council of Ministers as of April 1996 was as follows:

President of the Republic	Maaouiya Ould Sid'Ahmed Taya (q.v.)
Prime Minister	Cheikh El-Afia Ould Mohamed Khouna

Ministers

Minister of Civil Service, Labor, Youth, and Sports	Sidi Mohamed Ould Mohamed Vall
Minister of Commerce, Handicrafts, and Tourism	Boidel Ould Houmeid
Minister of Contacts and Relations with Parliament	Rachid Ould Saleh
Minister of Culture and Islamic Orientation	Limam Ould Teguedi
Minister of Defense	Abdellahi Ould Abdi
Minister of Equipment and Transport	Sow Mohamed Deina
Minister of Finance	Kamara Ely Gueladio
Minister of Fisheries and Maritime Economy	Baba Ould Sidi
Minister of Foreign Affairs and Cooperation	Mohamed Salem Ould Lekhal
Minister of Information	Ahmed Ould Khalifa Ould Jiddou
Minister of the Interior, Post, and Telecommunications	Mohamed Lamine Salem Ould Dah
Minister of Justice	Othmane Sid'Ahmed Yessa
Minister of Mines and Industry	N'Gaide Lamine
Minister of Education	Lemrabott Sidi Mahmoud Ould Cheikh Ahmed
Minister of Public Health and Social Affairs	Ch'bih Ould Cheikh Melanine
Minister of Rural Development and Environment	Sow Abou Demba

Minister of Planning   Sidi Mohamed Ould Biya
Minister of Energy and Water   Mohamed Lamine Ould Ahmed
  Supply

CURRENCY. Mauritania's attainment of independence from France on November 28, 1960, did not mean the end of close financial and other ties with the former metropole, as the new state, led by President Mokhtar Ould Daddah (q.v.), badly needed continuing support from Paris to run its economy and civil administration. From the beginning, therefore, Mauritania was a member (along with eleven other ex–French colonies) of the *Communauté Financière Africaine* (CFA) (q.v.), which oriented his country's monetary affairs toward dependence upon the French franc. It also made the Mauritanian economy more sensitive to external subsidies, due to the fact that France heavily underwrote the value and convertibility of the CFA franc, at least until the early 1990s. In addition, Mauritania was a member of the West African Monetary Union (*Union Monétaire Ouest-Africaine*, UMOA), which gave France an additional degree of control over the Mauritanian economy but which was a relatively secure arrangement since Paris thus guaranteed the value of the government's foreign exchange holdings. As Mauritania became flush with additional revenues, notably those derived from the extraction of iron ore (q.v.) in the late 1960s, the yoke of the CFA and UMOA began to chafe uncomfortably as Ould Daddah contemplated a more nationalistic and independent foreign relations (q.v.) line. In 1971, an extraordinary congress of the governing *Parti du Peuple Mauritanien* (PPM) (q.v.) voted either to renegotiate or to repudiate the various 1960 agreements with France that the country had signed before formal independence, including those dealing with monetary matters. A meeting in June 1972 of the PPM's *Bureau Politique National* (BPN) (q.v.) ratified this decision, the BPN and the PPM as a whole being in any event under the complete domination of President Ould Daddah. After attempts to renegotiate the monetary treaty with France failed, Mauritania decided to withdraw from the CFA franc zone and issue its own national currency, the *ouguiya* (q.v.). On June 30, 1973, the financial divorce from France was made official, with the ouguiya replacing the CFA franc, although the ouguiya's value was for a time fixed in relation to the French franc. Starting in the late 1980s, however, in response to demands from the World Bank and the International Monetary Fund (IMF) that the ouguiya, like the currencies of other developing countries, be cut loose from fixed exchange rates in order to reflect more accurately its value, the ouguiya was steadily devaluated against other leading world currencies, a trend that appears to have accelerated in the 1990s.

DAKHLA. Virtually the only population center of consequence in Mauritania's former portion of Western Sahara (q.v.), an area it called Tiris el-Gharbia (q.v.), the town of Dakhla is situated at the end of a long peninsula on the desert territory's 875-kilometer Atlantic coastline. Dakhla had its origins as the trading and fisheries (q.v.) settlement of Villa Cisneros, which was founded by Spain in 1884 but which was largely abandoned until 1895 after the Spanish suffered attacks by Saharawi (q.v.) tribesmen. For several decades thereafter, Villa Cisneros remained part of Madrid's colony of Río de Oro (q.v.), and was commercially unviable and almost wholly isolated. In this period, the total number of residents often did not exceed 200. With the drought-induced decline in nomadism in Western Sahara, the population increased to at least 5413 Saharawis and 3000 Europeans by 1974, the year Spain conducted its last census.

By the terms of the Madrid Agreement (q.v.) of November 14, 1975, under which Spain agreed to withdraw from its last African colony and convey it to the governments of King Hassan II (q.v.) of Morocco and President Mokhtar Ould Daddah (q.v.) of Mauritania, Villa Cisneros (which soon reverted to its Arabic name, Dakhla) fell within the Mauritanian zone of occupation. But ironically, Moroccan troops were the first to enter Dakhla, doing so on January 9, 1976, three days before Mauritania's armed forces (q.v.). The vast majority of the Saharawi populace fled Dakhla upon the outbreak of war between Morocco, Mauritania, and the pro-independence Polisario Front (q.v.).

In a secret addendum to the Algiers Agreement (q.v.) of August 5, 1979, by which Mauritania's CMSN (q.v.) government made peace with the Polisario Front and renounced its claim to Western Sahara, it was stipulated that upon Mauritania's withdrawal from Tiris el-Gharbia, the territory would be transferred directly to Polisario control. But this did not happen. On August 6, Morocco occupied Dakhla immediately after Mauritania departed and formally annexed it eight days later.

DAKHLET-NOUADHIBOU. One of Mauritania's smallest (22,000 square kilometers) yet relatively most prosperous administrative régions (q.v.), Dakhlet-Nouadhibou was formerly called Baie du Lévrier by the French colonial authorities, after the name of its enclosed harbor formed by the Cape Blanc peninsula, one of the few such protected shorelines in that area of West Africa. The province has several sources of economic activity, all centered on the région's capital, Nouadhibou (q.v.). Fisheries (q.v.) activity is intense, with fleets from around the world partaking (not always legally) of the huge numbers of fish that dwell on the area's large and shallow continental shelf. The province is also the terminus of the railway (q.v.) line running from the iron ore diggings near Zouerate (qq.v.) to the *Port Minéralier* (q.v.) ten kilometers south of Nouadhibou, generating employment in the mineral extraction industry and allied occupations. Merchant shipping also takes advantage of Nouadhibou's position as one of the only major ports (q.v.) in the vicinity. The presence of the *Parc National du Banc d'Arguin* (q.v.) in the province also makes it attractive to tourists (q.v.).

In 1977, the région boasted only about 23,000 inhabitants, a figure that almost tripled to an officially reported 63,030 in 1988, of whom the vast majority lived in or near the city of Nouadhibou, the rest of the province being a trackless desert wilderness with a nomadic population (q.v.) of only 800 or so. One small exception is the settlement of Nouamghar along the Atlantic coast, home of Mauritania's unique Imraguen (q.v.) fishing tribe.

DEPARTEMENT. Also called by their Arabic name, *Moughataas,* the *départements* are the former *sous-préfectures* (q.v.) which serve as the middle level of local and regional administration in Mauritania, below that of the *régions* (q.v.) but above that of the *arrondissements* (q.v.). The départements were established on July 30, 1968, as part of the sweeping changes instituted that year by President Mokhtar Ould Daddah (q.v.), and were identical to the sous-préfectures except for a few minor adjustments. The chief administrator in each département was a *préfet,* who, along with the civil servants under his direction, was subordinate to the regional governor, who was in turn appointed directly by the President of the Republic in Nouakchott (q.v.), preserving the tightly centralized system inherited from French colonialism. After the *coup d'état* of July 10, 1978, which displaced Ould Daddah in favor of direct rule by the country's armed forces (q.v.), the départements lost what limited authority they had and were placed under the control of regional military commanders who were answerable only to (and sometimes members of) the CMRN or the CMSN (qq.v.). As part of the liberalization of Mauritanian politics initiated by the last CMSN chairman, Colonel Maaouiya Ould Sid'Ahmed Taya (q.v.), the départements, like other local bodies, were revitalized, although the general organization of the government still reserved most actual power in Nouakchott.

DESERTIFICATION. The most serious and pervasive natural phenomenon to affect Mauritania since its independence, desertification's symptoms include the gradual conversion of relatively fertile grasslands (pasturelands), black-earth agricultural (q.v.) lands, and even forests into arid or semiarid wastelands upon which crop raising or livestock (q.v.) herding is difficult or impossible. In the place of trees, crops, or bushes anchoring the topsoil, sandy desert moves in, supporting only a few hardy varieties of plants that usually have no economic value. Animal life migrates or becomes extinct, and the human population (q.v.) leaves the land, often permanently, and moves to cities and towns.

Meteorologically, the process of desertification can be traced through the rainfall (q.v.) pattern, which, in the case of Mauritania, manifested itself in the movement of the 150-mm isohyet line (at which the rainfall is the same amount in a given year) southward by about one hundred kilometers during the 1970s and early 1980s. Beyond these observable characteristics, the cause and permanency of desertification have been disputed among many experts. One school of thought, dire in its predictions, holds that desertified zones, made so by overgrazing, overuse of land for agricultural purposes, and general overpopulation, tend to remain that way indefinitely. Moreover, these experts believe that droughts (a cyclical phenomenon in Africa as elsewhere) are perpetuated by the existence of desert, which reflects solar energy back into the skies immediately, without the moisture and vegetation-generating carbon dioxide that would eventually be converted into clouds and rainfall. In short, the "microenvironment" created by the desertification of a small area or a Sahelian fringe zone is duplicated and enlarged by climatic processes. If the vegetation in an area has already been denuded by livestock grazing or human activity, a vicious cycle is established that is extremely difficult to overcome, and desertification can be expected to continue until it claims vast tracts of land and even entire countries. In the early 1990s, however, an alternative theory of desertification was circulating in the international community. According to this view, rainfall cycles do produce desert or desert-like conditions, but once the drought situation improves, grasslands will reestablish themselves and the desert itself will be "pushed back." In the African context, this pattern, some believe, has been present for 10,000 years and the 1968–88 period was merely a periodic oscillation, albeit one exacerbated by overpopulation and poor land management. This theory, which utilizes satellite-derived data as well as long-range climatological observations, holds out rather more hope that countries like Mauritania will be able to preserve their pastoral economic sector as wet years alternate with dry spells, leading to more fertile conditions and slowing or stopping the Sahara's encroachment.

Whatever the actual theoretical situation or future prospects, droughts and attendant desertification have had calamitous consequences for Mauritania. Beginning with the great Sahelian drought in the late 1960s and early 1970s, agricultural output fell drastically and rains came late if at all. Thousands of people were driven off their rural lands and into the cities and towns, notably Nouakchott (q.v.), and sand dunes began to invade hitherto unaffected areas of the country. Shortages of electricity and petroleum (qq.v.) made a bad state of affairs worse by forcing many Mauritanians to use firewood for cooking and heating purposes, taking a huge toll on the trees of the southern régions (q.v.) especially, eliminating up to 80 percent of the forest cover in the Senegal River Valley. This necessitated a determined, and partially successful, effort to plant additional trees to stem the desert's tide. According to one estimate, 21,000 hectares of trees would have to be planted every year until 2000 just to keep pace with the removal rate and preserve existing forests. Netting and selective plantings along affected areas, including adjacent to the road (q.v.) system, have also been tried with some success, but it was the more plentiful rains that fell in the country's agricultural zones that gave observers some cause for optimism in 1995, even as a population symposium held in Nouakchott the year before predicted that the Sahara would advance from six to ten kilometers southward annually for the foreseeable future. In any event, much damage had already been done: increased competition for what cultivable land remained led to tensions between the traditional farmers of the southern régions, the Halpulaaren (q.v.) and other Black Africans, and their Moorish (q.v.) counterparts, including the *haratines* (q.v.) or "Black Moors" who were in desperate need of economic sustenance after being emancipated from slavery (q.v.). More intangibly, the seemingly endless droughts and the onward march of the Sahara has led to feelings of wounded pride and deep pessimism among many Mauritanians, as a lack of income has forced a fiercely independent people to rely upon food and other aid from Arab and Western donors, without any prospect of ever resuming a normal rural life. The practical as well as social and psychological problems associated with desertification are thus a preoccupation of the Mauritanian government irrespective of political circumstances.

DIOUF, ABDOU. Senegal's second president was born in 1935 and was educated at the *Lycée Faidherbe* and at the universities of Dakar, St. Louis, and Paris. Beginning in 1960, when the country was given its independence from France, he occupied a wide variety of governmental positions, including those in the ministries of defense, foreign affairs, and planning and industry. He was prime minister of Senegal from 1970 to 1980 under the country's first president and paramount political figure, Léopold Sédar Senghor (q.v.), with whom he became closely associated. In what was widely remarked as a first in postcolonial African politics, he peacefully succeeded Senghor as president in January 1981. In contrast to his predecessor's deeply pro-Moroccan, anti-Polisario Front (q.v.) stance on the Western Sahara conflict (q.v.), Abdou Diouf pursued a more evenhanded set of policies towards the Arab Maghreb, sharing Senghor's affinity with Morocco's King Hassan II (q.v.), but working actively to bring the Western Sahara dispute to an end through the good offices of the United Nations (q.v.). As for Mauritania, he showed a willingness at first to accommodate the wishes of his northern neighbor, expelling from Dakar many Mauritanians belonging to the opposition *Alliance pour une Mauritanie Démocratique* (AMD) (q.v.) after the organization's coup attempt against the government of Colonel Mohammed Khouna Ould Heydallah (q.v.) on March 16, 1981. But later, around 1986–87, President Diouf showed a sympathetic attitude toward black Mauritanians who wished to carry on, from exile, various activities against the CMSN (q.v.) regime. Most prominently, the *Forces de Libération Africaine de Mauritanie* (FLAM) (q.v.) was allowed to make Dakar its African headquarters.

Abdou Diouf, like Mauritania's President, Maaouiya Ould Sid' Ahmed Taya (q.v.), was apparently caught off guard by the incidents along the Senegal River border area in early April 1989 which touched off the Senegal-Mauritania Crisis (q.v.) and which led to hundreds of deaths in intercommunal rioting, a massive airlift of persons fleeing the strife, and mass expulsions of Senegalese from Mauritania and of mainly Moorish (q.v.) Mauritanians who had long resided in Senegal. Over the next several months, the Nouakchott (q.v.) government and Abdou Diouf constantly traded accusations to the effect that each country was being subjected to hostile or subversive acts instigated by the other. President Diouf was not able to resist pressures to sever diplomatic relations with Mauritania on August 21, 1989, but, according to some reports, was able to disregard the urgings of certain Senegalese who advocated taking stronger measures, including war, against what they perceived as racist policies emanating from the Beydanes (q.v.) in Mauritania. Eventually, tensions were partly defused through the vigorous diplomatic intervention of the Organization of African Unity (OAU) and the Arab League (q.v.), and formal relations with Mauritania were resumed on April 22, 1992. Despite this apparent thaw, "misunderstandings" along the Senegal River Valley border continued, seemingly ensuring a period of tension lasting well into the 1990s. Since the apparent resolution of the crisis situation with Mauritania, Abdou Diouf has devoted most of his attention to domestic troubles, as when Senegal's currency, the CFA (q.v.) franc, was devaluated in mid-January 1994, plunging the country (along with much of the rest of Francophone Africa) into severe economic difficulties.

DIRECTION D'ETUDES ET DE LA DOCUMENTATION (DED). The Department of Research and Information, Mauritania's primary intelligence agency, was established after the December 1984 accession to power of Colonel Maaouiya Ould Sid'Ahmed Taya (q.v.) as head of state, replacing the formidable and widely-feared *Bureau* *d'Etudes et de la Documentation* (BED), which had reportedly become an instrument of repression and intimidation under President Ould Taya's predecessor, Colonel Mohammed Khouna Ould Heydallah (q.v.). Although the DED's exact level of staffing, collection resources, and budget remains unknown, it is believed that it possesses independent capabilities both inside and outside of Mauritania and was tasked with analyzing foreign and domestic developments affecting the country and coordinating this data with that gathered by the intelligence divisions (*deuxième bureaux*) of the various branches of the Mauritanian armed forces (q.v.) as well as the *Gendarmerie Nationale* (q.v.). These synthesized reports would then be presented to President Ould Taya, who, according to some reports, took a keen interest in the agency's work, a probable outgrowth of his own experience as a Mauritanian army intelligence officer in the 1960s and 1970s. Indeed, the head of the DED in 1996, Commandant (Major) Mohamed Cheikh Ould El-Hady, held the position of Counselor to the President of the Republic, a post that may well have afforded him privileged personal access to Ould Taya regarding the entire range of security issues Mauritania faced in its fourth decade of independence. Headquartered in a nondescript two-story residential-type building near one of Nouakchott's (q.v.) largest mosques, it was unclear to outsiders whether the DED possessed the powers of arrest, interrogation, and imprisonment of its forerunner, the BED, or whether it placed primary reliance upon human or technological means of acquiring information.

DJIBRIL OULD ABDELLAHI. One of independent Mauritania's most prominent and powerful leadership figures was born Gabriel Cimper in 1943 in Kiffa (q.v.), the son of a French administrator stationed there who converted to Islam (q.v.), married a Moorish (q.v.) Mauritanian woman, and adopted the name Abdellahi. After receiving a primary education in Mauritania, Gabriel Cimper attended secondary school at the *Lycée Van Vollenhoven* in Dakar, Senegal, and also in Nouakchott (q.v.), deciding in 1963 to become an officer in the country's embryonic armed forces (q.v.). After graduating from the *Ecole d'Application de l'Armée Blindée* at St. Marie, France, he served a stint as a sublieutenant in the city of Atar (q.v.) from 1964 to 1966 before traveling once again to France to receive additional advanced military training at the *Ecole d'Application du Matériel* at Bourg, receiving his diploma in 1970. As a specialist in administration and logistics, he served the next eight years (until 1978) as the Mauritanian army's director of materiel and supply. In the aftermath of the country's involvement in the Western Sahara conflict (q.v.) and the displacement of the civilian regime of President Mokhtar Ould Daddah (q.v.) by a military council, he was promoted to captain in

January 1979 and placed in command of the Sixth Military Region, in effect becoming the military governor of Nouakchott. He remained in that key post until 1980, when, in addition to becoming a commandant (major) in the armed forces, he was tapped by the chairman of the army ruling council, the *Comité Militaire de Salut National* (CMSN) (q.v.), Colonel Mohammed Khouna Ould Heydallah (q.v.), to be deputy chief of staff of Mauritania's military establishment. After Ould Heydallah successfully put down a violent coup attempt mounted by the exiled *Alliance pour une Mauritanie Démocratique* (AMD) (q.v.) in March 1981, he selected Gabriel Cimper (on April 27) to be minister of the interior with responsibility for internal security, a post that included membership in the CMSN itself. In March 1982 he was transferred, becoming minister of equipment and transport, occupying that position during the peaceful "restructuring" of the CMSN which deposed Ould Heydallah in favor of a fellow officer, Colonel Maaouiya Ould Sid'Ahmed Taya (q.v.). In January 1985, after being promoted to the rank of lieutenant colonel the previous year, Gabriel Cimper was given back the Interior portfolio, playing a major role, as one of Ould Taya's closest advisers, in instilling a new discipline into the Mauritanian domestic scene and in the restoration of diplomatic relations with Morocco on April 13, 1985, healing a rift that had begun four years earlier. Djibril Ould Abdellahi—the name that he increasingly began to use—was appointed army chief of staff in late 1985, his place at the Interior Ministry being taken by a prominent Halpulaar (q.v.) officer, Lieutenant Colonel Anne Ahmadou Babaly (q.v.). Eight months later, on August 31, 1986, Ould Abdellahi's penchant for firmness toward suspected adversaries of the CMSN enabled him to recapture the job of minister of the interior for the third time, after some on the governing body had come to suspect Anne Ahmadou Babaly of laxity in locating the authors of the controversial pamphlet, *Le Manifesto du Négro-Mauritanien Opprimé* (q.v.), issued by the *Forces Libération Africaine de Mauritanie* (FLAM) (q.v.), many of whose activists were, like Colonel Babaly, Halpulaaren from the sensitive Senegal River Valley. Another officer with a nonideological, professional outlook, Lieutenant Colonel Ahmed Ould Minnih (q.v.), was chosen army chief of staff, leaving Ould Abdellahi free to conduct a massive search for FLAM militants, a hunt that led in 1987 and 1988 to the arrest, trial, and imprisonment of those thought to harbor antigovernment feelings. Throughout the 1986–1990 period when he headed the Interior Ministry, Ould Abdellahi became the unquestioned second-in-command of the Mauritanian regime, widely known as "Taya's strongman" and reportedly cultivating support among the country's ex-slaves, the *haratines* (qq.v.), in an effort to secure his own political base. In addition to being by now a full colonel, a cabinet reorganization in March 1989 reaffirmed Ould Abdellahi's position as minister of the interior.

As one of the CMSN's most influential members, Ould Abdellahi had a major part in the unfolding events of April 1989 that directly led to the Senegal-Mauritania Crisis (q.v.). After a series of "incidents" in the Senegal River border area had resulted in outbreaks of violence against Mauritanian Moors in Senegal, he flew to Dakar to hold (unsuccessful) talks with André Sonko, his Senegalese counterpart. On April 26, in the midst of uncontrolled rioting against Mauritanians in Senegal and, to a lesser extent, against Senegalese in Nouakchott and in Nouadhibou (q.v.), Ould Abdellahi stayed very much in the public eye, delivering a forceful radio and television address in which he warned that Mauritanian rioters would face dire consequences if they did not cease attacking Senegalese nationals. For the remainder of 1989, according to some reports, he was perhaps one of Senegal's most forceful opponents within the CMSN, urging a hard line against the government of Abdou Diouf (q.v.) and resisting concessions. But on February 4, 1990, Ould Abdellahi was suddenly and without explanation dismissed as interior minister, his post being assumed by Lieutenant Colonel Sidina Mohamed Ould Sidiya from Boutilimit (q.v.). Four days later, on February 8, Ould Abdellahi's dismissal from the CMSN was announced, as was the news that he had been placed under house arrest in his birthplace of Kiffa.

The sacking and detention of Ould Abdellahi caused intense speculation on the part of outside observers. Some maintained that President Ould Taya removed his longtime colleague as a conciliatory gesture toward Senegal, given that the two countries were hovering dangerously close to war at this time. Others had Ould Abdellahi losing out in an internal power struggle with the pro-Iraq partisans of Mauritania's Arab Baath Socialist Party (ABSP) (q.v.), who used the crisis with Senegal, an upsurge in FLAM activity, and heightened ethnic tension to attempt to move Mauritania farther down the road to complete Arabization (q.v.). Whatever the actual reasons, Ould Abdellahi was released from detention later in 1990, only to re-enter the political scene on June 6, 1991, when he was arrested and imprisoned along with the leaders of the semi-clandestine, illegal opposition group, the *Front Démocratique Uni des Forces du Changement* (FDUC) (q.v.). Along with the FDUC leaders (with whom he was not associated), Ould Abdellahi was set free on July 29, 1991 and then devoted himself to a variety of business ventures both in the Mauritanian capital and in Kiffa. In 1995, though, it was rumored that he was seeking to stage a political comeback, stories which were given added credence by his publicized reconciliation meeting with President Ould Taya at about the same time, the first since Ould Abdellahi left the government in 1990.

ECOLE MILITAIRE INTERARMES D'ATAR (EMIA). Located on the outskirts of its namesake city near a former French fort, the Combined Military Academy of Atar was established in November 1976, after the start of Mauritania's involvement in the Western Sahara conflict (q.v.), which necessitated a more rapid pace in the training of officer candidates for the country's armed forces (q.v.). France, the former colonial power, played a major role in the establishment of the EMIA. In 1977, there were as many as sixty French instructors there, their number sharply declining after the Algiers Agreement (q.v.) of August 1979, by which Mauritania pulled out of the Western Sahara dispute. Officers went through a two-year course of study, while noncommissioned officers (NCOs) faced only one year of academic work before assignment. The EMIA teaches traditional military subjects, including tactics, firearms training, engineering, signals, logistics, and general administration. The academy conducts all training for the Mauritanian armed forces within the country except for a small school for the navy (q.v.) in Nouadhibou (q.v.). The commander of the EMIA is usually a colonel, and until 1992 he was often a member of Mauritania's former military government, the *Comité Militaire de Salut National* (CMSN) (q.v.).

ECOUVILLON, OPERATION. See Operation Ouragon

EDUCATION. Mauritania's system of primary and secondary schooling has been characterized since independence by low enrollments, sometimes deficient physical facilities, and shortages of trained teachers and administrators. In addition, educational life, from about 1966 onward, was overlaid by political considerations, as it was a prime focus of the Arabization policies (q.v.) of successive governments. A paucity of money, classrooms, and teachers meant that only a small proportion of the school-age Mauritanian population (q.v.) was enrolled at any given time: by 1995, the figure stood at a modest 36 percent. Although this number is an improvement over prior decades, when foreign aid for Mauritania's schools had yet to make itself felt and a predominantly nomadic way of life effectively precluded many Moorish (q.v.) children from receiving an education, it ensures that the country's overall literacy rate (17 to 25 percent in the late 1980s) will remain low for the foreseeable future. In the 1985–86 academic year, there were about 141,000 pupils in primary schools scattered throughout Mauritania and roughly 35,000 in secondary and vocational institutions usually situated in the capitals of the twelve administrative régions (q.v.), where they functioned essentially as boarding schools because of the large distances separating the country's cities and towns. Islamic (q.v.) education, a traditionally strong point in Mauritania, continued its popularity into the 1990s, based in Boutilimit, Chinguetti, Nouakchott, Oualata, and Tidjikja (qq.v.), using substantial libraries of Muslim texts and enjoying private funding and a dedicated faculty. But a Koran-based curriculum was not sufficient to supply a skilled workforce and a well-rounded intelligentsia, so in 1966 an indigenous Mauritanian secular college, the *Ecole Nationale d'Administration* (ENA), opened its doors for the first time, as did the *Institut Supérieur Scientifique* twenty years later. In addition to these major higher institutions, the Université de Nouakchott, which was set up in 1981 and which includes faculties of Law and Economics and Letters and Humane Sciences, comprises the country's only general institution of higher learning. The University of Nouakchott had about seventy professors and 2800 students in 1995. Education of a more specialized nature is provided by several additional schools, among them the veterinary and agricultural (q.v.) college, the *Ecole Nationale de Formation et Vulgarisation Rurale* (ENFVR) located in the riverbank town of Kaédi (q.v.), and the main military academy, the *Ecole Militaire Interarmes d'Atar* (EMIA) (q.v.) in its namesake city. Nationalistic considerations were a prominent factor in the establishment of these schools as well as the University of Nouakchott, but the budgetary (q.v.) toll was considerable, as it was estimated that accommodating a student at university level in Mauritania cost up to 250 percent more than sending him or her abroad to be educated. Government financing provides the vast majority of educational resources, but private schools are not forbidden, and indeed, several have established themselves, for primary and secondary pupils alike, in Nouakchott, Nouadhibou (q.v.), and several other locations.

Outside of recurrent difficulties over staffing, administration, and curriculum, the most controversial aspect of Mauritanian schools has concerned the increasing use of Hassaniya (q.v.) Arabic as the language of instruction. This emphasis began in January 1966, when the country's first president, Mokhtar Ould Daddah (q.v.), decreed that Arabic would be mandatory beyond the primary level in all the nation's schools. To the Moorish majority, this new orientation was perceived as necessary, since under colonial rule the use of Arabic was officially discouraged in favor of French, ensuring that upon independence in 1960, a preponderance of the infant country's educated men and women (as well as teachers) were not Arabic-speaking. However, Ould Daddah's new policy angered some black Mauritanians, who believed not only that languages such as Fulani, Sarakolé, and Wolof (qq.v.) were being shortchanged, but that French was being deemphasized as well—a language that, despite negative connotations resulting from colonialism, was a major international tongue that many Mauritanians needed for professional advancement. Despite the extensive protests that greeted the 1966 ordinances, Arabization in education continued to be the rule throughout the 1970s, with French continuing to be an unofficial language of instruction and the country's system of schools still largely patterned after that of France. Some retreat from full-scale Arabization was evident during the 1980–84 period under the armed forces (q.v.) government of Colonel Mohammed Khouna Ould Heydallah (q.v.), who in 1980 set up an Institute of National Languages to train teachers and translate and publish textbooks in traditional Black African tongues, while at the same time making use of the *Structures pour l'Education des Masses* (SEM) (q.v.) to promote increased literacy. Teacher training programs were reorganized, and the renewed attention to Fulani and other Black African languages had the added benefit of decreasing Mauritania's reliance on expatriate instructors from Algeria, Egypt, Morocco, and the Gulf states. Ould Heydallah's measures pleased black Mauritanians, but Arabization in general was sharply condemned by the black opposition group, the *Forces de Libération Africaine de Mauritanie* (FLAM) in *Le Manifesto du Négro-Mauritanien Opprimé* (qq.v.). Arabic, though, seemed destined to be the country's primary language in education, as evidenced by its designation as the official language of the state in the Constitution of July 20, 1991 (q.v.).

ELECTRICITY. See Société Nationale d'Eau et d'Electricité (SON-ELEC)

EL-HOR (Arabic: "Free Man"). A semiclandestine organization claiming to represent the interests of Mauritania's freed slave class, the *haratines* (q.v.), as well as opposing the persistence of slavery (q.v.) within the country, El-Hor was founded in 1974 by a group of intellectuals and officers in the Mauritanian armed forces (q.v.) who were dissatisfied with the policies of President Mokhtar Ould Daddah (q.v.) relative to the slavery issue and who blamed the Mauritanian head of state for not allocating sufficient resources to address the needs of haratines, in particular allegedly not providing agricultural (q.v.) land for ex-slaves and their families. El-Hor's demands were for a total and effectively enforced abolition of slavery, compensation for those enslaved, new labor laws to prevent exploitation of haratines by their former Beydane Moor (qq.v.) masters, increased social services and educational (q.v.) opportunities, and a full acceptance by Mauritanian society of haratine cultural identity. Although the haratines were black, they had largely assimilated to the Arab way of life over the years. El-Hor, moreover, tended to describe itself as a social and political, not a racial, grouping, and throughout its history always took either a neutral or equivocal stance on the contentious matter of the status of the free Black African population (q.v.) in the Senegal River Valley.

El-Hor's early years were devoted to both the distribution of pamphlets and word-of-mouth agitation, but although the organization was not subjected to severe repression by President Ould Daddah, it initially made little progress toward its goal of garnering mass support, with some observers blaming this on apathy and indifference on the part of the haratines themselves, as well as the great distances and difficult communications (q.v.) with Mauritania. Beginning in late 1978, though, the group assumed greater prominence, staging a protest march in Nouakchott's (q.v.) *cinquième* (fifth) district in November after two escaped slaves were detained by police pending a possible return to their owner. In August 1979, antislavery slogans, written by El-Hor supporters, were displayed on placards in Nouakchott during a march celebrating Mauritania's signing of the Algiers Agreement (q.v.), by which the country withdrew from the Western Sahara conflict (q.v.). These two public displays went forward without a significant government response, but this was soon to change under Colonel Mohammed Khouna Ould Heydallah (q.v.), who assumed full powers as head of the ruling *Comité Militaire de Salut National* (CMSN) (q.v.) in January 1980. Spurred on by the attempted sale of a young slave woman in a public marketplace in Atar (q.v.) in February 1980—an event which generated a 300-strong demonstration in the city's streets—El-Hor stepped up its efforts, holding protests on March 14 not only in Nouakchott, but in Nouadhibou and Rosso (qq.v.) as well. Ould Heydallah struck hard at the organization, briefly jailing about one hundred of its backers and forcing certain others into exile. But in his characteristic fashion, the Mauritanian leader also sought to satisfy some of El-Hor's demands. Reacting to the group's protests, which also generated international attention to the problem of slavery in Mauritania, the CMSN issued a statement on July 5, 1980, abolishing slavery in the country, a step which was followed, on November 9, 1981, by an ordinance (No. 81.234) formalizing the abolition, although it also specified that slaveowners had a right to compensation after setting their subjects free, a provision that angered El-Hor greatly. A similar conciliatory move toward haratine interests was made on June 5, 1983, when a new Land Reform Act (q.v.) was promulgated, a controversial law that was partially intended to increase farming opportunities for former slaves.

Despite these substantial measures, El-Hor remained mainly underground and its fortunes fell into decline. From 1981 to 1984, the group loosely attached itself to a pair of illegal exiled opposition groups, the *Alliance pour une Mauritanie Démocratique* (AMD) and the *Mouvement National Démocratique* (MND) (qq.v.), although El-Hor never became completely identified with any larger organization and always maintained a separate existence. El-Hor, along with the AMD and MND, welcomed the accession to power, on December 12, 1984, of Colonel Maaouiya Ould Sid'Ahmed Taya (q.v.) in a bloodless putsch that deposed Ould Heydallah. Thereafter, El-Hor's leaders and sympathizers carried out their activities primarily as a "current" or "tendency" within other groups, a process hastened by the appointment, by both Ould Heydallah and Ould Taya, of certain El-Hor members to high government posts. El-Hor continued to be present within other political parties in Mauritania in the 1990s, including the short-lived *Front Démocratique Uni des Forces du Changement* (FDUC) (q.v.), founded in June 1991, and in the *Union des Forces Démocratiques* (UFD) (q.v.), which by early 1992 had become Mauritania's primary opposition party. On June 6, 1994, however, El-Hor announced that it was leaving the UFD, citing an "excessive centralization of power" in the hands of the party's leader, Ahmed Ould Daddah (q.v.). After over a year in the political wilderness, El-Hor stated, on August 22, 1995, that it and other UFD dissidents were forming a new organization, *Action pour le Changement* (Action for Change).

ENTENTE MAURITANIENNE. Mauritania's first political party was formed in mid-1946 under the auspices of the French Socialist Party, and among whose members was Senegal's future president, Léopold Sédar Senghor (q.v.). The party remained loosely organized and without any real mass support for its entire existence, a state of affairs some observers ascribed to the personality of its first leader, Horma Ould Babana (q.v.), an ardent backer of Moorish (q.v.) interests and of ties to, or integration with, Morocco. But immediately after its founding, the Entente decisively defeated a French candidate (Ould Babana getting 6076 votes of a total of 9611 in November 1946) and thus made its mark as the first purely Mauritanian group to sit in the French National Assembly. Ould Babana, however, chose to spend most of his five-year parliamentary term in Paris, where he was isolated from the currents of Mauritanian politics. Meanwhile, tribal and regional interests, fearing the Entente's nationalist platform, formed the *Union Progressiste Mauritanienne* (UPM) (q.v.) in February 1948. In 1951, Ould Babana lost his seat in the French Assembly to a UPM representative, and then went into self-exile in Dakar, Senegal. The Entente's fortunes then suffered a severe decline from which it never recovered. Ould Babana tried to win a seat in the French-sponsored *Conseil Général* (q.v.) in 1956, but lost heavily, polling fewer than 20,000 votes of a total of over 100,000 cast. Ould Babana went again into exile, eventually ending up in Morocco, where he actively supported the "Greater Morocco" aspirations of Allal el-Fassi (q.v.). For this, the other members of the Mauritanian Entente expelled him from the party. The elements of the Entente who had fallen out with Ould Babana subsequently agreed, at the Congress of Aleg (q.v.) held in May 1958, to merge their organization with the UPM and a few other smaller groupings to form the *Parti de Regroupement Mauritanien* (PRM) (q.v.), headed, as was the UPM, by the country's future president, Mokhtar Ould Daddah (q.v.).

FAIDHERBE, LOUIS. As French colonial governor of Senegal from 1854 to 1861 and again from 1863 to 1865, Louis Faidherbe played a major role in the early French attempts to penetrate and "pacify" modern-day Mauritania. Like his counterpart almost half a century later, Xavier Coppolani (q.v.), he advocated indirect rule as the best approach to the territory's governmental problems, and suggested leaving in place traditional Mauritanian institutions. Almost as soon as he arrived in Dakar, Faidherbe, under orders from Paris, militarily conquered great portions of the modern provinces of Brakna and Trarza (qq.v.) and successfully defended the town of St. Louis from a counterattack by Moorish (q.v.) tribesmen in 1856. He forced the defeated Moors to recognize French sovereignty over the north bank of the Senegal River, although the areas encompassed were largely left without anything more than a very thin European presence. After his military victories, Louis Faidherbe turned his attention to mapping and surveying Brakna and Trarza and publishing his observations in a book (see Bibliography). His surveys later extended farther north into the province of Adrar (q.v.), which he believed would be the focal point of any future effort by France to occupy Mauritania fully.

F'DERIK. The administrative center of Mauritania's vast northern région of Tiris Zemmour (qq.v.), F'Derik was known during the French colonial period as Fort Gouraud, named after General Henri Gouraud (q.v.) who in the early twentieth century successfully "pacified" the area (see ADRAR CAMPAIGN). After the advent of Mauritanian independence in 1960, the town found itself largely overshadowed by the nearby iron ore (q.v.) mining center of Zouerate (q.v.). In 1977, F'Derik was estimated to have a population (q.v.) of only about 800 people.

FISHERIES. The Atlantic waters off Mauritania's 754-kilometer coastline are home to an almost bewildering variety and quantity of fish, giving rise to one of the country's two most critical industries, the other being iron ore (q.v.) mined in the administrative région of Tiris Zemmour (qq.v.). As a general rule, the aquatic life inhabiting the sea floor (demersal fish) is the most highly prized to consumers, while the fish that swim the open seas more freely (the pelagic species) are both more plentiful and less difficult to catch. Demersal varieties in Mauritania include octopus, cod, sole, squid, shrimp, and lobster. The number of pelagic species is also high and includes the horse mackerel, sardines, trout, herring, and tuna, among many others. Despite this huge abundance of a major renewable natural resource, however, the exploitation of these fisheries has been fraught with problems throughout Mauritania's history as an independent nation. Perennial drawbacks have included a lack of infrastructure to support expanded outputs and revenues, overfishing caused by poaching in the poorly monitored territorial waters of the country—in turn caused by a small, ill-equipped Mauritanian navy (q.v.)—and by a very small domestic market for fish, many Mauritanians continuing to dislike fish as part of their daily fare. In addition, Mauritania suffers from an almost total lack of a maritime tradition, with only the small Imraguen (q.v.) tribe engaging in fishing as a vocation. This has led to a high degree of reliance upon foreigners for equipment, expertise, and vessels, and all too often, foreign interests have taken much more than they contributed to the Mauritanian economy.

For about the first two decades of its independence (1960 to 1979), Mauritania depended upon a patchwork of individual licensing arrangements with foreign fishermen and mainly European fishing fleets. This policy was never successful, for a variety of reasons. In the first place, many foreign interests simply ignored the licensing requirement and either stationed their boats beyond the thirty-nautical-mile limit of Mauritanian sovereignty, or else violated the maritime boundary with impunity. Secondly, shore facilities for storing and processing fish were inadequate during this period, with the port city of Nouadhibou (q.v.) even lacking a dependable supply of electricity (q.v.). Furthermore, Nouadhibou offered little to the overseas crews of fishing vessels—they almost invariably preferred Las Palmas in the Spanish-controlled Canary Islands as a place to rest after their grueling tours of duty afloat. Las Palmas, too, had better facilities for processing and storing the catch, and for this reason never felt challenged by Nouadhibou, which could accommodate only 50,000 to 80,000 tons of fish per year. Still, it was a measure of the sheer plentitude of fish off of Mauritania that the fisheries sector became the second pillar of the country's economy quite early on.

Urgently seeking increased revenues in the aftermath of Mauritania's disastrous involvement in the Western Sahara conflict (q.v.) between 1975 and 1979, the country's ruling CMSN (q.v.) military council took several momentous steps in 1979 to rehabilitate the fishing business. After extending its territorial waters outward to form a 200-nautical-mile Exclusive Economic Zone (EEZ), the armed forces (q.v.) body, headed by Colonel Mohammed Khouna Ould Heydallah (q.v.), largely scrapped the old individual licensing agreements with overseas fleets and instead required interested countries to form joint ventures with the Mauritanian government. Some of the most important joint-stock companies, formed mostly in the late 1970s, were:

- the *Compagnie Mauritano-Coréenne de Pêche* (COMACOP), founded with the participation of the Republic of Korea (South Korea);
- the *Mauritanienne-Soviétique des Ressources Maritimes* (MAUSOV), partly owned by the government of the former Soviet Union and

which accounted for over half of the total tonnage of fish exports from Mauritania by 1988, due in large part to the USSR's large, well-equipped, and wide-ranging fishing fleet and associated factory ships. However, the breakup of the USSR caused MAUSOV's fortunes to decline precipitously by late 1994;

- the *Société Algéro-Mauritanienne des Pêches* (ALMAP), in existence since 1974 and manifesting the close ties between Mauritania and Algeria;
- the *Société Arabe Libyenne-Mauritanienne des Resources Maritimes* (SALIMAUREM), formed in 1978;
- the *Société Arabe Mauritano-Irakienne de Pêche* (SAMIP), set up in 1979 with Iraq and reportedly enabling that country to ensure a steady supply of fish for its troops during the 1980–88 war with Iran; and
- the *Société Industrielle Mauritano-Roumaine de Pêche* (SIMAR), a large Mauritanian-Romanian joint venture that was responsible for about 18 percent of total fish exports in the 1985–87 period.

Even though these arrangements were sometimes little more than a façade—the Mauritanian share of the joint enterprises was often lent by foreign donors or by the participants themselves—business increased almost at once and soon employed thousands of people, an increasing proportion of them Mauritanians who were beginning to overcome their traditional aversion to work in maritime-related fields.

Although no real restrictions were placed on the taking of pelagic fish, demersal fish, by a CMSN decree in 1983, had to be offloaded in Nouadhibou, where they would be marketed by a newly formed parastatal, the *Société Mauritanienne du Commercialisation du Poisson* (SMCP) (q.v.), which held a legal monopoly on the valuable demersal trade that was often honored in the breach. A second governmental agency, the *Société des Frigorifiques Mauritaniens* (SOFRIMA), augmented refrigeration and storage facilities in and near Nouadhibou. These measures mostly had the desired effect, as fisheries income outstripped iron ore revenues beginning in 1983, with pelagic species accounting for 80 percent of the total catch by 1987. Many difficulties remained despite these successes, though: Nouadhibou's infrastructure continued to compare unfavorably to that of Las Palmas; corruption was never entirely absent; larger trawlers and factory ships still could not use the harbor at Nouadhibou; and up to 10,000 tons of fish were still harvested illegally every year.

By the early 1990s, the problems in the fishing sector had begun to multiply, and so an additional round of reforms was undertaken by the government of President Maaouiya Ould Sid'Ahmed Taya (q.v.). The SMCP monopoly was ended by 1992, more foreign investment was welcomed, and a new ship repair yard at Nouadhibou, built with assistance from Saudi Arabia, was opened in 1989, a step which gave rise to the hope that Mauritania's own consistently underutilized fishing fleet would be seaworthy once again. Mauritanian fisheries were also helped by the influx, after the initial stages of the Senegal-Mauritania Crisis (q.v.) in April 1989, of Moors (q.v.) who had been expelled or repatriated by the Senegalese regime of Abdou Diouf (q.v.). Many resettled people found employment in fishing-related areas. On the negative side, overfishing (and resultant bankruptcies of fishing companies) clouded the outlook for Mauritania's most robust foreign exchange earner, with catches for some species such as mackerel being reduced by nearly three-quarters from the high levels of two decades before. But by 1995, the Mauritanian fishing sector continued to be a relatively healthy one, providing many economic opportunities and playing a key role in President Ould Taya's plans to deregulate and further open the country's economy to foreign participation, all the while compelling him to pay an inordinate amount of attention to the industry's weaknesses and its inherent low degree of susceptibility to centralized control.

FOOLAN. An alternative name sometimes given to the Fulbe (q.v.), one of Mauritania's Black African groups. The Fulbe are closely related to the Halpulaaren (q.v.), another more numerous category of Mauritanian blacks. Both the Fulbe and the Halpulaaren, in turn, speak Fulani (q.v.), a language prevalent throughout West Africa.

FORCES DE LIBERATION AFRICAINE DE MAURITANIE (FLAM). The African Liberation Forces of Mauritania was formed in March 1983 to protest what the group saw as a pervasive system of racial discrimination in Mauritania practiced by the politically dominant Beydane Moors (q.v.). It also attacked the persistence of slavery (q.v.) in the Mauritanian hinterland as well as the lack of political and economic opportunities for the former slave class, the *haratines* (q.v.), who according to FLAM were still in a quasi-servile status. Four smaller antecedent groups made up FLAM, and the organization's program of action went considerably beyond the reform of existing governmental structures. Instead, it urged the overthrow of the regime, by armed force if necessary, and its replacement by a nondiscriminatory, "nonracial" government. Although FLAM at first saw itself as a mainly political force, its declared willingness to engage in an armed struggle against the CMSN (q.v.) caused the governing military council formally to declare the organization illegal in 1984, driving it underground and to offices in Paris and in Dakar, where its members were welcomed by certain Senegalese politicians. Little more was heard of FLAM until April 1986, when the group's members operating clandestinely in Nouakchott (q.v.) issued a fifty-page, forcefully argued pamphlet entitled *Le Manifesto du Négro-Mauritanien Opprimé* (q.v.), which detailed alleged abuses and injustices inflicted by the "Beydane system" since Mauritania's independence in 1960. In addition to attacking what it saw as racist patterns in employment, education (q.v.), and foreign relations (q.v.), the Manifesto also criticized the government of President Maaouiya Ould Sid'Ahmed Taya (q.v.) for accelerating the process of Arabization (q.v.) and for allegedly expropriating the lands of Halpulaaren (q.v.) and other Black Africans in the Senegal River Valley by means of a selective and racially biased application of the Land Reform Act of June 5, 1983 (q.v.). Government corruption and purported racial discrimination in the armed forces (q.v.) of Mauritania were also detailed.

After a series of armed attacks on Mauritanian government vehicles and buildings in Nouadhibou (q.v.) and elsewhere in the country, reportedly mounted by FLAM activists in September 1986—but which caused little damage and no loss of life—the Ould Taya regime responded harshly. On September 4 and 5, at least thirty people, many of them prominent black intellectuals who were suspected of membership in FLAM, were arrested, of whom twenty were later given prison sentences. Over the following several weeks, another one hundred or so black Mauritanians were detained by the authorities, at which time, according to reports issued by human rights organizations such as Africa Watch and Amnesty International (see Bibliography), they were subjected to torture and mistreatment, the first such instances since Ould Taya assumed power in December 1984. Furthermore, some black prisoners, including former Minister of Health Djigo Tafsirou and the well-known writer Téné Youssouf Guéye, were transferred to a remote jail located in Oualata (q.v.), where at least four were to perish in September 1988 due to the exceedingly poor conditions and brutal treatment they encountered there. The resurgence of FLAM also had the effect of casting suspicion upon members of the government for alleged sympathy with the outlawed group. One such person was a prominent Halpulaar officer and CMSN member, Lieutenant Colonel Anne Ahmadou Babaly (q.v.), who was dismissed as minister of the interior in August 1986 supposedly for disregarding evidence of FLAM's activities. He was replaced by Lieutenant Colonel Djibril Ould Abdellahi (q.v.). Other highly placed Halpulaaren were also dismissed, including the director of the *Banque Internationale pour la Mauritanie* (BIMA), and the army soon underwent a full-scale purge of suspected FLAM militants. For its part, the CMSN regime described FLAM's followers as "misled persons" who were aiming to destroy the cohesiveness of the country. The government also accused some of FLAM's leaders (''a small nucleus of only

about forty persons," according to Ould Abdellahi) of being politicians and military officers who had fallen into disfavor due to corruption or other misconduct while in office, and who joined the organization to satisfy personal ambitions.

The hard line against FLAM activity continued into 1987, with additional trials of alleged FLAM supporters taking place, often resulting in prison sentences of up to five years for the defendants. But these
events were eclipsed by the CMSN's announcement, on October 17,
1987, that it had uncovered a conspiracy within the armed forces
to overthrow President Ould Taya and establish a separate, black-
dominated "Walo Republic" in southern Mauritania. This shook the
regime to its foundations, and guaranteed a strong response. Between
November 18 and December 3, 1987, fifty black Mauritanian army officers were tried before a special military tribunal at the J'reida barracks north of Nouakchott. The trials, attended by outside observers,
were conducted pursuant to the provisions of Mauritania's Penal
Code. On December 3, the verdicts were rendered: although seven of
the accused (including Anne Ahmadou Babaly) were acquitted, eighteen were sentenced to life imprisonment (two of whom later died at
Oualata), nine were given twenty years in jail, five received ten years,
and three others were sentenced to five years. Six other officers were
given suspended sentences, with stiff fines, and ordered to remain in
their home villages in the Senegal River Valley. There was no right of
appeal. But the ultimate punishment was reserved for the convicted
ringleaders of the coup plot, Lieutenants Sy Saidou, Bâ Seydi, and
Sarr Ahmadou. Although some Mauritanians (including the Moorish
imam of Nouakchott's main mosque) protested that their degree of
guilt did not warrant the death penalty, all three were executed on December 6. Reportedly, President Ould Taya was personally reluctant
to carry out these shootings (the first use of capital punishment during
his time in office), but acceded to them under pressure from certain
CMSN colleagues, including Djibril Ould Abdellahi and the influential Director of the Police, Captain Ely Ould Mohamed Vall, who were
anxious that the threat from FLAM be quickly eliminated. These trials and executions subjected Mauritania to additional international
criticism, contributed to a tense atmosphere within the country, and
encouraged some Moors, notably those affiliated with the Arab Baath
Socialist Party (ABSP) (q.v.) to step up the pace of Arabization and
allegedly redouble their efforts to acquire black-owned land in southern Mauritania.

The Senegal-Mauritania Crisis (q.v.), which began in April 1989,
resulted in a rapid escalation of FLAM's activities. To oppose what
FLAM saw as a developing pattern of antiblack repression within
Mauritania, the organization, starting in early 1990, staged violent

military attacks against Mauritanian army units stationed near the Senegal River. A FLAM spokesman described on May 8, 1990, an assault that transpired on April 21 and 22 in the village of Sabouala, near Kaédi (q.v.), that was claimed to have resulted in the deaths of fifty-one Mauritanian soldiers. Another major attack took place on the night of September 26–27, 1990, this time at Bofel, about forty-five kilometers west of Bogué, near the border with Senegal. FLAM stated that forty-nine "enemy" troops had been killed (against three of FLAM's own) and six army vehicles had been destroyed.

By the time of the end of the Gulf Crisis (q.v.) in March 1991, the governmental position on FLAM had softened somewhat. Just a few days after the end of hostilities in Iraq and Kuwait (March 7), Ould Taya announced a wide-ranging amnesty of most remaining political prisoners in Mauritania in an effort to ease his country's estrangement from Arab states and the West. FLAM detainees were included in the gesture, and on April 15, 1991, the head of state went further: he outlined a program of political liberalization, the promulgation of a new constitution (q.v.), and elections to a bicameral legislature consisting of a National Assembly and a Senate (qq.v.). Impressed by these concessions from the regime, FLAM's leadership announced that they were suspending their armed struggle until the group could appraise the status of the democratization process. Over the next several months, however, FLAM watched with rapidly diminishing patience as the character of Ould Taya's political opening fell short of its expectations. On January 15, 1992, FLAM announced that it would resume its armed actions against the government and urged a boycott of all forthcoming elections. After President Ould Taya's election victory (on January 17), FLAM continued to stand aloof from the institutions of Mauritania's Second Republic (q.v.), repeatedly stating that any dialogue with the regime was "impossible," although its armed activities did not immediately resume and its degree of popular support remained uncertain.

FOREIGN RELATIONS. Since attaining independence on November 28, 1960, Mauritania has been obliged, by geographical and political circumstance, to pursue a balanced approach in its external relationships, primarily between Black Africa to the south and the Arab-populated Maghreb to the north, a necessity mirrored by the country's own internal situation, in which Moorish (q.v.) Mauritanians share the same territory with black groupings such as the Halpulaaren, Soninké, and Wolofs (qq.v.). In addition, the degree of orientation toward one region of Africa or another has varied over time, although since in the mid-1960s, a leaning in favor of Arab Africa was carried into practice by successive governments. This, in turn, sometimes heightened internal controversies, and made the maintenance of a balanced foreign policy difficult to achieve, especially when the attitudes of certain European and other actors had to be considered by Mauritanian decision makers. Finally, a series of territorial claims against Mauritania, advanced with various degrees of seriousness by Mali, Morocco, and Senegal, significantly affected the conduct of Mauritania's foreign relations.

When the French colonial regime officially departed in November 1960, Mauritania faced an uncertain future, due in considerable part to a claim to its entire territory by Morocco, based upon supposed historical ties between the country's Berber (q.v.) inhabitants and the early Moroccan sultans, an irredenta first articulated by the nationalist politician Allal el-Fassi (q.v.). Such was the popularity of el-Fassi's "Greater Morocco" concept among the Moroccan public, moreover, that his claims were embraced by Morocco's first post-independence monarch, King Mohammed V, and by his son Hassan II (q.v.), who ascended the Rabat throne upon the death of his father in 1961. Both Mohammed V and Hassan II enjoyed great international esteem during this period, and consequently were able to ensure that Mauritania would remain unrecognized by nearly all the states of the Arab League (q.v.), Tunisia being the most prominent exception. Spurned by the Arab world, the country's first president, Mokhtar Ould Daddah (q.v.), turned instead to sub-Saharan Africa for diplomatic support, realizing that the countries of Black Africa were sometimes suspicious of the Arab north, and feared the eruption of similar territorial claims among themselves, jeopardizing their hard-won independence. In 1963, Ould Daddah played an active role in the founding of the Organization of African Unity (OAU), which had a majority Black African membership and whose Charter explicitly ruled out territorial rearrangements that were at variance with the boundaries inherited from colonial rule. Furthermore, the Mauritanian head of state felt obliged to accept the presence of French military installations and troops in his country until 1966, confident that Paris's involvement in Mauritania's security would checkmate any Moroccan move against his infant nation. President Ould Daddah also settled Mali's far less substantial claims to his country by negotiating and signing the Treaty of Kayes (q.v.) in February 1963, and on a theoretical level sought to put the best face possible on a still difficult situation, offering his country as a "bridge" or "hyphen" between North Africa and Black Africa as at least a potential path to a greater harmony and understanding between the two regions.

But Mauritania's identification with Black Africa was not destined to last through the 1960s. More and more Arab countries recognized Mauritanian independence over the next several years, discrediting Morocco's claim and leaving the Rabat monarchy isolated on this issue. Also, King Hassan II had not been able to prevent Mauritania's admission to the United Nations (q.v.) in 1961, an early sign that his efforts would be unsuccessful. With growing Arab acceptance of Mauritania behind him, Mokhtar Ould Daddah was able, by about 1966, to begin to rely on the Arab League's superior oil-generated wealth as an alternative means of support and development aid for Mauritania's economy. This shift was felt within the country, too — the government began its controversial Arabization policy (q.v.) in the mid-1960s, requiring the use of Hassaniya (q.v.) Arabic as the language of instruction in the educational (q.v.) system, drawing protests from Halpulaaren and other black Mauritanians, who up to then had made up a preponderance of the country's educated elite. But Arabization brought about barely a ripple on the international scene, largely because of Ould Daddah's talent in portraying the pro-Arab measures as incremental, and because of his continuing close interest in the OAU.

With the countries of the Arab League, Ould Daddah displayed a catholic taste: money and diplomatic backing was solicited from all states, ranging from Saudi Arabia's conservative monarchy to one of the most "radical" countries in North Africa, Colonel Muammar el-Qadaffi's Libya. Possibly prodded by Algeria's president, Houari Boumedienne (q.v.), with whom Ould Daddah had an exceptionally harmonious relationship, the Mauritanian head of state became more vocal in championing many developing-world concerns, including apartheid in South Africa and the Israel-Palestinian conflict. Friendship with Houari Boumedienne also brought with it an invaluable advantage: the Algerian leader helped bring an end to the long breach with Morocco, and formal diplomatic ties were established by the two former adversaries in April 1970. Mauritania was finally admitted to the Arab League in October 1973. President Ould Daddah's popularity among Arab nationalists was further bolstered by his nationalization of the French-dominated MIFERMA iron ore (qq.v.) mining consortium in November 1974 and his pullout from the French-controlled CFA (q.v.) franc zone in 1973 and the issuance of a new, purely Mauritanian medium of exchange, the *ouguiya* (q.v.). For the first time since independence, Mauritania's foreign relations seemed to have reached an equilibrium, both with Africa and the wider world.

The impending decolonization of the adjacent Spanish territory of Western Sahara (q.v.), however, threw all of Mauritania's prior political calculations into question. President Ould Daddah's stance on this issue had been ambiguous in that he claimed the entire colony for Mauritania while at the same time advocating a plebiscite of self-determination for the native Saharawis (q.v.). But his real concern, according to some observers, was to keep Morocco out of at least the southern part of Western Sahara if possible, reasoning that if King

Hassan's army could establish itself there, they would be only a stone's throw from his country's economic center of Nouadhibou (q.v.), and only slightly more distant from the critical iron ore mines. This could have enabled Morocco—under a pessimistic scenario—to hold Mauritania to virtual ransom if it so chose.

After briefly (and embarrassingly) matching Mauritania's claim to Western Sahara against Morocco's, President Ould Daddah agreed to divide the Spanish colony with the southern one-third, a tract of desert known as Tiris el-Gharbia (q.v.), going to Mauritania. Once the principle of partition had been settled, it remained for a formal treaty to be signed. This document, the Madrid Agreement of November 14, 1975 (q.v.), was consummated by Mauritania, Morocco, and Spain and made no reference to Saharawi self-determination. Not only did this treaty formally ally Mauritania with King Hassan's Morocco after only a five-year rapprochement, but it also immediately alienated Algeria, whose head of state, Houari Boumedienne, had fallen out with his friend, Ould Daddah, over the Western Sahara issue and had become the staunchest supporter of the Polisario Front (q.v.), a Saharawi nationalist organization founded in May 1973 which strove to establish an independent state in the disputed territory. For his part, Ould Daddah felt that Polisario was not a movement with mass popular support, and he was confident that most Western Saharans would willingly accept Mauritanian sovereignty over Tiris el-Gharbia, conscious of the tribal ties between the Moors and some Saharawis. Intensely worded appeals from President Boumedienne and the Polisario leader, El-Ouali Mustapha Sayed, consequently fell on the deaf ears of Ould Daddah and his pro-Moroccan foreign minister, Hamdi Ould Mouknass (q.v.).

The Western Sahara conflict began in earnest in early 1976 with the withdrawal of Spanish troops from the territory and the nearly simultaneous proclamation of an independent Saharan Arab Democratic Republic (SADR) (q.v.) by Polisario on February 27, and quickly turned into a near-rout for Mauritania's small and ill-equipped armed forces (q.v.). The highly motivated and mobile forces of the Polisario Front, seeing a fairly vulnerable foe, soon staged attacks not only in Western Sahara but inside Mauritania as well, at times disabling the railway (q.v.) line running from the iron ore mines to Nouadhibou, making exports of the vital commodity highly irregular. Few places in the country were safe from Polisario incursions, and the Front humiliated Ould Daddah further by two spectacular Nouakchott raids (q.v.) in June 1976 and July 1977 in which mortar rounds were fired into the presidential palace. An additional, perhaps more important blow was struck on May 1, 1977, when the mining town of Zouerate (q.v.) was captured for several hours by the Saharawis, who encountered no resistance from its 1000-strong Mauritanian garrison.

Aside from the military aspects, the Zouerate raid was a diplomatic crossroads for Mauritania's civilian leadership. Recognizing that its own military resources were insufficient to the task, the Ould Daddah regime signed a Moroccan-Mauritanian Defense Committee (q.v.) agreement a fortnight later, a move which gave King Hassan the right to station Moroccan troops in northern Mauritania. Upwards of 9000 Moroccans were in the country several months later. By late 1977 France had staged its own air strikes against Polisario forces (see OPERATION LAMANTIN) in an effort to stem the tide, but they—like the Moroccan presence—could not make a real difference. Politically, though, the defense pact with Morocco and Operation Lamantin may have sealed President Ould Daddah's fate. Both the French and Moroccan affiliations were unpopular with many Mauritanians, due not only to King Hassan's claim to the country, only recently buried, but also because reliance on Paris marked the reversal of one of Mauritania's proudest achievements—namely, the distancing of the country from the ex-metropole. Ties to the OAU and Black Africa were also severely frayed.

Partly because they felt affronted by their country's inability to defend itself, and because they saw little prospect for an end to Mauritania's international isolation or an improved economy under civilian rule, a group of high-ranking military officers, led by the army chief of staff, Colonel Mustapha Ould Mohammed Salek (q.v.), peacefully deposed Mokhtar Ould Daddah on July 10, 1978. Forming themselves into a new government, known as the *Comité Militaire de Redressement National* (CMRN) (q.v.), they pledged an end to Mauritanian involvement in Western Sahara. This was to prove extremely difficult in practice. For almost a year, the CMRN remained paralyzed over what to do to ensure a final, face-saving exit from the destructive conflict. Ould Salek himself, according to some reports, could not deliver a settlement alone, as he was faced with divergent attitudes toward the problem on the part of some CMRN members, who advocated either a unilateral withdrawal from Tiris el-Gharbia and a peace treaty with the Polisario Front, a continued sympathetic stance towards King Hassan's Saharan policy, or some other alternative. It proved impossible to reconcile these differences, and on April 6, 1979, Ould Salek was stripped of all real power, his place taken by Lieutenant Colonel Ahmed Ould Bouceif (q.v.), head of a new *Comité Militaire de Salut National* (CMSN) (q.v.), which replaced the CMRN. But Ould Bouceif could not make peace either, and his death in a plane crash near Dakar, Senegal, on May 27, 1979, led to further factional infighting in the governing council, out of which emerged Lieutenant Colonel Mohammed Khouna Ould Heydallah (q.v.) as effective head of state. Although Ould Heydallah hailed from a Saharawi tribe, the Arosien, and had long been suspected of pro-Polisario feelings, he, too, got off to a slow start, mindful, among other things, of the 9000 Moroccan soldiers still in the country. But after the Polisario Front ended its year-long cease-fire against Mauritanian targets in July 1979, the CMSN finally capitulated, signing the Algiers Agreement (q.v.) with Polisario on August 5, 1979. Relations with Algeria were soon restored, and Ould Heydallah took the precaution of requesting that French paratroopers guard the vital port (q.v.) facilities at Nouadhibou. Morocco's *Forces Armées Royales* (FAR) eventually left Mauritania by late 1980, although King Hassan annexed Tiris el-Gharbia to his kingdom as soon as Mauritanian troops departed.

With peace achieved in Western Sahara, balance in Mauritanian foreign affairs had been partially restored. Indeed, the early 1980s were characterized by increased diplomatic interchanges with African and "progressive" and conservative Arab countries alike, and cooperative arrangements with Romania, the Soviet Union, and other states in the fisheries (q.v.) sector were strengthened. However, a violent coup attempt against the government on March 16, 1981, led by two exiled ex-CMSN members, Lieutenant Colonels Ahmed Salem Ould Sidi and Mohammed Ould Bah Ould Abdel Kader (qq.v.), fueled President Ould Heydallah's suspicions that Morocco was seeking revenge for his country's peace treaty with the Polisario Front. Diplomatic relations with Rabat were severed, obliging the CMSN to move squarely into the Algerian orbit, with the seal on this new state of affairs set on December 13, 1983, when Mauritania adhered to an earlier Algerian-Tunisian agreement, the Treaty of Fraternity and Concord (q.v.). Concurrent with this, Ould Heydallah repeatedly threatened to recognize the SADR formally if Morocco did not agree to allow the OAU to hold a referendum of self-determination in Western Sahara. When King Hassan did not do so, the Mauritanian leader extended full recognition to the Saharawi state on February 27, 1984, irritating some CMSN colleagues who feared a Moroccan counterresponse and the possible triggering of Mauritania's reentry into the Saharan war, with disastrous consequences for a country already in poor economic condition due to persistent droughts, desertification (q.v.), and mismanagement. These more cautious officers, most prominently Lieutenant Colonel Anne Ahmadou Babaly and Colonel Maaouiya Ould Sid'Ahmed Taya (qq.v.), wanted a strict neutrality in Mauritania's relations with the Maghreb, and so led a bloodless "restructuring" on December 12, 1984, that ousted Ould Heydallah and put Ould Taya in his place.

Very quickly, the forty-one-year-old CMSN chairman reoriented Mauritanian foreign relations. Diplomatic ties and airline (q.v.) links with Morocco were restored within a few months, and Mauritania's traditionally good relations with Gulf states such as Kuwait and Saudi

Arabia were reanimated after having undergone a period of tension under Ould Heydallah. The number of French troops in the country, primarily in a training role, was also increased significantly. Moreover, Ould Taya paid more attention to Mauritania's most significant links to Black Africa, the Economic Community of West African States (ECOWAS), and, most importantly, the *Organisation pour la Mise en Valeur du Fleuve Sénégal* (OMVS) (q.v.), whose water resource (q.v.) management projects embodied the country's best hope for its long-suffering agricultural (q.v.) sector. More immediate economic benefits related to foreign policy measures were the construction by the People's Republic of China of Nouakchott's Friendship Port (q.v.) and the considerable assistance given by the Gulf emirates to fisheries and other infrastructural improvements. Generally, President Ould Taya's early days at the helm were distinguished by a lack of ideological posturing, a clearly neutral stance on Western Sahara, and a willingness to accept development assistance from virtually any state, including Brazil, whose engineers completed the final stretch of the *Route de l'Espoir* (q.v.) running from Nouakchott to Néma (q.v.) by the mid-1980s.

By the spring of 1986, though, the foreign relations outlook began to dim once again. Clearly, the revived activities of the *Forces de Libération Africaine de Mauritanie* (FLAM) (q.v.) and the issuance of its forceful antigovernment tract, *Le Manifesto du Négro-Mauritanien Opprimé* (q.v.), were related to internal conditions, but they had a decided effect externally in at least two ways. First, the CMSN could not overcome the suspicion that FLAM's actions were orchestrated (or at least tacitly backed) by either the Senegalese regime of Abdou Diouf (q.v.) or by opposition elements in Dakar, who consistently urged a stronger stance toward Mauritania. Hence, the usually correct relationship between Senegal and Mauritania could not help but suffer, especially when it become apparent that Dakar was home to many exiled Mauritanians who opposed the CMSN's policies. Secondly, some of the harsh measures taken by the ruling council against suspected FLAM militants and other dissenters caused international human rights organizations to focus an unusual degree of attention on the country, often reporting on detentions without trial, deaths in the remote Oualata (q.v.) prison fortress, and other allegations of torture and mistreatment.

Somewhat related to this deteriorating domestic situation and its international repercussions were Mauritania's growing ties with Saddam Hussein's Iraq, whose Mauritanian branch of the Arab Baath Socialist Party (ABSP) (q.v.) had been active in the country since around 1980 and which, in spite of periodic spells of repression, became a major political force from 1988 onward. As a relatively wealthy, technologically advanced Arab state that enjoyed considerable prestige in the Arab League because of its perceived victory over Iran after an eight-year war, the CMSN believed that friendship with Iraq carried few risks *vis-à-vis* its standing with the other Gulf countries, and that there was less chance of Iraqi interference in Mauritanian affairs than could be the case with an adjacent state. Therefore, by 1989, Mauritania had become quite close to Baghdad, taking deliveries of military equipment, accepting aid from Iraq to improve its communications (q.v.) network, and enhancing cooperation in the fisheries sector. Moreover, in February 1989, Mauritania decided to join the *Union du Maghreb Arabe* (UMA) (q.v.), confirming the country's emphatic affiliation with North Africa. Together with heightened Baath Party influence, UMA membership seemed to serve as the capstone to an increasingly pan-Arab foreign policy.

Against this backdrop, the Senegal-Mauritania Crisis (q.v.) erupted in April 1989 and rapidly escalated into the severest foreign policy test for Mauritania since the end of the Western Saharan war. Beginning with a limited dispute over livestock (q.v.) in the Senegal River Valley between the citizens of both states, a pattern of assaults, robberies, arson, and killings was soon established in which Senegalese nationals in Mauritania, as well as Moors in Senegal, were set upon by inhabitants of each country who blamed them for the violence taking place across the border. After diplomatic efforts to end the crisis had failed early on, it was mutually decided, in late April 1989, to repatriate any Mauritanian or Senegalese resident who wished to leave. Hundreds of thousands of people, made destitute by the violence, were airlifted or taken by road to safety. The successful repatriation program, however, did not lead to an end to the impasse. Senegal charged that the CMSN was exploiting the confusion generated by the dispute to deport large numbers of black Mauritanians to Senegal, allegedly to make way for Moorish agriculturalists and livestock herders. The Nouakchott government denied that any deportations had taken place, and stated that it had merely fulfilled the terms of the population transfer agreement, while conceding that some mistakes had been made. President Ould Taya also accused Senegal of encouraging FLAM militants to mount attacks on Mauritania from its territory. Over the following few months, Senegalese-Mauritanian relations sank to an all-time low, as they closed their common border, ended their thriving interstate commerce (q.v.), embarked on a military buildup, severed diplomatic relations, and moved close to all-out war, which was only avoided by strenuous international mediation. The Baath Party, for its part, advocated a hard line against Senegal, and their influence grew so much by 1990 that some commentators remarked that Mauritania stood some chance of becoming an Iraqi dependency. As a measure of Baathist power, the party's leader, Mohammed Yehdih Ould Breideleil (q.v.), became by 1990 the executive secretary of the CMSN, the highest civilian post in the entire government.

Matters essentially stood at this point on August 2, 1990, when Saddam Hussein sent his forces crashing into neighboring Kuwait, conquering the emirate in less than twenty-four hours. At a stroke, Mauritanian foreign relations were totally transformed. The exiled Kuwaiti monarchy and its Saudi and other Gulf associates made clear that any nation that sided with Baghdad or failed to oppose the invasion would be diplomatically ostracized and would suffer a cessation of economic aid. Since the majority of Mauritanians (like most other people in North Africa) were sympathetic to Iraq's position, and because the pro-Iraq Baath Party was so active in Nouakchott, the country bore a heavy burden of odium in the eyes not only of Gulf interests, but also of the United States, which was in the process of dispatching to the Gulf a 550,000-troop expeditionary force to compel Saddam Hussein to leave Kuwait. Faced with this parlous situation—and mindful that frontier incidents with Senegal were still going on—the CMSN took immediate steps to defuse what was promising to become another full-bore crisis, one in which the CMSN was powerless to affect the outcome. As the Gulf Crisis (q.v.) wore on into the beginning of 1991, Mauritania's foreign minister, Hasni Ould Didi (q.v.), reiterated that his country opposed Iraq's annexation of Kuwait and that it had no objection to the U.S.-led counterinvasion force, and he expressed a willingness to see the resolutions of the United Nations on the subject carried out. The comprehensive international isolation of Baghdad also cut Saddam Hussein off from his Mauritanian Baathist clients, so much so that the more moderate members of the CMSN, led by Ould Taya himself, were able to rally and clarify the country's external relationships as the standoff in the Gulf moved toward a violent conclusion in January and February 1991. In spite of Mauritania's diplomatic campaign to distance itself from Baghdad, however, it was shunned for a time by financial institutions such as the World Bank and the International Monetary Fund (IMF), organizations in which Western countries carried considerable weight. Bilateral relations with the U.S. remained strained even into 1994, officially because of the alleged persistence of slavery (q.v.) in Mauritania but, in the opinion of some commentators, due to the American perception of the country as having been unhelpful to its policies in the Gulf.

After embarking on wide-ranging democratic reforms during 1991 which culminated in the inauguration of the Mauritanian Second Republic (q.v.) on April 18, 1992, with a newly elected President Ould Taya in charge, Mauritania's external relations largely settled into a regular pattern. Capping a months-long warming of attitudes, Mauritania and Senegal decided, on April 24, 1992, to reestablish diplomatic relations and hold talks on the reopening of border crossings and commercial links. The Second Republic's first foreign minister, Mohammed

Abderrahmane Ould Moine, who enjoyed access to the ruling circles of the Gulf monarchies, played a key role in 1992 and 1993 in restarting the nearly moribund state of relations with Kuwait and Saudi Arabia, eventually dispelling those countries' anger at the Nouakchott government. On April 27, 1994, a visit was made to the Mauritanian capital by Kuwait's foreign minister, Cheikh Sabah al-Ahmed al-Jabir, presaging a resumption of economic assistance to Mauritania and a regularized political interchange. The Ould Taya regime also undertook to provide humanitarian aid to Rwanda by dispatching several doctors to that civil war–racked state, and also decided, in a highly publicized move in September 1993, to adhere to the terms of the Treaty on the Non-Proliferation of Nuclear Weapons, even though Mauritania never had any nuclear installations or aspirations.

FORT GOURAUD. See F'Derik

FORT TRINQUET. See Bir Moghrein

FRENTE POPULAR PARA LA LIBERACION DE SAGUIA EL-HAMRA Y RIO DE ORO (POLISARIO FRONT). The Popular Front for the Liberation of Saguia el-Hamra and Río de Oro—referring to the two constituent regions of Western Sahara (q.v.) located, respectively, in the north and south of the territory—was founded on May 10, 1973, by a group of young, educated Saharawis (q.v.) from the Spanish colony. At the time of its formation, the Front's goals were mainly anti-Spanish and apparently did not exclude the possibility of some sort of federation of Western Sahara with Mauritania, and it did not expressly seek, as it would later, the formation of an independent Saharan state. Mauritania's president, Mokhtar Ould Daddah (q.v.), was not wholly unsympathetic to the Polisario Front at first, since its anticolonial stance was largely congruent with his own rhetoric on the subject. He may have also believed that Polisario's efforts would result in the colony's being conveyed into Mauritanian hands, something Ould Daddah always favored. But the Mauritanian head of state probably did not take the Saharawi organization very seriously, and his territorial desires were such that he was later (on November 14, 1975) to sign the Madrid Agreement (q.v.) with Spain and Morocco, under which Western Sahara would be partitioned, with Mauritania receiving the southern one-third of the territory, a desert wasteland known as Tiris el-Gharbia (q.v.).

Polisario's reaction was swift. From late 1975 onward, the Front's highly motivated fighters ranged far and wide across Mauritania, causing considerable destruction, great economic hardship, and hundreds of casualties. The Polisario Front's rhetoric reflected an intense dislike bordering on condescension for the Mauritanian leader, Ould Daddah, whose armed forces (q.v.) proved unable to contain the guerrillas' depredations, and who was forced to call on Morocco (and later France) for military assistance. Mauritania's people, whether or not they harbored sympathies for their tribal brethren on the Saharawi side, were increasingly weary of what they saw as an unnecessary and futile war.

It was with a good deal of satisfaction that the Polisario Front witnessed the July 10, 1978, overthrow of President Ould Daddah and his replacement by a military council, the CMRN (q.v.), headed by Colonel Mustapha Ould Mohammed Salek (q.v.). Immediately, the Front declared a unilateral cease-fire against Mauritanian targets while hoping that the army regime would disengage from Tiris el-Gharbia and recognize its government-in-exile, the Saharan Arab Democratic Republic (SADR) (q.v.). For a variety of reasons, however, a peace treaty with Mauritania did not come until August 5, 1979, when both the CMSN (q.v.) (the CMRN's successor) and the Saharawi nationalists signed the Algiers Agreement (q.v.), renouncing, in word and deed, all Mauritanian claims to Western Sahara. The agreement was made possible, in large part, by the accession to power in June 1979 of Lieutenant Colonel Mohammed Khouna Ould Heydallah (q.v.), a Mauritanian officer who hailed from a Saharawi tribe, the Arosien.

Under the Ould Heydallah government, Mauritanian-Polisario relations were to reach their highest level, with the seal set upon them by Mauritania's formal diplomatic recognition, on February 27, 1984, of the SADR. This decision, which Ould Heydallah apparently made on his own, was not received favorably by all CMSN members, who feared Moroccan reprisals against the country. These concerns played a role in the governing council's bloodless *coup d'état* of December 12, 1984, deposing Ould Heydallah and putting in his place a more cautious and pragmatic colleague, Colonel Maaouiya Ould Sid' Ahmed Taya (q.v.).

After Ould Taya's assumption of the Mauritanian presidency, the country's relations with the Polisario Front became somewhat ambivalent. The Front's activities inside Mauritania were curtailed and the CMSN was careful to strike a balance in its relations with Morocco and all the other Maghreb states. Diplomatic and moral backing for Polisario, on the other hand, continued. Ould Taya did not try to revoke his predecessor's recognition of the SADR, and sometimes, as a gesture of support, Mauritania sent representatives to the Saharawi organization's general popular congresses, plenary policymaking gatherings held, on average, every three years.

FRIENDSHIP PORT (of Nouakchott). Although Mauritania's capital city is located only about five kilometers from the country's Atlantic coastline, there was until the mid-1980s no high-capacity deepwater port (q.v.) facility in the area, as there were no natural harbors between Dakar, Senegal, and Nouadhibou (q.v.). Consequently, Mauritania was forced after its independence to continue to rely upon Senegalese ports to provision Nouakchott, a situation which, aside from its political dimensions, increased transportation costs and overburdened the modest Mauritanian road (q.v.) system. Although Nouakchott's small existing port was refurbished in the late 1970s using funds from Kuwait and the World Bank (almost $30 million), a lasting solution to the shipping problem required a more ambitious project. So, in the early 1980s, the People's Republic of China designed and constructed an entirely new port facility near the Mauritanian capital at a cost of $150 million, financed by a fifty-year interest-free Chinese loan. The Friendship Port was built under extremely difficult conditions, as over 400 Chinese workers had to position about 100,000 concrete blocks, each weighing twelve tons, along the rugged, unprotected shoreline, beset by high winds and waves, sandstorms, and strong currents. Despite these hardships, the jetties and other parts of the facility were completed by September 17, 1986, and the port was opened several months ahead of schedule. The port's capacity was 500,000 tons per year, with up to three large merchant ships, of 10,000 tons each, able to be moored at once. By 1988, the Friendship Port was operating at 80 percent of capacity, and it was envisioned that Mali, Mauritania's landlocked eastern neighbor, could utilize the facility for some of its own imports and exports.

FRONT DE LA RESISTANCE POUR L'UNITE, L'INDE PENDANCE ET LA DEMOCRATIE EN MAURITANIE (FRUIDEM). One of a number of clandestine political groups claiming to represent the interests of black Mauritanians formed during the Senegal-Mauritania Crisis (q.v.) and the accompanying racial tensions in the country, the Resistance Front for Unity, Independence, and Democracy in Mauritania was founded on August 24, 1989, and had as its goal the overthrow of the regime of President Maaouiya Ould Sid'Ahmed Taya (q.v.) and the ending of repressive measures against blacks by what FRUIDEM regarded as a government dominated by Beydane Moors (qq.v.). According to its founding communiqué issued in Paris, FRUIDEM also called for the immediate release of all prisoners who were "victims of the chauvinism of the state" and the arrest and trial of all Mauritanians believed to be responsible for crimes against the Halpulaaren (q.v.) and other blacks. FRUIDEM also wanted a new government based on federalist principles, replacing the tightly centralized, authoritarian system that had existed since independence in 1960. In the following two years, the group seemed to have attracted rather little in the way of popular support, but when President Ould Taya attempted, beginning in early 1991, to liberalize Mauritanian political life and allow the formation of multiple political parties, the Executive Committee of FRUIDEM, in a statement issued on October 10, 1991, announced that the group would merge with an established, legal opposition party, Ahmed Ould Daddah's *Union des Forces Démocratiques* (UFD) (qq.v.).

FRONT DEMOCRATIQUE UNI DES FORCES DU CHANGE-MENT (FDUC). The United Democratic Front of Forces for Change, an illegal, short-lived opposition grouping that included a variety of Mauritanian political tendencies, was founded on June 5, 1991. A loosely organized umbrella organization rather than a political party in the strict sense, it demanded the democratization of Mauritania beyond that envisioned by the country's president, Maaouiya Ould Sid'Ahmed Taya (q.v.), who had announced in April that a new constitution would be submitted for popular ratification, and multiple political parties and a free press would be permitted for the first time since the country's independence in 1960. FDUC urged that a national conference be held to decide the future course of the nation, asked for Ould Taya's resignation and an investigation into alleged human rights violations, and wanted a further relaxation of state controls. A total of six factions made up FDUC's membership, with the influential *Mouvement National Démocratique* (MND) (q.v.) as well as El-Hor (q.v.), the organization claiming to represent Mauritania's *haratines* (q.v.), who comprised a significant presence in its ranks. On June 6, 1991, the day after FDUC first announced its existence, its leaders were arrested and detained, the authorities using as a pretext a series of destructive riots in Nouadhibou (q.v.) four days earlier, which had been generated by sharp increases in bread prices as well as by other local political grievances. The detained personalities included FDUC's president and former minister of education, Hadrami Ould Khattri, El-Hor leader Messaoud Ould Boulkheir, another former cabinet minister, Diop Mamadou Ahmadou, and Béchir el-Hassen, another prominent member of the opposition. The remainder of the Front's members still at liberty mounted a domestic and international campaign to free its leaders, an effort that bore fruit on July 25, when Ould Taya ordered the unconditional release of the detainees. Afterwards, FDUC's membership quickly dispersed, with many finding a home in one of the legal political parties formed beginning in August 1991, most notably the *Union des Forces Démocratiques* (UFD) headed by Ahmed Ould Daddah (qq.v.), and the *Rassemblement pour la Démocratie et l'Unité* (RDU) led by Ahmed Ould Sidi Baba, the former mayor of Atar (q.v.).

FRONT NATIONAL DE LIBERATION MAURITANIEN (FNLM).
The Mauritanian National Liberation Front was a small, narrowly based political party set up in Morocco in the summer of 1956 under the leadership of Horma Ould Babana (q.v.), who, as Mauritania's first deputy in the French National Assembly, had earlier helped to form the territory's first party, the *Entente Mauritanienne* (q.v.). Ould Babana's political fortunes, however, took a sharp turn for the worse in the early 1950s Mauritanian elections, which were won handily by the *Union Progressiste Mauritanienne* (UPM) (q.v.). As a result, Ould Babana and his followers fled to Morocco to found the FNLM, whose platform openly supported the "Greater Morocco" aspirations of Allal el-Fassi (q.v.). The FNLM also acted as a surrogate for the Army of Liberation (q.v.), leading the UPM leader and future president, Mokhtar Ould Daddah (q.v.), to call for French assistance in halting their guerrilla campaigns. This was accomplished in February 1958 by the joint French-Spanish military expedition, Operation Ouragon (q.v.).

FRONT UNI POUR LA RESISTANCE ARMEE EN MAURI-TANIE (FURAM). Created by a group of black Mauritanians on May 1, 1990, during the Senegal-Mauritania Crisis (q.v.) that began in April of the previous year, the United Front for Armed Resistance in Mauritania, according to its founding manifesto, had as its primary objective the launching of an armed struggle to overthrow the regime of President Maaouiya Ould Sid'Ahmed Taya (q.v.), which it held responsible for the expulsion of hundreds of Halpulaaren (q.v.) and other Black Africans from the country, the deaths of many others in detention, and for "ignoring black Mauritanian cultural identity." FURAM appeared to attract a lesser degree of support than did its larger counterpart, the *Forces de Libération Africaine de Mauritanie* (FLAM) (q.v.), and it greeted President Ould Taya's democratization measures which began in mid-1991 with disbelief, saying that the measures announced were a "confession of failure" by the ruling CMSN (q.v.) military council.

FULANI. Fulani is a term sometimes used in Mauritania to describe the Halpulaaren (q.v.), the country's most numerous Black African grouping. Somewhat confusingly, it is also the name of one of West Africa's primary languages. Fulani is spoken not only by Halpulaars in Mauritania, but also by their ethnic kinsmen in Mali, Nigeria, and Senegal.

FULBE (variants: Foolan, Fulani). One of Mauritania's Black African population (q.v.) groupings, the Fulbe are related by a common language and set of customs to the Halpulaaren (q.v.), the country's largest group of blacks. Their origins are obscure. Some historians believe that they came originally from Senegal and then migrated eastward and northward, while others say the opposite—that they came from the Sudan and traveled westward, in small groups, over a period of about 800 years. The Fulbe are found across a wide expanse of central Africa from the Sudan to Senegal, and only a minority reside within Mauritania. The Fulbe share many common attributes with their other black Mauritanian counterparts: they practice polygyny, have a historically rigid caste and occupational system, and for their livelihoods are reliant upon the herding of livestock (q.v.). Unusual for black Mauritanians, however, a great many Fulbe lead a nomadic or seminomadic life, living temporarily in huts or tents near the Senegal River Valley and then moving on in search of new pastureland. The wealthier Fulbe, by contrast, were the first to opt for a sedentary existence after Mauritania's independence, with drought and desertification (q.v.) accelerating the trend. As with all Mauritanians, the Fulbe adhere fervently to Islam (q.v.). Within Mauritania, most Fulbe live in the administrative région of Trarza (qq.v.).

GENDARMERIE NATIONALE. As Mauritania's main paramilitary police force, the *Gendarmerie Nationale* is responsible for law enforcement in both urban and rural areas, the latter also under the jurisdiction of the National Guard (q.v.). In 1994, it comprised about 3000 men organized into six regional companies covering the entire country. When it was formed after Mauritania's independence in 1960, the Gendarmerie was considered part of the regular armed forces (q.v.), but was later separated from the army and given its own commander and headquarters. Answerable to the minister of the interior, it is equipped with mainly small arms and lightly armored vehicles, and as a measure of its importance, the commander of the Gendarmerie was usually a member of Mauritania's governing military council until 1992, the CMSN (q.v.).

GENERAL COUNCIL. See Conseil General

GHAZZI. In the harsh Saharan regions of Mauritania as recently as the early twentieth century, raiding and pillage by rival Moorish (q.v.) tribes against one another often served as the only perceived way to avoid disaster when food and water were short. The *ghazzi* was an elaborately prepared and executed raid against the "enemy" tribe in which camels and other equipment were borrowed from allies, and booty taken in the campaign was meticulously divided among the participants. In Mauritanian and Saharawi (q.v.) tribes alike, ghazzis over time began to be seen as an efficient way to enhance a group's wealth and influence. As a consequence, the practice was very difficult to eradicate, and it was only after the complete French "pacification" of the Adrar (q.v.) in 1934 that armed tribesmen found their activities effectively restricted. As France insisted that disputes among tribes be settled by arbitration, many Moors were forced to channel their energies elsewhere, often by joining the French army, which offered them increased social mobility and better standards of living.

GOLD. Gold in commercial quantities was first discovered in Mauritania in 1991 in the tailings pile of a former copper (q.v.) mine in the vicinity of Akjoujt (q.v.). According to an article in the *Australian Financial Review* (July 23, 1992), General Gold Resources NL, a subsidiary of Rothschild Australia Ltd., had a plurality (42.5 percent) stake, with the Mauritanian government and other Arab investors holding smaller shares in the extraction project. Operated by *Mines d'Or d'Akjoujt* (MORAK), the $10 million venture was projected to net at least 204,000 ounces of gold over a five-year period. By early 1993, output at Akjoujt had increased about 60 percent over the previous year, with the new plant averaging a monthly production of 2800 ounces. MORAK, which employed about one hundred people at the site, thus enabled $7 million to be added to Mauritania's export revenues for 1992, a figure that rose quickly to $13.8 million in 1993 and $15.4 million in 1994, with further increases possible due to improved extraction techniques. Moreover, the Mauritanian *Bureau des Recherches Géologiques et Minières* (BRGM) was exploring for gold deposits elsewhere in the région of Inchiri (qq.v.) which it estimated could amount to over one million ounces of the precious metal. Australia's General Gold Resources was believed by some analysts to be a prime candidate to exploit these reserves, since it was already the largest Western mining concern operating in Mauritania.

GORGOL. A Mauritanian région bordering the Senegal River Valley, Gorgol covers an area of about 14,000 square kilometers and supports significant agriculture and livestock (qq.v.) activity by virtue of its being one of the country's best-watered areas. Its location on the Senegal River also makes it the site of considerable cross-border commerce (q.v.) with Senegal. Ethnically, Gorgol is a stronghold of black Mauritanian groupings, notably the Fulbe and Halpulaaren (qq.v.), a fact that made the région a zone of high tension during the Senegal-Mauritania Crisis (q.v.) of 1989–1990. The province's population (q.v.) stood at an officially reported 184,359 in 1988, an increase from an estimated 149,000 in 1977.

GOURAUD, HENRI. After the May 12, 1905, assassination of the French governor-general of the Mauritanian terrritory, Xavier Coppolani (q.v.), in Tidjikja (q.v.), French plans to "pacify" and administer the country as a colonial possession went through a period of soul-searching. Individuals with the stature of Coppolani, who skillfully blended inducements to the Mauritanian inhabitants of Brakna and Trarza (qq.v.) with the application of military force, were difficult to locate. Finally, in 1907, French forces in Mauritania were placed under the command of Colonel Henri Gouraud (later promoted to General), a flamboyant yet highly professional officer who was prepared to use more frankly military means to bring the rest of the country, notably the Adrar (q.v.), under French suzerainty. Mindful that the most aggressive opponent of France, Cheikh Ma el-Ainin (q.v.), had a considerable popular following as well as a large army, Gouraud laid his plans for the capture of Adrar carefully, drawing on his previous military successes against similarly intransigent Islamic (q.v.) tribesmen in adjacent "Soudan" (Mali) several years before. He aimed first to occupy the strategic town of Atar (q.v.) and then attack Ma el-Ainin's forces and defeat them piecemeal with what he believed was vastly superior French firepower. On January 9, 1909, he launched his *Colonne d'Adrar,* or Adrar Campaign (q.v.). He quickly captured Atar, but nearly met disaster against the more skilled and motivated men under Ma el-Ainin's command. After an inconclusive series of skirmishes that lasted through June, Gouraud revised his strategy, cutting off the rebel forces from their crucial *wadis* (q.v.) and date palm groves, then attacked them frontally. By July 28, 1909, Idjil and Chinguetti (q.v.) had been taken and most resistance had been crushed, sending Ma el-Ainin back to Morocco. The following year, Gouraud published a diary/memoir of his experiences in Mauritania (see Bibliography), and later went on to command French forces in World War I.

GRAND CONSEIL D'AOF. The Grand Council of the Federation of French West Africa (*Afrique Occidentale Française* [q.v.] or AOF) was created in 1925 to assist the Paris-appointed governor-general (*commissaire de gouvernement*) in his administration of France's vast West African colonies which included Mauritania. When the Grand Council was established, its members were appointed by the governor-general according to corporatist principles, with only military officers, businessmen, and civil servants, along with a few others, represented. Even with this narrow and undemocratic base, the council had no real power and served only to advise the governor-general on matters primarily of local political and economic interest. The Grand Council of AOF was based in Dakar, Senegal, as was a parallel institution, the *Conseil de Gouvernement* (q.v.), which had a slightly broader (but still appointive) membership that encompassed all eight territories of AOF. The Grand Council did acquire some additional influence, however, on October 26, 1946, when a French decree transferred to it most of the consultative powers formerly held by the Council of Government and at the same time reorganized it, giving five persons from each AOF territory (including Mauritania) places in the Grand Council. Thus, Mauritania was separated administratively from Senegal at this time, although its capital continued to reside at St. Louis until the founding of Nouakchott (q.v.) over a decade later.

GUELB. The name given to a relatively large, isolated peak situated on a plateau in Mauritania's Saharan zone. A prominent guelb known as Kediet d'Idjil is located near the towns of F'Derik and Zouerate (qq.v.) in the administrative région of Tiris Zemmour (qq.v.) and at over 900 meters is the highest point in the entire country. Guelbs have often turned out to be rich in mineral deposits, notably copper and iron ore (qq.v.).

GUIDIMAKA. Mauritania's smallest région (q.v.) and probably the one with the best agricultural (q.v.) resources, Guidimaka covers an area of about 10,000 square kilometers. The province counted a population (q.v.) of 83,000 in 1977, rising to 116,436 by an official 1988 census. Very few of its residents are nomadic, as most are sedentary farmers in the fertile Senegal River Valley, often from the Soninké (q.v.), one of the country's Black African groupings. As Mauritania's southernmost province, Guidimaka has been affected least by the droughts and desertification (q.v.) that have plagued the country, but it has not proved totally immune: in the 1980s, it received only about two-thirds of its normal rainfall (q.v.). Sélibaby (q.v.), the provincial capital, is the only population center of note, and the town is linked to the rest of the région by a small network of roads (q.v.).

GULF CRISIS AND WAR (August 2, 1990–March 3, 1991). Although Mauritania is located thousands of kilometers from the Gulf region, the crisis caused by Saddam Hussein's invasion of Kuwait on August 2, 1990, and lasting until March 3, 1991, when Iraq formally surrendered to the United States–led coalition forces of Operation Desert Storm after having been forcibly ejected from Kuwait, presented the country with one of its most intense foreign relations (q.v.) challenges since the achievement of Mauritanian independence in 1960. The crisis also happened at a time when the CMSN (q.v.) regime of Colonel Maaouiya Ould Sid'Ahmed Taya (q.v.) was under severe pressure from two other directions: the still unfriendly relations with its southern neighbor, Senegal, as part of the Senegal-Mauritania Crisis (q.v.) that began in April 1989, and the high level of influence that was being exerted upon the governing armed forces (q.v.) committee by the Mauritanian branch of the Arab Baath Socialist Party (ABSP) (q.v.), closely allied with Iraq. Consequently, Mauritania found itself under heavy international scrutiny due to its friendship with Baghdad and the hostility felt by many of its people toward the U.S.-organized campaign against Iraq, which succeeded in liberating Kuwait after several weeks of air strikes beginning on January 16, 1991, and a ground assault lasting one hundred hours launched in late February, encountering only sporadic Iraqi resistance.

For many years prior to the Iraqi invasion, Mauritania, whether under the civilian government of President Mokhtar Ould Daddah (q.v.) or the military regimes that had followed it since July 1978, had never found it necessary to differentiate politically among Arab countries when it came to seeking development assistance or diplomatic support and protection. From the conservative Gulf monarchies to the "radical" governments of Algeria and Libya, relations were usually amicable, and the donors themselves were quite tolerant of the political leanings of successive regimes in Nouakchott (q.v.). At a time when both Kuwait and the West were actively courting Saddam Hussein as a bulwark against the Islamic fundamentalist government of Iran, Mauritania sought and obtained fruitful relations with both Iraq and Kuwait. But following the end of the Iran-Iraq war in mid-1988, Iraqi influence in Mauritania grew steadily, spurred on by Baghdad's added prestige as an alliance partner due to its perceived victory over Teheran, and later, by the CMSN's need for a steady supply of arms during the crisis with Abdou Diouf's (q.v.) Senegal. However skeptical President Ould Taya may have felt about such a wholehearted embrace of Iraq, he was induced to hold two summit meetings in Baghdad with Saddam Hussein in December 1988 and October 1989. Soon, visits by Iraqi representatives were increasingly frequent, the persistent efforts of Iraqi Foreign Minister Tariq Aziz appeared to be paying off for both countries, and some worried observers began to speak ominously about Mauritania's becoming a satellite of Iraq. The Baath Party's uncompromising, decidedly pro-Moorish (q.v.) attitude at a time of ethnic tension related to the Senegal situation, and resultant pressures to intensify the policy of Arabization (q.v.) in the country further affected Mauritania's internal scene. But the CMSN's foreign policy calculations with other Arab and Islamic nations were not altered significantly.

All this changed overnight beginning on August 2, 1990, when Iraqi forces, led by the elite Republican Guard, overran Kuwait City and the rest of the small sheikhdom in a blitzkrieg operation lasting only twenty-four hours. The now exiled Kuwaiti monarchy, as well as Saudi Arabia and the other states of the Gulf, made clear that countries (especially Arab/Islamic ones) that did not express at least rhetorical disapproval of Saddam Hussein's actions would find their financial assistance eliminated or drastically curtailed, regardless of their past relationship. In spite of this, Mauritania sought to straddle the diplomatic fence by abstaining on votes taken by the Arab League (q.v.) on August 3 and by the Islamic Conference a day later, making itself one of the few Arab (and African) states that did not immediately condemn the invasion. During the next week, though, intense pressures were exerted by Arabs and Western states alike upon Nouakchott to change its course, so that at the next emergency meeting of the Arab League (August 9–10), Mauritania sided with the majority to demand the full restoration of Kuwaiti sovereignty. However, it did express "reservations," a gambit designed to mollify the still powerful Baathists and take into account the overwhelmingly pro-Iraq sentiments of the Mauritanian people. In the weeks following the hectic diplomatic activity that the invasion triggered, a comprehensive array of economic and other sanctions (including a naval quarantine) were levied against Baghdad, cutting the Baathists in Mauritania off from their patrons in Iraq and allowing the CMSN to take a less ambiguous attitude to the anti-Iraq effort, which soon blossomed into the assemblage of a large and diverse thirty-nation coalition that included over 500,000 American troops to prepare for military action if peaceful means to remove Iraq from Kuwait failed. In late October 1990, Mauritanian Foreign Minister Hasni Ould Didi (q.v.) stated that "the presence of fraternal and friendly forces in the Kingdom of Saudi Arabia is legal and legitimate, because it came at the request of a fully sovereign state and falls within the context of the United Nations resolutions."

From an economic standpoint, the Gulf Crisis could not have come at a worse time for Mauritania. On top of the existing cutoff in trade with Senegal that had begun in 1989, there was also a cessation of economic aid, as well as of trade, with the Gulf countries due to Kuwaiti and Saudi anger at Nouakchott's perceived sympathies for Baghdad. These donors provided fully 40 percent of Mauritania's total assistance, and the inability of Kuwait to deliver aid (due, of course, to the invasion) was reportedly used as a pretext by other nations to slow or stop the flow of money to Mauritania. Western countries, most prominently the United States, were also unsure of the Ould Taya government's real loyalties, and their influence with financial institutions such as the World Bank and the International Monetary Fund (IMF) caused Mauritania's ostracism in banking circles for the duration. The Kuwait crisis also produced a temporary disruption of petroleum (q.v.) supplies, with a consequent steep rise in oil prices in the months after August 2. Mauritania, like most developing countries with few energy resources of their own, saw the bill for importing its oil skyrocket from $50 million in 1989 to an estimated $100 million in 1990. With iron ore (q.v.) prices in a slump and the new mines at M'Haoudat not yet operational, the condition of the Mauritanian economy looked bleak to a degree not seen since the early 1980s after the country had extricated itself from its ruinous involvement in the Western Sahara conflict (q.v.).

In the final weeks before the outbreak of war in the Gulf on January 16, 1991, the political situation became extremely tense. Irrespective of the reassuring statements coming from President Ould Taya and Foreign Minister Hasni Ould Didi, popular opinion in Mauritania grew more anti-Western. As it increasingly looked as though the U.S.-led coalition would resort to all-out war to force Saddam Hussein out of Kuwait, hostility to French and American interests increased to the point where Paris urged all of its roughly 1600 nationals in the country either to take refuge in its Nouakchott embassy or to leave Mauritania entirely. Pro-Iraq demonstrations had, in fact, taken place in front of the French embassy before hostilities began, but all were broken up by police using tear gas. The United States embassy in the capital, located as it was near President Ould Taya's large residential and office compound and thus heavily policed by the *Bataillon de la Sécurité Présidentielle* (q.v.), was less affected by protests, although the U.S. State Department urged all Americans to leave Mauritania as early as December 15, 1990. All Mauritanian educational (q.v.) institutions were also ordered closed by the CMSN, but despite this flurry of activity, events in Mauritania were rapidly relegated to the distant background in the coverage of the Gulf War. There was speculation, spurred by the unexpected arrival at Nouakchott's airport (q.v.) of two Iraqi Airways Boeing 707s on January 16, 1991, that the Ould Taya regime was giving refuge to certain members of Saddam Hussein's family, but this was firmly denied.

The rapid defeat of Iraq at the hands of the West was greeted with keen disappointment in Mauritania, but the end of the conflict caused political events to move rapidly. In a determined effort to capitalize on the discrediting of the Baath Party, and mindful of the necessity to improve relations with the West and the Gulf sheikhdoms and generally to restore equilibrium to the foreign and domestic situations, President Ould Taya announced a wide-ranging amnesty for political prisoners within days of the Iraqi surrender. Following this, the president announced on April 15, 1991, that a new constitution (q.v.) would be promulgated and that the political system would be liberalized to permit the formation of multiple political parties. Many members of the Baath Party, including the executive secretary of the CMSN, Mohammed Yehdih Ould Breideleil (q.v.), were dismissed from the government, and a moderate figure with good ties to the Gulf countries, the veteran civil servant and former Mauritanian ambassador to Kuwait and counselor to the Kuwaiti Fund for Development between 1981 and 1990, Mohammed Abderrahmane Ould Moine, was appointed foreign minister, leaving that post in September 1993 after successfully mending fences with the restored Kuwaiti regime as well as with Saudi Arabia and other aid donors and trading partners. But although Mauritania was soon invited back into discussions with the world financial community, lingering ill-feeling regarding the country's supposed alignment with Iraq during the Gulf Crisis continued to negatively affect bilateral relations between Mauritania and the United States into the mid-1990s.

GYPSUM. Mauritania possesses some of the world's largest deposits of gypsum (estimated at 4 billion tons), but exploitation of these reserves has been plagued with difficulties over the years. In 1973 the state mining company, SNIM (q.v.), began operations at a quarry at N'-Drahamcha in the administrative région of Trarza (qq.v) about fifty kilometers north of the capital, Nouakchott (q.v.). After extraction, the material was exported by road (q.v.) to Senegal for cement production. This endeavor was successful for almost a decade, but high transportation costs forced a halt to the operation in 1981. Three years later, a joint-stock Mauritanian-Kuwaiti company, the *Société Arabe des Industries Métallurgiques Mauritano-Koweitienne* (SAMIA), resumed mining after an infusion of fresh capital from the Gulf emirate, and achieved a production level of 19,400 tons in 1987. But this output could not be sustained due to technical problems at the site, and all activity had ended by 1989.

HALPULAAR (pl. Halpulaaren; variants: Fulani, Toucouleur). The most numerous of Mauritania's Black African population (q.v.) groups, the Halpulaaren are, like all their compatriots, adherents to Islam (q.v.) and belong largely to the Tidjaniya religious brotherhood. They speak Fulani, a language found throughout West Africa, including in Mali, Nigeria, and Senegal, areas outside Mauritania where the Halpulaaren are also present. Like their Black African brethren (but unlike the Fulbe [q.v.], their closest black ethnic kinsmen), they are mainly sedentary agriculturalists (q.v.), often alternately cultivating land on both sides of the Senegal River. In common with most other black Mauritanians, as well as with their Moorish (q.v.) Arab counterparts in the country, traditional Halpulaar society was highly stratified, with a recognized institution of slavery (q.v.), although it had vanished almost entirely among the black Mauritanian population before the country's independence in 1960. At the pinnacle of the social order were the learned men concerned mainly with religious scholarship and propagation; further down was a substantial middle class and lower middle class which included fishermen, farmers, traditional warriors, and tradesmen. Not as highly regarded in Halpulaar society were the craftsmen, jewelers, woodworkers, musicians, and weavers, who constituted separate castes. The lower middle class also included bards, held in low esteem but nonetheless respected for their talents. Except for slaves, the lowest stratum was composed of manual laborers and servants, who were often former slaves who held a position analogous to the so-called Black Moors, or *haratines* (q.v.). Although the rigid caste structure among the Halpulaaren was gradually modified by, among other factors, somewhat greater economic mobility over the years, the extended patrilineal family remained an extremely strong institution. Intermarriage generally took place within the particular caste group.

Because their numbers relative to the total population of Mauritania were so high (though hotly disputed), the Halpulaaren were found more than any other group of Black Africans in the ranks of the Mauritanian civil service, the armed forces (q.v.), and the diplomatic corps. Well-known Halpulaaren in the government have included Dieng Boubou Farba, an economist, former minister of energy, and in 1996 president of the Mauritanian Senate (q.v.); Lieutenant Colonel Anne Ahmadou Babaly (q.v.), until 1986 a full member of the CMSN (q.v.) governing body and holder of key portfolios in the Council of Ministers (q.v.); and Kane Mohamed Fadel Cheikh and Sow Abou Demba, the ministers of finance and justice, respectively, in the 1994 cabinet. On the other hand, Halpulaaren were also prominent in the leadership (and rank and file) of the *Forces de Libération Africaine de Mauritanie* (FLAM) (q.v.), formed in 1983 to protest alleged racial discrimination by Moorish elements in the country. Consequently, this group was sometimes subjected to investigation, arrest, and imprisonment by the government, which greatly feared FLAM infiltration into the Mauritanian bureaucracy, and especially the army. In turn, FLAM pointedly accused the CMSN of attempting to divide Halpulaaren from their Fulbe cousins, as well as from Mauritanians belonging to the Bambara, Soninké, and Wolof (qq.v.) groups, supposedly by giving non-Halpulaar groups preferential treatment and sparing them from repression.

HAMDI OULD MOUKNASS. One of independent Mauritania's most prominent political personalities and a long-serving foreign minister, Hamdi Ould Mouknass was born in 1935 in Port-Etienne (q.v.), the son of a Moorish (q.v.) chieftain. After receiving a primary and secondary education both in Port-Etienne and in Boutilimit (q.v.), he joined the French colonial government around age twenty-one and achieved great distinction, soon being promoted to *chef de cabinet* in the Ministry of Civil Service. In 1960 he left Mauritania for France, acquiring a *baccalauréat* from the *Collège Michelet* in Nice, a law degree from the *Faculté de Droit* in Paris, and an advanced legal degree (*diplôme d'études supérieures*) from the same institution in 1965. Returning to Nouakchott (q.v.), he quickly became one of President Mokhtar Ould Daddah's (q.v.) closest advisers, first serving as legal counsel to the presidential office. He also joined Ould Daddah's *Parti du Peuple Mauritanien* (PPM) (q.v.), and was elected to the PPM's governing body, the *Bureau Politique National* (BPN) (q.v.), a sign of the trust reposed in him by the Mauritanian head of state. Hamdi Ould Mouknass held a variety of increasingly responsible positions over the following three years, including commissioner for state security, high commissioner for youth and sports, social chargé d'affaires, and by January 1968, minister of youth, information, and culture. He only held this last portfolio for a few months, however, because in July 1968 he was selected by President Ould Daddah to be minister of foreign affairs, a post Ould Mouknass was to hold uninterruptedly for the next ten years. As head of the Foreign Ministry, he played a critical role in the reformulation of Mauritania's basic foreign relations (q.v.) orientation that was underway during this time. This included loosening military and economic ties with France, assuming a more nonaligned, nationalistic stance at the United Nations (q.v.), and moving closer to the Arab states of the Maghreb and the Middle East, a goal consummated in October 1973, when Mauritania finally joined the Arab League (q.v.).

As foreign minister, Hamdi Ould Mouknass faithfully enunciated Mauritania's long-standing territorial claim to the neighboring Spanish colony of Western Sahara (q.v.), but by the early 1970s, the hitherto somnolent desert dependency became the focus of more and more of President Ould Daddah's attention as it was becoming apparent that Madrid's ability and willingness to remain in "Spanish Sahara" were doubtful. For about two years, Mauritania and Morocco's King Hassan II (q.v.) each pursued their own mutually exclusive claims to the entire colony, which caused considerable embarrassment. But in October and November 1974, the impasse was broken during a visit by Ould Mouknass to the United Nations in New York, where, upon being sounded out by Moroccan diplomats, he reacted positively to a proposal to partition Western Sahara between Mauritania and Morocco. After the idea had been cleared by President Ould Daddah, a tentative understanding was reached the next month, and early in 1975, the two countries agreed to make a joint approach to the International Court of Justice (ICJ) to attempt to have their Saharan claims legally accepted. Ould Mouknass thereafter became quite close to Morocco, playing a prominent part in the negotiation and signing of the Madrid Agreement (q.v.) on November 14, 1975. The Madrid accords, which were kept secret, provided that after Spain's withdrawal from Western Sahara in February 1976, Mauritania and Morocco would each take control of allotted portions of the Great Britain–sized territory. The treaty took no account of the wishes of the indigenous Saharawi (q.v.) population of Western Sahara, as the ICJ had demanded in an advisory opinion issued that same month.

Mauritania's annexation of Tiris el-Gharbia (q.v.) was to prove far from painless, however, and soon pitted the small, underequipped Mauritanian armed forces (q.v.) against the guerrilla fighters of the Polisario Front (q.v.). Ould Mouknass continued to lobby the UN, the Organization of African Unity (OAU), and other international fora on behalf of President Ould Daddah's policies, but his long tenure as foreign minister came to an abrupt end on July 10, 1978, when officers of the war-weary Mauritanian army, led by Colonel Mustapha Ould Mohammed Salek (q.v.), overthrew Ould Daddah and instituted military government in the form of the *Comité Militaire de Redressement National* (CMRN) (q.v.). Ould Mouknass, who was in Khartoum, Sudan, at the time of the bloodless *coup d'état,* returned to Mauritania on July 13 and was immediately placed under arrest by the new regime. He remained in detention until April 1979, when he was freed and allowed to return to his home city of Nouadhibou (q.v.). After a long subsequent period of exile and political inactivity, he emerged along with Ahmed Ould Daddah (q.v.) as one of the country's leading opposition politicians in the wake of the liberalization of Mauritania's institutions begun by President Maaouiya Ould Sid'Ahmed Taya (q.v.) in early 1991. During the period leading up to the January 1992 presidential elections, Ould Mouknass aligned himself with the *Union des Forces Démocratiques* (UFD) (q.v.), the largest opposition party, but after Ould Taya emerged victorious as president, and after the head of state's *Parti Républicain, Démocratique et Social* (PRDS) (q.v.) won a landslide parliamentary victory partly as a consequence of a UFD boycott, Ould Mouknass, along with several other well-known figures, decided in early 1993 to break away from the UFD and start their own political party, the *Union pour le Progrès et la Démocratie* (UPD) (q.v.). Reportedly, Ould Mouknass was keen to distance himself from Ahmed Ould Daddah, and also wished to adopt a more conciliatory tone toward the Ould Taya regime than the UFD was willing to contemplate. The UPD was formally registered with the government on June 15, 1993. Later that month, Ould Mouknass reentered the international spotlight when he was briefly detained by the authorities in regard to a recent invitation he had received from King Hassan to visit Morocco and to his role in arranging a visit to Rabat by Mokhtar Ould Daddah, by now living in retirement in France. Apparently, the government wished to interrogate him on the subject of possible foreign (i.e., Moroccan) financial backing for the UPD, such contributions being forbidden by Mauritanian law. Upon his release,

Ould Mouknass, unrepentant, clearly articulated his sympathies: "We must have good relations with all our neighbors, but it seems to me that these should be privileged as regards Morocco. It is a great country with a long history whose king is among the world's most prestigious heads of state."

HARATINE (sing., hartani). In post-independence Mauritania, haratines (literally in Arabic, "plowmen") constitute a unique stratum in the country's societal framework. Generally speaking, a hartani is one who either has been in slavery (q.v.) and is no longer subject to a master's direction in any form, or is a "part-slave"—that is, formally emancipated by his or her Beydane Moorish (qq.v.) overseers, but remaining within the Moorish family unit in a servile or semiservile state. Due to their long proximity to Moorish Mauritanian society and their consequent isolation from the free Black African groups such as the Halpulaaren and the Soninké (qq.v.) in the Senegal River Valley, the haratines, although black, usually have fully assimilated to Arab culture, speak Hassaniya (q.v.) Arabic as their mother tongue, bear Arab names and have sometimes intermarried with Beydanes. Their origins as inhabitants of the country's northern régions (q.v.) can be traced to about the sixteenth century, when most blacks, formerly subjects of the Ghana and Mali Empires, were displaced to the south by Arab invaders from the north and the east. Black Africans who remained behind or who were captured by the invaders became slaves working mostly in small-scale agricultural or livestock (qq.v.) herding activities supervised by Moors. Their servile condition continued into the twentieth century, until the gradual erosion of the strict Moorish caste system, a phenomenon partly brought on by French penetration of Mauritanian territory and the abolition of slavery that Paris decreed. But many stayed enslaved in the 1960–75 period, and some slavery persisted into the 1990s, although the extent of its prevalence was extremely controversial. Despite gaining a measure of freedom, a hartani faced an unpromising future: continued dependence upon a "white" Moorish family that was itself often desperately poor, nearly nonexistent economic opportunities, especially with the decline in agriculture caused by desertification (q.v.), and the unenviable distinction of occupying nearly the lowest rung on the Moorish social ladder. On the other hand, growing emancipatory attitudes in Mauritania, coupled with extensive population (q.v.) shifts to the cities and towns of the country and greater social mobility, meant that haratines were increasingly found, as time went on, in the professions, as owners of land, and as officers and enlisted men in the Mauritanian armed forces (q.v.). Ironically, they sometimes outstripped their Beydane counterparts in educational (q.v.) attainments and earning capacity.

Still, the hartani's lot was a disadvantaged one, and in 1974, certain intellectuals in the ex-slave community came together to form El-Hor (q.v.), an organization intended to protest slavery and all forms of discrimination against "Black Moors." Although El-Hor was politically active only between 1978 and about 1983, and its degree of popular support was uncertain in the eyes of independent observers, the group managed to focus domestic and international attention upon the haratines' special problems. It was probably due to El-Hor's pressure, for example, that the CMSN (q.v.) government of Colonel Mohammed Khouna Ould Heydallah (q.v.) issued a decree in July 1980 formally reabolishing slavery and in June 1983 promulgated a Land Reform Act (q.v.) that had as one of its goals the placement of haratines on fertile farmland in the Senegal River Valley.

The political ramifications of the haratine phenomenon went beyond their economic condition or the activities of El-Hor. Many free blacks who opposed the CMSN, notably those connected to the *Forces de Libération Africaine de Mauritanie* (FLAM) (q.v.), hoped to enlist the ex-slaves as allies in their campaign to overturn the "Beydane system" or "Mauritanian apartheid" (as FLAM put it), but such a goal was problematic, as the haratines nearly always felt a closer affinity with the Moorish way of life. And as with all population groups in the country, the number of haratines relative to other citizens was greatly disputed. In addition, in the course of the Senegal-Mauritania Crisis (q.v.) that began in April 1989, opposition elements charged that haratines were being used by the CMSN to intimidate and expel Halpulaaren from their lands along the Senegal River, either for their own use or on behalf of Beydanes. The existence of a "haratine militia," reputedly the brainchild of Djibril Ould Abdellahi (q.v.), then minister of the interior, was strongly denied by the Mauritanian authorities, who maintained that haratines who lawfully acquired land under the 1983 Land Reform Act were merely defending themselves against armed FLAM militants and other "troublemakers." Whatever the actual situation, it was clear by the mid-1990s that the haratine question would not go away, if for no other reason than that the difficulties the former slaves faced, both social and economic, were often the same as those confronted by the Mauritanian people as a whole.

HARMATTAN. A dry, hot wind which in Mauritania generally blows westward toward the coastal areas from the Sahara. It gives rise to the *irifi* (q.v.), the dreaded sandstorms which afflict the country for hours or days at a time. (See CLIMATE.)

HASNI OULD DIDI. A Mauritanian administrator whose career has spanned nearly a generation of civilian and military governments,

Hasni Ould Didi was born in 1945 in Tidjikja (q.v.), and between 1950 and 1956 received his primary education there. Then, beginning in 1956, he attended secondary schools in Rosso and Nouakchott (qq.v.), graduating in 1961, a year after his country's independence. He then moved to Paris, studying at the prestigious *Ecole des Hautes Etudes d'Outre-Mer,* receiving a diploma in administration in 1963. Almost immediately, Ould Didi began working in a variety of bureaucratic positions under the civilian regime of President Mokhtar Ould Daddah (q.v.). In 1967 and 1968 he served as Director of Labor and National Security at the young age of twenty-two. In the following two years, he occupied a rapid succession of high-level jobs, including secretary-general at the Ministry of Planning, minister of rural development, minister of public employment and training, and minister of finance. In 1971, President Ould Daddah rotated him out of the Council of Ministers (q.v.), making him governor of the administrative région of Dakhlet-Nouadhibou (qq.v.). In 1974, he was recalled to the capital to lead the effort to construct the first stage of the *Route de l'Espoir* (q.v.), a high-quality paved road that would eventually extend all the way across Mauritania, from Nouakchott to the eastern city of Néma (q.v.). By January 1976 he had once again moved on, becoming minister of trade and transport, and a year later (in 1977) he was named minister of justice for a brief time at the height of the Western Sahara conflict (q.v.). Later in 1977, Ould Didi was again dropped from the cabinet and was chosen governor of the important southern région of Gorgol (q.v.), remaining there despite the *coup d'état* of July 10, 1978, in which officers of the Mauritanian armed forces (q.v.) forced President Ould Daddah from office and replaced him with the *Comité Militaire de Redressement National* (CMRN) (q.v.). Despite the fact that he had no military background and was close to Mokhtar Ould Daddah, Ould Didi's abilities were sufficiently respected by the army establishment that on April 30, 1979, he was named secretary-general at the Presidency of the Republic under the short-lived *de facto* leadership of Lieutenant Colonel Ahmed Ould Bouceif (q.v.), who had helped abolish the CMRN a fortnight earlier and form a new ruling body, the *Comité Militaire de Salut National* (CMSN) (q.v.). After Ould Bouceif's death on May 27, 1979, and the ensuing power struggle that brought Lieutenant Colonel Mohammed Khouna Ould Heydallah (q.v.) to prominence for the first time, Ould Didi was named minister of education on June 22, replacing Lieutenant Colonel Mohammed Ould Bah Ould Abdel Kader (q.v.). From June 1979 until early 1990, he retained the education portfolio, enjoying an exceptionally long tenure in office and remaining in favor past December 1984, when Ould Heydallah was replaced as head of state by Colonel Maaouiya Ould Sid'Ahmed Taya (q.v.). As minister of education,

Ould Didi was a proponent of the government's Arabization policy (q.v.) and worked to make Hassaniya (q.v.) Arabic Mauritania's *lingua franca*. In the spring of 1990, Ould Didi left the Ministry of Education to become foreign minister, possibly as part of a reshuffle designed to put officials with more moderate credentials into place during the Senegal-Mauritania Crisis (q.v.), which had begun in April 1989. As head of the Ministry of Foreign Affairs, Ould Didi also had the task of clarifying his country's diplomatic stance during the Gulf Crisis (q.v.), which was the outgrowth of the invasion of Kuwait on August 2, 1990, by Iraq's President, Saddam Hussein, and which alienated Mauritania for a time from some Arab League (q.v.) members due to the country's perceived pro-Iraq attitudes. When the Mauritanian Second Republic (q.v.) was installed on April 18, 1992, Ould Didi left the Foreign Ministry, his place taken by Mohammed Abderrahmane Ould Moine, a longtime administrator and politician with close ties to the Kuwaitis and to the other Gulf emirates. Ould Didi then became minister of the interior, but on January 3, 1993, Mauritania's prime minister, Sidi Mohamed Ould Boubacar (q.v.), carried out a reorganization of the government, displacing Ould Didi at the Interior Ministry with Lemrabott Sidi Mahmoud Ould Cheikh Ahmed. In late 1993, Ould Didi was made head of the State Audit Bureau, a body charged with exposing governmental waste, corruption, and mismanagement.

HASSAN. As the dominant social stratum among Mauritania's Moors (q.v.), the *hassan,* or warrior tribes, are descended from Arab invaders originating in Yemen who, after a series of conflicts ending with the Char Bobha (q.v.), fought between 1644 and 1674, defeated the Berbers (q.v.) of the region, who were thereafter forced into vassalage as *znaga* (q.v.), or tributaries. The only exceptions to the hassan tribes' undisputed mastery were the *zawiya* (q.v.), or religious tribes, who themselves were often more Arab than Berber and who enjoyed protection from the hassan due to their knowledge of Islam (q.v.). Even before the start of vigorous French penetration of Mauritania in the late nineteenth century, the distinction between hassan and zawiya tribes was beginning to lose some of its importance due to intermarriage and other factors, and the policies of the French governor-general of Mauritania between 1901 and 1905, Xavier Coppolani (q.v.), who tried to elevate the zawiya to a higher social position relative to the hassan, lessened it still further.

HASSAN II. Born in 1929 and educated in France, Hassan II became King of Morocco in 1961 upon the death of his father, Mohammed V, the country's first post-independence leader. From the beginning of his long occupancy of the Moroccan Alawite throne, he displayed a consistent and at times controversial preoccupation with Mauritania. Partly in an effort to consolidate his grip on power at home and in an attempt to formulate an "anticolonial" foreign policy, King Hassan continued to embrace his father's "Greater Morocco" aspirations, which had first been urged upon the Rabat government by the prominent nationalist leader, Allal el-Fassi (q.v.) in the 1950s. King Hassan thus enunciated a Moroccan claim not only to western Algeria and the then-Spanish colony of Western Sahara (q.v.), but also the entire territory of the newly independent Mauritanian state. As a consequence, King Hassan refused to extend diplomatic recognition to Mauritania throughout the 1960s and mounted an aggressive campaign to deny the country admission to the United Nations (q.v.) and to bar it from the Arab League (q.v.). For a time, the Moroccan effort bore fruit: no Arab country other than Tunisia at first supported Mauritania's existence, and the Moroccan monarch was able to buttress his historically based designs on the country by attracting the loyalties of certain Mauritanian political personages, notably Horma Ould Babana (q.v.) and elements of the Nadha (q.v.) party.

From the Mauritanian point of view, this Moroccan—and Arab—nonrecognition was to exert a profound influence upon the country's foreign relations (q.v.) strategy during the first years after its release from French rule. President Mokhtar Ould Daddah (q.v.) was careful to retain very close political and military ties to the former metropole, and relied heavily on the more sympathetic attitudes of Black African states, gaining admission to the Organization of African Unity (OAU) when it was founded in 1963. The Moroccan king persisted in his effort to annex Mauritania, creating a separate ministry within his government for Mauritanian (and Western Saharan) affairs in 1966 to pave the way for the "return" of these territories to the Moroccan fold. But King Hassan's endeavor waned as it became apparent that the Ould Daddah regime enjoyed too much international recognition, even—increasingly—among Arab League countries, and was thus unlikely to be absorbed by Morocco. Moreover, King Hassan by then felt a good deal more confident of his own position inside Morocco, reaching the point where he could afford to ignore the hard-line irredentist political parties in the country, notably the *Istiqlal* (Independence) Party. Relations were on the mend with Algeria as well. On January 15, 1969, King Hassan and President Houari Boumedienne (q.v.) held a summit conference at Ifrane, Morocco, and agreed in principle to resolve their border and other differences peacefully. This Algerian-Moroccan entente also had a positive effect on Mauritania. Through the intervention of Boumedienne and other Arab leaders, Hassan II and Mokhtar Ould Daddah met for the first time in Rabat in September 1969, and the definitive abandonment of the Moroccan claim to Mauritania came in early 1970, when the two heads of state signed a convention establishing formal diplomatic relations. After this, ties developed quickly, with Morocco supplying economic assistance to the Mauritanians, including a crucial loan that enabled Ould Daddah to compensate the French and other shareholders of the giant MIFERMA iron ore (qq.v.) consortium, which was nationalized in November 1974.

King Hassan retained his claim to Western Sahara, however, and sought to avoid a possible confrontation with President Ould Daddah, who also claimed the entire colony for his country. After a period of equivocation (and attempted dissuasion by Houari Boumedienne and the nascent Polisario Front [q.v.], which wanted an independent Western Saharan state), the Mauritanian president decided in November 1975 to join with his erstwhile adversary and agree to the partition of the Spanish territory between the two countries. On November 14, Mauritania, Morocco, and Spain signed the Madrid Agreement (q.v.), which divided the colony, but which made no reference to the Saharawi (q.v.) self-determination that the International Court of Justice (ICJ) had earlier demanded. On April 14, 1976, the Moroccan-Mauritanian Conventions (q.v.) were signed, formally delineating the two states' respective zones, a document which left Mauritania with an almost valueless tract of desert known as Tiris el-Gharbia (q.v.), while Morocco took over the phosphate-rich northern two-thirds of Western Sahara, Saguia el-Hamra (q.v.).

The Western Sahara conflict, which began even before the Madrid Agreement and which pitted Mauritania's minuscule armed forces (q.v.) against the motivated troops of the Polisario Front, affected the Ould Daddah government the most severely. Polisario units raided virtually every population (q.v.) center in the country's northern and central régions (q.v.), showing up the limitations of the Mauritanian army and forcing President Ould Daddah ever further into the embrace of King Hassan. After a series of disastrous military defeats and the near collapse of Mauritania's economy, a Moroccan-Mauritanian Defense Committee (q.v.) was set up on May 13, 1977, allowing Moroccan troops to station themselves in both Tiris el-Gharbia and within Mauritania itself to try to secure Ould Daddah's grip on his outgunned nation. Soon, nearly 9000 of Hassan II's soldiers were in Mauritania, virtually relegating the country to the status of Morocco's junior partner in Western Sahara. This deepening alignment with Morocco rekindled latent suspicions among some Mauritanians that the king had never really reconciled himself to their country's independence. The large Moroccan presence, even with French air strikes against

Polisario in late 1977, was insufficient to turn the tide, though, and on July 10, 1978, Mokhtar Ould Daddah was overthrown by his disillusioned army in a bloodless putsch.

King Hassan reacted to the coup in Nouakchott (q.v.) with considerable concern, fearing a loss of resolve by Mauritania to hold onto its Saharan acquisition. But he was pleased that the chairman of the new military governing council, the *Comité Militaire de Redressement National* (CMRN) (q.v.), Colonel Mustapha Ould Mohammed Salek (q.v.), was reluctant to pull out of Western Sahara unilaterally and sign a separate peace with the Polisario Front. However, Ould Salek, though not from want of trying, could not entice the Moroccan monarch into joining him in a "global" settlement of the Saharan dispute, and as a result had little to show for his efforts by April 1979, when he was stripped of power by his fellow Mauritanian officers and eventually replaced as paramount leader by Lieutenant Colonel Mohammed Khouna Ould Heydallah (q.v.). After a few months, the new CMSN (q.v.) chairman took the step that had eluded his predecessors, and on August 5, 1979, Mauritania put its signature to the Algiers Agreement (q.v.), by which the country renounced its claim to Western Sahara and made peace with Polisario. The thousands of troops Morocco still had inside Mauritania were quickly obliged to leave, although Rabat moved into Tiris el-Gharbia as Nouakchott's troops withdrew, annexing Mauritania's former share of the territory a week later.

Despite Ould Heydallah's strenuous attempts to explain his policy shift personally to King Hassan, the Algiers Agreement evoked the monarch's wrath, especially given the Mauritanian head of state's reported sympathy for the Saharawi cause. As a result, Hassan II welcomed to Rabat members of the exiled anti-CMSN opposition group, the *Alliance pour une Mauritanie Démocratique* (AMD) (q.v.), and allegedly allowed them to conspire against Ould Heydallah as a way of seeking revenge on his "pro-Polisario" government. Matters came to a head on March 16, 1981, when AMD members staged a violent coup attempt in the streets of Nouakchott, killing several people before loyal army units defeated them. President Ould Heydallah broke off diplomatic relations with Morocco a few days later and moved his country progressively closer to Algeria and Polisario. Three years later, on February 27, 1984, the Mauritanian leader formally recognized the Polisario Front's government-in-exile, the Saharan Arab Democratic Republic (SADR) (q.v.), further antagonizing King Hassan. Soon after, in a move which was met with undisguised satisfaction by the Moroccan royal palace, Colonel Maaouiya Ould Sid'Ahmed Taya (q.v.) unseated Ould Heydallah on December 12, 1984, and signalled a desire to assume a more neutral stance on Western Sahara. Diplomatic relations were restored a few months later, although friendly ties with Algeria were sustained and the recognition of the SADR was not rescinded. Finally, in February 1989, President Ould Taya brought Mauritania into the *Union du Maghreb Arabe* (UMA) (q.v.), a five-nation unity arrangement which included Morocco and which replaced the implicitly anti-Moroccan Treaty of Fraternity and Concord (q.v.), which Ould Heydallah had signed on December 13, 1983.

Although the overall state of relations between King Hassan and the Ould Taya regime was regularly described as "excellent" by diplomats from both countries in the late 1980s and early 1990s, irritants remained. The CMSN registered a strong protest with Hassan II when he ordered the extension of Morocco's "defensive wall" (earthen barrier) system in Western Sahara to within a few kilometers of Mauritania's borders in early 1987, which raised the specter of a powerful Moroccan army camped within a stone's throw of the economically vital Zouerate-Nouadhibou railway (q.v.) line. Moroccan attitudes during the Senegal-Mauritania Crisis (q.v.), which began in April 1989, also caused the Nouakchott government anxiety, for King Hassan had made Senegal one of his closest allies in sub-Saharan Africa, and according to some observers was not prepared to support Mauritania, a fellow Maghreb state, against the government of Abdou Diouf (q.v.).

HASSANIYA. As the dialect of Arabic spoken in Mauritania, Hassaniya, as its name indicates, was imported by the *hassan* (q.v.), or warrior tribes, who finally subjugated the country in the late 1600s in the Char Bobha (q.v.) against the Berbers (q.v.). The Hassaniya dialect is one of the purest in the Arabic language, coming perhaps closest to classical Arabic. Despite the predominance of Hassaniya, many local place names in Mauritania, as well as some words in everyday use, retain their Berber antecedents.

HEALTH. Since independence, Mauritania's public health situation has remained at a substandard level, with the prevalence of waterborne and insect-transmitted diseases made worse by extreme poverty, sparse hospital and clinic facilities even in major population (q.v.) centers, and a lack of trained personnel and equipment. In the mid-1990s, life expectancy stood at a very low forty-five years for men and fifty-one years for women (q.v.), while the infant mortality rate, already at a level of 102 per 1000 live births in the late 1980s, deteriorated to 125 deaths per 1000 births by 1993. On the other hand, both the civilian government of President Mokhtar Ould Daddah (q.v.), who held office from 1960 to 1978, and successor regimes from the country's armed forces (q.v.), made strenuous efforts to improve health conditions. Great strides, for example, were made in facilitating the education (q.v.) of doctors, nurses, midwives, and other health care providers, with a National School of Nurses and Midwives established in 1966 and a National Health Center in 1977, tasked with research into infectious diseases and their prevention. By the early 1990s, consequently, there was one doctor for every 13,350 Mauritanians, an improvement from the 1965 ratio, one doctor for every 36,580. In the mid-1990s, the country's health and hospital infrastructure consists of a modern 500-bed facility in the capital, Nouakchott (q.v.) (the staff of which includes many French expatriate doctors), a dozen smaller hospitals situated mostly in the capitals of Mauritania's administrative régions (q.v.), and a variety of clinics, maternal units, and mobile health care and education vehicles that traverse the country's rural areas. The armed forces are also involved in health care, with army hospitals, dispensaries, and personnel being used as providers in the countryside, all in an effort to heighten the army's visibility and so (it is hoped) foster a sense of national unity and transcend regional and ethnic differences. Nearly all of Mauritania's hospitals, however, lack sufficient medicines and supplies and are inadequate to deal with the number of patients who need their services.

Throughout the post-independence period, many infectious diseases have been endemic to Mauritania. Generally, the northern part of the country is healthier, although measles and tuberculosis as well as a variety of respiratory ailments are more common there. The southern régions have considerably greater incidence of disease, with malaria, schistosomiasis, cholera, yellow fever, Rift Valley fever, hepatitis, and parasitical illnesses found in the fertile (and tropical) Senegal River Valley. Other diseases such as poliomyelitis, meningitis, and typhoid are found across the whole country. Dysentery from impure water (q.v.) supplies is also a problem. Nearly all Mauritanian governments have undertaken extensive vaccination programs, especially for children, but improvements in overall public health have often been slow to materialize.

HIVERNAGE. The rainy season in Mauritania, generally extending from July to September, is called the *hivernage* ("wintering"). Wide regional variations exist in rainfall (q.v.) amounts—Nouadhibou (q.v.), for example, has less than 30 mm of rain per year, while the southern régions of Gorgol and Guidimaka (qq.v.) register far more, making these areas suitable for agriculture (q.v.). In some of Mauritania's territory, it is not unusual for several years to pass with little or no rainfall. (See CLIMATE.)

HIZB ESH-SHAAB AL-MORITANY. See Parti du Peuple Mauritanien (PPM)

HODH ECH-CHARGUI. Covering about 183,000 square kilometers in Mauritania's far east, the Eastern Hodh has been subject to what some observers have called "centrifugal forces" emanating from adjacent Mali, a political concern that prompted successive governments to pay greater attention to this administrative région (q.v.), as when the *Route de l'Espoir* (q.v.) was extended through Hodh ech-Chargui to the provincial capital, Néma (q.v.), in the early 1980s using extensive foreign aid. In 1977, the région's population (q.v.) was estimated at 157,000 persons, rising to an officially reported 212,203 in 1988, most of whom were sedentary in the towns. Because of its remoteness, the province was also used as a place of political exile and imprisonment; for example, Mauritania's first President, Mokhtar Ould Daddah (q.v.), spent almost a year in Oualata (q.v.) after he was ousted as head of state by the armed forces (q.v.) on July 10, 1978. Apart from Néma and Oualata, the only population centers of consequence are Timbédra (west of Néma), Amourj (south of Néma) and Bassikounou (far to the southeast near the Malian border). A small network of roads (q.v.) of uncertain reliability connects these towns, but the rest of Hodh ech-Chargui is trackless desert with an extremely harsh climate (q.v.).

HODH EL-GHARBI. One of Mauritania's most populous administrative régions (q.v.) because of its proximity to portions of the fertile Senegal River Valley, the Western Hodh had a population (q.v.) of about 124,000 in 1977, a figure that increased, according to an official census, to 159,296 in 1988. The province has an area of 53,000 square kilometers fairly evenly divided between desert in the north and savanna grassland in the south, where Hodh el-Gharbi shares a border with Mali. Agriculture and livestock (qq.v.) herding are practiced there, although both occupations have been affected negatively since the mid-1970s by drought, overgrazing, and desertification (q.v.). Due to its partly agricultural economic base, the province has a substantial number of black Mauritanian farmers. Also, a refugee (q.v.) problem exists with Mali — a delay of only a few weeks in the *hivernage* (q.v.) often leads to mass migrations from the région to more hospitable areas south of the border. The provincial capital, Ayoun el-Atrouss (q.v.), is the only important town. Hodh el-Gharbi is served by the Trans-Mauritanian Highway (q.v.), which was constructed to bind it more closely to the rest of the country and promote feelings of national unity. The province is also the site of the ruins of the great trading center of Aoudaghost (q.v.), capital of the Sanhadja Confederation (q.v.) beginning in the ninth century A.D., which fell to the Almoravids (q.v.) around 1054.

HORMA OULD BABANA. One of Mauritania's first native politicians and leader of its first political party, the *Entente Mauritanienne* (q.v.),

Horma Ould Babana was a member of the Idaw 'Ali tribe and originally worked as an interpreter for the French colonial administration,
AOF (q.v.). Though he had earned a reputation for impetuosity, he was
selected by the French Socialist Party to stand as that organization's
candidate in the November 1946 elections to the French National Assembly in Paris, in which each AOF territory would be entitled to one
seat. It was believed at the time by the Section Française de l'Internationale Ouvrière (SFIO) that Ould Babana would work to lessen the influence of traditional Moorish (q.v.) chieftains and tribal authorities in
Mauritania and promote the ascendancy of more "modern" elements.
In part because Ould Babana was a Mauritanian running against a
Frenchman (Yvon Razac), and also due to generous financial contributions from France and Senegal, Ould Babana won the election handily, with roughly two-thirds of the 9611 ballots being cast in his favor.
However, his political fortunes waned rapidly during his five-year term
in the French parliament, as he chose to spend most of his time in Paris
and was thus isolated from events in Mauritania. In addition, frictions
soon developed between Ould Babana and the traditional Muslim personalities in the country, who were suspicious of the Entente's
"radical" and "socialist" programs. But according to Alfred Gerteiny
(see Bibliography), he acted almost as a French nationalist himself on
occasion, neither favoring an end to France's colonial empire nor
Mauritania's eventual independence. He also emerged as a strong de-
fender of Moorish interests in the country, making some black Mauritanians nervous. In the meantime, Ould Babana was gradually deserted
by the French Socialist rank and file, and he left the SFIO in 1948, ostensibly because of that group's sympathies with the newly independent State of Israel, but possibly due to Ould Babana's perception that
his ambitions were being thwarted by the Socialists. Also in 1948, the
conservative and regionally based interests in Mauritania founded a
new political party, the *Union Progressiste Mauritanienne* (UPM)
(q.v.). The UPM was specifically intended to oppose Ould Babana's
Entente, and was headed by Sidi el-Mokhtar N'Diaye, who was part
Moor and part Wolof (q.v.), thus enhancing his appeal to the voters.

The Entente Mauritanienne and the UPM ran against one another in
the 1951 elections to the *Conseil Général* (q.v.) and the UPM emerged
the winner, N'Diaye winning with 29,323 votes to Ould Babana's
23,649. In 1956 Ould Babana tried again to be elected to the General
Council, but was once again defeated, this time by a greater margin,
getting only 17,371 votes to N'Diaye's 106,603. Thereafter, Ould Babana wholeheartedly embraced Allal el-Fassi's (q.v.) "Greater Morocco" concept, which envisioned the nearly complete absorption of
Mauritania into Morocco. This stance heightened tensions in the country, and Ould Babana soon left Mauritania, first traveling in the sum-

mer of 1956 to Cairo and then settling in Morocco, where he helped to create the *Front National de Libération Mauritanienne* (FNLM) (q.v.), a segment of the Army of Liberation (q.v.), which hoped to reclaim Mauritania for the Moroccan kingdom. The Army of Liberation's activities forced Mauritania's dominant politician, Mokhtar Ould Daddah (q.v.), to call upon France for military assistance, which was forthcoming in the form of Operation Ouragon (q.v.) in February 1958. Because of his pro-Moroccan stance, Horma Ould Babana was around this time expelled from the Entente, and he remained in Morocco, becoming a strong supporter of King Hassan II (q.v.) and serving as a royalist member of the Moroccan parliament in the 1960s.

HOUSING. Mauritania has suffered from a severe shortage of housing that was greatly aggravated by a series of droughts beginning in the 1970s, as well as by the process of desertification (q.v.). Together, these phenomena have forced many of the country's inhabitants out of rural areas and into the major urban centers, most notably the national capital, Nouakchott (q.v.). These persons, virtually internal refugees (q.v.), sometimes live in tents on the outskirts of the towns or along major roads (q.v.). Often, though, the displaced agriculturalists and livestock (qq.v.) herders would resort to constructing rough, lean-to shelters of scrap metal and wood. From the late 1970s onward, shanty-towns (*kébés*) sprang up and expanded at a fast pace on Nouakchott's periphery to the point where fully one-third of the entire Mauritanian population (q.v.) was supposedly living somewhere in or around the capital. Although food, distributed through the state relief agency, the *Commissariat à la Sécurité Alimentaire* (CSA) (q.v.), has been in reasonably good supply, there is little chance that the new arrivals can readily gain access to adequate water resources and health care (qq.v.), not to mention sanitary facilities and other amenities. A high rate of population growth—over 2 percent per year throughout the 1975–1990 period—does not help matters, and ensures that governmental efforts to improve the housing situation would be little more than palliatives.

Mauritania's first president, Mokhtar Ould Daddah (q.v.) recognized the need for new housing construction, and so created a new state agency, the *Société de Construction et de Gestion Immobilière de Mauritanie* (SOCOGIM) in 1974. Due to a lack of funding, corruption and mismanagement, and other factors, however, few additional low-cost dwellings were built, with cost overruns and the prices of imported building materials rendering the houses too expensive for the average Mauritanian. No improvements were evident under successive armed forces (q.v.) governments; indeed, rather than try to house new and existing residents of Nouakchott, the regime for a time prohibited the construction of permanent structures in the shanty-towns, hoping to induce the people living in them to "return to the land," a highly uncertain prospect. A more imaginative approach to the problem was attempted between 1977 and 1982 near the town of Rosso (q.v.). In a cooperative scheme, houses were to be constructed using local materials by the same people who were to occupy them. Funding and expertise were provided by a variety of foreign sources. After an impressive beginning, in which over 500 units were built with room for about 4500 people, the project was allowed to lapse and SOCOGIM soon became the object of corruption allegations. More recently, Mauritania has turned to foreign, especially Arab, donors for direct assistance. In 1985, Kuwait and Saudi Arabia agreed to fund about 1000 new homes, with the People's Republic of China doing likewise, but compared to the magnitude of the overall problem, these were little more than drops in the proverbial bucket. And due to a lack of materials and skilled labor, those attempting to maintain and improve the country's existing housing stock were largely on their own.

IMRAGUEN. Mauritania's smallest ethnic grouping and the one with the most obscure origins, the Imraguen number no more than 1500 and are found between Nouadhibou (q.v.) and the settlement of Nou-amghar on the southern edge of the country's wildlife preserve, the *Parc National du Banc d'Arguin* (q.v.). Unlike other Mauritanians, the Imraguen engage in fishing (q.v.) as their vocation along the largely unspoiled Atlantic coastline, which limits their contact with outsiders. Black-skinned and physically well-built, they are believed by some historians to be the descendants of the Bafour, a pastoralist, proto-Berber (q.v.) people who migrated into the area during Neolithic times, when Mauritania had not yet succumbed to the process of desertification (q.v.). After the Berbers were defeated in the Char Bobha (q.v.) in 1674 by the *Beni Hassan* (q.v.), the Imraguen were reduced to the status of *znaga* (q.v.) to the victorious *hassan* (q.v.) tribe, the Oulad Bou Sbaa. Like other Moorish (q.v.) Mauritanians, the Imraguen speak mainly Hassaniya (q.v.) Arabic.

INCHIRI. Located in the southwest of Mauritania and occupying a total area of 47,000 square kilometers, Inchiri is one of the country's most sparsely populated administrative régions (q.v.), registering just 18,000 people in 1977 and declining to only 14,613 a decade later (1988). The province lies within the Saharan zone, meaning that it has a hot, dry climate (q.v.) and very little vegetation. The only town of real importance is Akjoujt (q.v.), the site of extensive copper and gold (qq.v.) mining operations conducted by the Mauritanian parastatal companies SNIM and SOMIMA (qq.v.). A substantial paved road (q.v.) links Akjoujt with the capital, Nouakchott (q.v.), as well as with the province of Adrar (q.v.) farther north.

INDUSTRIAL DEVELOPMENT. The great majority of Mauritania's industrial infrastructure, from independence onward, has been related to iron ore and fisheries (qq.v.), the two largest contributions to the country's economy; there is also a fairly small oil refining and distribution sector (see PETROLEUM) centered in Nouadhibou (q.v.). Aside from these, efforts to develop Mauritanian industries have been severely hampered by a lack of money and a consequent dependence on the priorities of foreign aid donors, the absence of a significant pool of skilled labor, and a thin domestic market for finished products resulting from very low incomes. Starting in the early 1970s, the first Mauritanian president, Mokhtar Ould Daddah (q.v.), like his counterparts elsewhere in the developing world, embarked on the construction of large-scale state-sponsored industrial enterprises which would attempt to produce goods that, it was envisioned, would obviate the need for at least some imports. Hence, the *Société Arabe des Industries Métallurgiques Mauritano-Koweitienne* (SAMIA) was set up with Kuwaiti participation in 1974 to build an indigenous steel industry that looked forward to producing 500,000 tons of steel and copper (q.v.) products annually by 1980. However, only a single mill was eventually built with a capacity of 36,000 tons per annum, mostly steel reinforcing rods for the construction trade. For a variety of reasons, the enterprise ran into immediate trouble and never produced anything near its planned output: in 1985 it turned out only 5,300 tons, and it closed the same year. After a reorganization carried out by the new government of Colonel Maaouiya Ould Sid'Ahmed Taya (q.v.), the mill reopened in 1987 with Kuwaiti and Jordanian assistance, but production remained low and SAMIA was scheduled for privatization by 1994 to improve efficiency.

Besides steel, mining, oil, and fishing, Mauritania's only other significant foray into industrial development (excluding a few small leather-tanning and textile mills that were liquidated in 1991 and 1992 after finding no private buyers) has been in sugar refining, for which a large facility in Nouakchott (q.v.) opened in 1977. However, the plant confined itself to processing and packaging imports, and closed after only six months of operation. In 1982, the sugar mill opened its doors again with help from Algeria, but shut down again in 1991 after years of substandard performance.

The Ould Taya regime, stung by all these reverses, shifted decisively away from large-scale import-substitution projects and instead tried to encourage smaller private enterprises that would gradually form the foundation for an indigenous Mauritanian industry. By the early 1990s, special industrial zones had been established, notably in and near Nouakchott and Nouadhibou, and preferential treatment was given to serious-minded entrepreneurs, whether domestic or foreign. In the mid-1990s it is too early to ascertain whether these endeavors will bear fruit, and even under the most optimistic calculations, the number of persons employed by these new industries would still account for only a small proportion of the total Mauritanian workforce.

IRIFI. The Arabic word for a severe sandstorm, the *irifi* is one of the harshest and most costly aspects of Mauritania's climate (q.v.). The fine sand of the Sahara, thrown up by the wind, often reduces visibility to near zero and clogs roads (q.v.) as well as entering homes and other buildings. In some years, the irifi makes itself felt nearly 50 percent of the time in the country's capital, Nouakchott (q.v.), impeding air traffic and bringing much human activity to a halt.

IRON ORE. In the late 1940s, a series of French aeromagnetic and other surveys revealed the existence of great quantities of high-grade iron ore in Mauritania's northeast, near the French military outpost of Fort Gouraud (q.v.) and contained in a series of *guelbs* (q.v.) or raised geological formations. In particular, the deposits at Kediet d'Idjil, a few kilometers east of Fort Gouraud, were thought to be especially promising for commercial exploitation, with an estimated 125 million tons of 65 percent pure iron ore available. In addition, there were 1 billion tons of lower-quality (25 to 30 percent purity) ore believed to be present nearby. In all, over fifty individual ore-bearing sites were identified by French geologists. Several years later, efforts to mine the ore advanced further, with the formation in 1952 of the *Société Anonyme des Mines de Fer de Mauritanie* (MIFERMA) (q.v.), a Paris-dominated international consortium that also included British, West German, and Italian investors with an initial capitalization of $52 million. However, the actual start-up of mining operations had to wait until the attainment of Mauritanian independence, which occurred on November 28, 1960. Just a few months before, on March 17, a $66 million loan was granted by the World Bank, with France and Mauritania guaranteeing repayment. The Mauritanian government headed by Mokhtar Ould Daddah (q.v.) had already agreed, moreover, in September 1959, on the overall terms of the operation and financing of the venture. Although many logistical and technical problems had to be resolved before the iron mines could become productive, construction moved fairly rapidly. By early 1963, not only had a 650-kilometer railway (q.v.) line been finished between the mine sites near Zouerate (q.v.) and the coastal city of Nouadhibou (q.v.), but also a brand-new docking facility, the *Port Minéralier* (q.v.), had been built to accommodate the large ships into which the ore would be loaded for export. In April 1963, MIFERMA's operations began in earnest, injecting millions of dollars into an infant Mauritanian economy that had hitherto been almost wholly dependent upon revenue from agriculture, fisheries, and livestock (qq.v.).

Mining procedures at Kediet d'Idjil were relatively simple. After being blasted from the sides of the guelbs with large amounts of explosives, the ore was shovelled into 100-ton trucks for the journey to the railhead, where the ore was placed into hopper cars. Once loaded, the train would begin its slow trip to Nouadhibou, taking approximately sixteen hours to reach the Port Minéralier. In Nouadhibou, ships would be waiting to transport the ore for steelmaking in Europe and North America. The empty train would soon return to Zouerate, as operations went on around the clock and often necessitated two daily railway runs from the mines. MIFERMA intentionally automated as much of the operation of the mines as possible, due in large part to a shortage of qualified Mauritanian workers and a desire to reduce labor costs.

The Zouerate-area iron ore mines were an immediate economic success story for Mauritania. Having extracted over 4 million tons of ore in 1965, two years after start-up, production soon surpassed 7 million tons annually, and by 1966, an overwhelming 92 percent of Mauritanian exports were accounted for by the iron ore deposits. In budgetary (q.v.) terms, the mine's operator turned a clear profit every year from 1966 to 1976, and through taxes and remittances from sales of the ore itself, the mining sector provided fully 30 percent of all Mauritanian government revenues by the early 1970s. Indirect economic benefits were also significant. The MIFERMA workers and their dependents soon created a market for housing (q.v.), food, transport, and other items, further contributing to the flush atmosphere in the country, especially in the late 1960s. A few years later, iron ore revenues earned the Ould Daddah regime an additional prize: Mauritania was reclassified by the World Bank and the United Nations (q.v.) from a "least developed country" to a "moderate-income developing country," contributing not only to national prestige but also to the government's ability to seek financing for an ambitious program of industrial development (q.v.).

To be sure, though, the huge iron reserves were not an unmixed blessing for Mauritania. Attempts to diversify exports were spotty at best, the iron mining industry consumed 40 percent of the country's expensive imports of oil (q.v.), and revenues derived from MIFERMA were often placed in overambitious and unsuccessful projects, while the southern régions (q.v.) of the country, practically the only areas of Mauritania that possessed arable land, were not allocated development monies proportional to their economic importance. Politically, too, the mining sector was problematic. Throughout the 1966–72 period, periodic strikes and protests shook MIFERMA, with students from Nouadhibou and the capital, Nouakchott (q.v.), often joining the strikers, who resented the continued domination of Mauritania's most important industry by French interests, and who also disliked MIFERMA's slowness in recruiting Mauritanian workers, especially in the middle and upper management levels of the company. As a result, the mines were sometimes shut down for days or even weeks at a time, and there was some loss of life as well as many injuries and arrests when demonstrations were suppressed by the Mauritanian police and armed forces (q.v.), particularly in 1966, a year that witnessed the first mass-scale opposition to President Mokhtar Ould Daddah's one-party government.

Seeing that foreign domination of the iron mines had great potential for becoming a focus of opposition to his regime, and irritated that MIFERMA revenues were not being remitted to Mauritania to the extent he felt reasonable, President Ould Daddah decided to nationalize the industry, a step that was taken on November 28, 1974. MIFERMA was abolished and all mining and associated activities were taken over by a Mauritanian parastatal, the *Société Nationale Industrielle et Minière* (SNIM) (q.v.). The changeover from MIFERMA to SNIM operation was uneventful and production was not disrupted. Government revenues—and the mines' profitability—increased substantially, and efforts were made to employ more Mauritanians in skilled positions. But the progress that was made by the nationalization of the industry was offset by two factors. The first, a worldwide slump in commodity prices, was beyond Mauritania's control. But the second, the disruption of mining operations caused by Mauritania's involvement in the Western Sahara conflict (q.v.), was something for which the regime itself was responsible. President Ould Daddah's adherence, on November 14, 1975, to the Madrid Agreement (q.v.) between Mauritania, Morocco, and Spain providing for the Spanish colony to be partitioned between the two Maghreb states, took no account of the attitudes of the Polisario Front (q.v.), a nationalist organization claiming to represent the Saharawis (q.v.) of the territory and which desired an independent Western Sahara. As soon as Mauritania's intentions to annex Tiris el-Gharbia (q.v.) became clear, Polisario's aggressive guerrilla fighters made the iron ore facilities one of their first targets.

The Polisario Front struck first at the railway line, which ran within a few kilometers of the Western Saharan border and which could not be patrolled effectively due to its great length and the remote areas it traversed. Zouerate was also greatly affected: after a series of smaller-scale attacks, a massive assault by Polisario against the town was mounted on May 1, 1977, laying waste to mining and railway equipment. Iron ore production and exports fell drastically, a situation illustrated by the following export statistics (expressed in millions of metric tons):

1968	1973	1978
7.7	10.5	7.1
1969	1974	1979
8.4	11.9	9.1
1970	1975	1980
9.1	8.6	8.7
1971	1976	1981
8.6	9.6	8.8
1972	1977	1982
8.6	7.5	7.3

Even allowing for continued low iron ore prices during the early 1980s, a phenomenon that impeded Mauritania's recovery from the effects of the Western Sahara war, which the country formally exited by means of the Algiers Agreement (q.v.) signed on August 5, 1979, the figures show the damage inflicted by the conflict. The fall in production and exports drove the fragile Mauritanian economy to virtual bankruptcy and played a major role in the overthrow of President Ould Daddah on July 10, 1978 and his replacement by Colonel Mustapha Ould Mohammed Salek's *Comité Militaire de Redressement National* (CMRN) (qq.v.).

The end of Mauritania's involvement in the Western Sahara conflict did not lead to the resumption of the high revenues and profits that had characterized the late 1960s. Low prices on the world market were a constant impediment, as was the fact that the Kediet d'Idjil mines were nearing exhaustion (they ceased entirely in early 1992), an event for which Mauritania was not fully prepared, as its economy was still greatly dependent upon the Zouerate reserves. Consequently, in 1984 the CMSN (q.v.) government embarked on the $360 million Guelbs Project, targeting large iron ore reserves at el-Rhein, about thirty kilometers northeast of F'Derik (q.v.), for exploitation. An extension of the railway was spiked down to the new mine sites, and for a while the deposits at el-Rhein were more than adequate, with total annual iron ore production being as follows from 1983 to 1994 (in millions of metric tons):

1983	1989
7.5	11.3
1984	1990
9.2	11.6
1985	1991
9.3	10.5
1986	1992
9.3	8.0
1987	1993
9.0	9.8
1988	1994
10.2	10.3

As can be seen, the yield of the iron ore mines rose sharply between 1984 and 1991. But various technical problems at el-Rhein, coupled with the low quality (38 percent purity) of some of the ore, caused output to fall to 8 million tons in 1992. With $200 million in support from Arab and other international donors, the attention of SNIM shifted to much larger ore reserves at M'Haoudat, about fifteen kilometers east of el-Rhein. It was estimated that these deposits, whose extraction began in 1993, would keep one of Mauritania's most vital industries viable for several decades to follow, as they were believed to total over 100 million tons and had an iron content of over 60 percent, eliminating any need to construct concentration and beneficiation facilities at the site to improve the ore's quality. But the M'Haoudat deposits still did not restore iron ore to quite the central position it possessed earlier. Already by 1983, the sum of iron ore exports had fallen below 50 percent of the country's total for the first time since 1963, falling further to 40 percent by the early 1990s, as a reorganized and more prosperous fishing industry overtook mineral extraction as Mauritania's prime revenue source.

ISLAM. Islamic religious and cultural identity has formed the bedrock of Mauritanian life since the faith was introduced to northwest Africa by Arab merchants in the tenth century A.D. Fairly soon after this time, virtually all Mauritanians, whether black or Moorish (q.v.), considered themselves Muslims, adhering by the nineteenth century to the Malekite Sunni school of Islamic law. Mauritania has also been, from an early date, noted for its citizens' membership in various religious brotherhoods, hierarchical yet relatively informal organizations that provide spiritual guidance to their flock. The Qadiriya and Tidjaniya brotherhoods are the most important such groups, although smaller brotherhoods, such as the Chadeliya, centered in Tagant (q.v.), and the Goudfiya, found in Adrar, Hodh ech-Chargui, Hodh el-Gharbi, and Tagant (qq.v.) also exist as do various *sufi* (mystical) movements. The Islamic brotherhoods acquired a great deal more influence in the early twentieth century when, as part of the French colonial government's "pacification" strategy, led most prominently by Xavier Coppolani (q.v.), the monastic or *zawiya* (q.v.) tribes were favored over their more militaristic *hassan* (q.v.) counterparts. Independent Mauritania's first president, Mokhtar Ould Daddah (q.v.), came from a religious tribe, the Oulad Berri of Boutilimit (q.v.), as did many other officials of the new state.

Early on, Ould Daddah and his French and Mauritanian backers recognized the key role of Islam in the societal arrangements of the country. The Islamic faith was essentially the only thing the various racial, tribal, and regional groupings had in common, and thus religion was constantly emphasized as a powerful tool in building national unity where none had existed before. The name of the country, the Islamic Republic of Mauritania, symbolized this overriding concern, and was the very first state in the Arab-Islamic world so named. Yet this identity, coupled with the formal constitutional designation of Mauritania as a Muslim country, did not imply the existence of a theocratic government, since its governmental structures were Western-oriented and liberal democratic in form from 1960 onward. In addition, its legal and judicial system (q.v.) gave short shrift to the *sharia* (q.v.) except in certain domestic relations matters. The Ould Daddah regime also went out of its way to guarantee that the presence and practice of other religions would be tolerated; hence, freedom of religion was guaranteed pursuant to the Constitution of Mauritania of May 20, 1961 (q.v.). Given that almost 100 percent of Mauritanians were Muslims, this was a perhaps superfluous provision, but it has given the small Roman Catholic community—about 4000-strong in 1995, mainly expatriates from France—leeway to maintain its own house of worship and conduct various humanitarian activities, both in Nouakchott (q.v.) and to a limited degree elsewhere in the country.

After the overthrow of President Ould Daddah on July 10, 1978, and his replacement by a group of officers from the armed forces (q.v.) who organized themselves into the *Comité Militaire de Redressement National* (CMRN) (q.v.), very little changed in terms of the government's attitudes toward Islam until 1980, when the chairman of the CMRN's successor council, the *Comité Militaire de Salut National* (CMSN) (q.v.), Colonel Mohammed Khouna Ould Heydallah (q.v.), decided to enhance greatly the state's adherence to the sharia to the point where some of the more severe provisions of Islamic jurisprudence, such as amputations, whippings in public, and even execution, became relatively commonplace. These measures drew a storm of domestic and international protest and were suspended in February 1984.

Ould Heydallah's successor as head of state from December 12, 1984, Colonel Maaouiya Ould Sid'Ahmed Taya (q.v.), adopted a much more cautious attitude toward Islam, disparaging Muslim militants while extolling the unifying powers of a religion in which all Mauritanians had a place. A balanced approach was also adopted by the government as a whole: Koranic education (q.v.) continued to be supported and encouraged by the state, and indigenous resources as well as foreign donations were utilized for the construction of new mosques. At the same time, the outlook of the regime remained secular, with bureaucratic and administrative values and procedures basically emulating Western models. The same was true of the country's foreign relations (q.v.): although ties to Islamic countries and members of the Arab League (q.v.) took pride of place, overidentification with any one foreign nation or bloc was for the most part avoided.

As of 1996, Mauritania had largely been spared the effects of the upsurge in Islamic militancy that swept much of the rest of North Africa, notably Algeria and Egypt. Purely religious political parties were outlawed by a statute enacted pursuant to the July 20, 1991 Mauritanian Constitution (q.v.), were excluded from the institutions of the Second Republic (q.v.), and were repressed on occasion by the Ould Taya government. Even with these legal prohibitions, however, a few Islamist organizations sprang up in 1993, among them a branch of the Iran-based Hezbollah (Party of God), the Ummah Party which advocated the forcible overthrow of the regime, and the Mauritanian Muslim Brotherhood, thought to be influenced by like-minded militants in Egypt. Members of these groups were implicated in attacks on two Catholic priests in October 1993 and in the death of a policeman the following month. The governmental response was uncompromising: meeting halls used by the militants were shut down, foreign (especially Algerian) Islamic militants were deported, and some Mauritanian Islamists were prosecuted. In addition, some sixty suspected Muslim fundamentalists were arrested on September 30, 1994 and charged with unauthorized political activity and receiving funds and advice from foreign interests, purportedly Iranian and Sudanese. These accusations were extremely serious ones in the context of Mauritania's political system, but on October 11, after ten of the defendants confessed their actions on national television the previous day and promised not to again break the law, President Ould Taya pardoned all sixty Islamic activists. But by this series of arrests and detentions, Ould Taya gave every indication that he intended to enforce the legal prohibition against religious parties, and indeed had publicly stated, about a year before the September arrests, that "we have no lessons to learn about Islam or our Arab roots from religious radicals who know less than us about the language of the Prophet or about our religion."

JAICH AT-TAHRIR. See Army of Liberation

JUDICIAL SYSTEM. Mauritania's legal and judicial institutions have suffered from shortages of resources and qualified personnel, conflicting lines of jurisdiction between French-based and Islamic (q.v.) law, and a lack of political independence. After the end of the French colonial period, the country's legal code was almost entirely French except for a few areas, notably domestic relations, that had traditionally been under the purview of Muslim *qadis* (judges) whose authority continued to be protected. To ensure continuity, the Constitution of Mauritania of May 20, 1961 (q.v.), provided that French laws would apply until a purely Mauritanian system could be instituted. Progress, however, was extremely slow, with the European codes never being entirely replaced and with indigenous lawyers few in number. Moreover, appellate courts were nearly nonexistent and there was no one to examine legislation for its conformity to the constitution. In the early 1970s, new codes were enacted by the government of President Mokhtar Ould Daddah (q.v.) which covered both civil and criminal matters as well as regulatory areas such as labor, administrative and nationality law, and commercial arbitration. Cases brought into court were handled with an almost glacial slowness, a phenomenon that, in the penal area, often entailed long pretrial detention periods. Beyond practical concerns, the court system was never a truly autonomous branch of the government, as the executive invariably held sway over wide areas of Mauritanian life. For example, in January 1966, the signers of the so-called "Manifesto of 19," black Mauritanians who complained to Ould Daddah about perceived racial discrimination and the nascent Arabization policy (q.v.) of the regime, were arrested and detained without charges or trial for six months under a broadly worded national security statute that accorded few rights to the defendant. In 1978, while Mauritania was embroiled in the Western Sahara conflict (q.v.) and just before a *coup d'état* mounted by the armed forces (q.v.) overthrew his civilian government, Ould Daddah pushed legislation through a compliant *Assemblée Nationale* (q.v.) enabling him to detain indefinitely anyone believed to be a threat to public order.

Mauritania's military regimes, the CMRN and the CMSN (qq.v.), who governed the country between July 1978 and April 1992, often disregarded legal processes. Persons could be apprehended and incarcerated without judicial sanction. In addition, the Supreme Court of Mauritania, which had some authority on constitutional matters before 1978, fell under the shadow of the army, whose officers appointed a fixed number of its judges. One area in which the CMSN leader from 1980 to 1984, Colonel Mohammed Khouna Ould Heydallah (q.v.), devoted great energy was the imposition in 1980 of the Islamic *sharia* (q.v.) in criminal cases such as theft, murder, rape, and adultery. The sharia courts, however, suffered from the same maladies as their secular counterparts—untrained personnel, a lack of formalized procedures, and uneven decisions. The rapid infliction of severe punishments was also commonplace, and often included whipping, amputation of feet or hands, and execution by firing squad. Domestic and international pressure forced a halt to these drastic measures in early 1984, and plans to extend the sharia's application to civil and commercial areas never got off the ground.

During the 1980s, the Mauritanian legal system languished. The bloodless "restructuring" of the ruling CMSN that displaced Ould Heydallah and brought Colonel Maaouiya Ould Sid'Ahmed Taya (q.v.) to power on December 12, 1984, did for a time result in an end to arbitrary detention, but few steps were taken to augment the country's slender judicial resources or to improve administration. Pretrial (and extrajudicial) imprisonment was utilized against suspected followers of both the Arab Baath Socialist Party (ABSP) and the *Forces de Libération Africaine de Mauritanie* (FLAM) (qq.v.) during the late 1980s, and trials were often held in a cavalier fashion, with a limited right to defense counsel and with few opportunities to appeal the decision of the tribunal. Of particular concern to some Mauritanian lawyers was the government's liberal use of the summary procedures afforded by the legal rule of *flagrant délit* (literally, "caught in the act"); ordinarily intended to apply only to cases in which a defendant was observed committing an illegal act in the presence of a law enforcement officer, the CMSN extended the doctrine to conspiracy cases and other secret or inchoate crimes. Suspected Baathists or FLAM militants, civil servants, workers, and army officers all were subjected to unchecked governmental power at one time or another, with a low point reached between 1989 and 1991 when the upheavals caused by the Senegal-Mauritania Crisis (q.v.) and a variety of coup plots resulted in the arrest of hundreds, some of whom died in detention.

The Mauritanian Second Republic (q.v.), inaugurated on April 18, 1992, and based on the constitution which had taken effect on July 20, 1991 (q.v.), possesses an expanded and formally independent judicial system. Titles VII and VIII of the constitution set forth, in broad outline, the court structure, including at its apex a High Court of Justice (Article 92), selected jointly by the National Assembly and Mauritania's Senate (q.v.). Below the High Court, tribunals exist in each *département* (q.v.) in the country; these courts have a judge assisted by two laypersons. At one level above these *tribunaux des Moughataas,* each région (q.v.) of the country has its own court, divided into two parts: a "mixed" chamber and a section handling civil and commercial cases. Criminal courts are a separate branch, and there are Courts of Appeal in Nouakchott, Nouadhibou, and Kiffa (qq.v.). A special tribunal exists for adjudicating matters arising out of the labor code: two assessors, one from the employer's side and one from the workers', assist the single magistrate. One other quasi-judicial institution has drawn considerable attention: the Constitutional Council, established under Articles 81–88. Meant to oversee the smooth functioning of the election laws of the Second Republic, as well as to issue opinions when requested on the constitutionality of proposed legislation (Article 86), it has six members serving a nonrenewable term of nine years and appointed either by the President of the Republic or by the parliament's presiding officers. Mauritania's new judicial system is quite sophisticated and the constitution guarantees many basic civil liberties, but the practical impact of the judiciary on the country's affairs remains uncertain in the mid-1990s.

KAEDI. One of Mauritania's largest population (q.v.) centers and the capital of the administrative région of Gorgol (qq.v.), Kaédi is located on the north bank of the Senegal River and is linked by a basic but improving system of roads (q.v.) to the rest of the province. The city saw substantial growth in the 1980s: the government's official statistics showed 30,515 residents in 1988, up from about 20,000 a decade before. It was there that the country's first president, Mokhtar Ould Daddah (q.v.) solidified his hold on Mauritania at a meeting of the ruling *Parti du Peuple Mauritanien* (PPM) (q.v.) held in January 1964 (see KAEDI, CONFERENCE OF). The city is also home to a library of Islamic (q.v.) scholarly works dating back several centuries, and has been a center of commerce (q.v.) in the post-independence period owing to its proximity to Senegal. The central government in Nouakchott (q.v.) devotes considerable efforts to improving agricultural (q.v.) output near Kaédi through its parastatal organization, the *Société Nationale pour le Développement Rural* (SONADER) (q.v.), which set up several large-scale (500 hectares or greater) farming projects to take advantage of the construction of dams and irrigation works by the *Organisation pour la Mise en Valeur du Fleuve Sénégal* (OMVS) (q.v.). Earlier, in 1968, the Ould Daddah regime had set up in Kaédi a National School for Training and Rural Extension (*Ecole Nationale de Formation et Vulgarisation Rurale,* ENFVR) to provide veterinary and other services for livestock (q.v.). There were serious instances of civil unrest in Kaédi after the executions on December 6, 1987, of three Halpulaar armed forces (qq.v.) officers convicted of complicity in a coup attempt a fortnight earlier, protests possibly engineered by the primary black Mauritanian opposition group, the *Forces de Libération Africaine de Mauritanie* (FLAM) (q.v.). Kaédi was also very tense during the Senegal-Mauritania Crisis (q.v.) which began in April 1989 and had a heavy impact on the entire southern part of the country.

KAEDI, CONFERENCE OF (January 28–29, 1964). A key event in post-independence Mauritania's political evolution, the Kaédi Conference was held at the instigation of the country's first president, Mokhtar Ould Daddah (q.v.), and was announced as a seemingly routine meeting of the *Bureau Politique National* (BPN) (q.v.), the top governing body of the ruling *Parti du Peuple Mauritanien* (PPM) (q.v.). But not all could (or would) attend, and when all the BPN members who had decided to come were seated, the area was reportedly sealed off by units of the Mauritanian armed forces (q.v.). President Ould Daddah then took it upon himself to deliver a lengthy speech, denouncing the PPM's "inertia" and "indiscipline" in carrying out his policies and demanding better communication between the party and ordinary Mauritanians. He also called for greater surveillance by PPM supervisors over the rank and file. Ould Daddah then turned his attention to the *Assemblée Nationale* (q.v.), the PPM-dominated national legislature. He criticized "electoralism," by which he apparently meant the practice of trading favors for favorable votes on matters of constituent interest. Henceforth, the president declared, there would be no more free selection of candidates for the National Assembly — the electoral slate would now be approved by the BPN, and all deputies would be required to submit an undated resignation letter to the President of the Republic, which Ould Daddah could invoke at his pleasure. Without any contingent of PPM members who might have questioned these authoritarian measures, the Kaédi Conference fully endorsed them. The conference's outcome marked the end of any semblance of autonomy for the Mauritanian People's Party; thenceforth, until it was disbanded by the army in July 1978, it had little substance other than as conduit for the execution of policy decisions made elsewhere — that is, by Mokhtar Ould Daddah himself.

KAYES, TREATY OF (February 16, 1963). When Mauritania became independent on November 28, 1960, it faced two major foreign relations (q.v.) difficulties. The first was Morocco's territorial claim to the entire country, a problem that was not resolved until April 1970, when diplomatic relations were finally established, and the second was poor relations with Mali, Mauritania's neighbor to the south and east, with whom it shared a land and riverine border of almost 2000 kilometers. Much of the frontier area was in sharp dispute, with serious armed clashes between the armed forces (q.v.) of Mauritania and the Malian army breaking out in 1960 and 1961. These engagements were the direct result of disagreements over the rights of the nomads of the Saharan zone straddling the two states to water resources (q.v.) and pastureland. In addition, the unregulated nature of cross-border commerce (q.v.) was causing anxiety, especially in Mali, whose currency difficulties placed it at a significant disadvantage. Finally, Mali's foreign policy at the time was closely aligned with that of Morocco's King Hassan II (q.v.), who had assumed the throne in 1961, and Mali's President, Modibo Keita, had taken to harboring Mauritanian dissidents who were highly critical of the regime of President Mokhtar Ould Daddah (q.v.). As a consequence, both countries were under considerable pressure to resolve the border question and regularize their troubled relationship.

Discussions regarding the Mali-Mauritania frontier were focused upon two areas, both of them in the far east of Mauritania: the administrative régions of Hodh ech-Chargui and Hodh el-Gharbi (qq.v.). In these zones, boundary lines were fixed solely by the French authorities (as they were throughout Francophone Africa), but since the writ of the colonial government did not effectively operate in these two remote areas, the dividing line was never rigorously laid out. Furthermore, Hodh ech-Chargui had been part of Mauritania only since July 5, 1944, when the governor-general of AOF (q.v.) transferred it from Mali (then known as "Soudan") for reasons of military security related to the availability of troops to quell an intertribal conflict that broke out, for reasons still obscure, in 1940. On October 28, 1944, the AOF authorities made another adjustment of the border at Mali's expense, transferring a substantial portion of Hodh el-Gharbi to Mauritania, abolishing the former frontier line along the Ouadou River south of the town of Ayoun el-Atrouss (q.v.). Very few areas of the border were actually marked, and both states, after independence in 1960, quickly fell into a cycle of misunderstandings, border incidents, and resultant ill-will. Although a convention had been signed by Mali and Mauritania in 1958 essentially freezing the status quo by guaranteeing the nomads of the Hodh free access to the wells of both countries, the problem demanded a lasting solution.

Negotiations were begun between the Keita and Ould Daddah governments after independence, and resulted in the Treaty of Kayes, which was signed at a ceremony at Bamako, the Malian capital, on February 16, 1963. The agreement took its name from the place where the talks were held, in a Malian town located about 110 kilometers southwest of Sélibaby (q.v.). The outcome of the talks was relatively favorable for Mauritania, as it did not have to relinquish significant amounts of territory, although a thin strip of Hodh ech-Chargui in the extreme east was ceded to Mali, as were a few pockets of land in the Western Hodh, usually involving wells upon which the Sahelian nomads in the area depended for survival. Rights of free movement and the system of priorities to the water resources in the Hodh were continued as under the 1958 convention. In the economic sphere, the Treaty of Kayes provided that, to avoid hardships to each country due to the weakness of Mali's currency, the French franc would be the basic unit of exchange between Mali and Mauritania. Also, imports and exports from each state were to be categorized according to the amount of tax or duty that would be levied on each, reportedly with the objective of discouraging "consumption in transit"; that is, a diversion of goods imported through Dakar to Senegalese interests at the expense of others. As a general rule, however, cross-border commerce was to be as free of restriction as possible.

With the signing of the Treaty of Kayes, the Mali-Mauritania relationship was free to develop normally, but uncertainties over the exact location of the long common border continued for the next twenty-five years and were not resolved until May 31, 1988, when Malian and Mauritanian delegations, meeting in Bamako, agreed to delineate comprehensively the frontier. This process was completed about six years later, and on September 12, 1993, the interior ministers of both countries, meeting again at Kayes, signed a convention finalizing the border after discussions that lasted four days. This treaty underscored the generally good relations between the two Sahelian neighbors in the 1980s and early 1990s, although differences with regard to the problem of Tuareg refugees (q.v.) were an irritating factor.

KHOUM. The *khoum* is a subunit of Mauritania's national currency, the *ouguiya* (qq.v.), which was established on June 30, 1973, following the country's decision to withdraw from the French-dominated CFA (q.v.) franc zone. Five khoums make up one ouguiya under this monetary arrangement, and a coin worth one khoum was issued, but given the steady devaluation of the ouguiya over the years, the value of the khoum soon became rather slight.

KIFFA. The administrative center of the Assaba région (qq.v.) of Mauritania, Kiffa's population (q.v.) was put at 29,292 in 1988 according to official statistics, but the real number was probably greater than that, due to the continuing influx into the towns throughout the country caused by drought and desertification (q.v.). The town is located approximately halfway along the *Route de l'Espoir* (q.v.), a paved artery running from the capital, Nouakchott, to Néma (qq.v.). Because of its location on the fringes of southern Mauritania where agriculture (q.v.) is a mainstay of the economy, Kiffa has a mixed Moorish (q.v.) and black population. The town has always been a center of commerce (q.v.) in the area, and has an improved airport (q.v.) with regular service to the rest of the country via the national carrier, Air Mauritanie. Kiffa has also given Mauritania more than its share of political leaders, notably Mustapha Ould Mohammed Salek and Ahmed Ould Bouceif (qq.v.), the country's first two military heads of state, as well as Djibril Ould Abdellahi (q.v.), the influential minister of the interior from 1985 to 1990.

KOUMBI SALEH. One of the most important cities in ancient Mauritania, Koumbi Saleh was the commercial and political center of the Kingdom of Ghana, which flourished in the southern part of the country from about the fifth century A.D. until 1076, when it was defeated, and Koumbi Saleh occupied, by the Almoravids (q.v.), led by the great Islamic (q.v.) campaigner, Abdallah Ibn Yacin. The Kingdom of Ghana, dominated by the Soninké (q.v.), controlled, along with the

Berber Sanhadja Confederation (q.v.), substantial caravan trading routes that passed through Koumbi Saleh on their way to various destinations in Mali and also in the Maghreb. Chroniclers of the period speak of the city's being the most populous and cosmopolitan to be found anywhere in the region, and of its being divided into two sections, one Berber and Muslim and the other Ghanaian. Houses, both palatial and more modest, were constructed of stone by the Berbers, while the Soninké used mud and thatch for their dwellings. Large mosques were also present.

After the sacking of Koumbi Saleh in 1076, the city rapidly lost its importance, although the Kingdom of Ghana remained in existence for another hundred years. A shift in caravan trading patterns away from the area and toward other routes that afforded more convenient access to the European-occupied *entrepôts* along the Mediterranean coast, sealed the fate of the city, but its companion trading towns in Mauritania, Aoudaghost and Oualata (qq.v.), continued to be important centers well into the sixteenth century. Koumbi Saleh quickly fell into ruins after the Almoravid conquest, and is today of purely historical interest, with no permanent inhabitants. It is situated about seventy kilometers southeast of Timbédra in the administrative région of Hodh ech-Chargui (qq.v.) and about twenty-five kilometers from the border with Mali. Reached by a gravel road (q.v.) which branches off the *Route de l'Espoir* (q.v.) at Timbédra, it is one of Mauritania's most significant archeological sites.

LA GUERA. Located within Western Sahara (q.v.) near the southwestern tip of the Cape Blanc (Ras Nouadhibou) peninsula about three kilometers from the city of Nouadhibou (q.v.), La Guera served from about 1920 to 1975 as a small fishing port and military base, its importance always overshadowed by Nouadhibou as well as by the larger Spanish town of Villa Cisneros (q.v.) farther up the coast. Its population was only about 1200 in 1974. As part of Spain's colony, the settlement was included in the Mauritanian sector of Western Sahara pursuant to the Moroccan-Mauritanian Conventions of April 14, 1976 (q.v.), which formalized the division of territory agreed upon by the two claimant states in the Madrid Agreement (q.v.) of the previous November. Spanish troops were quickly pulled out of La Guera, leaving it briefly in the hands of the guerrillas of the Polisario Front (q.v.), who were in turn displaced by Mauritania's armed forces (q.v.) on December 19, 1975. For the remainder of Mauritania's involvement in the Western Sahara conflict, La Guera was considered part of Tiris el-Gharbia (q.v.), although technically it was administered as part of the région of Dakhlet-Nouadhibou (qq.v.). After undergoing severe military and economic reverses at the hands of Polisario as well as a change of regime in Nouakchott (q.v.), Mauritania made peace with the Saharawi (q.v.) nationalist organization and relinquished its claim to Tiris el-Gharbia by means of the Algiers Agreement (q.v.) in August 1979. But after Mauritania's military rulers saw Morocco immediately occupy all of their country's former zone after they had withdrawn, they declined to leave La Guera, fearing the presence of Moroccan troops only a stone's throw from the vital fishing and iron ore (qq.v.) facilities of Nouadhibou. Stating that Mauritanian troops would remain only until a definitive settlement to the Western Sahara question was reached, and insisting that no territorial claim was implied, a small garrison was stationed there, its uneventful presence disrupted only by a brief shelling by a Moroccan gunboat on January 20, 1983, which resulted in no casualties. La Guera remained under Mauritanian control in 1996.

LAMANTIN, OPERATION. See Operation Lamantin

LAND REFORM ACT (of June 5, 1983). Promulgated as Ordinance 83.127 by the ruling military council of Mauritania, the CMSN (q.v.), then headed by Colonel Mohammed Khouna Ould Heydallah (q.v.), the Land Reform Act was intended to regularize the relationship of the country's citizens to the fertile agricultural (q.v.) land along the Senegal River Valley, and in so doing open substantial new tracts of land to cultivation. But the language of the law and the manner in which it was reportedly applied affected more than Mauritania's output of urgently needed foodstuffs: it elicited questions about the relations between the Moorish population (qq.v.) of the country and the Black African groups in the southern administrative régions (q.v.). Secondarily, the act raised issues concerning the application of the Islamic *sharia* (qq.v.) to those persons who had not traditionally structured their land tenure patterns around it, but had instead relied upon a more communal set of customs that sometimes predated the conversion of those Mauritanians to the Muslim faith.

The economic motivations for the regime of President Ould Heydallah to pass the law was, in the opinion of many outside observers, beyond question, given that the 1970s and early 1980s were exceedingly difficult ones for Mauritanian agriculture, with crop yields in virtually every région that would support a pastoral economy registering steep declines. This phenomenon was traceable to severe, extended droughts and the seemingly inexorable process of desertification (q.v.), which caused an exodus of rural inhabitants to the country's cities and towns, where they became dependent on foreign food assistance. Furthermore, much arable land situated in the provinces of Assaba, Brakna, Gorgol, Guidimaka, and Hodh el-Gharbi (qq.v.) was fallow or in the hands of no clearly identifiable owner, whether black or Moorish. Finally, it was envisioned by the CMSN that the dam projects in the Senegal River Valley constructed by the *Organisation pour la Mise en Valeur du Fleuve Sénégal* (OMVS) (q.v.) would, when completed (as they were in the late 1980s) result in additional hectarage being available for agricultural purposes. Therefore, it was felt imperative that as much unproductive land as possible be brought into use to feed growing numbers of Mauritanians, and that ownership of those lands be given to those persons willing to improve them.

The most important—and controversial—parts of the law were the first four articles:

Article 1: The land belongs to the nation and to every Mauritanian without discrimination of any kind who may, in conformity with the law, become the owner of part thereof;

Article 2: The State recognizes and guarantees the private ownership of land which, in accordance with the sharia, must contribute to the social and economic development of the country;

Article 3: The traditional system of land tenure is hereby abolished;

Article 4: Any right of ownership which is not directly connected with an individual or with a legal entity, or which does not arise from a legally protected development, is hereby declared nonexistent.

Other sections of the new law stated that "dead" (unused) tracts of land, or those which had no owner, were to revert to state ownership (Articles 9 and 11), that under some circumstances the state could take land under the principle of eminent domain (Article 21), and that the water resources (q.v.) of the country would be opened to public use if they lay outside a legally recognized property interest (Article 22).

By abolishing "traditional" systems of land tenure, the CMSN laid itself open to charges of racial discrimination, since this system, in which land was passed through the generations as the property of extended families, was common among black Mauritanians. This system did not strictly conform to the sharia, which was a more individually based, recorded method of real estate purchase and sale not wholly dissimilar from that found in Western societies. To drive this point home, the law stated that "individual ownership shall be mandatory" (Article 6).

By the 1983 Land Reform Act, the governing military committee appeared to be providing a powerful new tool for land purchases which could benefit most Mauritanians, but it also allegedly made it more difficult for Black Africans to prove ownership of land they had cultivated for decades, and conceivably lose their land to wealthy Moors who would purchase legally vacant land, register their interest in accord with the sharia, and then cultivate it, with the former black Mauritanian possessors reduced to the status of tenants. On the other hand, the opening of new lands for cultivation did provide many economic opportunities for the *haratines* (q.v.), the ex-slaves who, upon gaining freedom from their servile status, often had few or no prospects for an independent existence. Resentment by black Mauritanians of the Land Reform Act was not universal; moreover, prosperous black farmers near the Senegal River saw its passage as a chance to increase their own holdings. It was also considered possible by some commentators that some black Mauritanian groups owned their lands communally, but in the name of the chief of the clan or village, thereby satisfying the law's requirement of individual ownership.

Despite a land tenure system that appeared to be in considerable flux by the early 1990s and which lent itself to varying interpretations, some Black Africans in Mauritania saw the Land Reform Act as a legal artifice meant to dispossess them as part of a conscious government strategy of Arabization (q.v.). The law was strongly condemned by the country's primary black opposition group, the *Forces de Libération Africaine de Mauritanie* (FLAM) (q.v.), in its forcefully argued pamphlet, *Le Manifesto du Négro-Mauritanien Opprimé* (q.v.) issued in April 1986. Problems over land issues may also have been at least partly responsible for the increase in ethnic tension that became part of Mauritanian political life in the late 1980s, and according to some even played a role in igniting the Senegal-Mauritania Crisis (q.v.) in April 1989, which led to a condition of near-war between the two countries.

Ironically the Land Reform Act of June 1983 seemed, by the early 1990s, to have been something of a success story—crop yields were generally on the increase, and the Mauritanian government, led since December 1984 by Maaouiya Ould Sid'Ahmed Taya (q.v.), was earmarking more national resources to the black-dominated south. Still, troubling questions remained concerning the imposition of one system of land ownership at the expense of other methods adhered to by substantial numbers of Mauritania's citizens.

LE MANIFESTO DU NEGRO-MAURITANIEN OPPRIME. See Manifesto du Negro-Mauritanien Opprimé

LIVESTOCK. Traditionally, animal husbandry has served as a critical means of economic support in Mauritania, although herd size has fluctuated greatly due to the country's harsh climate (q.v.) and the process of desertification (q.v.), which both have a severe impact on the availability and quality of pasturelands. Several species of animal are raised, with Moorish (q.v.) Mauritanians centered in the northern régions (q.v.) relying mainly on camels and goats, while the Halpulaaren (q.v.) and other Black Africans in and near the Senegal River

Valley possess herds of sheep and cattle as well as goats. Also present throughout Mauritania are a limited number of horses and donkeys, although these, like the camel, are often utilized only as beasts of burden. The predominant species of cattle is the zebu, divided into two varieties: the lighter, short-horned *Maure,* owned by nomadic Moors in the north, and the heavier, long-horned subspecies, the *Peul,* which is found in the south and prefers a riverine environment. Long-horned cattle also tend to be the choice of black Mauritanians to supplement their often precarious agricultural (q.v.) holdings.

Mauritania's livestock sector first began to suffer serious problems in the early 1970s, when droughts afflicted the entire Sahel. According to some estimates, between 65 and 70 percent of the sheep, 30 to 40 percent of all cows and goats, and 15 to 20 percent of all camels had perished by 1975, with the efforts made by the government of President Mokhtar Ould Daddah (q.v.) to replenish herds and prevent overgrazing proving almost totally ineffectual. Overgrazing also exacerbated the desertification problem, further decimating herds and driving their owners off their rural lands and into the already overcrowded cities and towns. By 1981, herd size had decreased by as much as 50 percent and the number of people engaged in animal husbandry fell to about 35 percent, only half the 1973 ratio. Furthermore, the attitudes of successive governments often ensured the neglect of the rural sector, as preference was given, until 1985, to industrial development (q.v.) programs that often proved uneconomic. Droughts also caused many herders to move to the better-watered precincts of Mali and Senegal, if they were not compelled to slaughter their herds to stay alive. The CMSN (q.v.) regime of Colonel Mohammed Khouna Ould Heydallah (q.v.) did make some effort to rebuild herds and provide rural extension services, but its primary response to the crisis was to form a state agency, the *Société Mauritanienne de la Commercialisation du Bétail* (SOMECOB), with a legal monopoly on the marketing and export of beef, augmented by a system of guaranteed prices. This proved unworkable in practice, as patterns of commerce (q.v.) in Mauritania had long eluded any effort to exert centralized control. The livestock crisis still seemed impervious to a solution by 1984, with drought, desertification, and out-migration of herds combining to render an estimated 70 percent of the country's 800,000 cattle vulnerable to extinction, a predicament also shared by 5 million goats and sheep and half a million otherwise resilient camels.

The government's priorities changed drastically after the accession to power of Colonel Maaouiya Ould Sid'Ahmed Taya (q.v.) as head of state on December 12, 1984. Almost at once, the rural areas of Mauritania were targeted for a greater share of state expenditures.

SOMECOB's formal monopoly was ended by the early 1990s, and rural agencies, especially the *Direction Nationale d'Elevage* (DNE) and the *Société Nationale pour le Développement Rural* (SONADER) (q.v.), were reorganized. The DNE, for example, was instructed to devote more of its energies to animal vaccination to enable cattle to resist disease. Helped by increasing rainfall and a slowing of desertification, herd size began to recover in the late 1980s, though by 1987 the number of goats and sheep was still 20 percent less than it had been a decade earlier. After 1987 livestock resources rapidly rebounded, so much so that many herders moved their animals back into Mauritania from Mali and Senegal. By 1991 there were an estimated 1.4 million cattle and 7.5 million sheep and goats in the country's pasturelands, accounting for fully 20 percent of Mauritania's total gross domestic product (GDP). By the mid-1990s, herds had multiplied almost back to predrought levels, and although the threat of another drought was ever-present, the outlook for the livestock sector appeared reasonably bright.

LOCAL COUNCILS. See Conseils Locaux

LOI CADRE. Promulgated by the French government of Premier Guy Mollet in June 1956, the *loi cadre,* an "outline" or "enabling" law, provided the basic framework for the future independence of most of France's African colonies, including Mauritania. In practical terms, the loi cadre abolished the highly centralized *Grand Conseil d'AOF* (q.v.) which had been set up in 1946 by the Fourth French Republic, and strengthened the role of the native populations in the *Assemblées Territoriales* (q.v.) which had existed since 1952 and which had themselves replaced the *Conseils Généraux* (q.v.). In addition, local councils (q.v.) were also restructured to give more representation to Africans, and henceforth three to six "ministers" were to be chosen by the Territorial Assemblies, supposedly by a form of indirect universal suffrage. However, the authority of these bodies was still restricted by the fact that France continued to possess full powers over matters of defense, foreign affairs, and certain economic questions. At the apex of this revamped structure was the *Conseil de Gouvernement* (q.v.) whose president was still a Frenchman but whose vice-president would be the territory's most prominent politician, a position filled in Mauritania by Mokhtar Ould Daddah (q.v.). More broadly, the passage of the loi cadre signalled the end of France's proclaimed effort to integrate its colonies culturally and politically with the metropole, and indicated a realization by Paris that, far from producing contentment, its *mission civilistrice* had created resentments and nationalist aspirations that could not be indefinitely ignored or suppressed.

MAAOUIYA OULD SID'AHMED TAYA. Mauritania's fifth military leader since the assumption of power by the armed forces (q.v.) in July 1978 and the first head of state in the country's history to institute limited democratic reforms, Maaouiya Ould Sid'Ahmed Taya was born in 1943 in the vicinity of Atar (q.v.) into a small Moorish (q.v.) tribe of traders and merchants, the Semissides. When he was aged five years, Ould Taya, like a great many of his compatriots, received a rigorous Islamic (q.v.) education, studying the *Koran* and other Muslim texts for upwards of ten hours a day for the next three years. In about 1951, he was enrolled in a "regular" school in Atar, where he developed an aptitude for mathematics and caught the eye of the school's director, who recommended to his parents that he attend a *lycée* in the town of Rosso (q.v.) in the Senegal River Valley. Thus, from November 1955 to June 1959, Ould Taya was a student at this institution, which prided itself on training a future Mauritanian (and other West African) administrative elite, since independence for those territories was at that time clearly imminent. In early 1960, diploma in hand, the teenaged Maaouiya decided to enlist as an officer candidate in the embryonic army of his homeland. With the encouragement of his father, he made his way to St. Louis, Senegal, then the governmental center of Mauritania, to enroll, and from there he was dispatched to Atar, where he took five months of basic military courses. His performance there so impressed his instructors, reportedly, that he was chosen to attend the prestigious *Ecole Militaire de Cavalérie* at Saumur, France. Graduating in May 1961 (after entering in November 1960), Ould Taya returned to Mauritania where, as a newly-commissioned lieutenant in command of a small unit of men, undertook a 1000-kilometer patrol of the rugged, sometimes obstreperous administrative régions of Hodh ech-Chargui and Hodh el-Gharbi (qq.v.), the results of which gave President Mokhtar Ould Daddah (q.v.) a clearer idea of the political and social conditions prevailing in the far east of Mauritania. Ould Taya returned to Nouakchott (q.v.) at the age of twenty-one.

Ould Taya's military career had by this time achieved distinguished dimensions. At the end of 1963, he was again selected to travel to France, this time to attend the *Ecole d'Application de l'Infantérie* at St. Maxen on a nine-month course, during which time he met many of his future officer colleagues, including Mohammed Ould Bah Ould Abdel Kader and Mustapha Ould Mohammed Salek (qq.v.). Upon receiving his degree from that institution, he once more returned to Rosso, Mauritania, where, in the absence of an immediate army posting, he was a teacher at a secondary school for about the next two years. From 1966 to 1974, though, Ould Taya began to occupy a series of increasingly responsible positions in the small Mauritanian officer corps, including command of a unit at Nouadhibou (q.v.), a period of service in the *deuxième bureau* (intelligence corps) in Nouakchott, a prized posting as President Ould Daddah's *aide-de-camp,* and assignment as *chef de poste* in Akjoujt and F'Derik (qq.v.). At the end of 1974, moreover, Ould Taya traveled to France for a third time, to attend the top-ranked *Ecole supérieure de guerre* in Paris. He acquitted himself well there, but the Mauritania to which he returned in December 1975 was about to be changed forever. His country stood on the brink of full-scale involvement in the Western Sahara conflict (q.v.), which President Ould Daddah had made inevitable by his adherence, with Morocco, to the so-called Madrid Agreement of November 14, 1975 (q.v.), by which the former Spanish colony was partitioned between Rabat and Nouakchott without reference to either the desires of the native Saharawi (q.v.) people or to the threats of armed action by the nascent Western Saharan liberation movement, the Polisario Front (q.v.).

Only a matter of days after Commandant (Major) Maaouiya Ould Sid'Ahmed Taya arrived back in Mauritania after his spell in France, Polisario's guerrilla forces staged some of their first attacks against Mauritanian targets, striking at the economically vital (and militarily vulnerable) iron ore railway (qq.v.) line running from Nouadhibou to Zouerate (q.v.). President Ould Daddah, realizing that he and his small nation could be headed for a serious war, immediately sent Ould Taya back to Paris, where he held urgent consultations with the French government with a view to acquiring much-needed weaponry for the country's army. After successfully fulfilling his mission in France, Ould Taya got his first real taste of combat in early 1976, when he was successively appointed deputy chief of military operations and commander of the vital Mauritanian garrison at Bir Moghrein (q.v.). In the latter assignment especially, the full ramifications of the Saharan war were driven home, as the whole area was under nearly constant assault by Polisario. Gradually, and in common with many of his fellow officers, Ould Taya became frustrated with the seemingly endless and unwinnable Western Sahara war and reportedly shared in the suspicions felt by many that Mauritania was risking its very independence as a nation, in part by allowing Morocco to station its troops in the country pursuant to the agreement setting up the Moroccan-Mauritanian Defense Committee (q.v.), which was signed on May 13, 1977 after a period of particularly sharp military reverses.

Consequently, Ould Taya fully supported the nonviolent *coup d'état* of July 10, 1978, which displaced President Ould Daddah and instituted military rule in the form of the *Comité Militaire de Redressement National* (CMRN) (q.v.). The CMRN, led by Colonel Mustapha Ould Mohammed Salek, counted Ould Taya as one of its members from the start, and by January 1979, although not yet a full colonel, he was appointed the ruling council's permanent secretary in charge of the Defense Ministry, in effect becoming minister of defense. He held that post only for the next two months, however, as Ould Salek was forced to relinquish his powers on April 5, 1979, after his assumption of near-dictatorial authority on March 20 had alienated many in the government. Lieutenant Colonel Ould Taya, although still a member of the *Comité Militaire de Salut National* (CMSN) (q.v.), the CMRN's successor, left the government and became commander of the *Gendarmerie Nationale* (q.v.). He held that post until early in 1980, by which time a series of complicated maneuvers within the CMSN had ended with the assumption of most real power in mid-1979 by Lieutenant Colonel Mohammed Khouna Ould Heydallah (q.v.).

Throughout this extremely unstable period in the post-independence history of Mauritania, Ould Taya retained his reputation as a diligent, honest, and relatively non-political soldier with a thoroughly professional and nationalistic outlook. Importantly, he managed to remain aloof from the ethnic and tribal infighting that characterized the early years of army governance, a phenomenon aggravated by the division of the officer corps into pro-Polisario and pro-Moroccan factions, among others. After the accession of Ould Heydallah and his consolidation of power in January 1980, Ould Taya was restored to favor, becoming army chief of staff. In that position, he narrowly escaped death at the hands of the conspirators of the exiled *Alliance pour une Mauritanie Démocratique* (AMD) (q.v.), who staged a bloody coup attempt against the CMSN on March 16, 1981, in the process taking Ould Taya prisoner. But he escaped from captivity in time to help rally loyalist forces to defeat the plotters, who were mostly rounded up in the next few days and executed. Ould Heydallah, in recognition of his counterpart's role in preserving his government, promoted him to prime minister and minister of defense in April 1981, by way of returning to direct military rule and dismissing a civilian cabinet chosen in December 1980. This reshuffle made Ould Taya the second most powerful person in Mauritania.

For the moment, Ould Taya and Ould Heydallah were colleagues with a close working relationship, but this state of affairs was not destined to last. The Mauritanian head of state soon embarked on a personalized and—according to some—high-handed form of government, reportedly tolerating corruption and instituting frequent changes in the regime's personnel to keep various factions in check. In the area of foreign relations (q.v.), Ould Heydallah leaned increasingly toward the Polisario Front after Mauritania's successful exit from the Western Sahara conflict in August 1979, when the Algiers Agreement (q.v.) was negotiated with the Saharawi nationalists. Above all, Ould Heydallah was perceived by some CMSN members as eroding the carefully-crafted collegiality and collective decision-making that they believed essential. Ould Heydallah went so far as to recognize formally Polis-ario's government-in-exile, the Saharan Arab Democratic Republic (SADR) (q.v.) on February 27, 1984, apparently without telling Ould Taya or any of his fellow officers of the decision. Ould Taya, who reportedly had some reservations about setting up diplomatic ties with the SADR, was demoted back to army chief of staff two weeks later in early March after he spoke his mind on this and other issues.

On December 12, 1984, while Ould Heydallah was out of the country, Ould Taya, assisted by Lieutenant Colonel Anne Ahmadou Babaly (q.v.), a leading CMSN member and a Halpulaar (q.v.) from the Senegal River Valley, staged a bloodless coup in which he assumed the presidency. Almost immediately, he made his mark: he distanced himself from his predecessor's recognition of the SADR, restored diplomatic relations with Morocco which had been severed after the March 1981 coup attempt, freed most political prisoners, and enacted firm measures against those engaged in corrupt practices and influence-peddling on behalf of foreign interests, including Libya. He also moved somewhat closer to France and the conservative Gulf monarchies as a means of preserving traditional sources of urgently needed financial assistance. In sum, Ould Taya's first years appeared to signal a return to a consensus-based style of CMSN rule, greater regularity in domestic and foreign policy, and less frequent changes on the Council of Ministers (q.v.).

But even as Colonel Ould Taya embarked on a cautious process of democratization by holding remarkably free municipal elections in December 1986, the situation within the country was worsening. Ethnic tensions were on the rise, and Ould Taya found it desirable to repress the activities of the influential Arab Baath Socialist Party (ABSP) (q.v.), which had been active in Mauritania since about 1980 but which was enjoying greater visibility due to the growing strength of its main backer, Iraqi President Saddam Hussein. In September 1987 and July 1988, many Baathists, including a former minister of information, Mohammed Yehdih Ould Breideleil (q.v.), were jailed, allegedly for acting on behalf of Baghdad. Similar measures were also taken against the resurgent (and exiled) black Mauritanian opposition group, the *Forces de Libération Africaine de Mauritanie* (FLAM) (q.v.). However much these actions generated criticism amongst human rights professionals and other international observers, they were entirely in keeping with Ould Taya's strongly nationalistic orientation, which manifested itself in the 1980s in a suspicion of most foreign attempts to gain an inordinate degree of influence in the CMSN's councils, whether in the form of the Iraq-sponsored Baath Party or the FLAM organization, whose leaders were seen by the regime as separatists acting as agents of Senegal and other states.

President Ould Taya's most difficult period as the Mauritanian head of state still lay ahead of him. The Black African criticism of his government did not abate, and the Baathists showed little sign of being cowed by the CMSN's clampdown, since they were trained by their Iraqi sponsors for precisely such an eventuality. It was at this point, according to some observers of Mauritania's political landscape, that Ould Taya began to lose influence and become progressively isolated. An invidious dynamic appeared to be at work: the more strident advocacy of Black African interests by the FLAM led to a reaction among some Beydane (q.v.) Moors in favor of the pan-Arab Baath Party, by degrees tightening the screws on the black opposition, in turn further heightening Baathist influence within and close to the CMSN. For his part, President Ould Taya felt obliged to follow up his own visit to Iraq in December 1988 with another *tête-à-tête* with Saddam Hussein in October 1989, during the first, most intense stages of the Senegal-Mauritania crisis (q.v.).

Iraq's invasion of Kuwait on August 2, 1990, which touched off the Gulf Crisis and the Gulf War (q.v.), was a time of acute economic and political hardship and uncertainty for Mauritania, but it also provided an opportunity for Ould Taya. With Saddam Hussein progressively isolated by economic sanctions, quarantined by a United States-led military buildup on Iraq's borders, and forcibly ejected from Kuwait in January and February 1991, Iraq was prevented from exercising sway over Mauritania, allowing Ould Taya's men—that is, those of a nationalist and "neutralist" proclivity—to reassert themselves. Soon after the end of the Gulf War, President Ould Taya surprised many commentators by announcing the legalization of multiple political parties in the country for the first time since 1960, the holding of a referendum for a new constitution (enacted on July 20, 1991) (q.v.), and contested presidential elections, the first instance of this in any Arab state. When the elections were finally held on January 17, 1992, the president emerged triumphant, winning over 62 percent of the votes cast. Although opinion was divided over whether the election was completely free and fair, the fact that Ould Taya's main opponent, Ahmed Ould Daddah (q.v.), finished with a respectable 33 percent seemed to rule out the possibility of a preordained outcome.

Bestowed with a degree of legitimacy unprecedented in Mauritanian history, President Ould Taya moved swiftly to hold elections for the *Assemblée Nationale* and the Senate (qq.v.), the two chambers of Mauritania's bicameral legislature. But this phase of the democratization process was marred by an opposition boycott motivated by allegations of fraud in the voting for president. Consequently, Ould Taya's political organization, the *Parti Républicain, Démocratique et Social* (PRDS) (q.v.), had little trouble in taking the lion's share of the seats in each house (thirty-six out of fifty-six in the Senate and sixty-seven of seventy-nine in the National Assembly). On April 18, 1992, Ould Taya was inaugurated as President of the Mauritanian Second Republic (q.v.), an act which was accompanied by the formal disbanding of the CMSN and the installation of a new civilian cabinet headed by a respected financial specialist and economist, Sidi Mohamed Ould Boubacar (q.v.), and in which the only military representative was Colonel Ahmed Ould Minnih (q.v.), who held the defense portfolio.

By 1996, President Ould Taya's position appeared to be fairly secure. However, the problems facing Mauritania, including tribal and ethnic divisions, desertification (q.v.), a troubled economy, the uncertain relations with Senegal, and a worrying emergence of Islamic fundamentalist activity in 1994 and renewed Baathist agitation in October 1995, ensured that his attentions were always fully engaged. Through all of these difficulties, Ould Taya's governing strategy has combined the symbolic and the substantive, in that he has attempted, in his low-key, unpretentious manner, to serve as the focus of national unity in a still-divided country while ceaselessly balancing many separate and competing interests. These were, in fact, functions which the Mauritanian presidency has performed since independence.

MADRID AGREEMENT (Of November 14, 1975). A still secret treaty signed by the representatives of Spain, Morocco, and Mauritania, under the terms of which Madrid's colony of Western Sahara (q.v.) would be handed over to the governments of King Hassan II and Mokhtar Ould Daddah (qq.v.). Spain officially denied that it was transferring full sovereignty over its Saharan possession—it merely stated (in a six-paragraph declaration of principles that was made public) that it was ceding only temporary administrative authority to the two claimant states pending a referendum or other type of consultation with the indigenous Saharawi (q.v.) population. The Madrid Agreement marked a new spirit of *entente* between Hassan II and Ould Daddah, who by signing the accord buried their often embarrassing duplicate claims to all of Western Sahara, settling instead for a roughly two-thirds/one-third division of the territory, with the largest and most useful part going to Rabat, a partition finalized by the Moroccan-Mauritanian Conventions of April 14, 1976 (q.v.).

For Spain, the crisis over Western Sahara came at a particularly delicate moment. Longtime Spanish dictator Francisco Franco had fallen gravely ill on the eve of what could have become a military showdown with Morocco, since, on November 6, King Hassan had sent tens of thousands of unarmed civilians across the border into Saguia el-Hamra (q.v.) in a so-called "Green March" to claim its "amputated Saharan province." Under intense political pressure and preoccupied with internal affairs (Franco eventually died on November 20), Spain embraced the concept of a trilateral accord excluding the Saharawis with alacrity.

For Mauritania, the signing of the Madrid Agreement marked the beginning of a disastrous venture that came close to unraveling the country, since President Ould Daddah's armed forces (q.v.) proved unable to fend off attacks by the Polisario Front (q.v.), a Saharawi nationalist organization that advocated an independent Western Saharan state. After the country's virtual defeat at the hands of Polisario, Mauritania formally ceased to be a party to the Madrid accord, signing the Algiers Agreement (q.v.) on August 5, 1979, under which it renounced its claim to Western Sahara. The Madrid Agreement also contained a number of subsidiary clauses providing for joint Spanish-Mauritanian-Moroccan fisheries (q.v.) and phosphate extraction projects, but these were not implemented and were quickly forgotten.

MA EL-AININ, Cheikh. One of northwest Africa's most prominent anticolonial leaders, Cheikh Ma el-Ainin (whose name means "water of the eyes") was born around 1830–31 in southeastern Mauritania, possibly in the modern-day région of Hodh ech-Chargui (qq.v.). Originally called Mohammed Sidi el-Mustapha, he quickly acquired a reputation for physical stamina and intellectual accomplishment, particularly because of his extensive knowledge and practice of Islam (q.v.). After being sent by his family to be educated in Morocco (around 1847), he engaged primarily in commercial activities from 1852 to about 1885, but increasingly became disturbed at the growing incursions of the Spanish government into Western Sahara (q.v.) at the time. At the beginning of the twentieth century, he shifted his attentions farther south, to Mauritania, where certain groups, notably the Oulad Berri, a *zawiya* (q.v.) tribe, were succumbing to the blandishments of the French, led by Xavier Coppolani (q.v.), and allowing Paris to establish sovereignty over Brakna and Trarza (qq.v.) in 1902. As a step in the direction of consolidating his already great influence, Ma el-Ainin set to work building the city of Smara, located in eastern Saguia el-Hamra (q.v.) where Spanish control had not yet been established. He then decided to use all possible means to repel French incursions in the Adrar (q.v.), deducing—correctly—that Xavier Coppolani's next campaign would be focused there. On May 12, 1905, a detachment of men loyal to the cheikh succeeded in killing Coppolani at his home in Tidjikja (q.v.). For a few years, the French advance toward the Adrar was stopped as Paris reassessed its strategy, eventually opting for a purely military solution to the problem, in contrast to Coppolani's mix of peaceful and more violent means. The years 1907 and

1908 marked the zenith of Ma el-Ainin's fortunes in Mauritania, due in large part to his success in procuring weapons from Spain and Germany, who were anxious to curb French influence. This period was characterized by a series of brutal campaigns waged by the cheikh's followers not only against France but also against those Mauritanian tribes who chose to ally themselves with Paris. These raids, however, failed to budge the French from Tagant (q.v.), and a parallel anticolonial effort by Moulay Idriss, the uncle of Moulay Abdelaziz, the Moroccan sultan, was equally inconclusive. In the meantime, Xavier Coppolani had been replaced as governor-general of France's Mauritanian colony by Colonel (later General) Henri Gouraud (q.v.), who with several years of "pacification" experience in "Soudan" (Mali) behind him, launched a massive endeavor to subdue the Adrar beginning in January 1909 (see ADRAR CAMPAIGN). Gouraud's men proved too much for Ma el-Ainin's forces, which were led by two of his sons, Hassena and el-Oueli, the cheikh himself remaining well out of harm's way in Smara. By July 1909, the cheikh's resistance had been decisively crushed, leaving Ma el-Ainin with little alternative but to return to Morocco, where he continued to oppose any moves toward compromise with the French by the new sultan (from 1908), Moulay Hafid. In what turned out to be the cheikh's last effort to assume undisputed spiritual and political leadership in the region, he proclaimed himself sultan in 1910 and rallied a force of Saharawi (q.v.) and other tribesmen to depose Moulay Hafid. But Ma el-Ainin was defeated on June 23 by the French army and he then retired to Tiznit, southern Morocco, where he died on October 28, 1910.

MANIFESTO DU NEGRO-MAURITANIEN OPPRIME. Circulated both inside Mauritania and abroad beginning in April 1986, the appearance of the Manifesto of the Oppressed Black Mauritanian marked the start of an intense round of ethnic disharmony in Mauritanian society and politics, and was also the clearest indication up to that time of the determination of the exiled (and illegal) black opposition movement, the *Forces de Libération Africaine de Mauritanie* (FLAM) (q.v.) to battle by whatever means it considered necessary the CMSN (q.v.) government headed by President Maaouiya Ould Sid'Ahmed Taya (q.v.). The Manifesto itself was a French-language pamphlet, approximately fifty pages in length and polemical in tone, that detailed alleged racial discrimination against black Mauritanians, especially the Halpulaaren (q.v.), since the country's independence in 1960. After recounting Mauritania's earlier instance of conflict between Black Africans and Moors (q.v.) under the regime of President Mokhtar Ould Daddah (q.v.) in 1966, which involved a decided shift in governmental policy toward Arabization (q.v.), the FLAM document stated that most government ministries were controlled by Moors, and that the numbers of black Mauritanians in the bureaucracy and in the officer corps of the armed forces (q.v.) were far less than their proportion of the total Mauritanian population (q.v.). The highest positions in the army, for example, supposedly nearly always went to Beydanes (q.v.). FLAM argued that similar discrimination also existed in Mauritania's diplomatic representation in other countries: it believed that diplomats (and especially ambassadors) were overwhelmingly Moorish, and that the country maintained diplomatic missions in a far greater number of Arab League (q.v.) states than Black African countries. In Mauritania's economic life, particularly the "modern" sector, the situation was much the same in the eyes of the writers of the Manifesto. FLAM charged that the heads of the major parastatal companies in Mauritania were almost entirely Moors, as were the officers and higher-ranking employees of the country's important banking system (q.v.). The document also condemned Mauritania's foreign relations (q.v.) orientation toward the Arab League and away from Black Africa, and alleged that the Mauritanian communications (q.v.) media, especially radio, were guilty of discrimination by not sponsoring sufficient programming in languages spoken predominantly by black Mauritanians, such as French, Fulani, Sarakolé, and Wolof (qq.v.).

FLAM's manifesto saved two aspects of Mauritanian life for particularly vehement criticism. It alleged racism in the application of the Land Reform Act of June 5, 1983 (q.v.), which modified the land tenure system in the agricultural (q.v.) region of the country in the Senegal River Valley and gave the state a greater role in allocating "dead" or fallow hectarage in southern Mauritania. The Manifesto characterized the law as a means by which black Mauritanians, who adhered to a land ownership system sometimes at odds with the Islamic *sharia* (qq.v.), could be dispossessed in favor of Moorish immigrants from the north. FLAM also feared that, by a series of legal artifices, large blocks of land would be awarded to Beydane-dominated agribusinesses and force their Black African or *haratine* (q.v.) former owners into the status of tenants, and that some CMSN members and well-connected government officials—many of whom it identified by name—would be the prime beneficiaries of the new land ownership arrangements. Mauritania's system of education (q.v.) was also castigated: the Manifesto accused the minister of education for most of the 1980s, Hasni Ould Didi (q.v.), of aggressively Arabizing the schools, neglecting the teaching of African languages beyond the primary level, imposing Arabic language and culture upon a whole generation of Black Africans, and of sabotaging the reforms in educational life that were introduced in the early 1980s by the then-chairman of the CMSN, Colonel Mohammed Khouna Ould Heydallah (q.v.).

Whatever the merits of the arguments it presented (many of which were dependent upon the actual numbers of black Mauritanians in the country), the appearance of the Manifesto of the Oppressed Black Mauritanian facilitated a quantum jump in the level of publicity accorded FLAM, helped in large part by the distribution of its pamphlet at international conferences, notably those held by the nonaligned movement and the Organization of African Unity (OAU). But the effect of the FLAM document was felt most clearly inside Mauritania itself, where its publication touched off a massive search for its authors, an effort reportedly led by a powerful CMSN member, Lieutenant Colonel Djibril Ould Abdellahi (q.v.), who was able soon afterward to reassume his old post as minister of the interior, wrestling the key portfolio out of the hands of a prominent Halpulaar officer, Lieutenant Colonel Anne Ahmadou Babaly (q.v.). The Black African chairman of the *Banque Centrale de Mauritanie* (BCM) (q.v.) was also sacked, and many other dismissals in the army and civil service followed. In September 1986 a total of twenty-one black Mauritanians were brought to trial in Nouakchott (q.v.) and charged with being the authors of the Manifesto, with belonging to an illegal organization (i.e., FLAM), and with holding unauthorized meetings. The defendants denied their guilt, but all were convicted on September 25 and sentenced to between six months' and five years' imprisonment, in proceedings that lasted only a single day. Several of those convicted were later to die in detention (in September 1988) at the remote prison fortress at Oualata (q.v.) in circumstances that elicited severe international criticism. The Manifesto's appearance had given the Ould Taya regime its first real shock, and FLAM activity, the government's response, and the question of the support for FLAM given by Senegal contributed to a delicate situation that exploded into intercommunal violence in April 1989 at the start of the Senegal-Mauritania Crisis (q.v.).

MAQIL. See Beni Hassan

MAURE. See Moor/Moorish

MAURITANIAN KHADIHINE PARTY. See Parti des Khadihines de Mauritanie (PKM)

MAURITANIAN MUSLIM SOCIALIST UNION. See Union Socialiste des Musulmans Mauritaniens (USMM)

MAURITANIAN NATIONAL LIBERATION FRONT. See Front National de Libération Mauritanienne (FNLM)

MAURITANIAN NATIONAL RENAISSANCE PARTY. See An-Nadha al-Wataniyya al-Mauritaniya (Nadha)

MAURITANIAN NATIONAL UNION. See Union Nationale Mauritanienne (UNM)

MAURITANIAN PEOPLE'S PARTY. See Parti du Peuple Mauritanien (PPM)

MOHAMMED KHOUNA OULD HEYDALLAH. Mauritania's fifth head of state was born in 1940 in Port-Etienne, later called Nouadhibou (q.v.) and was a member of a Saharawi (q.v.) tribe, the Arosien, a fact that led to some reports placing his birthplace farther north inside Western Sahara at the settlement of Bir Enzaren. After receiving a primary and secondary education in Mauritania, he joined the country's armed forces (q.v.) in 1962 and received officer training in France at the St. Cyr military academy, later supplemented by a stint at St. Maxen after being commissioned a second lieutenant in July 1964. He rose steadily in the officer corps, becoming commandant (major) at the time of the start of Mauritania's involvement in the Western Sahara conflict (q.v.) in late 1975. Several months after the beginning of the war, he underwent his first real combat test as deputy to Lieutenant Colonel Ahmed Ould Bouceif (q.v.) while assigned to help defend the country's vast northern area from the activities of the Polisario Front (q.v.). In June 1976, Polisario launched the first of two daring Nouakchott raids (q.v.), and Ould Heydallah was one of the first to learn of the Saharawi nationalists' intentions when his men ambushed a diversionary Polisario column near his headquarters at Zouerate (q.v.). The early warning provided by Ould Heydallah did not prevent the guerrillas from briefly shelling the residence of President Mokhtar Ould Daddah (q.v.), but it did ensure that Polisario's success would come at a high price, as Mauritania's army relentlessly pursued the retreating fighters, killing the front's leader, El-Ouali Mustapha Sayed, and decimating a Polisario relief force sent to link up with Nouakchott's attackers. This feat and several other displays of command prowess earned Ould Heydallah a promotion to lieutenant colonel, but he suffered two severe setbacks in 1977. On May 1 of that year, Polisario units fought their way into the center of Zouerate for several hours, causing extensive damage and taking several French expatriate workers prisoner. As commander of Zouerate's 1500-man garrison, Ould Heydallah was away on business in Nouakchott at the time and the soldiers he left there surrendered without resistance, a grave embarrassment. Afterwards, he was charged by a court-martial in Atar (q.v.) with "collusion" with the Polisario Front, due not so much to the debacle at Zouerate as to the allegation that some of his Mauritanian relatives had joined the front. His career almost ended there and then, but Ould Heydallah's established reputation for honesty and competence saved him and the charges were dropped, although his superiors thought it best to transfer him to a less sensitive post as commander of the Fifth Military Region, headquartered in Néma (q.v.) far to the southeast.

As an officer familiarized at first hand with the severe military reverses his country was suffering, and realizing that the Western Saharan war also meant the virtual collapse of the Mauritanian economy, Ould Heydallah fully supported the planning and execution, on July 10, 1978, of the *coup d'état* that overthrew Mokhtar Ould Daddah and installed the first Mauritanian military governing body, the *Comité Militaire de Redressement National* (CMRN) headed by Colonel Mustapha Ould Mohammed Salek (qq.v.). Simultaneously, Ould Heydallah became the army's chief of staff, and appeared for a time to work harmoniously with Ould Salek, whose preferred strategy for exiting the Western Sahara imbroglio was to construct a comprehensive peace agreement among all the interested parties, eschewing a unilateral deal with the Polisario Front and the rapid abandonment of Mauritania's claim to Tiris el-Gharbia (q.v.). But although Polisario halted its attacks on Mauritania while the CMRN pondered the country's future, Ould Heydallah, along with some of his colleagues, became more critical of Ould Salek's stewardship, not only with regard to Western Sahara but also in the areas of interethnic relations and economic policy. As a result, on April 6, 1979, Ould Salek, although still nominally the head of state, found himself deprived of all real authority in a palace coup led by Lieutenant Colonel Ahmed Ould Bouceif, who felt obliged to appoint Ould Heydallah minister of defense as well as a full member of the new Mauritanian ruling body, the *Comité Militaire de Salut National* (CMSN) (q.v.).

Ould Heydallah's fortunes, temporarily clouded by Ould Bouceif's assumption of power, suddenly shifted a few weeks later (on May 27, 1979), when Ahmed Ould Bouceif was killed in a plane crash near Dakar, Senegal. After a four-day power struggle notable for its intensity and presided over by the CMSN's vice-chairman, Lieutenant Colonel Ahmed Salem Ould Sidi (q.v.), Ould Heydallah became prime minister on May 31 and four days later, on June 3, ousted Ould Salek as titular head of state and appointed another figurehead to that position, Lieutenant Colonel Mohammed Mahmoud Ould Louly (q.v.). He also retained the defense portfolio in the revamped CMSN, and set about looking for a face-saving way out of Western Sahara. Mindful of the competing factions in the ruling council as well as in the country at large, however, he still shied away from a unilateral agreement with the Polisario Front, and it looked for a short time as though Ould Heydallah would be no more successful than his predecessors in resolving this critical foreign relations (q.v.) question. But in the end, the Saharawi nationalists forced his hand by abrogating their yearlong cease-fire and attacking targets in Tiris el-Gharbia. This galvanized Ould Heydallah into action, and on August 5, 1979, Mauritania finally pledged, in the Algiers Agreement (q.v.), to abandon all claims to Western Sahara and to make peace with the Polisario Front. The Algiers peace treaty was greeted with great relief by the vast majority of Mauritanians, and it enabled Ould Heydallah to consolidate further his position and, he hoped, to redirect his energies toward national rehabilitation.

Despite these aspirations, however, the next four years were to be stressful ones for Ould Heydallah, who had by this time been promoted to full colonel. He was able, on January 4, 1980, to ease Ould Louly out of the government and assume for himself the formal title of president, as well as to conduct the first of countless reshuffles in the CMSN and in the Council of Ministers (q.v.) in which all of the country's many groupings—Black African, *haratine,* or Moorish (qq.v.), or pro-Moroccan or pro-Polisario—underwent alternate periods of favor, disgrace, imprisonment, and restoration to positions of responsibility. Having named a mostly civilian cabinet in December 1980 as an attempt to legitimate his rule, he felt obliged to institute a purely military regime in April 1981, after a serious and violent coup attempt in Nouakchott that he alleged had Moroccan support and which was led by the exiled *Alliance pour une Mauritanie Démocratique* (AMD) (q.v.). This event deepened Ould Heydallah's suspicions that King Hassan II (q.v.) and his allies were intent on extracting revenge for his separate peace with Poliario. In response, he cultivated increasingly close ties to Algeria, and became more wary of domestic factions that he believed might be linked to outside powers. Diplomatic links with Morocco were severed and the overall relationship remained very tense, as King Hassan accused Mauritania of allowing its territory to be used by the Polisario Front as a staging ground for its continuing attacks on Moroccan forces in Western Sahara. Another coup attempt, this time in January 1983 and thought to originate with Libya's sympathizers, further muddied the waters, as did the increased influence of the Arab Baath Socialist Party (ABSP) (q.v.) aligned with Saddam Hussein's Iraq. Domestically, the Ould Heydallah years were marked by considerable energy. Being more religiously inclined than any of his counterparts, he instituted Islam's (q.v.) legal code, the *sharia* (q.v.), in 1980, but its application (stonings, floggings, and amputations were carried out) led to international protests and resistance at home and so was relaxed. More auspiciously, on November 9, 1981, the practice of slavery (q.v.) was reabolished, and the educational (q.v.) system was reformed, with relatively less attention being paid to Arabization (q.v.) and with African languages such as Fulani, Sarakolé, and Wolof (qq.v.) given additional emphasis in primary and secondary schools. Finally, Ould Heydallah organized grass-roots organizations at the family/neighborhood level in order to prepare for an eventual return to civilian government. Known as the *Structures pour l'Education des Masses* (SEM) (q.v.), they had some initial success but became a conduit over time for patronage activities and a high level of Libyan influence, necessitating swift measures after Ould Heydallah had passed from the political scene.

Although Ould Heydallah himself was universally thought to be beyond reproach, the early 1980s saw him take a tolerant line toward corrupt practices in his regime. When added to the severe droughts, advancing desertification (q.v.), and slumping commodity prices, notably for iron ore (q.v.), it came as little surprise to outside observers that he became increasingly unpopular. Impulsive decision making also became the norm, the head of state increasingly acted on his own, bypassing the rest of the CMSN and relying on the Mauritanian secret intelligence service, the *Bureau d'Etudes et de la Documentation* (BED), to keep opposition elements off balance. By 1984, the mood in the country approached one of despair, and changes in the regime's personnel became frequent and sometimes difficult to fathom for Mauritanians, with some commentators ascribing them to Ould Heydallah's lack of a secure regional or tribal power base. Foreign pressures did not abate either. Relations with Libya and Morocco remained broken, strains were developing with France and the United States (where much of Mauritania's food aid originated), and the government's increasingly pro-Polisario diplomatic stance was costing it support in the Gulf monarchies. Only relations with Algeria remained close. On February 27, 1984, Ould Heydallah took the step that many had predicted and which he had always warned of: Mauritania formally recognized the Polisario Front's government-in-exile, the Saharan Arab Democratic Republic (SADR) (q.v.), after the failure of the Organization of African Unity (OAU) to resolve the Western Sahara conflict peacefully through its good offices. Not only did this step alienate those who feared a possible Moroccan military response to Nouakchott's recognition of the Saharawi state, but it also angered the rest of the CMSN, who reportedly had not been informed of Ould Heydallah's impending decision, nor even consulted on its merits. For those in the leadership who had been concerned for some time about the president's inordinate independence from the governing council, the recognition of the SADR was almost the last straw. Sensing this, Ould Heydallah reorganized his cabinet in early March 1984 (for the fourth time in the previous twelve months), awarding himself the posts of prime minister and minister of defense and demoting the previous occupant of those offices, Colonel Maaouiya Ould Sid'Ahmed Taya (q.v.), to army chief of staff because of Ould Taya's reservations about the diplomatic recognition to the SADR. Ould Heydallah believed he had solidified his position, but the opposite was true—Ould Taya and his supporters almost immediately began plotting his downfall. On December 12, 1984, while Ould Heydallah was out of the country attending a Franco-African summit conference in Burundi, an efficient and bloodless putsch removed him as president and put Ould Taya in his place. After learning that he was no longer the head of state, Ould Heydallah chose to return to Mauritania and was placed under arrest in a military barracks. Despite some reports that he would be placed on trial for corruption, he was never charged and was freed in December 1988. In the early 1990s Ould Heydallah was once more in the political spotlight, this time as one of the leaders of the *Parti Mauritanien pour Renouveau* (PMR) (q.v.), but in spite of this, he did not seek office in the Mauritanian Second Republic (q.v.) and gradually played a less prominent a role in the PMR's affairs. But in the spring of 1995, he held a reconciliation meeting with President Ould Taya, an event which was believed by some observers to be a reaction to statements emanating abroad from the exiled former head of state, Mokhtar Ould Daddah, which had the (unintended) effect of causing many opponents of the government to close ranks with the ruling *Parti Républicain, Démocratique et Social* (PRDS) (q.v.).

MOHAMMED MAHMOUD OULD LOULY. Mauritania's third head of state was born in 1943 at Tidjikja (q.v.), the son of a prominent local merchant family. After completing his secondary education in the country, he spent a year studying economics at the university level, but in 1960 joined the embryonic Mauritanian armed forces (q.v.), where he soon demonstrated a talent for administrative work. After enlisting in the army, he was seconded to the French military academy at St. Cyr (and later to the *Ecole Supérieure d'Intendance*) and graduated as an officer, holding several responsible positions by the early 1970s, including unit commander and director of the supply corps. Like his colleagues, he was drawn into his country's involvement in the Western Sahara conflict (q.v.), which pitted Mauritania against the guerrillas of the Polisario Front (q.v.). By then a lieutenant colonel and deputy director of army budgetary affairs, he supported the *coup d'état* of July 10, 1978, which deposed President Mokhtar Ould Daddah (q.v.) and replaced his regime with the *Comité Militaire de Redressement National* (CMRN) (q.v.), of which he was a full member and also minister of control and investigations. He held this post until January

16, 1979, when he was placed in charge of the permanent secretariat of the CMRN. After only a short time there, he was appointed minister of civil service, higher education, and vocational education. Then, on April 6, 1979, with the accession to power of Lieutenant Colonel Ahmed Ould Bouceif (q.v.), Ould Louly was chosen minister of general employment in the new Council of Ministers (q.v.) appointed by the CMRN's replacement body, the *Comité Militaire de Salut National* (CMSN) (q.v.). On May 27, Ould Bouceif was killed in a plane crash near Dakar, Senegal, and in the brief, intense round of factional infighting that followed, Ould Louly's fortunes improved when he was chosen by the CMSN as President of Mauritania. However, real power resided with the prime minister and minister of defense, Lieutenant Colonel Mohammed Khouna Ould Heydallah (q.v.). Hence, Ould Louly's position as head of state was in reality little more than a sinecure. Under his (titular) leadership, Mauritania finally disengaged from the Western Sahara conflict, signing the Algiers Agreement (q.v.) on August 5, 1979. By January 4, 1980, Ould Heydallah felt sufficiently confident to assume for himself the presidency of the country, gently easing his colleague, Mohammed Mahmoud Ould Louly, out of the government.

MOHAMMED OULD BAH OULD ABDEL KADER. As a Lieutenant Colonel and commander of Mauritania's small air force (q.v.) during the period of his country's involvement in the Western Sahara conflict (q.v.), Mohammed Ould Bah Ould Abdel Kader participated extensively in the war in Tiris el-Gharbia (q.v.) against the guerrillas of the Polisario Front (q.v.). Unlike most other high-ranking Mauritanian officers, he did not support the *coup d'état* of July 10, 1978, that brought down the civilian regime of President Mokhtar Ould Daddah (q.v.) and replaced it with a new government, the *Comité Militaire de Redressement National* (CMRN) (q.v.). Nevertheless, although not a member of the CMRN, he was appointed minister of culture, information and communications in March 1979. Two weeks later, on April 6, when Lieutenant Colonel Ahmed Ould Bouceif (q.v.) had outmaneuvered his rivals on the CMRN's replacement body, the *Comité Militaire de Salut National* (CMSN) (q.v.), Ould Abdel Kader became a member of the CMSN as Ould Bouceif attempted to find Mauritania's way out of the ruinous Western Saharan war. But after Ould Bouceif was killed in a plane crash near Dakar, Senegal, on May 27, 1979, Ould Abdel Kader lost influence with the new CMSN strongman, Lieutenant Colonel Mohammed Khouna Ould Heydallah (q.v.). He was appointed minister of education, but in mid-June 1979 he fled to Morocco. There, in addition to forming a "free officers movement" in opposition to the CMSN and advocating a greater role for Islam (q.v.) in Mauritanian life, he joined an exiled political grouping, the *Alliance pour une Mauritanie Démocratique* (AMD) (q.v.). He strongly opposed the Algiers Agreement (q.v.) of August 5, 1979, by which Mauritania relinquished its claims to Western Sahara and made peace with the Polisario Front, and urged a continued Mauritanian alignment with Morocco. In league with another dissident former CMSN member, Lieutenant Colonel Ahmed Salem Ould Sidi (q.v.), he secretly reentered Mauritania to mount an uprising against Ould Heydallah's leadership. On March 16, 1981, the putsch was attempted but failed, and Mohammed Ould Bah Ould Abdel Kader was captured, and ten days later, executed.

MOHAMMED YEHDIH OULD BREIDELEIL. One of independent Mauritania's most durable civilian politicians, Mohammed Yehdih Ould Breideleil was born in 1944 in Akjoujt (q.v.). After receiving a primary education there between 1952 and 1958, he attended secondary schools in Kaédi, Rosso, and Nouakchott (qq.v.), graduating in the early 1960s. Ould Breideleil then moved to France, where he studied at the *Ecole Supérieure du Journalisme* at Lille, receiving his *licence* in 1967. Back in Mauritania, he spent the years from 1967 to 1969 as an editor for the official government newspaper (q.v.) *Ech-Chaab* (The People), moving up to become director of *Ech-Chaab* from 1969 to 1973. In that year, he quit journalism and served until 1976 as one of the leading members of the *Bureau Politique National* (BPN) of the ruling *Parti du Peuple Mauritanien* (PPM) (qq.v.) under the overall guidance of President Mokhtar Ould Daddah (q.v.). From 1976 until the bloodless *coup d'état* of July 10, 1978, that removed Ould Daddah and instituted rule by the Mauritanian armed forces (q.v.), he held the job of administrative director of a public works organization. Despite being a strong supporter of Mokhtar Ould Daddah and a prominent PPM member, his journalistic background called him to the attention of the *Comité Militaire de Redressement National* (CMRN) (q.v.), which named him minister of culture and information the day after the July 10 putsch. On March 17, 1979, however, he apparently lost favor with the governing military council, and was dropped from the Council of Ministers (q.v.) entirely, although in February 1980 he was made governor of the important administrative région of Trarza (qq.v.) by the new Mauritanian head of state, Lieutenant Colonel Mohammed Khouna Ould Heydallah (q.v.). In December of that year, Ould Breideleil was recalled to Nouakchott to become secretary-general of the Presidency, concurrent with Ould Heydallah's drafting of a Provisional Constitution (q.v.) meant to serve as the framework for the eventual return of civilian rule. But when Ould Heydallah dismissed his civilian cabinet in April 1981, a month after a violent coup attempt against his regime by the exiled *Alliance pour une Mauritanie Démocratique* (AMD) (q.v.), Ould Breideleil was again dismissed from the government, returning to private life. By then he had developed marked sympathies for the influential, pro-Iraq Arab Baath Socialist Party (ABSP) (q.v.), and had become one of the party's leading lights by 1982, when he was imprisoned by Ould Heydallah as part of the Mauritanian president's periodic roundups of opposition personalities that characterized his tenure as CMSN (q.v.) chairman. Ould Breideleil remained jailed until December 1984, when he was freed in a general amnesty of all political prisoners by the new head of state, Colonel Maaouiya Ould Sid'Ahmed Taya (q.v.), who had displaced Ould Heydallah in a peaceful "restructuring" of the ruling council on December 12. After his release, Ould Breideleil remained a staunch Baathist, running afoul of the CMSN once again in July 1988, when he (along with many other civilians and army personnel) was placed on trial for conspiracy on behalf of a foreign power, a charge that amounted to espionage and otherwise acting in the interests of the Iraqi leader, Saddam Hussein. Although the accusations were extremely serious, he reportedly provided the authorities with information on the Baathist organization in Mauritania and so escaped with the lenient sentence of two years' imprisonment. While Ould Breideleil was incarcerated, however, the Ould Taya regime's alliance with Baghdad deepened, especially after the severe stresses placed upon the CMSN by the Senegel-Mauritania Crisis (q.v.) of 1989 and 1990. It was a measure of Baathist influence, in the opinion of some observers, that Ould Breideleil was released from prison in December 1989 and soon made an astonishing political comeback, being catapulted back into his old post, secretary-general of the Presidency, a position that carried with it *ex officio* membership in the CMSN itself, making him the highest-ranking civilian in the entire Mauritanian government. Newly reanointed, Ould Breideleil did his best to move the Ould Taya regime even closer to Iraq, but after Saddam Hussein's invasion of Kuwait on August 2, 1990, his fortunes rapidly went into eclipse, as the ensuing defeat of Iraq at the hands of a United States–led expeditionary force during the final stages of the Gulf Crisis (q.v.) discredited the Mauritanian Baathists. Not long after the end of the Gulf War in March 1991, Ould Breideleil quit the ABSP and became, in late August 1991, one of the founding members of the *Parti Républicain, Démocratique et Social* (PRDS) (q.v.), an organization closely identified with President Ould Taya. After the party's lopsided victory in parliamentary elections held in early 1992, Ould Breideleil moved into a new political post, that of secretary-general of the PRDS-dominated *Assemblée Nationale* (q.v.). But adding to a reputation for unpredictability, he was arrested and detained by the government on October 23, 1995 for alleged pro-Iraq and pro-Baath activities along with some one hundred others, upwards of twenty of whom were, like Ould Breideleil himself, affiliated with the ruling PRDS. He was released in early November after most of the accused Baathists had the charges against them commuted by Mauritania's public prosecutor.

MOKHTAR OULD DADDAH. As Mauritania's most prominent and successful politician in the country's pre-independence period who went on to become president from 1960 to 1978, Mokhtar Ould Daddah was born on December 25, 1924, in Boutilimit (q.v.), where his family belonged to an influential *zawiya* (q.v.) tribe, the Oulad Berri. He was raised in a devoutly Islamic (q.v.) atmosphere, receiving a primary education at the Medersa Koranic school in Boutilimit and going on to study at the *Ecole des Fils de Chefs* in St. Louis, Senegal, where he graduated in 1940. The onset of the Second World War interrupted his schooling, and he consequently worked as an interpreter for the French colonial administration, the AOF (q.v.). After the war, he traveled to France to complete his education, first studying in Nice and then in Paris, where he obtained a *baccalauréat* and a law degree. Finally, he obtained a diploma (in Arabic) from the *Institut National des Langues Orientales* also in Paris. Returning to West Africa, he first settled in Dakar, where he became a member of the bar in 1955 and was employed by the law firm of Boussier, Palun. However, his ambitions shifted to his home country, where he caught the eye of the French government, which was then in the process of preparing Mauritania for independence in close association with France. As the territory's only lawyer, his soft-spoken integrity and evident political skill earned him the position of Territorial Counselor of Adrar (q.v.) in May 1957, followed by his election to the *Conseil de Gouvernement* (q.v.) on May 20, in which the dominant party, the *Union Progressiste Mauritanienne* (UPM) (q.v.), consolidated its lead over other political groupings, notably the by now fractured *Entente Mauritanienne* (q.v.). Since Ould Daddah had been absent from Mauritania during the earlier years of infighting between the Entente, the UPM, the *Association de la Jeunesse Mauritanienne* (AJM) (q.v.), and other groupings, he could distance himself from the quarrels of those around him and concentrate on a straightforward program: to unify all the country's factions, overcome differences between its Moorish (q.v.) and Black African citizens, and prepare new Mauritanian political institutions for eventual independence. To that end, Ould Daddah tirelessly urged the various parties in Mauritania to come together and reject any move toward "union" with either neighboring Black African states or with Morocco, which had begun an effort to "reclaim" all of the country's territory. In May 1958, in a step which displayed his considerable persuasive powers, Ould Daddah organized the Congress of Aleg (q.v.), at which the UPM, elements of the Entente, and the black-oriented *Bloc Démocratique du Gorgol* (BDG) (q.v.) agreed to merge into a new political organization, the *Parti de Regroupement Mauritanien* (PRM) (q.v.), in which Ould Daddah was the acknowledged leader.

But this newfound unity did not last. Four months later, disaffected youths and other members of the PRM broke away from Ould Daddah, piqued at his pro-French policies, and formed the Nadha (q.v.) party, a pan-Arab group under the leadership of Ahmed Baba Miské (q.v.). Although the Mauritanian public approved membership in the French Community by a large margin, Mokhtar Ould Daddah once more had to deal with competing political tendencies in the country as the Islamic Republic of Mauritania was declared in October 1958. On November 28, 1960, Mauritania finally achieved full independence from France, and Ould Daddah became prime minister, albeit with a cloudy internal political situation and a poor foreign relations (q.v.) outlook, since Morocco and other countries of the Arab League (q.v.) continued to deny the legitimacy of the infant state. By the summer of 1961, though, there were no viable challengers to Ould Daddah's rule, and through a combination of co-optation and persuasion he managed to win election as Mauritania's first president overwhelmingly, on August 20, 1961. By the provisions of the constitution approved on May 20, 1961 (q.v.), the presidential office enjoyed great power, and the state administration remained highly centralized. Barely two months later, on October 4, he consolidated his domination of the political scene by holding the Congress of Unity (q.v.), which combined the PRM, Nadha, and several other smaller groups into a new *Parti du Peuple Mauritanien* (PPM) (q.v.), in which Ould Daddah was the paramount leader.

The PPM quickly secured a monopoly over the Mauritanian governmental apparatus, and decision making was almost entirely confined to a small coterie of Ould Daddah supporters, the *Bureau Politique National* (BPN) (q.v.). Still, rival politicians continued their activities (some within the PPM), and Ould Daddah decided that this state of affairs must end, both to ensure the unity of the country and to buttress his own position (as he saw it) as a "chieftain" capable of balancing various ethnic, regional, and tribal interests which he believed had been selfishly exploited by other political parties. On January 28 and 29, 1964, he called loyal BPN members together at the Conference of Kaédi (q.v.), which led to the outlawing of all non-PPM political parties. Also at Kaédi, the PPM itself was sternly reminded by Ould Daddah to lessen the distance between it and ordinary Mauritanians, and that corruption had to be stamped out. With this move,

Mauritania became a virtual one-party dictatorship, and although the state did not immediately become repressive, Ould Daddah was willing, on occasion, to use the Mauritanian police and armed forces (q.v.) to quell strikes and demonstrations, particularly those connected with his developing Arabization policy (q.v.) instituted a few years later.

Over the following decade (from 1964), Ould Daddah's leadership accumulated considerable achievements. Exports of iron ore (q.v.) carried out by the MIFERMA (q.v.) consortium yielded large revenues, as did, for a short time, the copper reserves near Akjoujt (qq.v.). Some progress was made in the construction of roads (q.v.), the supply of water and electricity (qq.v.), and in improvements to the country's ports and communications (qq.v.) facilities. Agriculture (q.v.), however, was neglected, as Ould Daddah adhered to the philosophy then current in developing nations that priority should be given to large industrial development (q.v.) projects at the expense of the countryside. In foreign affairs, too, Ould Daddah succeeded in having a greater number of states—especially Arab ones—acknowledge the legitimacy of Mauritania, and was one of the few leaders of Muslim nations of North Africa to take the Organization of African Unity (OAU) seriously. His efforts to align Mauritania with the Arab world received a massive boost in April 1970, when Morocco's King Hassan II (q.v.) dropped his claim to the country and formally established diplomatic ties. After this favorable development, Ould Daddah displayed many of the same political skills that he used to his advantage in the pre-independence period domestically: he sought—and usually received—development assistance, grants, and loans from many Arab League members without regard to their political leanings. Thus he was able to sustain particularly close links with President Houari Boumedienne (q.v.) of Algeria while building a web of beneficial relations with Saudi Arabia and the other conservative Gulf monarchies. Bolstered by this friendlier international environment, Ould Daddah embarked on a policy of ending France's privileged position in Mauritanian affairs, nationalizing MIFERMA in 1974, revising French-Mauritanian economic and military arrangements dating to 1960, and on June 30, 1973, leaving the French-controlled *Communauté Financière Africaine* (CFA) (q.v.) and issuing a separate Mauritanian currency, the *ouguiya* (qq.v.). For a thinly populated, ethnically diverse nation that observers only a few years earlier had been calling an artificial construct that could not survive, Mauritania under Mokhtar Ould Daddah's stewardship attracted little but praise from the Third World, and Mauritania's future appeared reasonably bright.

Ould Daddah, however, had not forgotten his territorial claim to the neighboring Spanish colony of Western Sahara (q.v.) that he first enunciated in 1957, and it was this preoccupation that was to prove his undoing. In 1973 and 1974, when it became obvious that Spain's determination to remain in its colony was slipping, Ould Daddah, after some temporizing, moved to cement his relations with Morocco, Western Sahara's co-claimant, by agreeing with King Hassan to divide the territory, with Morocco getting the northern, resource-rich two-thirds, and Mauritania receiving Tiris el-Gharbia (q.v.), a largely useless expanse of desert. This arrangement was formalized by the Madrid Agreement (q.v.) of November 14, 1975. In opting for partition, Mauritania ignored the demand of the nascent Saharawi (q.v.) nationalist movement, the Polisario Front (q.v.), that "Spanish Sahara" become independent. Polisario, in response, soon began a wide-ranging, highly destructive military campaign against the country's fragile economy and its small army. Beginning in late 1975, almost every population center in northern Mauritania was set upon by well-armed Polisario units, often bringing iron ore exports to a halt due to raids on Zouerate (q.v.) as well as on the long, vulnerable railway (q.v.) line running to the commercial center of Nouadhibou (q.v.). Budgetary (q.v.) problems also multiplied, as the size of the armed forces had to be quadrupled virtually overnight. From 1976 to 1978, Ould Daddah suffered one humiliation after another: his residence in Nouakchott (q.v.) was attacked twice by Polisario (see NOUAKCHOTT RAIDS), his standing at the United Nations (q.v.) dropped precipitously, and he was forced to ally ever more closely with Morocco and with France, from which he had proudly distanced himself only a few years before. But all the diplomatic shifts, military assistance (including Operation Lamantin [q.v.], a series of French air strikes against Polisario), and internal reorganizations could not salvage Mauritania from its dire circumstances. Finally the one-party PPM regime, which earlier had perhaps helped to channel the aspirations of many Mauritanians, now effectively blocked any discussion of political alternatives.

The end of Ould Daddah's presidency came in the early hours of July 10, 1978. A specially selected force of the disenchanted Mauritanian army, commanded by Colonel Mustapha Ould Mohammed Salek (q.v.), deposed him, abolished the PPM and the toothless *Assemblée Nationale* (q.v.), and suspended the 1961 constitution. Ould Daddah was arrested without violence by the armed forces, which then governed the country through a committee of officers, the *Comité Militaire de Redressement National* (CMRN) (q.v.). The former head of state spent the next thirteen months in detention, part of it in the remote town of Oualata (q.v.). In August 1979 he was released, and two months later he was allowed to go into exile in France, where he was given asylum by the government of President Valéry Giscard d'Estaing. The ex-president made no secret of his dissatisfaction with political events back home, and for a time (until about 1981) he was loosely affiliated with an exiled opposition group, the *Alliance pour une Mauritanie Démocratique* (AMD) (q.v.). Ould Daddah, though, reportedly became unhappy with the constant infighting within the AMD's ranks. Moreover, the accession to power of François Mitterrand as French President in 1981 made Ould Daddah less welcome in France, and so he moved (temporarily, as it turned out) to Tunisia. In the meantime, in November 1980, he was sentenced *in absentia* to life imprisonment at hard labor on charges of high treason and economic mismanagement leveled by the new Mauritanian head of state, Colonel Mohammed Khouna Ould Heydallah (q.v.). He remained a wanted man in his country until December 1984, when Ould Heydallah was ousted and replaced by Colonel Maaouiya Ould Sid'Ahmed Taya (q.v.), who promptly amnestied Ould Daddah and many others. Despite this, Ould Daddah chose not to return to Mauritania and continued to live in retirement in Nice, France.

With Mokhtar Ould Daddah now living outside his homeland on a seemingly permanent basis, and with a whole generation of Mauritanians having come of age since his overthrow in 1978, his political influence might have been thought to have been in eclipse, notwithstanding the fact that his brother, Ahmed Ould Daddah (q.v.) was one of the foremost leaders of the opposition to the Ould Taya government and was head of a major political party, the *Union des Forces Démocratiques— Ere Nouvelle* (UFD) (q.v.). But this situation changed suddenly in early 1995. In January, Mokhtar Ould Daddah began giving a series of interviews with the news media, breaking a seventeen-year silence. The French radio address he recorded called merely for a renewed sense of national unity among Mauritania's citizens, but in a lengthy interview he gave to the Moroccan weekly *Maroc-Hebdo* during a visit to that country, he stated that conditions in Mauritania were worsening on several fronts, urged the opposition parties to coordinate their positions and activities, and said that freedom of expression and a free press did not exist in Mauritania. If the former president had wanted to generate a more cohesive counterpoise to the government, his statements actually achieved nearly the opposite effect in the eyes of many observers. Nationalists quickly noted that Ould Daddah had traveled to Morocco rather than Mauritania to make his most controversial statements, a fact that motivated others to close ranks behind President Ould Taya and his ruling *Parti Républicain, Démocratique et Social* (PRDS) (q.v.). Mokhtar Ould Daddah's interviews also made it more difficult for his brother Ahmed and the UFD, too: throughout 1995, a steady stream of PRDS opponents sought to align themselves with the regime in power. By late February 1995, moreover, the government itself stepped into the fray, alleging that Mokhtar Ould Daddah had spurned its offer of renewed Mauritanian citizenship as well as certain other perquisites.

Prime Minister Sidi Mohamed Ould Boubacar (q.v.), speaking for the regime, said (without mentioning the ex-head of state by name) that he found it "surprising" that "they falsify charges to inflict harm on their country at foreign gatherings," and that "anyone who blemishes the reputation of his country cannot be described as a democrat or patriot." These and other high-level statements indicated that the rift between the government and Ould Daddah, far from lessening, was in reality growing wider.

MOOR/MOORISH (variant: Maure). The preponderant ethnic group in Mauritania (and from whom the country takes its name), the Moorish peoples are in most cases of Arab or Berber (q.v.) extraction who use Hassaniya (q.v.) Arabic as their *lingua franca* and live primarily in the Saharan north of Mauritania, in the administrative régions of Adrar, Dakhlet-Nouadhibou, Inchiri, Tagant, Tiris Zemmour, and Trarza (qq.v.). Historically, the Moors were either nomadic herders of livestock (q.v.) or engaged in more sedentary occupations such as artisanry or agriculture (q.v.). Except for the substantial numbers of "Black Moors," known as *haratines* (q.v.), the Moors tended to be light-skinned and possessed "Caucasian" features, although significant intermarriage took place between "white," or Beydane (q.v.) Moors and the haratine population (q.v.). Furthermore, even if the differences between "white" and "black" Moors were put aside, the Arab-Berber community was far from monolithic; indeed, their society was traditionally highly stratified and segmented.

Modern Moorish life in Mauritania derives its character primarily from the outcome of the Char Bobha (q.v.), or Thirty Years' War, fought from 1644 to 1674 between the Berbers who formerly comprised the Sanhadja Confederation (q.v.), and the Arab warriors from the east. That conflict, which ended in utter defeat for the Berbers under the leadership of Nasir ad-Din, a noted Islamic (q.v.) cleric, forced them to "abandon the sword for the book" and become tributaries of the triumphant Arabs, most prominently the *Beni Hassan* (q.v.), who ranked at the top of the rapidly developing caste system and who were collectively termed *hassan* (q.v.), or warrior, tribes. Some defeated Berbers (and some Arabs, too) zealously devoted themselves to Islamic scholarship in an effort to retain their social status, and became *zawiya* (q.v.) (or *marabouts*, as they were called by French colonialists) and were respected for their learning even as they occupied a position just below that of the hassan. Over the years, the zawiya tended to intermarry less than the other castes.

Below the hassan and the zawiya were the *znaga* (q.v.), or tributary vassals. Made up for the most part of the defeated Sanhadja and other Berbers, they were firmly subordinate to the hassan tribes, spoke a different dialect of Hassaniya Arabic, and were obliged from time to time to pay tribute (known as *horma*) which could involve the provision of goods, personal services, or the education (q.v.) of children. The znaga were also divided into religious and warrior classes based primarily on their occupations before or during the Char Bobha. Some znaga were also impressed into slavery (q.v.) to their hassan counterparts, although it appears that this practice (as distinct from black Moorish slavery to Beydanes) died out in the early twentieth century. The znaga, more so than the hassan or zawiya, have intermarried extensively with Black Africans over the decades.

Ranking below all three groups of Moors are the so-called "occupational" castes, though their members' particular designations often do not describe present-day employment but rather a reputed historical status. These include artisans, craftsmen, weavers, tailors, and other practitioners of manual trades such as carpenters. Despite their lower standing, the craftsmen's talents made them valuable to the dominant groups, and in many cases they were allowed to live with other Moors almost as equals, a trend which gathered force after the arrival of the French. The occupational castes contained a final subgroup: the entertainers, including bards (poets), musicians, and storytellers, who were valued in Moorish society but were nonetheless viewed with suspicion due to their knowledge of recondite subjects and their alleged access to mystical or occult powers. As a result, "noble" Moors often had entertainers and mystics as companions, providing the protection that such persons were supposed to bring but without altering the patron-client relationship. Remaining outside the caste system almost entirely were occupations such as nomadic hunters and fishermen; in fact, the only Moorish tribe to practice fishing (q.v.) to any degree were the Imraguen (q.v.), believed to be Berbers traditionally dependent upon a hassan tribe, the Oulad Bou Sbaa.

Also near the bottom of the hierarchy of Moor society were the haratines who gradually gained their freedom from their "white" masters. In the process, they came to identify themselves almost entirely with Moorish culture and language. Due to a lack of economic opportunities in the country, the haratines often still worked for their former masters, blurring the line between actual slavery (the persistence of which is a fiercely controversial issue) and a merely servile status.

Whatever their place in the complex Moorish social world, all the groups have several attributes in common: the predominance of patrilineal kinship groups (and often extended families), the existence of polygyny, and the historical preference for marriage within one's clan or kinship group, although marriage within a prescribed degree of consanguinity is strictly enjoined. In addition, most Moors were traditionally partly or wholly nomadic. But with the onset of desertification (q.v.) in Mauritania during the 1970s and 1980s, many, like their Black African compatriots, were forced to abandon their way of life and migrate into the country's cities and towns, especially the capital, Nouakchott (q.v.), which by the 1990s had become a crossroads for all Mauritanians: Beydane, haratine, and Black African alike.

The following is a list of the principal Moorish tribes, confederations, and sub-tribes (fractions) in Mauritania, some of whose members are also found in neighboring Western Sahara and to some extent in northern Mali. The list is divided between tribes which were traditionally warriors (hassan) and those of a religious/monastic inclination (zawiya). It should also be kept in mind that the two large (hassan) Reguibat confederations counted a certain number of zawiya among their number, and some tribes (notably the Semissides of the Adrar) devoted themselves mostly to commerce and trade, although they are classed here as monastic.

Hassan Tribes
Brakna (includes the Ahel Yahya Ould Sidi Othman, the Oulad Abdallah, the Oulad Ahmed, and the Oulad Normach)
Idaw Aych
Kunta (also includes zawiya)
Mechdouf
Oulad Allouch
Oulad Ammoni (includes the Oulad Akshar and the Oulad Gaylan)
Oulad Bou Sbaa (includes Imraguen)
Oulad Delim
Oulad Lab
Oulad Nasir
Reguibat ech-Charg (also called Lgouacem; includes the Ahel Brahim Oulad Daoud, the Lebouihat, the Laiaicha, and the Foqra)
Reguibat es-Sahel (includes the Oulad Moussa, the Souaad, the Lemouedenin, the Oulad Borhim, the Oulad Cheikh, the Thaalat, and the Oulad Taleb)
Trarza (includes the Oulad Damman, the Oulad Ben Damman, the Ahel Mohammed, and El-Hbib)

Zawiya Tribes
Ahel Berikallah
Ahel Mohammed Fadel
Ahel Néma
Ahel Oualata
Ahel Sidi Mahmoud
Deiman
Djeiliba
Idab Lahsen
Idaw Ali
Idaw El-Hadj

Ideiboussat
Ideikoub
Idjeijiba
Laghlal
Messouma
Oulad Berri
Semissides
Tadjakant
Tagat
Tagnit
Tagounant
Tendgha
Tinaoudjuou

MOROCCAN-MAURITANIAN CONVENTIONS (of April 14, 1976). Pursuant to the Madrid Agreement (q.v.) of November 14, 1975, Morocco and Mauritania consented to drop their simultaneous claims to the entire territory of Western Sahara (q.v.) and partition it between them. However, the actual boundary of the Moroccan and Mauritanian zones remained unsettled until April 14, 1976, when an agreement was signed in Fez, Morocco, in the presence of the two countries' heads of state, King Hassan II and President Mokhtar Ould Daddah (qq.v.). The convention stated that "the frontier between the two countries shall be drawn by a straight line from the intersection of the 24th parallel north and the Atlantic coast to the intersections of the 23rd parallel north and the 13th meridian west, the intersection of this straight line with the present frontier of the Islamic Republic of Mauritania constituting the southeast limit of the frontier of the Kingdom of Morocco." In practical terms this meant that the new Mauritanian border would extend from the coast north of Dakhla (q.v.) to the prior border in the vicinity of the towns of F'Derik and Zouerate (qq.v.). All told, Morocco received two-thirds of Western Sahara (and the lion's share of its natural resources) while Mauritania received the southern one-third, practically bereft of resources, which was called Tiris el-Gharbia (q.v.).

Three and one-half years later, when Mauritania relinquished its share of Western Sahara to the Polisario Front (q.v.) by means of the Algiers Agreement (q.v.), Morocco unilaterally annexed Tiris el-Gharbia, renaming it Oued ed-Dahab. The 1976 boundary line set forth by the convention then lost whatever limited significance it previously had, since Moroccan troops had always been present within the Mauritanian sector, assisting in its defense.

MOROCCAN-MAURITANIAN DEFENSE COMMITTEE. When the former Spanish colony of Western Sahara (q.v.) was divided between Morocco and Mauritania by the Madrid Agreement (q.v.) in

November 1975, it was believed that Mauritania could occupy its allotted share of the territory without substantial outside assistance. But the Mauritanian president, Mokhtar Ould Daddah (q.v.), had badly underestimated the fighting skill and determination of the pro-independence Polisario Front (q.v.). Consequently, Ould Daddah was obliged almost from the start to allow Moroccan soldiers to assist their Mauritanian counterparts in defending Tiris el-Gharbia (q.v.). Later, the situation rapidly deteriorated, with Polisario guerrillas ranging far and wide across Mauritania, hitting and disabling the critical railway (q.v.) line from the interior to the Atlantic coast and even twice attacking the capital city (see NOUAKCHOTT RAIDS). On May 1, 1977, Polisario made a devastating attack on Zouerate (q.v.), and as uncomfortable as it was for Ould Daddah to seek outside help, he believed he had no choice. On May 13, a joint Moroccan-Mauritanian defense committee was set up and met on a monthly basis until the overthrow of Ould Daddah by members of his armed forces (q.v.) on July 10, 1978.

The agreement essentially merged the two countries' military high commands and, for the first time, permitted Morocco to place its own troops inside Mauritania's pre-1976 borders. By December 1977 there were about 6000 men of Morocco's *Forces Armées Royales* (FAR) in Mauritania proper; they were based at Akjoujt, Atar, Bir Moghrein, F'Derik, and Nouadhibou (qq.v.). In addition, the FAR's U.S.-built Northrup F-5 fighter jets were stationed at the Nouadhibou airport (q.v.), and Moroccans were posted along the vulnerable railway in the north. Although the capital, Nouakchott (q.v.), never hosted Moroccan troops, their presence gave considerable pause to the post–Ould Daddah government, the *Comité Militaire de Redressement National* (CMRN) (q.v.), which was actively seeking a dignified exit from the Saharan war without antagonizing Morocco. After the July 10, 1978, coup, most Moroccan soldiers were withdrawn after reaching a peak strength of about 9000. The agreement on the joint defense committee was renounced by the CMRN's successor body, the *Comité Militaire de Salut National* (CMSN) (q.v.), on August 23, 1979, a fortnight after the signing of the Algiers Agreement (q.v.), by which Mauritania made peace with the Polisario Front and abandoned its claim to Western Sahara. The last Moroccans, at Bir Moghrein, stayed in place until December 26, 1979, when they were finally repatriated after being the subject of strenuous Mauritanian protests.

MOUGHATAA. See Département

MOUVEMENT NATIONAL DEMOCRATIQUE (MND). A relatively small yet remarkably durable and influential political tendency, the National Democratic Movement was founded in 1968 as a semiclandestine organization, since the Mauritanian head of state at the time, President Mokhtar Ould Daddah (q.v.), tolerated no political activity outside of his own tightly structured *Parti du Peuple Mauritanien* (PPM) (q.v.). The MND, from its inception, always espoused a fairly left-wing agenda and articulated strong disapproval of Ould Daddah's domestic policies and foreign relations (q.v.) alignments, considering them exclusionary, conservative, and inordinately pro-Western. The National Democratic Movement found ready allies among the Saharawi (q.v.) and Mauritanian worker communities in the northern part of the country, particularly in Nouadhibou and Zouerate (qq.v.), locations which were heavily influenced by the vital iron ore (q.v.) industry, which itself was the subject of much organized labor activity at the end of the 1960s. Once he learned of the MND's existence, Mokhtar Ould Daddah dealt with the organization in his characteristic manner: repression (an MND-influenced strike by iron ore workers in Zouerate in 1968 was brutally put down with the loss of several lives) followed a series of nationalistic economic and political moves designed to mollify and eventually co-opt the regime's critics. These measures, outlined at an extraordinary PPM congress in June 1972, were to include the nationalization of the iron ore mines controlled by the MIFERMA (q.v.) consortium, Mauritania's withdrawal from the *Communauté Financière Africaine* (CFA) (q.v.) and the issuance of a new Mauritanian currency, the *ouguiya* (qq.v.), and a subtle reorientation of the country's foreign policy toward some of the "radical" members of the Arab League (q.v.). These measures did succeed in dampening domestic opposition to Ould Daddah, but the MND (which included small pro-Soviet and pro-Chinese Marxist elements) soon faced a dilemma—whether to support the nascent Saharawi nationalist organization, the Polisario Front (q.v.), which had been formed in May 1973. Many MND partisans had always supported a staunchly anticolonial line with regard to Western Sahara (q.v.) and many Saharawi workers and students were among the MND's members. Nevertheless, a majority of the National Democratic Movement voted, in August 1975, to merge with the ruling PPM, a move which reflected, by and large, its satisfaction with Ould Daddah's "progressive" policies. As part of its agreement to join the governing party, the MND also assented to the annexation by Mauritania of the southern one-third of Western Sahara, which was consummated three months later on November 14, 1975, when Ould Daddah, King Hassan II (q.v.) of Morocco, and the Spanish government signed the Madrid Agreement (q.v.). Only the Marxist minority within the MND declined the merger and openly supported Polisario.

The *coup d'état* mounted on July 10, 1978, by senior officers in the Mauritanian armed forces (q.v.) who were intensely frustrated by the seemingly endless and unwinnable war in Western Sahara against the Polisario Front's fighters, caused the remnants of the MND to retreat even further underground (and into exile), regaining its separate identity after the PPM was outlawed by the new ruling military junta, the *Comité Militaire de Redressement National* (CMSN) (q.v.). Despite its extremely low profile, the MND was still thought to command sympathy among businesspeople, civil servants, and even some army officers. The National Democratic Movement also enjoyed backing from both black and Moorish (q.v.) Mauritanians, lessening the ethnic divisions in the country. Repressed during the five-year rule of Colonel Mohammed Khouna Ould Heydallah (q.v.), the MND fully supported the nonviolent "restructuring" of the *Comité Militaire de Salut National* (CMSN) (q.v.) on December 12, 1984, which brought Colonel Maaouiya Ould Sid'Ahmed Taya (q.v.) to power. Despite having largely moderated its leftish views and being freed from most harassment, the MND led a somewhat nomadic political existence in the late 1980s and early 1990s, surviving more as a "tendency" or coalition partner with other groups than as an independent force in its own right. Immediately after President Ould Taya announced in April 1991 that multiple political parties would be legalized for the first time in Mauritania's history, the MND included itself in a hastily organized unofficial opposition group, the *Front Démocratique Uni des Forces du Changement* (FDUC) (q.v.), which was speedily suppressed by the CMSN after it was held responsible for a wave of unrest that swept Mauritania in June 1991, particularly in Nouadhibou. After this, the National Democratic Movement's backers were found in several places on the Mauritanian political scene, including in Ahmed Ould Daddah's *Union des Forces Démocratiques—Ere Nouvelle* (UFD) (qq.v.).

MURIBITUN. See Almoravids

MUSTAPHA OULD MOHAMMED SALEK. Mauritania's first military president was born in 1936 in Kiffa (q.v.) and entered the newly formed Mauritanian armed forces (q.v.) in 1961. His rise through the military hierarchy was rapid, especially after officer training at the Saumur and St. Maxen academies in France in the mid-1960s. After a stint as army chief of staff (1968–69), he was tapped by Mauritania's civilian president, Mokhtar Ould Daddah (q.v.), to become director of the *Société Nationale d'Importation et d'Exportation* (SONIMEX) (q.v.), the state trading company. However, he was recalled back into the army as a result of the country's involvement in the Western Sahara conflict (q.v.), in which the guerrilla fighters of the Polisario Front (q.v.) mounted destructive attacks against the thinly spread

Mauritanian army not only in Tiris el-Gharbia (q.v.), but within Mauritania itself. As a military commander, Ould Salek took part in the defense of the country's capital in June 1976 (see NOUAKCHOTT RAIDS). In recognition of his military skills, Ould Daddah appointed him, on July 15, 1977, as commander of the critical Third Military Region, with responsibility for defending the vulnerable northern towns of Akjoujt, Atar, and Chinguetti (qq.v.) against incursions by Polisario. But Mauritania's dismal fortunes on the battlefield were not reversed, and so, for the second time in his career, Ould Salek was appointed army chief of staff, a post which put him in a unique position to assess the increasingly unwinnable Western Saharan war. On July 10, 1978, consequently, he was the leader of the bloodless *coup d'état* that overthrew Ould Daddah and instituted army rule in the form of the *Comité Militaire de Redressement National* (CMRN) (q.v.). Colonel Ould Salek became head of the new government and promptly set about seeking an honorable exit from the Saharan conflict. Helpfully, the Polisario Front declared a unilateral cease-fire with regard to Mauritania immediately after the coup, allowing the CMRN some urgently needed breathing space.

But a solution to Mauritania's Western Saharan quagmire was to prove very difficult. Not only did the CMRN and Ould Salek have to contend with the presence of almost 9000 Moroccan troops on Mauritanian soil, stationed there under the provisions of the Moroccan-Mauritanian Defense Committee (q.v.) agreement of May 1977, but also they inherited a state in almost total economic disarray, caused in no small part by the largely nonoperational status of Mauritania's iron ore (q.v.) extraction and transport facilities. The situation was further complicated by Ould Salek's preference for trying to construct a "global" Western Sahara peace agreement in which the dispute would be resolved, at a stroke, among all the parties (Algeria, France, Mauritania, Morocco, and Polisario) interested in the outcome of the conflict. But a comprehensive peace of this type proved out of the question, and the strain in Nouakchott (q.v.) was beginning to show.

On March 20, 1979, Colonel Ould Salek prevailed upon his CMRN colleagues to grant him absolute powers. In an attempt to accord his regime some legitimacy, as well as to quell renascent racial tensions, he set up a National Consultative Council to advise the CMRN, but black Mauritanians were allegedly underrepresented in that body, and in any event its meetings were boycotted by forty of its 104 members. On April 5, 1979, Ould Salek found himself the victim of a nonviolent "palace revolution" which stripped him of all but the (titular) office of head of state and which installed Lieutenant Colonel Ahmed Ould Bouceif (q.v.) as prime minister. Colonel Ould Salek lingered on as the formal head of the government for another month until June 3, when he departed after having been succeeded by Lieutenant Colonel Mohammed Mahmoud Ould Louly (q.v.), who was in turn subordinate to the powerful minister of defense, Lieutenant Colonel Mohammed Khouna Ould Heydallah (q.v.).

After 1979, Ould Salek did not entirely forsake political activity. He still enjoyed enough favor within the newly formed *Comité Militaire de Salut National* (CMSN) to be invited to certain ceremonial functions, and he would occasionally vent his strong feelings of opposition to the governing council's policies. On February 6, 1982, he went so far as to become involved in a failed coup plot against Ould Heydallah, for which he was sentenced to ten years' imprisonment, a punishment remarkably mild in view of the fact that other such conspirators sometimes paid with their lives. After Ould Heydallah's replacement by Colonel Maaouiya Ould Sid'Ahmed Taya (q.v.) on December 12, 1984, Ould Salek was amnestied and released along with many other political prisoners. After a period of time outside the limelight, Ould Salek briefly rose to prominence again in January 1992, when he made a wildcat run for the Mauritanian presidency in the country's first contested elections since independence. He polled only 15,735 votes, less than 3 percent of the total.

NADHA. See An-Nadha al-Wataniyya al-Mauritaniya

NATIONAL ASSEMBLY. See Assemblée Nationale

NATIONAL GUARD. A small, lightly equipped paramilitary law enforcement unit, the National Guard is tasked with the maintenance of law and order primarily in the rural areas of Mauritania. The unit is answerable to the minister of the interior and numbers about 3000 men including auxiliary personnel.

NAVY. Established on January 25, 1966 as part of a series of measures taken by President Mokhtar Ould Daddah (q.v.) to increase Mauritania's autonomy, the country's naval arm is one of the smallest in the region, with a total strength of only about 500 men, thirty-eight or so of whom were officers. The flagship of the Mauritanian navy is the *Abubakr Ben Amer,* a French-built, 177-meter-long patrol vessel with displacement of 374 tons and a range of 4500 nautical miles. Ordered from the French shipyard of Leroux and Lotz in September 1992, it was commissioned on April 7, 1994. Mauritania held an option for the purchase of a second such ship in 1996. Also present in the fleet was *l-Nasr* (formerly *Le Dix Juillet*), another patrol ship with a displacement of nearly 150 tons and with a comparatively limited range of 1750 miles. In addition, there was one German-built *Neustadt*-class surveillance vessel acquired from the German navy in 1990, and three more Spanish-constructed boats of German design, each almost 119 meters in length and with a regular crew of nineteen. Purchased in the late 1970s, they were of dubious seaworthiness by 1988, but Mauritania could still count on the services of the *N'Madi*, a *Jura*-class 200-meter ship constructed in Great Britain in 1975 and leased to the Mauritanian armed forces (q.v.) in 1989 for the primary purpose of patrolling the country's abundant and heavily poached fisheries (q.v.). In the area of smaller vessels, Mauritania possessed about four British-built inshore boats of the *Mandovi* class delivered from India in 1990, but several other ex-French units, as well as a supply ship and a landing craft purchased from Senegal, had been removed from service by the early 1990s, a fate which also threatened some of the rest of the Mauritanian fleet, given a lack of finance for maintenance and a lack of trained personnel. Reportedly, no more than three of Mauritania's naval vessels were capable of performing their duties at any one time, causing the navy to be little more than a symbolic presence, all the more so since the country's Exclusive Economic Zone (EEZ) extends 200 nautical miles from the coastline.

Most of the navy's officers and men have been trained outside the country, at least for advanced studies; Algeria, France, and the United States have all undertaken some sort of naval education program. An indigenous naval training college is located in Nouadhibou (q.v.), the site of its only substantial base of operations, and a far smaller base also exists at Nouakchott (q.v.). The navy is usually commanded by a colonel in Mauritania's army, who was often a member of the country's governing military council until April 1992, the *Comité Militaire de Salut National* (CMSN) (q.v.).

NEMA. Mauritania's easternmost major population (q.v.) center and the administrative capital of the région of Hodh ech-Chargui (qq.v.). Néma had roughly 19,000 people in 1977, a figure that had, according to some sources, at least doubled by the late 1980s owing to drought and desertification (q.v.) in the area. By Mauritanian standards, the climate (q.v.) is relatively equable, with the often extreme heat and humidity tempered by an *hivernage* (q.v.) which typically lasts from June to October. Amenities in Néma are scarce: the town has no hotels and only a few markets and filling stations despite its location at the terminus of the *Route de l'Espoir,* (q.v.), the paved highway running 1100 kilometers from the capital, Nouakchott (q.v.). Néma also has an improved airport (q.v.), completed with West German assistance in the early 1980s.

NEWSPAPERS. With an overall literacy rate of only about 30 percent, the circulation of newspapers in Mauritania has been limited. Among the literate sector of the population (q.v.), however, the press has always played a significant role in the country's political evolution, beginning with *Al-Ittafaq* (q.v.), which was founded in 1948 and which served as an effective platform for the ambitions of Mokhtar Ould Daddah's *Union Progressiste Mauritanienne* (UPM) (qq.v.). After Mauritanian independence in 1960, the press gradually became more restricted. By the time Ould Daddah was ousted by the country's armed forces (q.v.) in July 1978, the only daily of consequence was *Ech-Chaab* (The People), a French-Arabic publication issued by the government, which carefully controlled its content. As part of the liberalization of Mauritania's political life initiated by President Maaouiya Ould Sid'Ahmed Taya (q.v.) in 1991, laws on the press and free speech were relaxed, and soon a substantial number of new publications, most in French but also some in Arabic, began to appear after they were given licenses by the government. In the mid-1990s, French-language newspapers and magazines include the weekly *Eveil-Hebdo* and the monthly *Le Temps,* a magazine, *L'Indépendant,* which appears twice a month, and *Le Peuple,* which is published six times per year. *Al-Bayane* was an Arabic-language newspaper (though it also had articles in French), and *El-Khyar* and *Muraat el-Moujtemaa* are also in circulation. On the governmental level, the Mauritanian Chamber of Commerce issues a regular bulletin, and the *Journal Officiel* serves as the Ministry of Justice's formal legal publication, issued fortnightly. (For Mauritania's television and radio services, see COMMUNICATIONS.)

NOMAD SECURITY GUARD. A small, paramilitary force of about one hundred men under the jurisdiction of the regular Mauritanian armed forces (q.v.), the Nomad Security Guard is assigned the task of policing the country's vast and often unmarked desert frontiers. In performing their duties, its members use camels as well as motor vehicles, a practice compelled by the extremely remote and forbidding terrain in its area of operations.

NOUADHIBOU. Mauritania's second-largest city and the economic center of the country, Nouadhibou—known as Port-Etienne during the French colonial period—had a population (q.v.) of 59,198 in 1988, according to official government census figures. The city accounts for the vast majority of the population in the otherwise sparsely inhabited région of Dakhlet-Nouadhibou (qq.v.), of which it is the capital. Nouadhibou is situated about halfway down the Cape Blanc (Ras Nouadhibou) peninsula, which Mauritania shares with the disputed territory of Western Sahara (q.v.), the Saharan side also including the settlement of La Guera (q.v.). The city of Nouadhibou faces the western portion of the Baie du Lévrier (q.v.), one of the only such protected areas on the West African coastline which gives the city its status as Mauritania's foremost port (q.v.) and home to the country's substantial fisheries (q.v.) industry. Aside from the *Port Minéralier* (q.v.) located several kilometers south of the city and used only by ships receiving cargoes of iron ore (q.v.), Nouadhibou has two port facilities in the 1990s, one of them older and dating from the colonial era, and the other more recently constructed and used mostly by fishing boats. Both were refurbished in the 1980s: the fishing port was improved in 1983 with the help of an $8 million loan from the World Bank, and a further improvement program completed in 1987 raised Nouadhibou's port capacity to 500,000 tons per year. Ashore, unloading and refrigeration facilities for the fishing fleet exist, although they are not generally considered as satisfactory as those in the Canary Islands, a competing fisheries center.

Nouadhibou's population is probably the most diverse in the country, due to the large number of West African and European immigrants, workers, and transients connected with the city's economy. Canary Islanders and the Asian crews of vessels from the Far East are also common, and Nouadhibou supports some tourist (q.v.) activity as well, mainly sport fishing and as a stopover for visitors to the *Parc National du Banc d'Arguin* (q.v.) situated to the south. Overland access to Nouadhibou is fairly difficult due to the lack of improved roads (q.v.), although there is a daily airline (q.v.) service to the Mauritanian capital, Nouakchott (q.v.).

Like the rest of Mauritania, Nouadhibou has had its share of political difficulties since independence. The city was a zone of tension during the Western Sahara conflict, when President Mokhtar Ould Daddah (q.v.) feared that it would be attacked by the Polisario Front (q.v.), a concern that led him to allow Moroccan troops to be stationed there. They were replaced by French paratroops in the early 1980s, as the successor military regime of Colonel Mohammed Khouna Ould Heydallah (q.v.) had by then come to fear a Moroccan attack near the city as a consequence of the Algiers Agreement (q.v.) of August 5, 1979, under which Mauritania made a separate peace with Polisario and relinquished its claim to Western Sahara. More recently, Nouadhibou was shaken by severe food riots on June 2, 1991, during which the city center was at the mercy of looters and protesters for over ten hours before order could be restored by the armed forces (q.v.) and the bread price increase that triggered the unrest could be rescinded.

NOUAKCHOTT. As Mauritania was preparing itself for independence from France in the late 1950s, the country—almost alone among the emergent nations of the Afro-Asian world—had no capital city on its own territory. Indeed, Mauritania was then administered from St. Louis, located just across the Senegal River in Senegal. Moreover, the country's leading politician (and future president), Mokhtar Ould Daddah (q.v.) desired that any capital city serve as a modern symbol of national unity, which precluded using several other cities and towns in the interior of Mauritania as the seat of government. In addition, there was the sensitive question of whether the capital would be located in an area populated predominantly by Moors (q.v.) or Black Africans.

After considerable study, Ould Daddah and his French and Mauritanian advisers settled on a site roughly halfway between St. Louis and the economic center of Port-Etienne, later renamed Nouadhibou (q.v.). Located on a small hill about six kilometers west of the Atlantic coast, Nouakchott ("place of the winds") was a sparsely inhabited *ksar* (fortified village) surrounded by flat, sandy terrain alternating with grassland. With French help, construction was begun in March 1958, and the rudiments of Mauritania's new capital were complete by the time of the country's independence on November 28, 1960. Nouakchott was designed to accommodate 15,000 people at most, as Ould Daddah understood that most commerce (q.v.) and other daily life would continue to be conducted elsewhere. A short distance west of the ksar, Nouakchott's business district was laid out with broad, grid-like streets but with little by way of significant architecture. A short distance south of this area lay the *cinquième* (fifth) district, which within a few years had a large open-air market and new housing (q.v.) developments. Both the fifth district and the business center tended, by the 1970s, to eclipse the old ksar in importance, and the headquarters of Mauritania's governmental ministries, as well as its parastatal commercial enterprises, were located there. Nouakchott's earlier years were fairly serene, and visitors remarked on the relaxed and orderly pace of life on its streets.

Beginning in the mid-1970s, Nouakchott's situation began to deteriorate. Years of droughts had made large swaths of land in the interior régions (q.v.) of the country uncultivable, and desertification (q.v.), proceeding inexorably from north to south, made a dismal agricultural (q.v.) outlook appear permanent. To escape their predicament, a sizeable portion of the Mauritanian population (q.v.) moved to the capital, where they contributed to some of the most severe problems of overurbanization in postcolonial African history. From 1975 to 1990, Nouakchott's population grew explosively—official census figures from 1977 showed 134,000 persons (already a strain on the facilities of the city), and by 1988, 393,325 were shown on the rolls, although that number was almost certainly an underestimate. Informal tallies put the population at 500,000 or more—roughly 25 percent of Mauritania's total population. City services such as water (q.v.) and sewerage as well as health (q.v.) care were strained to the breaking point, as the newcomers to Nouakchott continued to erect (legally and otherwise) crude houses and tents on the outskirts of areas built up by those who had come before. Unemployment was extremely high, and social dislocations were often profound. This concentration of people in a relatively compact location of about 1000 square kilometers did, however, make it easier for the state food relief agency, the *Commissariat à la Sécurité Alimentaire* (CSA) (q.v.), to distribute food aid efficiently and prevent deaths from starvation. To add insult to injury, the capital city itself was not immune to the effects of desertification by the mid-1980s: dunes sometimes forced their way into the city center, and sweeping sand from the insides of homes and offices became a daily ritual in some areas, especially during the *irifi* (q.v.), which reduced visibility for hours at a time.

Despite Nouakchott's straitened circumstances in the mid-1990s, the young city still possesses the most developed infrastructure in Mauritania, hosting some cultural life and a thriving private trade sector, and has an active political life, with most political parties and newspapers (q.v.) based in the capital. Nominally part of the région of Trarza (q.v.), the capital has had its own local administration and mayor beginning in the 1960s. Nouakchott's relative isolation was eased in the 1980s by the completion of several projects: road (q.v.) improvements in the direction of the Senegalese border, the construction of the *Route de l'Espoir* linking the city with areas to the east, the opening of the Friendship Port (q.v.) in 1986, and improvements to Nouakchott's airport (q.v.), the busiest in Mauritania. But these and other positive developments in the capital have to be balanced against a population problem that is not relenting and poses serious long-term questions for the city and its environs.

NOUAKCHOTT RAIDS. In June 1976 and July 1977, two audacious attacks against Mauritania's capital city were conducted by the guerrillas of the Polisario Front (q.v.), who were militarily contesting the Moroccan-Mauritanian partition of Western Sahara (q.v.) as envisaged by the Madrid Agreement (q.v.) of November 14, 1975. By the terms of the treaty, President Mokhtar Ould Daddah (q.v.) annexed the southern one-third of the former Spanish colony, land which Mauritania called Tiris el-Gharbia (q.v.). But the country immediately found itself embroiled (along with King Hassan II [q.v.] of Morocco) in an intense hit-and-run war in which the small Mauritanian armed forces (q.v.) found themselves outgunned and outmanned by the Saharawi (q.v.) nationalist fighters.

On June 2, 1976, the Polisario secretary-general, El-Ouali Mu-stapha Sayed, personally set out with a force of several hundred Sa-harawi guerrillas for the Mauritanian capital, hundreds of kilometers from the Front's staging areas in the Tindouf region of southwestern Algeria. Nouakchott was indeed an inviting target, as most of the army was far to the north, leaving few to guard the city, but on June 5, a pi-lot of Mauritania's minuscule air force (q.v.) located what turned out to be a Polisario diversionary column near Zouerate (q.v.). Informa-tion from prisoners captured in subsequent fighting with this unit dis-closed the Saharawis' real objective, although at first the intelligence was greeted with disbelief. The next day, though, the Mauritanian commander of the Zouerate region, Lieutenant Colonel Ahmed Ould Bouceif (q.v.), dispatched 400 men to race Polisario to the capital. A second Mauritanian army formation was also heading south from Tiris el-Gharbia to block the guerrillas. But they were not to arrive in time—Polisario reached the northern outskirts of Nouakchott by the morning of June 8, shelling the city for thirty minutes and returning later in the evening to aim a few projectiles into the garden of Presi-dent Ould Daddah's residence before withdrawing. Ould Bouceif's troops finally closed in on the retreating Polisario units at Bennichab, southwest of Akjoujt in the région of Inchiri (q.v.), on June 9, killing El-Ouali and many of the Front's fighters in the ensuing shootout. Another Mauritanian commander, Lieutenant Colonel Mohammed Khouna Ould Heydallah (q.v.), also successfully attacked a Polisario force in the north of the country that had been intended to relieve the attackers of Nouakchott.

The impact of this bold *ghazzi* (q.v.) was more psychological than mil-itary, as there were few Mauritanian casualties and little property dam-age and Polisario had been routed on its way home. But the attack was jarring for several reasons, not least of which was the fact that it brought into high relief the country's extreme vulnerability, as the attackers had all the advantages of speed, motivation, mobility, and surprise. The raid also helped to disabuse Mokhtar Ould Daddah of his prior belief that his Western Saharan takeover would be a largely painless affair.

After this raid, the focus of Polisario activity shifted farther north away from the Mauritanian capital, but two months after a devastating attack on Zouerate (May 1, 1977), the Front struck Nouakchott again, firing several mortar rounds near the presidential palace on July 3. The Polisario force, which had entered Mauritania from Western Sahara it-self, retreated to its home bases nearly without casualties. The second raid further undermined Mauritanian morale and contributed to Presi-dent Ould Daddah's overthrow by the armed forces barely a year later.

OIL. See Petroleum

OMBUDSMAN OF THE REPUBLIC. A somewhat uncommon institution in Africa which derives from Scandinavian practice, the post of Ombudsman was created on May 22, 1993, as one of the liberalizing measures taken before and after the advent of the Second Republic (q.v.), presided over by President Maaouiya Ould Sid'Ahmed Taya (q.v.). According to the official announcement that accompanied the formation of the post, the Ombudsman's function would be "to seek appropriate solutions to requests made by citizens over their unresolved disagreements with state administrations and any other body which is aiming to give public service."

OPERATION LAMANTIN. As the codename given by France to its aerial campaign against the armed units of the Polisario Front (q.v.) in late 1977, Operation Lamantin (Sea Cow) was launched in response to Mauritanian President Mokhtar Ould Daddah's (q.v.) increasingly desperate military situation caused by Mauritania's involvement, with Morocco, in the Western Sahara conflict (q.v.). This was brought into high relief on May 1, 1977, when Polisario fought its way into the iron ore center of Zouerate (qq.v.), capturing and holding the town for several hours, causing extensive damage to its vital facilities, and killing two French expatriate workers and taking six others captive in an attempt to force a change in French President Valéry Giscard d'Estaing's anti-Polisario policies. The French took little action until October 25, when two more French workers, seconded to the nearby railway (q.v.) line, were also taken prisoner by the Polisario Front. Two days later, Paris decided on direct military involvement at a meeting chaired by French Foreign Minister Louis de Guiringaud, and planning was begun for a program of air strikes against Polisario formations in northern Mauritania to try to restrict the Saharawi (q.v.) nationalists' hitherto untrammeled freedom of movement there. On November 2, 1977, French Mirage-4 and Breuget-Atlantic reconnaissance planes began flying over Mauritania in search of the Saharawi guerrillas.

Over the next few weeks, intensive diplomatic efforts were mounted to attempt to free the French prisoners. But Polisario held firm, hoping to entice Paris away from its unstinting support for Morocco's King Hassan II (q.v.) and Mokhtar Ould Daddah. France, in turn, conceded nothing, and a renewed raid on the iron ore railway on November 21 was enough to cause President Giscard d'Estaing to order the deployment of Jaguar fighter-bombers to Ouakkam air base near Dakar, Senegal. By the first of December there were six Jaguars deployed along with a pair of KC-135F midair refueling planes. The Jaguars first went into action on December 2, strafing a Polisario column which had again attacked the railway. On December 12, the French raids reached their peak with a two-day campaign against guerrilla concentrations near

Zouerate, resulting in significant casualties, including Mauritanian prisoners of war captured by the Saharawis. Another series of Jaguar sorties followed on December 18, but the Polisario Front had by this time decided to release its eight French captives under the auspices of the United Nations (q.v.). They were duly handed over to UN officials in Algiers on December 23, and Operation Lamantin was stood down.

OPERATION OURAGON. A brief, aggressive French-Spanish military campaign directed against the guerrilla forces of the Army of Liberation (q.v.) in February 1958, Operation Hurricane, as the French called the joint operation (the French arm of the assault was called *Ecouvillon* [Sponge] and the Spanish called their operation *Teide,* after the highest mountain in the Canary Islands), was executed partly at the request of Mauritania's paramount politician and president-to-be, Mokhtar Ould Daddah (q.v.), who was worried that the Army of Liberation's activities in northern Mauritania would disrupt his ongoing preparations for the country's independence from France. Ould Daddah was also mindful that the Army of Liberation contained an element, known as the *Front National de Libération Mauritanienne* (FNLM) (q.v.) led by a disaffected politician, Horma Ould Babana (q.v.), who had since the summer of 1956 openly allied himself with the "Greater Morocco" aspirations of the leader of the Moroccan *Istiqlal* (Independence) party, Allal el-Fassi (q.v.). Fulfillment of el-Fassi's territorial designs would entail the nearly complete absorption of Mauritania into Morocco, something that Ould Daddah was determined to prevent at any cost. France also had a substantial interest in subduing the rebels, as they were an embarrassment to France's former colony, Morocco, whose monarch, Mohammed V, had not yet succeeded in establishing full control over the southern part of his country, an area that the Army of Liberation was using to launch its attacks. The Spanish, then ensconced in neighboring Western Sahara (q.v.), were also feeling insecure, as the guerrillas were attacking their forces in the colony and were using "Spanish Sahara" as a sanctuary from which to mount raids on northern Mauritania. Spain at the time had few troops in its desert colony outside of a handful of major towns, and even these population centers were sometimes abandoned to the Army of Liberation's highly motivated fighters.

A collective military effort to rid the region of the guerrillas was the brainchild of the French general, Gabriel Bourgund, and it was assented to by the Spanish officer with responsibility for the area, General Mario Gomez Zamalloa, on September 20, 1957, at a meeting in Dakar, Senegal. Planning and the process of receiving high-level governmental approval for the scheme consumed most of the next few months, but on February 10, 1958, a force of 5000 French and 9000 Spanish troops (with dozens of combat aircraft between them) went into action against the Army of Liberation in Western Sahara, soon putting the irregulars to flight and securing the territory fully for the Spanish for the first time since Spain had established a permanent presence there in the 1880s. Ten days later (on February 20), additional French and Spanish units began a four-day "mopping up" operation, occupying Fort Trinquet (q.v.) and the settlement of Ain Ben Tili in extreme northeast Mauritania, effectively severing the supply lines of the guerrillas. Permanent bases for the troops of both countries were soon set up, often forcing the Saharawi (q.v.) tribes of the region to live for the first time under direct colonial rule. Although French and Spanish casualties in the campaign were light (about a dozen killed and fifty wounded in the entire affair), the Army of Liberation's losses were much higher, and many of its members were forced to settle in Morocco and elsewhere. The rebel movement, already suffering from grave internal dissention, completely disintegrated several months later. Freed from the guerrillas' distractions, Mokhtar Ould Daddah was able to hold the Congress of Aleg (q.v.) in May 1958, which consolidated several diverse political tendencies in Mauritania into a new organization, the *Parti de Regroupement Mauritanien* (PRM) (q.v.), which was to lead the country to full independence from France eighteen months later, on November 28, 1960.

ORGANISATION DES NATIONALISTES MAURITANIENS (ONM). An exiled political group, the Organization of Mauritanian Nationalists was formed around 1980 by blacks from Mauritania's southern régions (q.v.), and was based for the most part in Dakar, Senegal. With a mostly Halpulaar (q.v.) following, the party objected to what it perceived as favoritism toward Moorish (q.v.) Mauritanians and pledged to fight all types of racial discrimination. It also urged that the *haratines* (q.v.), the former black slaves (q.v.) in the country, join with their black Mauritanian counterparts in the south—an uncertain prospect since most "Black Moors" identified with their former Beydane (q.v.) masters and used Hassaniya (q.v.) Arabic as their *lingua franca*. The ONM was a tactical ally, in the early 1980s, of the *Alliance pour une Mauritanie Démocratique* (AMD) (q.v.), which opposed the domestic and foreign relations (q.v.) policies of the ruling *Comité Militaire de Salut National* (CMSN) (q.v.). It never formally joined the AMD, however, and publicly welcomed the accession to power, on December 12, 1984, of Colonel Maaouiya Ould Sid'Ahmed Taya (q.v.), as the ONM saw him as potentially more sympathetic to black Mauritanian aspirations.

ORGANISATION POUR LA MISE EN VALEUR DU FLEUVE SENEGAL (OMVS). The Senegal River Development Authority was founded on October 29, 1972, as a tripartite international organization comprising Mali, Mauritania, and Senegal; a fourth country, Guinea, declined to participate at first but was officially admitted to membership in 1987. All the member states of OMVS derive considerable benefits from their proximity to the Senegal River and its tributaries, often the only water resources (q.v.) in the area, yet are well aware of the limitations of the river for agricultural (q.v.) purposes. Seasonal flooding of the river, essential for crops, is nearly completely dependent upon an uncertain climate (q.v.), with the Senegal River either overflowing its banks excessively during the *hivernage* (q.v.) or not rising to flood stage at all during dry years. Moreover, salt water from the Atlantic Ocean enters the river at its outlet near St. Louis on the Senegal-Mauritania border, an occurrence that is harmful to agriculture and has a negative effect on long-term soil quality and freshwater fisheries (q.v.). Consequently, all three members of the OMVS agreed on the construction of an elaborate (and expensive) system of dams to regulate the flooding of the river and to ensure that additional tracts of arable land would be created. This was especially important for Mauritania, as droughts and the process of desertification (q.v.) had greatly reduced the proportion of its vast territory that was suitable for agriculture and livestock (q.v.) herding. It was also imperative to keep the Senegal River from flooding areas of high population (q.v.), such as the riverbank town of Kaédi (q.v.), during its annual rampages.

After a considerable planning process, it was decided by the OMVS membership that two major dam projects would be undertaken:

• The Diama Dam, located near a Senegalese village about fifty kilometers inland from the Atlantic coast and straddling the Senegal-Mauritania boundary line at a point where the river was 400 to 500 meters wide. This dam would be primarily intended to restrain the intrusion of salt water beyond the area, thus halting the degradation of the riverbed and the surrounding soil during the dry season. Alternatively, the dam could be used to regulate the seasonal release of water so as to extend agricultural growing times in Senegal's province of Dagana and in Mauritania's administrative région of Trarza (qq.v.).

• The Manantali Dam, situated in Mali on the Bofing tributary of the Senegal River about 250 kilometers south of the riverine Malian town of Kayes. A larger project than the Diama, the Manantali Dam would create a huge reservoir behind it, allowing for the controlled release of water downstream as well as creating additional cultivable land (400,000 hectares) in the vicinity. It was also envisioned that the dam would supply electricity (q.v.) to surrounding towns and villages through the use of hydroelectric generating techniques.

Over and above this array of major barrages, each OMVS member state undertook to build additional dams and reservoirs on their own territory. For Mauritania, this included dams on the Gorgol River (the only substantial tributary of the Senegal within the country) and elsewhere in the southwest and south-central régions. Although the articulation of these plans took relatively little time, financing these projects was to take considerably longer. Funding in excess of $500 million was eventually secured from various sources, including France, Germany, Libya, and Saudi Arabia and other Gulf countries as well as the World Bank and the European Community (EC). Construction was underway by the late 1970s and early 1980s, and the Mauritanian government's own dams were gradually brought into use, adding about 30,000 hectares to the country's total. Even with foreign help, the OMVS projects were a drain on its members' finances (the Gorgol Valley scheme in Mauritania cost $100 million), but the organization was able to open the Diama Dam in 1985 and the Manantali Dam in 1988, although the latter's hydroelectric plant was not begun until October 1992 owing to disputes over where the projected 800 megawatts of power would be distributed.

As it turned out, these new water-management arrangements were urgently needed. The Senegal River, swollen by increased rainfall amounts, flooded extensively in the early 1990s and damage to cropland was partly avoided by the judicious use of the new controlling works. Plans are under way also to make the Senegal River navigable to oceangoing vessels as far as Kayes, Mali, and the Manantali hydropower station was due to come on-line in 1996.

The Senegal River Development Authority also has a valuable political purpose for Mauritania: it symbolizes the country's commitment to the development of the southern régions largely populated by Black Africans, and thus serves as a counterpoise of sorts to Mauritania's Arabization policy (q.v.) and general orientation toward the Arab Maghreb. In addition, shared investments and interests in the Senegal River Valley may have played at least some role in the eventual lessening of tensions between Senegal and Mauritania following the violent and destructive events of April 1989 that began the Sengal-Mauritania Crisis (q.v.).

OUALATA (variant: Walata). As a small village of a few thousand people in Mauritania's extreme southeast about eighty kilometers north of Néma (q.v.), the administrative center of the région of Hodh ech-Chargui (qq.v.), Oualata served as a key commercial crossroads almost from the start of the recorded history of the area. By the ninth century A.D., three Berber (q.v.) ethnic groupings, the Djodala, Lemtuna, and the Messufa, had established the Sanhadja Confederation and effectively controlled the trading caravans from the city of Sijil-masa in the north to the Ghana Empire in the south. Oualata straddled the most efficient route between Sijilmasa and Ghana, and over time evolved into a trading center in its own right. It also served as an assembly point for Muslims setting out on the arduous pilgrimage (*hajj*) to Mecca. In the early eleventh century, the Sanhadja Confederation lost its influence after the introduction of a stricter variety of Islam (q.v.) to northwest Africa and was finally supplanted by the Almoravids (q.v.) around 1035. Some of the trading villages along the north-south trade route did not survive the Sanhadja period, but Oualata continued to thrive, becoming a center of Almoravid intellectual life and acquiring a large library of early Islamic literature and a renowned Islamic school that survives to the present. Despite their eventually being in control of a huge area extending from Senegal to Spain—and defeating the Ghana Empire along the way—the Almoravids could not resist the entry of Arab influences from the east, and steadily declined in importance until their final collapse around 1150. Trade routes were shifting as well—away from the interior and toward the Atlantic and Mediterranean coasts where Europeans were establishing themselves. By 1674, the year of the formation of the Adrar, Brakna, Tagant, and Trarza Arab dynasties, Oualata began to settle into the status of an increasingly remote provincial backwater, connected to the rest of Mauritania only by unimproved roads (q.v.).

In the late 1980s, Oualata suddenly became well known in a far grimmer context. In September 1988, it was disclosed that sixty-eight mainly black Mauritanians were being imprisoned under extremely harsh conditions at a former French fort just outside the town. Their number was divided between members of the armed forces (q.v.) who had been convicted of taking part in an unsuccessful coup plot allegedly hatched in October 1987, and blacks who were accused of associating themselves with the *Forces de Libération Africaine de Mauritanie* (FLAM) (q.v.), and in particular helping to draft FLAM's controversial pamphlet, *Le Manifesto du Négro-Mauritanien Opprimé* (q.v.). Reportedly, the prisoners were kept chained for most of the day, subjected to a regimen of forced labor in an almost unbearable climate (q.v.), given little food and no medical care, and regularly beaten by their guards. No communication with relatives, friends, or legal counsel was allowed. By September 1988, some inmates were so weak they could move about only by crawling, and some had taken to eating leaves and grass fetched from the prison grounds during exercise periods. The human rights organization Amnesty International was forthright in its criticism of the Mauritanian government regarding Oualata. In its November 1989 report on Mauritania (see Bibliography), it stated that "it appears that the cruel and inhuman treatment to which these prisoners were subjected was inflicted deliberately as an additional, extrajudicial form of punishment, rather than by accident or as a result of the inefficiency of the guards responsible for these prisoners."

For at least four Oualata inmates, the experience proved fatal. It was alleged—and the government gradually confirmed—that deaths at the prison had taken place. They included:

- Téné Youssouf Guéye, a sixty-year-old writer who came to Oualata with preexisting health problems after having been convicted in September 1986 of being a FLAM sympathizer. Serving a four-year term, he died in September 1988 of malnutrition and other causes.
- Bâ Alassane Omar, a black Mauritanian warrant officer serving a life term for his alleged association with the 1987 coup plot. He reportedly died on August 28, 1988.
- Abdul Ghandous Bâ, also associated with the October 1987 events, died on September 13, 1988.
- Djigo Tafsirou, an agricultural engineer and former minister of health who was convicted in 1986 of being a FLAM militant, died on September 27, 1988.

The Mauritanian government, headed by President Maaouiya Ould Sid'Ahmed Taya (q.v.), reacted to these disclosures by alleging that at least two of the deaths did not take place at the prison itself, but rather at a nearby hospital where the inmates were receiving medical attention. In addition, the regime began to allow visits to the jail by journalists and other observers, and apparently punished some prison guards and officials. By early 1989, all of Oualata's prisoners were transferred to another facility, with somewhat better conditions, located at Ayoun el-Atrouss (q.v.), and the fortress at Oualata was closed.

OUED ED-DAHAB. See Tiris el-Gharbia

OUGUIYA (UM). From June 30, 1973, the primary unit of Mauritania's currency (q.v.) after the country's pullout from the *Communauté Financière Africaine* (CFA) (q.v.), the *ouguiya* underwent steady devaluation in subsequent years, despite at first having had a fixed value of 10 to 1 relative to the French franc. The successive devaluations were due in part to Mauritania's often precarious economic condition, as well as pressure from financial institutions such as the World Bank and the International Monetary Fund (IMF), which advocated that currencies in developing countries not be of fixed valuation. In April 1996 the ouguiya's exchange rate stood at approximately 137 per U.S. $1.00. Simultaneous with the introduction of the ouguiya, a subunit, the *khoum* (q.v.) was issued with the value of 5 per ouguiya. In the mid-1990s, there exist coins with the value of 1, 5, 10, and 20 ouguiyas, and notes are issued by the *Banque Centrale de Mauritanie* (BCM) (q.v.) in the denominations of 100, 200, 500, and 1000 ouguiyas.

OURAGON, OPERATION. See Operation Ouragon

PARC NATIONAL DU BANC D'ARGUIN. Established in 1974 and encompassing approximately 12,000 square kilometers along Mauritania's Atlantic coast, the Banc d'Arguin National Park is situated about 150 kilometers north of Nouakchott (q.v.) along the unimproved road to Nouadhibou (qq.v.) and near the settlement of Nouamghar, which is home to the small Imraguen (q.v.) tribe of fishermen. The wildlife preserve includes inland areas, several islands, and coastal waters in which most fisheries (q.v.) activity is prohibited. The park is home to the world's largest concentration of wintering birds, some of which migrate in the autumn months all the way from Europe and North America. Shorebirds such as flamingoes, herons, and pelicans are common there, as are several rare species of seal, dolphin, and other seagoing mammals. It was estimated in the early 1990s by the United Nations Educational, Scientific, and Cultural Organization (UNESCO) that the park is populated by over two million birds comprising 250 different species. Because of its great natural beauty and relative ease of access from the capital city, visitors to the park account for a large share of Mauritania's tourist (q.v.) trade. The Mauritanian government sponsored an international conference on the Banc d'Arguin National Park in May 1993 in Nouakchott, with the objective of increasing the preserve's visibility at home and abroad and to ensure the continued protection of its natural assets.

PARTI DE REGROUPEMENT MAURITANIEN (PRM). In May 1958 the leader of the *Union Progressiste Mauritanienne* (UPM), Mokhtar Ould Daddah (qq.v.), decided to attempt to reconcile the varying political tendencies in Mauritania and form a single, inclusive organization that would add credibility to his country's quest for independence from France, and increase his own chances of acquiring predominant political power. In a *coup de grâce* that manifested considerable skill, Ould Daddah, at the Congress of Aleg (q.v.), persuaded the UPM, the *Entente Mauritanienne* (q.v.), and the black nationalist *Bloc Démocratique du Gorgol* (BDG) (q.v.) to forsake their separate identities and form the Mauritanian Regroupment Party. Nominally headed by Sidi el-Mokhtar N'Diaye as its president, Ould Daddah exercised decisive influence in PRM affairs through his secretary-generalship of the party. The PRM's platform was strongly nationalistic: it rejected both Morocco's territorial claim to Mauritania and all proposals for a federation of the country with any other state, and poured cold water on a French concept of uniting all its Saharan African territories into a Common Saharan States Organization dominated by Paris. However, the PRM did favor joining the French Community once Mauritania became independent, thereby paying off traditional Francophile elements within the Entente and the UPM. The party also insisted on a political balance between the Moorish (q.v.) tribes of the north and the Black Africans who lived mainly in the Senegal River Valley. To ensure both this and the inculcation of a spirit of national unity, Ould Daddah set up local PRM party committees open to participation by every citizen. In reality, the older, more conservative ex-UPM politicians remained firmly in control, and soon the PRM showed signs of authoritarianism by expelling, at a party congress in Nouakchott (q.v.) in July 1958, its more radical, anti-French and Arab nationalist members, who two months later (September 26) established the Nadha (q.v.) party, which soon received considerable backing and which fractured the unity that Ould Daddah had striven to achieve. But having triumphed massively (a reported 302,018 votes in favor to a mere 19,126 opposed) in his effort to produce an affirmative vote in the Mauritanian referendum of September 28, 1958, on the country's membership in the French Community, Ould Daddah maintained his leading position by revamping the structure of the PRM and moving closer to neighboring Mali, by way of seeking support against Morocco, which Nadha's pan-Arabists were ardently supporting. He also adopted a more flexible attitude toward France.

Soon after these changes, Ould Daddah was able to proclaim the Islamic Republic of Mauritania in October 1958 and present a new, interim constitution for approval on March 22, 1959 (q.v.). By this time, the fortunes of Nadha were in decline, and the Mauritanian Regroupment Party captured all forty seats in the elections to the *Assemblée Nationale* (q.v.) held on May 17, 1959, although this victory was not achieved without the proscription of all non-PRM political activity. Moreover, the party's central committee, packed with Ould Daddah loyalists, controlled all selections to the electoral lists. After the attainment of Mauritania's independence on November 28, 1960, most of the country's politicians rallied behind Mokhtar Ould Daddah, who reciprocated their support by naming Nadha members to his new Council of Ministers (q.v.) in September 1961. The following month, on October 4, Ould Daddah organized the Congress of Unity (q.v.), which merged the PRM, the remnants of Nadha, the *Union Nationale Mauritanienne* (UNM), and the *Union Socialiste des Musulmans Mauritaniens* (USMM) (qq.v.) into an entirely new political entity, the *Parti du Peuple Mauritanien* (PPM) (q.v.).

PARTI DES KHADIHINES DE MAURITANIE (PKM). A small, clandestine Marxist-Leninist movement, the Proletarian Party of Mauritania was founded in 1973 at a time of increasing opposition to President Mokhtar Ould Daddah (q.v.), whose basically conservative domestic and foreign policies had alienated many younger Mauritanians. The Khadihine Party advocated the overthrow of Ould Daddah's "feudal" and "imperialist" government, and, somewhat paradoxically, blended a Marxist platform with a denunciation of Ould Daddah for not adhering sufficiently to the precepts of Islam (q.v.). The PKM also criticized the monopolization of Mauritania's political life by the *Parti du Peuple Mauritanien* (PPM) (q.v.) and urged the formation of multiple political parties and youth organizations as part of a thorough liberalization of the country's politics. The party also had a newspaper, *The Cry of the Oppressed,* which circulated secretly in Mauritania, as freedom of the press did not exist in the country at that time. The Khadihine Party was at times loosely allied with the larger, more moderate *Mouvement National Démocratique* (MND) (q.v.) which served, from its formation in 1968, as an umbrella organization with various tendencies within it. The PKM, like much of the MND, at first strongly supported the efforts of the Polisario Front (q.v.) to create an independent state in Western Sahara (q.v.), but later rallied to the Ould Daddah regime after the president decided upon the annexation of Tiris el-Gharbia (q.v.), the southern one-third of the contested Spanish colony. Never well-organized and with only a thin base of popular support, the Khadihine Party fell into a rapid decline after 1975, although elements of the group were affiliated with the exiled *Alliance pour une Mauritanie Démocratique* (AMD) (q.v.) during the 1980s.

PARTI DU PEUPLE MAURITANIEN (PPM). The Mauritanian People's Party (known in Arabic as the *Hizb esh-Shaab al-Moritany*) was established under the guidance of the country's first president, Mokhtar Ould Daddah (q.v.), at the Congress of Unity (q.v.) held in October 1961, less than a year after Mauritania's independence from France. At the congress, a variety of political groupings, including Ould Daddah's *Parti de Regroupement Mauritanien* (PRM), the Nadha party, the *Union Nationale Mauritanienne* (UNM), and the *Union Socialiste des Musulmans Mauritaniens* (USMM) (qq.v.) were merged to form the PPM, evidence not only of Mokhtar Ould Daddah's skill at co-opting his opponents, but also of his insistence that only a single political party could preserve the unity of the fledgling country. Indeed, on December 25, 1961, the PPM was designated as the sole legal political organization in Mauritania, and thenceforth any dissent from Ould Daddah's policies could legally come only from within the party. Although the PPM was officially democratic in that all of its leaders and governing bodies were elected, the lack of any legal alternative and the screening of all candidates by the president and his protégés made this little more than a fiction. In practice, most decision making was entrusted to the *Bureau Politique National* (BPN) (q.v.), a small, dedicated group of Ould Daddah loyalists who gradually took over many state, as well as party, functions. Below the BPN were locally based committees in each of the *cercles* (later régions) (qq.v.) of the country, with all of them meeting regularly in a "federation" that was firmly subordinate to the BPN. The PPM also demonstrated from an early date that it intended to extend its reach into other areas of Mauritanian life; the *Union des Travailleurs Mauritaniens* (UTM) (q.v.) and the *Union Nationale des Femmes Mauritaniennes* (UNFM), respectively the state trade union and the women's (q.v.) organization, were soon operating under the PPM banner.

A further milestone on the PPM's path to becoming a virtually dictatorial "vanguard" party totally under the control of Mokhtar Ould Daddah was reached on January 28 and 29, 1964, at the Conference of Kaédi (q.v.). This PPM conclave, held under conditions of stringent security and which bypassed the National Assembly (q.v.) set up under the Mauritanian constitution of May 1961 (q.v.), featured a stern lecture delivered by Ould Daddah to the BPN's most reliable members, warning them of "electoralism" (trading votes for favors) and castigating them for their alleged lack of responsiveness to popular opinion. Ould Daddah decreed that thenceforth, every deputy of the *Assemblée Nationale* (which also had its separate budget abolished) would be selected from an approved list, relegating the Mauritanian parliament, a hotbed of opposition, to the sidelines. Finally, to ensure obedience, each member of parliament, as well as every PPM member and elected government employee, was required to submit, before assuming his duties, an undated letter of resignation which Ould Daddah could invoke at will. After the Kaédi Conference, state and party were nearly fully merged. National policies, including the first steps taken in the direction of Arabization (q.v.) and in the country's foreign relations (q.v.) and economic affairs, were formulated by Mokhtar Ould Daddah and his most trusted assistants with no popular consultation. The PPM's monopoly of most real power did not, however, ensure social peace. By the late 1960s, the continued control of a large part of Mauritania's economy by France caused large-scale protests and the formation of illegal opposition political parties. Although President Ould Daddah overcame this instability in the early 1970s by a combination of repression, "radical" public pronouncements, and the nationalization of the French-owned MIFERMA iron ore (qq.v.) mining consortium, Mauritania did not become more democratic, as the PPM was by now nearly coterminous with the state bureaucracy and Ould Daddah's reelection in a series of *pro forma* presidential ballots was never in doubt. With regard to the fate of the adjacent Spanish colony of Western Sahara (q.v.), the whole of which was always claimed by Mauritania, the PPM's role was quite subservient. After Ould Daddah had decided in principle to annex the southern one-third of the territory, ceding Morocco's King Hassan II (q.v.) the remainder, the PPM, at its Fourth Congress held in Nouakchott (q.v.) during August 15–20, 1975, endorsed, as expected, the president's move. A resolution passed at the meeting approved Ould Daddah's "wise and lucid policy pursued with a view to the liberation and return to the mother country that part of our national territory which is still occupied."

The days of the Mauritanian People's Party, as well as that of the Ould Daddah regime itself, were numbered, however. The war between the Mauritanian armed forces (q.v.) and the guerrillas of the Polisario Front (q.v.), which demanded an independent state in Western Sahara, nearly destroyed the country's fragile economy and caused the resurgence of social tensions that the PPM had fought to submerge. In the midst of the punishing Polisario attacks on Mauritanian targets, Mokhtar Ould Daddah was overthrown in a bloodless coup mounted by disaffected army officers on July 10, 1978. The PPM was immediately outlawed, as was all other political activity. Many PPM officials, like President Ould Daddah himself, eventually wound up in exile, where they were a significant force in the ranks of the opposition *Alliance pour une Mauritanie Démocratique* (AMD) (q.v.) in the 1980s.

PARTI MAURITANIEN POUR RENOUVEAU (PMR). A small opposition political grouping, the Mauritanian Party for Renewal was founded in 1991 in the wake of the unprecedented liberalization of the country's internal affairs initiated by President Maaouiya Ould Sid'Ahmed Taya (q.v.). After Ould Taya's victory in the presidential elections held on January 17, 1992, the PMR, unlike several other political parties, did not boycott the subsequent polling in March for the *Assemblée Nationale* (q.v.). However, the party captured only one seat of seventy-nine in Mauritania's lower house, the vast majority of slots being filled by President Ould Taya's *Parti Républicain, Démocratique et Social* (PRDS) (q.v.). A prominent figure in the PMR in the early 1990s was Mohammed Khouna Ould Heydallah (q.v.), who served as Mauritania's president between 1980 and 1984.

PARTI REPUBLICAIN, DEMOCRATIQUE ET SOCIAL (PRDS). Mauritania's Republican, Democratic, and Social Party was founded on August 29, 1991, a few months after President Maaouiya Ould

Sid'Ahmed Taya (q.v.) announced that for the first time since the country's independence in 1960, multiple political parties would be allowed to function and field candidates for the presidency and for seats in a bicameral parliament. Although the PRDS was nominally led by Cheikh Sid'Ahmed Ould Baba, a close associate of Ould Taya's from the armed forces (q.v.) and a former foreign minister and minister of the interior, it was clear that the Mauritanian head of state was the real force behind the party. As the PRDS candidate for president in the election held on January 17, 1992, Ould Taya easily defeated all his competitors, although opposition groups such as the *Union des Forces Démocratiques* (UFD) (q.v.) complained that the PRDS enjoyed privileged access to the resources of the state, ensuring its decisive victory in the presidential balloting. Greatly assisted by a boycott of the parliamentary elections in March and April 1991 led by the UFD and several other opposition parties, the PRDS consolidated its good fortune, winning sixty-seven of seventy-nine seats in the lower house of parliament, the *Assemblée Nationale* (q.v.), and garnering thirty-six of fifty-six places in the Mauritanian Senate (q.v.). The PRDS's power was strengthened two years later, when the party won all but thirty-six of the 208 seats of the municipal councils spread among the country's régions (q.v.), although the PRDS was rumored to be weak in Brakna, Gorgol, and Guidimaka (qq.v.), three régions where black Mauritanians lived in great numbers. In these locations, candidates from the opposition scored some successes. The senatorial elections (for one-third of that body) in April 1994 were a repeat performance: PRDS candidates received all but one of the seventeen contested seats. Despite claims by the opposition that the PRDS was merely a front organization for Ould Taya and his colleagues from the former military governing body, the *Comité Militaire de Salut National* (CMSN) (q.v.), the party was not immune to the forces that were steadily reshaping the country's political life in the mid-1990s. In late 1993, for example, it was learned that disputes had erupted inside the PRDS between the older, "traditionalist" leadership of Ould Baba and younger activists who wanted the party to be less set in its ways. The PRDS's stature, moreover, did not prevent certain of its members from being arrested by the security forces shortly before the January 1994 municipal elections and charged with conspiracy to commit electoral fraud. And although the party's fortunes were greatly on the rise in the 1994–95 period and were bolstered by critical defections from the opposition ranks, internal dissention continued, and a dozen or so PRDS members were among those arrested by the authorities on October 23, 1995 and accused of illegal political activity on behalf of the pro-Iraq Arab Baath Socialist Party (ABSP) (q.v.).

PARTY OF MAURITANIAN JUSTICE. A small, clandestine political grouping formed in 1974 at a time of unprecedented opposition to the single-party rule of President Mokhtar Ould Daddah's *Parti du Peuple Mauritanien* (PPM) (qq.v.), the Party of Mauritanian Justice was composed of dissidents who were somewhat more conservative than their counterparts in the *Mouvement National Démocratique* (MND) and the *Parti des Khadihines de Mauritanie* (PKM) (qq.v.), two other groups formed in 1968 and 1973, respectively. The party called for a federation between Mauritania, Morocco, and Senegal as a remedy for problems related to the country's economic development, urged a greater role for Islam (q.v.) in Mauritanian affairs, and condemned the PPM's monopoly of power. The party's influence was always very limited, but elements of the Justice Party were active in exile during the 1980s as one of several constituent parts of the *Alliance pour une Mauritanie Démocratique* (AMD) (q.v.).

PETROLEUM. Like the great majority of developing countries, Mauritania is totally dependent upon petroleum imports, as it has no known substantial oil resources of its own, either on land or offshore. Moreover, the importance (and cost) of oil imports acquired greater significance after about 1970, as a general rise in the demand for oil and oil-related products such as gasoline and kerosene placed great strains upon the country's small system of tank farms and distribution mechanisms, centered mainly in Nouadhibou (q.v.). The heaviest demand (about three-quarters) was for diesel fuel, needed to power trucks, the railway (q.v.) line, and equipment for the iron ore (q.v.) and other industries. Butane was also increasingly critical to the lives of ordinary Mauritanians as the 1980s ended, due to government efforts to decrease the use of wood for cooking purposes, a practice which had caused the deforestation of land in the southern régions (q.v.) of Mauritania and accelerated the process of desertification (q.v.). The fuel supply problem was somewhat offset, however, by the close ties the regime of President Mokhtar Ould Daddah (q.v.) had cultivated with oil-rich Arab League (q.v.) states such as Algeria, Iraq, Kuwait, and Saudi Arabia. These countries sometimes gave Mauritania access to some of their own vast supplies of oil at concessionary rates, and also provided technical advice and financing. In particular, the friendship between President Ould Daddah and Algerian President Houari Boumedienne (q.v.) paid especially handsome dividends for Mauritania. In 1978, an Algerian-financed, $140 million oil refinery complex opened in Nouadhibou. Algeria also provided a guaranteed supply of its light crude oil for the facility. This new refining capacity was only partially utilized, though, as technical problems and inadequate port (q.v.) facilities caused the plant to operate for only two years (1982 and 1983) and well under its designed capacity. It was shut down by 1984 while the Mauritanian government reassessed the situation and reorganized the entire petroleum sector.

In 1987, the Nouadhibou oil refinery reopened, after President Maaouiya Ould Sid'Ahmed Taya (q.v.) had agreed to allow Algeria a greatly increased role in his country's economic affairs. With a capacity of 1 million tons of crude oil per year, and with the facility operated by the Algerian parastatal, the *Entreprise Nationale de Raffinage et de Distribution des Produits Pétroliers* (NAFTAL), Mauritania's supplies seemed assured for some years to come. In addition, pipelines were laid to various new locations throughout the country, and significant investment was made, both in Nouadhibou and in Nouakchott (q.v.), to ensure that the vessels used in the critical fisheries (q.v.) sector had enough fuel to perform their work. But once again, the Nouadhibou refinery failed to live up to expectations, as managerial and technical problems cropped up and necessitated the import of already refined oil products at far greater cost. A relatively small domestic market for diesel fuel and gasoline in Mauritania (roughly 250,000 tons) exacerbated the problem, as it tended to obviate economies of scale.

The Gulf Crisis (q.v.), which began on August 2, 1990, with the invasion of Kuwait by Saddam Hussein's Iraq, had a severely negative impact on Mauritania. With its major oil suppliers, Iraq and Kuwait alike, cut off, Mauritanians soon felt the burden of extensive shortages and skyrocketing prices, aggravated by the Gulf states' alienation from the Ould Taya regime due to its perceived pro-Iraq diplomatic stance. After the end of the Gulf War, Mauritania simultaneously mended fences with the Gulf monarchies and turned toward even greater reliance upon Algeria in the financing and operation of its oil facilities. In early 1993, following a new round of fuel shortages in the country, it was announced that the Mauritanian state fuel distribution company, the *Société Mauritanienne de Commercialisation des Produits Pétroliers* (SMCPP), would be effectively merged with its larger Algerian counterpart, NAFTAL, with the Mauritanian government retaining only a 49 percent share, which in any event it intended to sell to private interests by 1995. Some Mauritanians voiced concern that the country was entering into an inordinately close relationship with a single oil supplier, but the Ould Taya regime hoped that Mauritania's fuel sector would be stabilized for good. At the same time, new tank farms were under construction near Nouakchott with financial help from the African Development Bank (ADB), a necessary step if the increasing number of fishing vessels plying Mauritanian waters were to be rapidly and adequately serviced.

PHOSPHATES. Surveys by an international consortium in the early 1980s revealed that phosphate deposits existed near Bofel, a small settlement in Brakna (q.v.) in the vicinity of the Senegal River. It was estimated that the site contained anywhere from 95 to 150 million tons of phosphates, but the projected high cost of exploitation (over $400 million in 1984) meant that by the mid-1990s no steps had been taken to begin mining operations.

POLISARIO FRONT. See Frente Popular para la Liberación de Saguia el-Hamra y Río de Oro (Polisario Front)

POPULAR FRONT FOR THE LIBERATION OF SAGUIA EL-HAMRA AND RIO DE ORO. See Frente Popular para la Liberacíon de Saguia el-Hamra Río de Oro (Polisario Front)

POPULATION. Unlike certain other African countries, Mauritania never suffered from overpopulation. According to a 1994 estimate, the country had only 2.11 million people, and its population density, at 1.8 per square kilometer, was one of the lowest on the entire continent, with vast swaths of the Mauritanian Sahara nearly devoid of human life. These statistics, however, belie a host of related characteristics. For example, Mauritania has one of the fastest population growth rates to be found anywhere in the developing world—2.9 percent per year over the decade of 1975–85 and believed to be on the increase. In addition, a combination of long, severe droughts and the seemingly inexorable process of desertification (q.v.) has caused massive migrations of formerly nomadic individuals, as well as herders and farmers, to the cities and towns, wreaking additional havoc on Mauritania's agricultural and livestock (qq.v.) sectors. In contrast with the early 1960s, when 90 percent of all Mauritanians, black or Moorish (q.v.), lived in the rural hinterland, by the late 1980s only 12 percent did so. Most of the remainder had moved to urbanized areas, where employment opportunities were minimal but which at least ensured an adequate supply of food. The Mauritanian capital, Nouakchott (q.v.), is the most prominent example of this demographic shift: planned for a population of 15,000 upon its founding in 1958, it had mushroomed (by unofficial estimates) to 500,000 or more by the early 1990s, probably accounting for a quarter or more of the country's people. Other centers, such as Atar, Kaédi, Néma, Nouadhibou, and Rosso (qq.v.), doubled or tripled in size between 1970 and 1985. Further overcrowding is forecast to be the rule rather than the exception, since estimates by the United Nations (q.v.) and other organizations put the rate of annual increase for the urban population at a staggering 9.8 percent. Rampant urbanization has caused many problems, particularly in Nouakchott, as successive governments have been obliged to allocate scarce resources to sustaining the new arrivals during the same period that rurally generated contributions to the national budget (q.v.) were steadily declining. And efforts to induce at least some of the displaced persons to return to their former occupations have been largely unsuccessful, since they hinge on climatic (q.v.) and other factors beyond any government's control. Mauritania's population is also predominantly youthful: in 1985, fully 72 percent were aged thirty or under, and an estimated 46.4 percent were under the age of fifteen. This has contributed to a troubled atmosphere, especially in the areas of education (q.v.) and politics.

The racial composition of the Mauritanian population has been the most controversial demographic matter. The government maintains that Moors make up about 80 percent of the total, with Black Africans comprising the remainder. Opposition groups, notably the *Forces de Libération Africaine de Mauritanie* (FLAM) (q.v.), have accused the regime of deliberately understating the black population in order to secure its grip on power. FLAM and its supporters claim that blacks comprise a majority in the country, although their numbers often include the so-called Black Moors, or *haratines* (q.v.), who have adopted Arabic culture over the years and who speak Hassaniya (q.v.) Arabic, exactly like their Beydane (q.v.) counterparts. Some independent observers believe that the Black African population is somewhat higher than 20 percent, with others alleging that the birth rate for Halpulaaren (q.v.) and other blacks is higher than that for Moorish Mauritanians. Regardless of the actual situation, the contentious disputes over the ethnic composition of Mauritania seem destined to continue. In addition, the government has been slow to collect and release census data due to a variety of administrative difficulties.

The official population statistics for Nouakchott and each of Mauritania's régions (q.v.) as of 1988 were as follows (see individual entries on each):

District of Nouakchott	393,325
Adrar	61,043
Assaba	107,123
Brakna	192,157
Dakhlet-Nouadhibou	63,030
Guidimaka	116,436
Gorgol	184,359
Hodh ech-Chargui	212,203
Hodh el-Gharbi	159,296
Inchiri	14,613
Tagant	64,508
Tiris Zemmour	33,147
Trarza	202,596

PORT-ETIENNE. See Nouadhibou

PORT MINERALIER (of Nouadhibou). An extensive port facility designed exclusively for the export of iron ore (q.v.) from the interior of Mauritania, the Port Minéralier is located ten kilometers south of the country's second city and economic center, Nouadhibou (q.v.). It features jetties, a mineral crusher, and other equipment suitable to accommodate large merchant vessels, and also serves as the terminus of the railway (q.v.) line from the mining center of Zouerate (q.v.) in northeast Mauritania. About four kilometers north of the port is Cansado, a town populated almost entirely by the employees of SNIM-SEM (q.v.), the Mauritanian parastatal that operates the mines, railway, and the Port Minéralier itself. The port was constructed by SNIM's predecessor company, the French-controlled MIFERMA (q.v.) consortium, and was slated for significant expansion in the mid-1990s, due mainly to the increased sizes of the ships serving the existing facility and the need to replace outdated and deteriorating equipment.

PORTS. Mauritania's 754-kilometer Atlantic coastline has no natural harbors except at Nouadhibou (q.v.), where the bulk of the country's fisheries (q.v.) industry is concentrated. In the early 1990s, the port facilities at Nouadhibou were elaborate, consisting of a 250-meter quay with a depth of three meters, a ninety-meter anchorage with a depth of seven meters, a 130-meter wharf with adjacent waters eight meters deep, and a quay 600 meters long that can accommodate vessels with a draft of under six meters. Smaller merchant ships use these wharves as well as ships connected with fisheries, but Mauritania's massive exports of iron ore (q.v.) are handled several kilometers south of Nouadhibou at the *Port Minéralier* (q.v.), which is the terminus of the railway (q.v.) line running from the interior. Along the Senegal River, a few small-scale ferry services and shallow-draft cargo vessels are in use, notably in the areas of Kaédi and Rosso (qq.v.), while the national capital, Nouakchott (q.v.), is serviced by the Friendship Port (q.v.) completed in September 1986.

PRESIDENTIAL GUARD. See Bataillon de la Sécurité Présidentielle

PROVISIONAL CONSTITUTION (Of December 1980). Less than a year after Colonel Mohammed Khouna Ould Heydallah (q.v.) had defeated his rivals for the Mauritanian presidency, he found his policies under severe attack from his colleagues on the ruling *Comité Militaire de Salut National* (CMSN) (q.v.). Furthermore, Mauritania had no constitution at the time, the last such document, dating to May 20,

1961 (q.v.), having been suspended upon the overthrow of the civilian regime of President Mokhtar Ould Daddah (q.v.) on July 10, 1978. Finally, the Ould Heydallah government totally lacked the stamp of legitimacy, even in the eyes of the country's elites. By way of confronting these criticisms, Ould Heydallah announced in December 1980 that a draft constitution would be submitted to a popular referendum and that a gradual return to civilian rule would be completed after its ratification. Without waiting for a new organic law, moreover, the Mauritanian leader the same month named a civilian Council of Ministers (q.v.) in which six of its eighteen members were black Mauritanians and in which only the minister of defense was a serving officer in the armed forces (q.v.).

When published, the provisional constitution resembled that of a parliamentary democracy. A National Assembly (q.v.) would be elected by universal suffrage, the head of state would stand for direct election to a six-year term, renewable only once, and a Constitutional Council would be appointed to supervise the implementation of its provisions. In addition, multiple political parties, independent trade unions, and other voluntary associations would be legalized, although groups formed on a strictly racial, religious, or tribal basis were to be banned. Citizens would be guaranteed freedom of expression and association.

The Provisional Constitution was destined never to be submitted to a plebiscite, much less implemented. On March 16, 1981, barely twelve weeks after its publication, a violent coup attempt against Ould Heydallah took place, led by two ex–CMSN members, Ahmed Salem Ould Sidi and Mohammed Ould Bah Ould Abdel Kader (qq.v.) under the aegis of the Moroccan-based *Alliance pour une Mauritanie Dém-ocratique* (AMD) (q.v.). Forces loyal to the regime quickly crushed the uprising, but the incident showed Mauritania's acute vulnerability to external pressures and highlighted the fragility of Ould Heydallah's position. Plans for the constitutional referendum were shelved, and the following month, the country's civilian cabinet was dismissed as Mauritania returned to the rigors of direct military rule.

RAILWAYS. The discovery in the late 1950s of vast deposits of iron ore (q.v.) near the towns of F'Derik and Zouerate (qq.v.) in the administrative région of Tiris Zemmour (qq.v.) necessitated the construction of a railway line to transport the ore from mines in the interior to a suitable transshipment point along the Atlantic coast. Although the French-dominated mining concern MIFERMA (q.v.) gave some thought to building the line in a northwesterly direction through Western Sahara (q.v.) to the port of Villa Cisneros (q.v.), the realities of Spanish colonial rule made this shorter route unfeasible. Instead, beginning at Mauritania's independence in 1960, MIFERMA constructed a single-track, four-foot, eight-and-a-half-inch gauge, 650-kilometer line from Zouerate southwesterly to Choum (where it traversed a short tunnel) and thence due west to the country's economic center of Nouadhibou (q.v.). The line, completed in 1963, was built to a very high standard, with welded track lengths and steel ties. Soon, some of the longest and heaviest trains in the world were in operation, consisting of three or more locomotives pulling over 200 wagons loaded with almost 20,000 tons of ore. After a journey of almost sixteen hours from the Zouerate mines, the train would reach MIFERMA's *Port Minéralier* (q.v.), ten kilometers south of Nouadhibou, where the wagons were emptied, the ore fed into a crusher and loaded onto ships, and the train sent back to the interior. By the late 1960s, the line was responsible for carrying nearly 80 percent of Mauritania's foreign exchange earnings, giving the country a dose of relative prosperity that would embolden President Mokhtar Ould Daddah (q.v.) to nationalize the mines and railway in 1974, replacing MIFERMA with the *Société Nationale Industrielle et Minière* (SNIM) (q.v.), a parastatal whose subsidiary, *Comptoir Minier du Nord* (COMINOR) (q.v.), performed day-to-day rail operations.

Traversing as it did a vast and virtually unpoliceable stretch of desert, the Zouerate-Nouadhibou railway proved to be an irresistible target for the guerrillas of the Polisario Front (q.v.) in its campaign, begun in late 1975, to eject Mauritania from Tiris el-Gharbia (q.v.), that portion of Western Sahara that President Ould Daddah had annexed pursuant to the terms of the Madrid Agreement (q.v.). At the beginning, the Saharawi (q.v.) nationalists merely tore up short lengths of track, but soon graduated to firebombing the trains themselves, destroying wagons and locomotives and bringing iron ore exports virtually to a halt by mid-1977. The presence of thousands of troops from the Mauritanian armed forces (q.v.) along the line, assisted by Moroccan soldiers, did little to stem the tide against Polisario. Not even direct intervention by the French air force in Operation Lamantin (q.v.) could alter the fact that the Front had succeeded in its objective of crippling Mauritania's economy and creating an atmosphere of insecurity and discouragement that contributed heavily to Mokhtar Ould Daddah's overthrow by the military establishment on July 10, 1978, and the country's abandonment of Tiris el-Gharbia a little over a year later.

With the war in Western Sahara finally over for Mauritania, French and other foreign assistance was provided to repair the railway, and it was back to operating normally in the early 1980s. Considerable investments were made in rolling stock, and additional track was laid to service new mining sites at el-Rhein and M'Haoudat, bringing the line's total length to 690 kilometers, not counting large marshalling yards at

Nouadhibou and Zouerate. About thirty diesel line-haul locomotives are in use, supplemented by eleven diesel units used for shunting the ore wagons, which number over 1300. And although the vast majority of its traffic is freight, the railway is also a significant transportation resource for the people in the area. SNIM owns several passenger coaches, which are attached to the ore wagons for the trip to Nouadhibou and Zouerate, the train running at least once a day. Fares are inexpensive—about 1 *ouguiya* (q.v.) per kilometer. Despite this, some passengers elect to travel more austerely (and dangerously) by riding without charge in the ore wagons themselves.

RAINFALL. See Climate

RASSEMBLEMENT POUR LA DEMOCRATIE ET L'UNITE (RDU). The Rally for Democracy and Unity was formed on August 24, 1991, becoming the first political party to be registered with the Mauritanian authorities since the liberalizing measures introduced by President Maaouiya Ould Sid'Ahmed Taya (q.v.) several months earlier. The party is led by Ahmed Ould Sidi Baba, a cousin of Ould Taya who was mayor of Atar (q.v.) and chairman of the Mauritanian Mayors' Association. From the beginning, the RDU was closely aligned with Ould Taya's *Parti Républicain, Démocratique et Social* (PRDS) (q.v.), and consequently did not propose a candidate of its own in the country's first contested presidential election, held on January 17, 1992. It chose instead to back Ould Taya's candidacy, although Ould Baba strongly denied that his organization was influenced by the PRDS. After Ould Taya, the incumbent, emerged victorious, the RDU, unlike the main opposition party, Ahmed Ould Daddah's *Union des Forces Démocratiques* (UFD) (qq.v.), chose to field candidates for election to the *Assemblée Nationale* (q.v.), the lower house of the Mauritanian legislature. But the party did poorly, winning only one seat in the seventy-nine-member body in the elections, which were held on March 6 and 13, 1992. Frustrated with his lack of success at the polls, Ould Baba announced that the RDU would boycott the next phase of the democratization process, the elections for the Mauritanian Senate (q.v.), and accused the government of conducting an "electoral parody," referring, presumably, to opposition allegations of voting fraud. By the spring of 1993, the RDU was in turmoil, suffering mass defections (including the departure of fifty-five prominent members) and eruptions of discontent on the part of younger party cadres who maintained that Ould Baba's attitudes were holding the party back from greater achievements. In addition, some RDU supporters were reportedly disappointed that Ould Taya had allegedly not repaid them for their support of his presidential candidacy by naming their representatives to the Council of Ministers (q.v.). Some observers, however, felt that what was happening was a more basic generational split in the ranks of all of Mauritania's political groups, including the PRDS, and that more defections and realignments could be expected. Ould Baba felt constrained to announce, on November 3, 1993, that the RDU would no longer boycott the institutions of the Mauritanian Second Republic (q.v.) and would instead participate as a formal ally of the PRDS in the municipal elections in the country's régions (q.v.) scheduled for January 1994. In those elections, the RDU presented candidates in only seven of Mauritania's 208 jurisdictions, all in conjunction with the PRDS.

RASSEMBLEMENT POUR LA RENAISSANCE DES NEGRO-AFRICAINS DE MAURITANIE (RENAM). The Rally for the Rebirth of Negro-Africans of Mauritania was founded in 1989 in the immediate aftermath of the destructive events of April of that year—riots between Mauritanians and Senegalese that had escalated into a full-fledged diplomatic imbroglio, the Senegal-Mauritania Crisis (q.v.), which brought Mauritania and the regime of Abdou Diouf (q.v.) to the threshold of war. Unlike its counterpart also led by black Mauritanians, the *Forces de Libération Africaine de Mauritanie* (FLAM) (q.v.), RE-NAM made no secret of its commitment to waging an armed struggle to overthrow the government of President Maaouiya Ould Sid'Ahmed Taya (q.v.) and force the secession of the black-majority régions (q.v.) in the south of the country. Despite its aggressive rhetoric and claims of a considerable popular following in Mauritania, RENAM appeared by 1995 to have mounted almost no armed actions and confined its activities to (limited) political organizing in France and Senegal.

REFUGEES. For almost the first three decades of its existence as an independent nation, Mauritania had only very slight refugee problems, although it had a great many "internal refugees" in the form of persons who were forced by drought and desertification (q.v.) to abandon their homes in the outlying administrative régions (q.v.) and settle in the cities and towns, particularly the capital, Nouakchott (q.v.). But with the Senegal-Mauritania Crisis (q.v.) of 1989 and 1990, the situation deteriorated dramatically, with up to 200,000 Moorish (q.v.) Mauritanian inhabitants of Senegal expelled by the regime of Abdou Diouf (q.v.). These people were obliged to move to Mauritania, where they placed enormous strains on the country's already inadequate housing (q.v.) stock and other social services. Nevertheless, by 1993 the U.S. State Department, in one of its annual human rights reports on Mauritania (see Bibliography) stated that most of these refugees had been successfully absorbed into the mainstream of Mauritanian life, often occupying land in the fertile Senegal River Valley which was vacated by

Halpulaaren (q.v.) and other blacks who departed, voluntarily or involuntarily, from Mauritania and who settled in Senegal. The Moorish expellees appeared to face a relatively stable future, but the same could not be said for the black Mauritanians who relocated to the Senegalese side of the river. Numbering an estimated 60,000 by 1991, they were given (according to some reports) a less-than-enthusiastic reception by the Diouf government while at the same time being reluctant to return home, since their citizenship was heatedly contested between the two countries. By 1995, only about 4000 or so had returned to Mauritania to engage in agricultural and livestock (qq.v.) activity. There were also fears by some observers that the returnees would not be able to reclaim their old lands, and would be reduced to wage labor on behalf of Beydane and *haratine* (qq.v.) owners who acquired legal title to the abandoned land in southern Mauritania by virtue of the controversial Land Reform Act of June 5, 1983 (q.v.). Unless questions regarding the citizenship of the relocatees could be answered and land ownership concerns allayed, the problem seems to defy resolution.

In 1991 and 1992, another refugee crisis struck the Nouakchott government. Seeking an escape from unrest in northern Mali, 46,000 or more Tuaregs, an independent, nomadic people who are often at odds with the central Malian authorities in Bamako, fled to hastily established camps in Mauritania's easternmost province, Hodh ech-Chargui (q.v.). The reaction by the United Nations High Commission for Refugees (UNHCR) was relatively swift, and the Tuaregs were reasonably cared for, so much so that efforts by the UNHCR and the Mauritanian government to send them back to Mali were hindered by the refugees' reluctance to abandon what had become a less precarious existence in Mauritania and return to the still unsettled Saharan zones of their own country.

Mauritania's third refugee problem was also its smallest and most easily managed. Beginning in 1975, several thousand Saharawis (q.v.) moved into northern Mauritania to escape the effects of the Western Sahara conflict (q.v.) in which the civilian regime of Mokhtar Ould Daddah (q.v.) had become involved and which was to persist into the mid-1990s. Given the often close ties of tribal affiliation between Saharawis and many Moorish Mauritanians, they were integrated into the country with little difficulty. Most of the Saharawi refugees either lived in encampments in the régions of Adrar or Tiris Zemmour (qq.v.) or led a sedentary lifestyle near the economic center of Nouadhibou (q.v.).

REGION (variants: Collectivité Territoriale, Wilaya). Mauritania's primary units of provincial administration acquired their name on July 30, 1968, when a decree issued by President Mokhtar Ould Daddah (q.v.) abolished the *cercles* and *communes* (qq.v.) which had been inherited from the French colonial period and which had for a variety of reasons proved unsuccessful in practice after Mauritanian independence in 1960. The *régions* were twelve in number, with each divided into *départements* (q.v.) that were generally coterminous with their older counterparts, the *sous-préfectures* (q.v.). The départements were further divided into *arrondissements* (q.v.), the smallest unit of local administration in the country, generally comprising a single town or settlement. From 1968 to 1978, there were elected assemblies for each région, made up of twenty to thirty people drawn exclusively from President Ould Daddah's *Parti du Peuple Mauritanien* (PPM) (q.v.). In reality, the change in terminology could not obscure the fact that the Mauritanian government remained tightly centralized, with the governors of the régions serving mostly to carry into execution the decisions taken by Ould Daddah in the capital, Nouakchott (q.v.). Thus, the régions had little real power, although they retained some oversight functions as to local budgets (q.v.) and the maintenance of provincial roads (q.v.).

Mauritania's two armed forces (q.v.) governing councils, the CMRN and the CMSN (qq.v.), which ruled the country from July 10, 1978 to April 18, 1992, relegated the régions to a position of even less importance. What few areas of autonomy the governors of each province had formerly enjoyed were eliminated, and the regional representative bodies were dismissed and abolished. Henceforth, provincial governors were either army officers themselves or civilians who depended directly upon guidance from a CMRN/CMSN member posted in the hinterland or stationed in Nouakchott. Only in December 1986 did this situation begin to change. In that month, the government of President Maaouiya Ould Sid'Ahmed Taya (q.v.) held the first regional and municipal elections since the advent of military rule. This balloting often surprised observers both by its impartial administration and by the sometimes intriguing results, particularly in the cities and towns. Individual political parties, however, remained banned until 1991, and the authority of the newly elected local councils was still no greater than before. Under the Constitution of Mauritania of July 20, 1991 (q.v.), the country's régions, called *collectivités territoriales* in that document, were mentioned in Title X, Article 98, although their precise functions (aside from their role in electing the Mauritanian Senate ([q.v.], set out in Article 47) were left unspecified. Whatever their formal legal status, it seems likely that Mauritania will, for the foreseeable future, continue to be administered mostly from Nouakchott, with the countryside playing only a minor role.

Mauritania's régions, excluding the separate District of Nouakchott, are as follows (see individual entries on each):

Adrar	Hodh ech-Chargui
Assaba	Hodh el-Gharbi

Brakna
Dakhlet-Nouadhibou
Gorgol
Guidimaka

Inchiri
Tagant
Tiris Zemmour
Trarza

RIO DE ORO. See Tiris el-Gharbia

ROADS. Despite Mauritania's great size (1,030,700 square kilometers), the road system is sparse, often of doubtful reliability, and difficult to maintain. In addition to severe budgetary (q.v.) constraints on the construction and maintenance of roads, geography has played a role too, as widely spaced population (q.v.) centers are separated by the nearly uninhabited reaches of the Sahara. In the mid-1990s, only about 1600 kilometers of road are paved, of a total of 7500 kilometers of marked roads and tracks. Paved roads connect the capital, Nouakchott (q.v.), with Akjoujt and Atar (qq.v.) in northeast Mauritania, while a good highway connects the capital with the Senegalese border at Rosso (q.v.). Other roads of more uncertain quality link Atar with the mining towns of F'Derik and Zouerate (qq.v.) as well as with Bir Moghrein (q.v.). Most of the remainder, however, are simply no more than tracks in the sand and gravel of the Sahara, upon which it is fool-hardy to venture alone or in anything less resilient than a heavy truck. One glaring omission in the national road system is the absence of a reliable road connecting Nouakchott with the economic center of Nouadhibou (q.v.)—the only method of traveling between the two cities is either by means of the airline (q.v.) service or by traversing a track along the Atlantic coast that is often flooded at high tide.

Without doubt, one of Mauritania's biggest public works projects in the 1980s was the 1100-kilometer Trans-Mauritanian Highway. Completed with Brazilian, European, and Arab financial assistance in 1985 and costing over $300 million, this showcase road extends eastward from Nouakchott, through Boutilimit, Aleg, Kiffa, and Ayoun el-Atrouss (qq.v.) before terminating in the town of Néma (q.v.). Meant to bind the country together more closely, the *Route de l'E-spoir,* or Road of Hope, as it was named, made possible much faster travel between the populated areas of south-central Mauritania, and also led to the more rapid alleviation of food shortages in those regions.

For the road system generally, the government decided in late 1993 to spend billions of *ouguiyas* (q.v.) to carry out improvements, in particular paving a long stretch between Aleg and Bogué and Kaédi (q.v.) along the sensitive Senegalese border. But no matter how many improvements are made, the need to remove drifting sand from the highways consumes upwards of 80 percent of the annual transportation budget.

ROSSO. One of the largest towns in southern Mauritania and the administrative capital of the région of Trarza (qq.v.), Rosso is the center of a brisk commerce (q.v.) between Senegal and Mauritania due to its strategic location on the Senegal River barely a kilometer from Senegalese territory, the two countries being linked by a frequent ferry service. Agriculture and livestock (qq.v.), in addition to overland trade, have made Rosso one of the most economically important towns in the area, although with the opening of the Friendship Port of Nouakchott (q.v.) in 1986, its significance receded somewhat, as supplies for Mauritania's capital city no longer need to be offloaded in Senegal's ports. Rosso also reflects the country's ethnic diversity, with Black Africans forming much of the population (q.v.), a fact that made it, along with other settlements along the Senegal River, the scene of considerable tension during the Senegal-Mauritania Crisis (q.v.) of 1989 and 1990, with the closing of the riverine border causing considerable economic hardship. A high-quality paved road (q.v.) connects Rosso with Nouakchott, and just across the border in Senegal, similar roads link it with Dakar. According to official government census figures, Rosso had a population of 27,783 in 1988.

ROUTE DE L'ESPOIR (ROAD OF HOPE). See Roads

SAGUIA EL-HAMRA (Arabic: "Red River"). Saguia el-Hamra is the name given by both the Spanish and the Saharawis (q.v.) to the northern one-third or so of Western Sahara (q.v.), situated roughly between Morocco's southern border, Mauritania's vast northeastern administrative région of Tiris Zemmour (qq.v.), the Atlantic coast, and what was until 1979 Mauritania's share of Western Sahara, Tiris el-Gharbia (q.v.). With its enormous phosphate deposits at Bou-Craa and its abundant fisheries (q.v.), Saguia el-Hamra is militarily occupied by Morocco beginning in late 1975, and was also the site of Smara, Western Sahara's only precolonial city, built between 1898 and 1902 by the Saharawi leader, Cheikh Ma el-Ainin (q.v.).

SAHARAN/SAHARAWI ARAB DEMOCRATIC REPUBLIC (SADR). Set up by the Polisario Front (q.v.) on February 27, 1976, immediately following the final withdrawal of Spain from its colony of Western Sahara (q.v.), the Saharan Arab Democratic Republic served as Polisario's state-in-exile, and possessed a Council of Ministers, a formal written constitution, and diplomatic representation abroad. Seventy-six nations had accorded the Saharawi (q.v.) state full recognition by 1996.

Mauritania at first refrained from formally recognizing the SADR, partly due to fears of Moroccan reprisals if such a step were taken. The clear preference of the country's ruling armed forces council, the CMSN (qq.v.), led after June 1979 by Colonel Mohammed Khouna Ould Heydallah (q.v.), was to allow more time for either the United Nations (q.v.) or the Organization of African Unity (OAU) to resolve the Morocco–Polisario conflict peacefully. It was the eventual failure of the OAU to advance its cease-fire and referendum plans for Western Sahara in late 1983 that impelled Ould Heydallah to modify his policy. On February 27, 1984, he formally recognized the SADR, and the move brought about no real Moroccan response. Ould Heydallah reportedly had not informed his CMSN colleagues in advance of his plans, however, alienating his more cautious colleagues and significantly contributing to the CMSN's decision to replace him with Colonel Maaouiya Ould Sid'Ahmed Taya (q.v.) on December 12, 1984, in a bloodless "restructuring."

SAHARAWI. As the term generally used to describe the Moorish (q.v.) peoples in what is now the territory of Western Sahara (q.v.), *Saharawi* is often used synonymously with the Arabic description, *Ahel es-Sahel* (people of the west)—that is, those tribes who live along the western margin of the Sahara. Due to the traditionally nomadic nature of the Moor lifestyle, Saharawis are found in Mauritania, southern Morocco, and southwestern Algeria as well as in Western Sahara, having disregarded, for the most part, the boundaries imposed by the European colonial powers in the late nineteenth and early twentieth centuries. More recently, the word came to acquire political significance, too: it was adopted by the Polisario Front (q.v.) to delineate Western Saharans as a separate and distinct people and thus deserving of independent statehood.

SANHADJA/SANHADJA CONFEDERATION. See Berbers

SARAKOLE. Sarakolé is the name often given to the westernmost branch of one of Mauritania's main Black African groups, the Soninké (q.v.). The term is also occasionally used to denote the language spoken by the Soninké in Mauritania as well as elsewhere in the region.

SECOND REPUBLIC. At a ceremony held on April 18, 1992, Mauritania's President, Maaouiya Ould Sid'Ahmed Taya (q.v.), formally proclaimed the Mauritanian Second Republic after fundamental changes were instituted in the country's political life beginning about a year earlier. The Second Republic, which replaced the first and is considered to have run from the time of independence from France on November 28, 1960, featured, among other things, a new constitution, the existence of legal political parties, a considerably greater degree of free speech, a freer press, and elections for president and for a bicameral Mauritanian parliament.

In April 1991 Mauritania's internal and foreign relations (q.v.) situation was highly uncertain. Not only had the country been forced to endure the severe economic consequences of the Gulf Crisis (q.v.) that began on August 2, 1990, with Iraq's invasion of Kuwait, but the crisis had also alienated Mauritania from key Arab sources of material and diplomatic support due to its perceived pro-Iraq position—and the Western attitude was almost equally negative. Moreover, the Gulf Crisis and subsequent war had taken place only about a year after the destructive Senegal-Mauritania Crisis (q.v.) of 1989 and 1990, which entailed serious internal shocks. This crisis had, in its earliest stages, involved great bloodshed followed by a massive exchange of people between the two countries, and soon led to a state of near-war between Mauritania and Senegal, coupled with increased international attention to the relations among Black African and Moorish (q.v.) Mauritanians. Finally, although President Ould Taya had, in December 1986, taken some steps toward eventual democratization by holding municipal elections, his regime, composed of armed forces (q.v.) officers sitting as the *Comité Militaire de Salut National* (CMSN) (q.v.), lacked popular legitimacy.

Given the historical lack of democratic institutions in Mauritania, therefore, it came as a complete surprise to many citizens when, on April 15, 1991, Ould Taya announced that a new constitutional order guaranteeing basic civil liberties and providing for a parliamentary democratic political system would be put into place. Even the country's primary exiled opposition movement, the *Forces de Libération Africaine de Mauritanie* (FLAM) (q.v.), which had been waging a low-key armed struggle against the "racist" CMSN government, was sufficiently impressed to suspend its war, at least until the contours of the political liberalization grew more apparent. Other Mauritanians, however, felt that Ould Taya did not go far enough. They wanted a national conference made up of all the country's interests to draft a constitution, followed by the CMSN's dissolution and a government of "reconciliation" to oversee free presidential and legislative elections. These sentiments were first manifested in a major way on June 6, 1991, when a newly formed, illegal political organization, the *Front Démocratique Uni des Forces du Changement* (FDUC) (q.v.), announced its existence on the heels of serious rioting in the economic center of Nouadhibou (q.v.). FDUC demanded additional democratization as well as an inquiry into alleged human rights abuses, but to little effect: the movement's leaders were arrested and imprisoned, although they were not mistreated and were released a few weeks later. In addition, a call by the country's main labor confederation, the

Union des Travailleurs Mauritaniens (UTM) (q.v.), for a general strike to spur further reforms and wage increases was mostly honored in the breach between June 19 and 21, 1991, the appointed dates for the stoppage.

Despite these outward signs of disharmony, President Ould Taya pressed on with his first order of business, promulgating a new constitution. In May and June 1991, in a series of interviews with *Le Monde* and with *Jeune Afrique,* the Mauritanian head of state explained that the CMSN, assisted by French and other jurists, had drafted a constitution that would be submitted for approval in July, with no real chance for popular comment before the referendum. There would also be no national conference. Ould Taya stated firmly that if some persons dissented from the draft constitution, "they may reject it in the referendum or amend the text if the legislative elections give them sufficient authority." As for the national conference, he dismissed the idea, calling it a "ridiculous and antidemocratic" concept.

Once it was made public, the new constitution was printed daily for two weeks in *Ech-Chaab,* the state-controlled newspaper (q.v.), to familiarize Mauritanians with its 103 articles, which provided for a bicameral legislature, a strong presidency on the French model, an Economic and Social Council, a nine-member Constitutional Council, and a High Islamic Council. On July 12, 1991, the promised referendum was held, with the government claiming that 85.2 percent of eligible voters had gone to the polls, with 97.9 percent of those endorsing the document. It was ratified by President Ould Taya on July 20 and immediately began to enter into force, with the formal authorization of independent political parties coming two weeks later, on July 25. A CMSN decree accompanying the new constitution provided that an unlimited number of political parties could register their intentions with the minister of the interior, at which time they would be required to pay a fee of 50,000 *ouguiyas* (q.v.), a sum that would be refunded only if the party received 10 percent or more of the popular vote. Purely Islamic (q.v.) parties were proscribed, "since Islam is the religion of the people and the state," and could never, in the regime's view, be the prerogative of a single organization.

Beginning in mid-August, new political parties began to form at a rapid pace. On August 22, the first party, the *Rassemblement pour la Démocratie et l'Unité* (RDU) (q.v.) was formed, followed by the creation of the grouping under whose banner Ould Taya would campaign, the *Parti Républicain, Démocratique et Social* (PRDS) (q.v.), on August 29. Many former FDUC members came together and founded the *Union des Forces Démocratiques* (UFD) (q.v.) in early October, while a smaller group, the *Parti Mauritanien pour Renouveau* (PMR) (q.v.) was set up, with ex-CMSN chairman Mohammed Khouna Ould

Heydallah (q.v.), who had been deposed by Ould Taya in December 1984, as one of its leading figures. Soon, over a dozen new parties were up and running. Independent candidates not connected with any party were also permitted under the new electoral law, and several persons announced their intention to run on their own. Among these were two presidential hopefuls: the economist and former mayor of Nouakchott (q.v.), Mohamed Mahmoud Ould Mah, who later went on to head the *Union Populaire Socialiste et Démocratique* (UPSD) (q.v.), and retired army colonel and first military leader Mustapha Ould Mohammed Salek (q.v.). Ahmed Ould Daddah (q.v.), the younger brother of the first Mauritanian president, also returned from exile abroad to run for president, officially alone but always with the UFD's *de facto* blessing. With the presidential election date of January 17, 1992, looming, the campaign quickly became a contest between Ould Taya and Ould Daddah. The latter promised a "new era" for Mauritania, a capitalist oriented economy, an investigation into the human rights situation, and the legalization of Islamist political parties. Ould Taya's speeches stressed themes of continuity, national unity, and reconciliation. As the election drew nearer, the UFD started to complain that Ould Taya's PRDS enjoyed an undue advantage by virtue of its allegedly privileged access to the resources of the state, and opposition politicians also charged that voters in the southern, Black African–dominated administrative régions (q.v.) of the country were being prevented from registering to cast ballots.

Election Day, January 17, went smoothly, with a reported voter turnout of 551,575 Mauritanian voters, or about 46 percent of the total, and President Ould Taya emerged triumphant. The official vote count was as follows:

Candidate	Total Vote	Percentage
Maaouiya Ould Sid'Ahmed Taya	345,583	62.65
Ahmed Ould Daddah	180,658	32.75
Mustapha Ould Mohammed Salek	15,735	2.85
Mohamed Mahmoud Ould Mah	7,506	1.36

Although Ahmed Ould Daddah's vote count was respectable, the defeated UFD candidate claimed that Ould Taya and the CMSN had cheated him of victory, and as a result, he announced on January 28, 1992, that the UFD would boycott the upcoming National Assembly and Senate (qq.v.) elections. FLAM militants, too, were defiant: they announced a resumption of their armed struggle even before the balloting and issued a call to Mauritanians to "do away quickly with this government," with whom "dialogue was impossible." With several other parties joining the walkout, it looked as though the whole democratization process might be aborted, but the government, undaunted, scheduled National Assembly elections for March 6 and 13, the latter date a runoff ballot for those candidates who failed to garner a majority in the first round. On the appointed dates, the legislative elections went forward, but the boycott had a telling effect: only 39 percent of the eligible electorate of 1,074,000 went to the polling stations on March 6, and a yet smaller number, 33 percent, showed up for the March 13 follow-on poll. However disappointing the turnout, the outcome was sharply apparent: the PRDS organization of President Ould Taya had easily captured sixty-seven of the seventy-nine *Assemblée Nationale* seats, with two nonboycotting parties, the PMR and the RDU, winning one seat apiece. Ten seats went to independents, but the party of the head of state had an overpowering majority. The senatorial elections also resulted in a PRDS sweep, winning thirty-six of the fifty-six seats on April 3 and 10, 1992. Having trounced the opposition, President Ould Taya proclaimed the Second Republic on April 18, an event that was accompanied by the convening of the new bicameral parliament, the inauguration of a broad-based Council of Ministers (q.v.) headed by a respected economist, Prime Minister Sidi Mohamed Ould Boubacar (q.v.), and the formal disbanding of the CMSN.

With these events, the transition to a more open Mauritania reached the end of its first phase. Ould Taya, now a civilian president with a six-year mandate ahead of him, encountered little resistance to instituting an economic "structural adjustment" program at the instigation of the World Bank and the International Monetary Fund (IMF). In June 1993 the PRDS-dominated parliament passed a general amnesty law, granting immunity from prosecution to all members of the police, army, and other individuals who might have committed human rights violations from early 1989 to mid-1991, not coincidentally the period of the crisis with Senegal. This legislation, which was advertised as an essential step toward national reconciliation, was strongly condemned internationally as well as by many Mauritanians, although the opposition parties' absence from parliament meant that they could not block the law's passage.

Mauritanian political parties themselves began also to undergo change, and a few new ones were founded, most notably the *Union pour le Progrès et la Démocratie* (UPD) (q.v.), formed on June 15, 1993, by former Foreign Minister Hamdi Ould Mouknass (q.v.) and other politicians who were reportedly upset with Ahmed Ould Daddah's leadership of the UFD. But the formation of the UPD and the UFD's subsequent decision to end its electoral boycott did not lead to a rise in the opposition's fortunes. In municipal elections held in January 1994, the governing PRDS won all but thirty-six of the country's 208 *arrondissements* (q.v.), and in April, balloting for one-third of the

Senate's seats went similarly for Ould Taya's organization, with the UFD winning just one of the seventeen contested seats. Another phenomenon, noted by outside observers, concerned the widening gap between the leadership cadres of most of the political parties (including the PRDS) and the younger, rank-and-file members. Splits were opening up as well in the UFD, UPD, RDU, and other groups by early 1995, and further such developments seem inevitable.

By and large, then, Mauritania's Second Republic by the mid-1990s has shown great differences from both the *ancien régime* of Mokhtar Ould Daddah (q.v.) and the CMRN/CMSN military councils in power from 1978 to 1992. But President Maaouiya Ould Sid'Ahmed Taya's incumbency has had a nearly decisive impact on many sectors of Mauritanian life, and the small, elite corps of army officers probably still exerts an outsized influence on political affairs. In spite of this, at least some representative institutions have been brought into being, and there appears to be a resultant rise in political awareness on the part of many of Mauritania's citizens.

SELIBABY. The administrative and commercial center of Mauritania's Guidimaka région (qq.v.), Sélibaby had a population of 8000 in 1977 according to official government census figures, a number which was widely believed to have increased during the 1980s. As the country's southernmost major town, it is dominated by black Mauritanian farmers of the Senegal River Valley, especially the Soninké (q.v.), and its economic viability is rooted in intensive agriculture and livestock (qq.v.) activities. During the Senegal-Mauritania Crisis (q.v.) of 1989 and 1990, the town was characterized by a high level of tension and, as were other locations along the Senegal River such as Kaédi (q.v.) and Bogué, it was closed to outsiders. Sélibaby is deeply influenced not only by Black African culture but also by events in Senegal and Mali, each country's border being only about forty kilometers from the town.

SENATE. One of the only such institutions of its kind in an African country, the Mauritanian Senate began its official existence on April 18, 1992, with the advent of the Second Republic (q.v.) and the simultaneous disbanding of the *Comité Militaire de Salut National* (CMSN) (q.v.), the country's governing armed forces (q.v.) council. Elections for the Senate had been held on April 3, 1992, with further runoff balloting on April 10. Partly because the legislative elections had been boycotted by some of the country's opposition parties, notably the *Union des Forces Démocratiques* (UFD) (q.v.), President Maaouiya Ould Sid'Ahmed Taya's *Parti Républicain, Démocratique et Social* (PRDS) (qq.v.) captured thirty-six seats in the fifty-six-member Senate, with seventeen going to independent candidates and three seats reserved for the representatives of Mauritanians living abroad, mainly in France and the Middle East. In a nation where regional, tribal, and clan-based loyalties remain strong, the Senate was designed by the drafters of the Mauritanian Constitution of July 20, 1991 (q.v.), to guarantee a minimum level of representation to all the country's ré-gions (q.v.) and municipalities. Pursuant to Article 47 of the Consti-tution, Senators must be at least thirty-five years old and are elected to a six-year term by indirect suffrage. Elections to the Senate are to be held every two years, meaning that the mandates of one-third of the chamber's membership are subject to renewal at those times. Sub-stantively, the Senate has joint responsibility for matters within the purview of the legislative branch, and has, along with Mauritania's lower house, the *Assemblée Nationale* (q.v.), the power to propose legislation. The Senate has its own president, who is chosen by its members every two years and who is, under Article 40 of the Consti-tution, the legal successor to the President of the Republic in the event of his death or incapacity for an interim period of ninety days, after which new presidential elections are required to be held. In early 1996, the Senate President was Dieng Boubou Farba, a Halpulaar (q.v.) who had served variously during the 1980s as Mauritania's minister of mines and energy, minister of economics and finance, and governor of the *Banque Centrale de Mauritanie* (BCM) (q.v.).

SENEGAL-MAURITANIA CRISIS (Of 1989–90). The Senegal-Mauritania Crisis was possibly the severest foreign relations (q.v.) prob-lem Mauritania faced since its independence in 1960, rivaled only by its 1975–79 involvement in the Western Sahara conflict (q.v.). Beginning as a localized dispute thought to have been rooted in the ownership and whereabouts of livestock (q.v.) herds, tensions rapidly escalated into vi-olent and sustained clashes between Mauritanian and Senegalese resi-dent nationals in each other's country, producing one of the largest pop-ulation (q.v.) transfers in modern African history and bringing Senegal and Mauritania to the brink of war, a dénouement avoided only by mu-tual restraint at the highest leadership levels in both states and by ag-gressive international mediation. And although the crisis, which began in April 1989 and continued for the rest of the year and into 1990, steadily abated starting in 1991, the long-term relationship between the two neighbors was permanently affected, with both Mauritania and Senegal paying a great deal more attention to a formerly relaxed border situation and to issues of citizenship and nationality.

In the decade prior to 1989, disputes between the successive CMSN (q.v.) governments in Mauritania and the Senegalese regime of Ab-dou Diouf (q.v.) had been confined almost entirely to the diplomatic sphere, excepting only local incidents over the migration of livestock and rights to the cultivation of land along the fertile, variably located frontier along the Senegal River. Politically, the Mauritanians had strongly protested the use of Senegalese territory by exiled dissidents, notably the *Alliance pour une Mauritanie Démocratique* (AMD) (q.v.) in the early 1980s and the *Forces de Libération Africaine de Mauritanie* (FLAM) (q.v.) from 1986 onward. The CMSN was also highly dismayed over what it perceived as support given to the AMD and FLAM by both the Dakar government and certain individuals and groups, particularly Abdoulaye Wade, Abdou Diouf's most prominent political opponent. Sometimes Mauritanian pressures were enough to make Senegal rethink whatever favorable intentions it may have had toward the CMSN's adversaries, other times not, but there was little in the past history of the two countries to indicate what was to happen next, nor what would be the consequences.

According to the Mauritanian government, which issued a "Book of Facts" (or "White Book") on the situation in August 1989 (see Bibliography), the crisis started on March 30, when Senegalese nationals or residents crossed the Senegal River into Mauritania's administrative région of Guidimaka (qq.v.) from an island village known as Diawara and carried away sheep and other animals belonging to the Halpulaar (q.v.) farmers of the area. Attempts over the next several days to resolve the matter proved unavailing, and on April 8 or 9, 1989, a group of Senegalese attacked Sunko, a village in Guidimaka, with the result that two persons were killed and thirteen others taken prisoner by the Mauritanian authorities. Senegal disputed this version of events, saying instead that the Mauritanian armed forces (q.v.) had entered Senegalese territory, inflicted injury there, and transported their "hostages" back to Mauritania. The CMSN insisted that its army was not involved, and maintained that the weapons used in the attack (hunting rifles and shotguns) were never issued to its troops. By April 10, the thirteen prisoners (and the bodies of the two dead men) were returned to Senegal, but already a violent popular reaction was beginning: on April 10 and 11, riots against some Moorish (q.v.) Mauritanians in the nearby Senegalese town of Bakel took place, with some loss of life and property damage. The Moors who were set upon by angry Senegalese in Bakel were not believed to have been involved in the riverbank incidents, but served as a prominent target for the resentments of villagers who perceived that the Moors, who were mostly small-scale traders, were depriving Senegalese citizens of their livelihood by exploiting their impoverished economic status.

Quickly, both governments worked to limit the impact of the rioting. On April 12, 1989, the interior minister of Senegal, André Sonko, flew to Nouakchott (q.v.) to meet with his Mauritanian counterpart, the powerful CMSN member Colonel Djibril Ould Abdellahi (q.v.). At their meeting, the two sides agreed to form a joint fact-finding commission to ascertain the origin of the dispute and compensate those victimized. Ould Abdellahi, for his part, sought to dampen popular emotions when he stated on television in Dakar on a reciprocal visit on April 18 and 19 that included a meeting with President Diouf, that the Diawara events, as well as the riots in Bakel and a few other villages, "should not be accorded an importance which surpasses reality." This statement backfired, as some Senegalese took the interior minister's comments to mean that he was making light of the deaths of their compatriots. In any event, the fact-finding commission had barely started work when events rapidly went out of control. During April 21–23, severe anti-Mauritanian violence broke out in Dakar, where the Mauritanian embassy was attacked, as well as all over the rest of Senegal, especially in the Senegal River Valley and in the towns of Kaolack, St. Louis, Thiés, and Ziguinchor. Shops and houses belonging to Moorish Mauritanians were looted and destroyed and their inhabitants beaten and in some cases killed by angry mobs, reportedly made up of Senegalese opposition supporters anxious to carry out the call from their leader, Abdoulaye Wade, for a tougher line against Mauritania. A hostile attitude toward Moors by Senegalese was not universal—some Dakar residents sheltered Mauritanians in their homes—but the situation deteriorated almost by the hour, as few Senegalese police or army personnel were to be seen, and Mauritania's Ambassador to Senegal, former Foreign Minister Mohamed el-Mokhtar Ould Zamel, apparently had great difficulty contacting Senegalese authorities to induce them to quell the violence. Ould Zamel and his embassy staff were also themselves threatened by the rioters on April 22 and 23, as the Diouf government showed, in the opinion of independent journalists, signs of complete paralysis, with a more sinister interpretation attached to this lack of activity by the Mauritanian regime of President Maaouiya Ould Sid'Ahmed Taya (q.v.).

Far worse violence was to follow. After news of the anti-Mauritanian riots in Senegal had reached Nouakchott on April 23 and 24, minor incidents took place against the substantial Senegalese population of the Mauritanian capital, spurred on, apparently, by false rumors and exaggerations over what had happened to Mauritanians across the border. Riots also occurred in the economic center of Nouadhibou (q.v.). Meanwhile, the number of disturbances was increasing in Senegal itself, still without what the Ould Taya regime believed should have been an adequate police response. Mauritania's minister of the interior, Ould Abdellahi, took to the airwaves on the evening of April 25 to try to discourage further violence against Senegalese in Mauritania. He sharply condemned the looting and assaults that had taken place over the previous twenty-four hours, exhorted his fellow citizens to "banish from their hearts the cowardly sentiment of revenge regardless of the pain they have suffered," and bade Mauritanians to realize that "these foreigners have no hand in the tragic and painful events experienced by our countrymen on the other side of the border." He sternly warned that further violence would not be tolerated, and to drive the point home, he announced a strict dusk-to-dawn curfew in Nouakchott and Nouadhibou. Despite this strong statement, accompanied by a large police and army deployment, the anti-Senegalese attacks went on for a time, and it was estimated that up to 300 expatriates were killed on the streets of Mauritania's two largest cities. Frightened for their lives, many Senegalese fled overland back to their home country, and when they arrived back in Dakar and other towns, they spread stories (again often false or exaggerated) of atrocities committed against their counterparts by Mauritanian Moors. Upon hearing this news, the Senegalese rioters in Dakar lost all restraint, and the looting and killing reached a crescendo on Friday, April 27 and continued through April 29. At least 300 Mauritanians were killed and property damage was enormous, with nearly the entire Mauritanian colony in Dakar left destitute either by arson or by (as the CMSN alleged) acquisitive Senegalese customs and police officials in border areas as well as at Dakar's Yoff airport and the International Trade Fairgrounds, where many Moors had fled. Finally, though, Senegal's police and armed forces were able to restore a semblance of order by April 29, in one case averting a castastrophe by barring a large crowd of angry Senegalese from the Dakar airport and nearby fairgrounds, where about 15,000 Mauritanians were encamped.

Senegal and Mauritania, resigned to the fact that their nationals could not, for the time being at least, safely remain in the other's country, arranged for a massive airlift in both directions, using many of Mauritania's airports (q.v.) as well as airliners and military transport planes from Algeria, Morocco, Spain, France, and the carriers Air Afrique and Air Mauritanie. For the next fortnight, the airports at both Dakar and Nouakchott handled an estimated 200,000 people, usually penniless refugees (q.v.). This number included many Mauritanians who had lived peacefully in Senegal for years, and Senegalese who had done likewise in Nouakchott and Nouadhibou. The task of providing for all these people promised to be extremely difficult for an already strapped Mauritanian government, and had severely adverse effects on Senegal's economy as well, with small retail shops hit especially hard. On top of the nearly 200,000 Mauritanians Senegal sent back home, 75,000 or so Senegalese were also put on planes and road transport by the Nouakchott government and repatriated. These Senegalese contributed to the problems of Abdou Diouf and his regime, as they too were almost without possessions when they arrived.

On an intergovernmental level, relations between Senegal and Mauritania deteriorated rapidly during May 1989. Dakar, for its part, accused the CMSN of deporting its own Black African citizens to Senegal as part of a racially discriminatory pattern of behavior by the dominant Moors, and claimed that there was government complicity in the anti-Senegalese rioting in Mauritania. The Ould Taya regime admitted that some *bona fide* Mauritanian citizens may have been sent to Senegal (and the United Nations High Commission for Refugees eventually seconded this), but that any such cases were either mistakes made in the confusion of the airlift program, or expulsions of individuals who had procured false Mauritanian identity documents. Other observers were not so sure, and Senegal continued to accuse Mauritania of such expulsions well into 1990. Mauritania returned these allegations with some of its own—that the Diouf government owed compensation to the Moors and others for the money and belongings they had left behind, that Senegal was behind an upsurge in activity by the outlawed FLAM organization (which included several attacks against the Mauritanian army in the Senegal River Valley), and that it was still encouraging anti-Mauritanian feelings among its own people. Conditions had reached such a low point by May 23, 1989, that Ould Taya felt compelled to recall his ambassador, Ould Zamel, from Dakar as a gesture of displeasure over what he perceived as Senegalese intransigence on the compensation issue and the failure of a mediation mission, under Malian sponsorship, at Bamako a few days earlier. A second meeting at Bamako (June 3–5) and a third (at Rosso [q.v.] on June 28) were equally fruitless, and in the coming weeks and months, it would be left to the Organization of African Unity (OAU) and its chairman, Egyptian President Hosni Mubarak, to continue what would become an extensive conciliation effort, aided critically by Algeria and France.

By the summer of 1989, the humanitarian situation in Senegal and Mauritania had stabilized somewhat, but the diplomatic side of the equation was another matter. A step backward, in the eyes of many outside observers, was taken in July, when Senegal announced that it would consider reopening a long-dormant border disagreement between the two states, asserting by implication a Senegalese claim to hundreds of thousands of hectares of Mauritania's prime agricultural (q.v.) land along the Senegal River. Although the legalities of the issue were complex and related partly to French colonial governmental actions taken at the beginning of the twentieth century, the Mauritanian response was swift and vehement—it categorically rejected Senegal's arguments and accused Abdou Diouf of creating an unfavorable climate for negotiations on other outstanding differences. Senegal's statements on the boundary issue, in any case, garnered no support from the OAU or others, and were quietly dropped months later. But enough damage had been done already: on August 21, 1989, the Senegalese ambassador to Mauritania was expelled after allegedly criticizing certain CMSN policies, and Dakar announced that effective that day it was breaking diplomatic relations completely. Morocco was chosen by Senegal to represent its interests in Mauritania, an act that irritated the CMSN, since in the crisis, King Hassan II (q.v.) had tended to side with Senegal, and the regime in any event felt that it had to be on its guard, given that no settlement had yet been reached in the nearby Western Sahara dispute. More generally, the autumn of 1989 was marked by the cessation of trade and airline links between the West African neighbors, the closure of most border crossings, and the militarization of the Senegal River Valley area. A combination of occasional artillery duels between Mauritanian and Senegalese forces, alleged mutual border incursions, reported deportations, and renewed FLAM activity conspired to make the riverine frontier increasingly insecure. At this stage, the primary risk appeared to be the outbreak of war, a course of action that was thought to be favored by influential voices in the Dakar government and military establishment (and by Senegalese opposition leader Abdoulaye Wade, who also favored Moroccan military intervention). War did not break out, partly because of the small size of the respective armies of the two states, and probably in part because of the calculation on both sides that warfare could prove to be economically calamitous and could perhaps threaten the underpinnings of their societies.

The year 1990 began inauspiciously, but in the view of some commentators, a conciliatory step toward Senegal was taken on February 4 with the sudden dismissal of Interior Minister Ould Abdellahi from the CMSN and his temporary "internal exile" to his birthplace of Kiffa (q.v.). Since Ould Abdellahi had been thought to be a relative "hardliner" on the Senegalese situation, his sacking was taken as a sign of a desire to reduce tensions. But other observers attached different interpretations to Ould Abdellahi's departure, and relations between Senegal and Mauritania remained frozen throughout the year. In fact, they were to suffer a sharp reverse in November 1990, when Senegal was accused by the CMSN of being behind an attempted coup against the Ould Taya regime, an allegation strongly denied by Abdou Diouf but which led to a wholesale purge in the Mauritanian armed forces, with many Halpulaar junior officers (and civil servants) being dismissed, imprisoned, or—according to some reports by human rights organizations—extrajudicially executed. For a time, it looked as though tensions were heating up again, with the political and economic strains caused by the Gulf Crisis (q.v.) of 1990 and 1991 providing an additional distraction for the Nouakchott government.

Dakar, too, still refused to recognize the center of the Senegal River as the definitive boundary between it and Mauritania, and Senegal charged that the CMSN was supporting separatist rebels in the unstable southern Senegalese province of Casamance, another allegation that the Ould Taya regime, in the person of Information Minister Mohammed Lamine Ould Ahmed, stoutly denied.

Despite the continuing "incidents" at the border, discreet contacts in Paris and elsewhere were in progress from mid-1991 onward, and managed to produce a thaw in relations. In late November 1991, Abdou Diouf and Maaouiya Ould Sid'Ahmed Taya met (briefly) for the first time since the start of the crisis at the annual meeting of Francophone African countries. Further contacts were conducted between lower-ranking officials of both states, and on April 24, 1992, it was announced that diplomatic ties between Mauritania and Senegal were to be resumed immediately, with trade and airline links to follow later. Reportedly, the accord reestablishing relations included provisions for payments for those who had suffered injury or property loss in the 1989 riots, the unblocking of Senegalese bank accounts held by repatriated Mauritanians, and the setting up of a joint commission of inquiry to address financial, border, and other questions as they arose. In addition, some attention was to be paid to the predicament of the 60,000 or so black Mauritanians allegedly expelled by the government and settled in refugee camps in Senegal. Dakar, however, did not insist that Nouakchott take back these supposed expellees, and showed a willingness not to allow this matter to cloud the overall diplomatic picture. One major concession by Senegal, moreover, was its tacit agreement to restrict FLAM activity in the Senegal River Valley and to increase patrols by its army with that objective in mind.

With the resumption of official relations between Senegal and Mauritania, one of the most severe challenges to the Nouakchott regime since independence had ended. The relationship, however, was to remain equivocal over the next two years, aggravated by occasional "misunderstandings" at the border (including an armed clash near Bogué in the province of Brakna [q.v.] in August 1993), and by continuing suspicions of each other's nationals. In the opinion of some students of the region, the increased attention being given by both Senegal and Mauritania to the citizenship status of persons within their respective frontiers is the most lasting legacy of the Senegal-Mauritania Crisis, a phenomenon that, among other things, threatens to hinder both commerce (q.v.) and normal human interchange along the common river boundary for the foreseeable future.

SENEGAL RIVER DEVELOPMENT AUTHORITY. See Organisation pour la Mise en Valeur du Fleuve Sénégal (OMVS)

SENGHOR, LEOPOLD SEDAR. One of the most prominent postwar Francophone African leaders and a cofounder of the *Entente Mauritanienne* (q.v.), Léopold Sédar Senghor was president of Mauritania's southern neighbor, Senegal, from its independence in August 1960 to his retirement in 1980. Under Léopold Senghor's leadership, the Senegal-Mauritanian relationship was relatively harmonious, as he and President Mokhtar Ould Daddah (q.v.) shared common attitudes on many issues. Concerning Western Sahara (q.v.), Senghor was instrumental in convincing Ould Daddah in late 1975 to embrace a deal with Morocco's King Hassan II (q.v.) under which the Spanish colony would be partitioned, with Mauritania receiving the southern one-third of the territory, Tiris el-Gharbia (q.v.), and the remainder going to Morocco. Senghor, however, like King Hassan and Ould Daddah, underestimated the willingness of the Polisario Front (q.v.) to resist the incursions of Mauritania and Morocco and press for an independent Saharan Arab Democratic Republic (SADR) (q.v.). Soon after Ould Daddah's armed forces (q.v.) began to suffer serious reverses at the hands of Polisario, Senghor attempted to mediate the dispute, but was not successful due to his pro-Morocco stance, which alienated him from the Saharawi (q.v.) nationalists as well as from Algeria, Polisario's main backer. His efforts to end the war rebuffed, Senghor significantly raised the stakes in December 1977, threatening to request "self-determination" for Mauritania's Black African groups if the regime in Nouakchott (q.v.) were to undergo a pro-Polisario "revolution." Although this gambit—in reality a challenge to Mauritania's territorial integrity—received no international support, Léopold Senghor did allow the French air force to mount Operation Lamantin (q.v.) from bases near Dakar in an attempt to bolster an increasingly insecure Mauritanian government. Senghor only reluctantly reconciled himself to the overthrow of Mokhtar Ould Daddah and his replacement by the *Comité Militaire de Redressement National* (CMRN) (q.v.) on July 10, 1978, but did adopt a somewhat lower profile on the Western Sahara conflict and internal Mauritanian affairs from that time onward. In what was heralded as one of the first peaceful transfers of power in postcolonial Africa, the seventy-four-year-old Senghor resigned as president of Senegal in late 1980 and was replaced in January 1981 by Abdou Diouf (q.v.).

SHARIA (variant: charia). The term used to denote the Islamic (q.v.) legal code, covering issues of civil, criminal, and commercial law in Muslim societies. Although there is no general body of Islamic law found in the Koran except for some domestic relations–related matters, a further source of jurisprudence is found in the *Hadiths*—the words and deeds of the Prophet Mohammed during his lifetime as they were recorded by his fellow believers. In addition, laws are also derived from the *ijma* (the consensus of Islamic beliefs) and the *qiryas* (elaborations on the intent and proper application of laws, on which significant differences exist among scholars).

In Mauritania, the application of the sharia has a history marked by some controversy. Although Islamic concepts were nominally considered to be the primary (or only) source of legislation since the country's independence in 1960, it was not until two decades later that a concerted effort was made to implement a Muslim legal code. In what many observers of Mauritanian political life saw as a device to legitimize the government of Colonel Mohammed Khouna Ould Heydallah (q.v.), then the head of Mauritania's governing military council, the CMSN (q.v.), the sharia was decreed, in early 1980, to be the sole law of the land, and a special Islamic court was added to the country's judicial system (q.v.) in May of that year to judge offenses under its provisions. It soon became apparent that Ould Heydallah, the most religiously inclined of Mauritania's heads of state, intended to use the sharia to crack down on an alleged crime wave afflicting the country, and that some of the sharia's harshest punishments, including whipping, amputation of hands, and the death penalty, would form a key part of its implementation. In September 1980 the Islamic courts handed down their first verdicts, which resulted in the execution of one man for homicide and the amputation of the hands of three others. Nine people were subsequently flogged in public for stealing. By February 1982, three people had been shot for murder, and dozens of petty thieves were publicly whipped at mass spectacles in the Nouakchott (q.v.) sports stadium, reportedly to the applause of thousands of onlookers. These severe punishments continued through 1983.

President Ould Heydallah's use of the more archaic sharia provisions touched off a firestorm of domestic and international criticism. Detractors alleged that many of those who were flogged for theft stole because they could not otherwise feed themselves, that the punishments were cruel and disproportionate to the offenses committed, and that those guilty of corruption in the government and private enterprise were never subjected to amputation or whipping. This was a telling point, since it was widely reported that Ould Heydallah's family and close friends were using their positions to enrich themselves. Under pressure from the Mauritanian public as well as his colleagues in the CMSN, Ould Heydallah halted these punishments in February 1984, several months before he was deposed by a fellow officer, Colonel Maaouiya Ould Sid'Ahmed Taya (q.v.). Upon his accession to power, Ould Taya showed more liberal attitudes on Islam than his predecessor, and the sharia's full application was indefinitely shelved. Recognizing that Mauritania's population (q.v.) was virtually all Muslim, yet at the same time mindful that the French civil law system, inherited from colonial days, continued to serve the country's needs in most situations, the Constitution of July 20, 1991 (q.v.), declared in its preamble that Mauritanian society would be "respectful of the precepts of Islam, the sole source of law, but responsive as well to the exigencies of the modern world."

SIDI MOHAMED OULD BOUBACAR. Mauritania's prime minister from April 1992 was born in Atar (q.v.) on May 31, 1957, hailing from the Oulad Ahmed tribe centered in the administrative région of Brakna (q.v.). He was educated primarily within his home country and in France, obtaining his *baccalauréat* in July 1976, and thereafter (in July 1980) receiving a university degree in financial management from the *Ecole Nationale d'Administration* (ENA) in Nouakchott (q.v.). A year later (in 1981) he was awarded a *diplôme des études approfondies* from the same institution. Almost immediately, he went into the Mauritanian state administration, serving first as general treasurer of the région of Dakhlet-Nouadhibou (qq.v.) from February to November 1983, and as treasurer of Mauritania in 1984. From 1985 to 1988, he held a variety of increasingly responsible positions, including director of the national budget, comptroller-general, and director of planning. In a periodic reorganization of the Council of Ministers (q.v.) carried out by President Maaouiya Ould Sid'Ahmed Taya (q.v.) on October 21, 1990, Ould Boubacar was appointed minister of finance at the age of only thirty-three. He occupied that high post in the midst of the severe dislocations caused by both the Senegal-Mauritania crisis (q.v.) of 1989 and 1990 and the Gulf Crisis (q.v.) of 1990 and 1991. He stayed on as head of the Finance Ministry until April 18, 1992, when, as part of President Ould Taya's appointments to the initial cabinet of the Mauritanian Second Republic (q.v.), he was named prime minister, at the age of thirty-five one of the youngest such officials anywhere in the world. His selection was greeted positively by financial agencies such as the World Bank and the International Monetary Fund (IMF), as Ould Boubacar had several years of experience in dealing with those institutions. Although he is a committed member of the ruling *Parti Républicain, Démocratique et Social* (PRDS) (q.v.), he worked mostly outside the national political spotlight, devoting himself to the preparation and presentation to the *Assemblée Nationale* (q.v.) of successive Mauritanian budgets (q.v.) as well as supervising the overall functioning of the government. He also remained a relatively nonpartisan figure, only seldom drawing criticism from Mauritania's opposition parties as he tried to set broad policy guidelines and navigate his way through the country's social and financial problems in the mid-1990s. Sidi Mahamed Ould Boubacar served as prime minister until January 1, 1996, when he was replaced by the former minister of fisheries and maritime economy, Cheikh el-Afia

Ould Khouna, and was almost immediately named secretary-general of the ruling PRDS.

SLAVERY (Arabic: sing., *Abd;* pl., *Abid*). Perhaps no single characteristic of modern Mauritanian society attracted such close attention as did the persistence, into the late twentieth century, of the institution of human bondage among a declining but significant number of the country's inhabitants. Indeed, slavery was often the only aspect of Mauritania that garnered any appreciable degree of coverage in the Western media, leading to a torrent of international criticism directed at successive Mauritanian governments for allegedly acquiescing in its continued existence. At various times, moreover, the conditions of those in a servile state, as well as those emancipated from that condition, have greatly affected Mauritania's internal political arrangements, complicating an already multivariate tribal, ethnic, and regional situation.

Slavery in Mauritania dates back at least several centuries to the time of Berber (q.v.) and later Almoravid (q.v.) domination, a period in which the black tribes of the north retreated before the superior weaponry and religiously motivated zeal of the Arabs, particularly the *Beni Hassan* (q.v.). The blacks who escaped in time settled permanently in the Senegal River Valley, but those who did not were impressed into domestic servitude, often as a spoil of war or as a form of punishment. Until the 1960s, slaves were more or less openly bought and sold among the Beydane Moorish (q.v.) segment of the population. By the same token, however, the blacks in the south of the country, groups such as the Bambara, Fulbe, Halpulaaren, Soninké, and Wolof (qq.v.), also practiced slavery against fellow Black Africans; it appeared, though, that the institution of intraracial slavery had practically vanished by about the time Mauritania became independent in November 1960.

. With the "white" Moors it was otherwise. Slaves (almost invariably black) continued to be kept as domestic servants and helpers in the fields and pastures of the new nation, and were only slowly freed, usually at the whim of their masters. At no time, however, did Mauritanian slavery resemble some of its counterparts elsewhere in the world, including, for example, the southern United States prior to 1865. Slaves in Mauritania mostly worked individually or in small groups, often for a Beydane family that was only slightly better off than they were. Expansive agricultural (q.v.) workings normally did not use slaves in large numbers, and a "plantation" economy, so conducive to slavery in Latin America and the U.S., never existed in Moor-inhabited Mauritania, with perhaps the single exception of the salt mines at Idjil in what is today the administrative région of Tiris Zemmour (qq.v.), a fairly large-scale extractive enterprise that used extensive slave labor. Despite the illegality of slavery in the country—it was always disapproved of by the French colonial government and was banned by the Mauritanian constitution of March 22, 1959 (q.v.) — slaves were seen by many Moors, particularly in rural areas, as vital to their continued prosperity.

In any event, it was not primarily legal or moral considerations that led to the decline of slavery, but rather the great social dislocations in Mauritania beginning in the early 1970s. Driven by severe droughts and the process of desertification (q.v.), thousands of Moors were forced off of their rural lands and into the country's already over-crowded cities and towns, where economic opportunities were extremely scarce and the viability of slavery virtually nil. But prospects for the ex-slaves, or *haratines* (q.v.), were also bleak, a circumstance that obliged many of them to continue serving their masters on an unpaid basis, perpetuating, many observers believed, a "psychology of slavery" that impeded their full emancipation even under better material conditions. Some haratines did manage to find their way independently, however, gaining full freedom through access to education (q.v.), by the intercession of sympathetic government officials or other Moors, or by simply escaping from their masters and using the improving Mauritanian road (q.v.) system to move far away. Many haratines were also conscripted into the armed forces (q.v.) beginning in 1976, when President Mokhtar Ould Daddah (q.v.) was obliged to increase vastly the size of the army after becoming embroiled in the Western Sahara conflict (q.v.). After the military officers who deposed Ould Daddah in July 1978 made peace with their Saharawi (q.v.) opponent, the Polisario Front (q.v.), in August 1979, the haratines and many others in the army were demobilized, a step which created considerable economic hardships but which by and large ensured that the ex-slaves no longer had anything to fear from their former masters.

However, the slavery problem did not abate in the early 1980s; in fact, it intensified. Spurred on by the increasing activities and prominence of the El-Hor (q.v.) movement made up of former slaves which had been formed clandestinely in 1974, the CMSN (q.v.) government of Colonel Mohammed Khouna Ould Heydallah (q.v.) found itself under increasing domestic and international pressure not only to move more forcefully against the existence of slavery, but also to ameliorate the lot of the haratines and assist their entry into the mainstream of Mauritanian society. Bowing to these influences, and after consulting with religious experts to make sure that the reabolition of slavery would conform to the Islamic *sharia* (qq.v.), Ould Heydallah issued the following ordinance (No. 81.234) on November 9, 1981:

Article 1: Slavery in all its forms is hereby definitively abolished throughout the territory of the Islamic Republic of Mauritania;
Article 2: In conformity with the sharia, this abolition shall give rise to compensation for persons entitled thereto;

Article 3: A National Commission consisting of ulema (religious experts), economists, and administrators shall be established by decree for the purpose of studying the practical modalities of such compensation. Upon completion of the study, the modalities in question shall be laid down by decree;
Article 4: The present Ordinance shall be published as a matter of urgency and shall be enforced as the law of the State.

However well-intentioned this decree may have been, it did little to quiet the slavery controversy or satisfy El-Hor's demands. International observers pointed out that most of the law was devoted to clarifying the principle of compensation for the slaveowners. This angered El-Hor, who asserted that it should have been the haratines themselves who would be economically assisted. Other more cautious officials opined that Ould Heydallah's ordinance was unnecessary, since it merely reiterated what was already the law—that slavery had always been illegal. In the midst of these contentious debates, Ould Heydallah took a more practical measure ostensibly to assist haratines. On June 5, 1983, he promulgated the Land Reform Act (q.v.), which modified land tenure regulations and gave the Mauritanian government a greater role in allocating unused cultivable hectarage, especially in the southern régions of the country. While haratines were helped by this development, the law proved intensely controversial, as it facilitated, in the eyes of some experts, the displacement of Halpulaaren and other free black Mauritanians from their ancestral holdings. Meanwhile, the number of people still in a servile or semi-servile condition in Mauritania was the subject of greatly varying estimates. The CMSN maintained that no more than a few thousand people were affected by Ould Heydallah's November 1981 decree, while studies published by international human rights organizations put the figure around 100,000, fully five percent of the country's total population (q.v.) of 2.1 million.

In January 1984, the United Nations (q.v.) stepped into the fray. A representative of the UN Sub-Commission on the Prevention of Discrimination and Protection of Minorities, Marc Bossyut, spent a fortnight in Mauritania, where he was received by government officials as well as by ordinary citizens and El-Hor supporters. Although Bossyut's report (see Bibliography) commended the CMSN for its reabolition decree of November 1981 and noted that slavery was in overall decline, it also pointed out that the regime was unwilling "to disturb the peace of the home" in rooting out enslaved individuals, and that this attitude, coupled with the purely domestic nature of Mauritanian slavery, made eradication more problematic. On top of this, the central role of the family in Islamic societies militated against more aggressive state action in this regard. In addition to advocating a less passive role on the part of the authorities, the UN report also strongly encouraged the wide dissemination of the reabolition ordinance throughout the countryside, favored the use of the *Structures pour l'Education des Masses* (SEM) (q.v.) toward that end, and stressed that "it is in the economic field that the greatest efforts must be undertaken." Specifically, the UN expert urged more access to arable lands and pastures for haratines, better educational opportunities, and targeted foreign development assistance, including the establishment of cooperatives and small businesses which would receive government start-up funds. Bossyut concluded that "the economic development of Mauritania will gradually bring about the disappearance of the traditional economy in which the slavery-like practices had developed."

Even with this relatively optimistic report, the issue of slavery would not go away. Some educated ex-slaves were appointed to cabinet-level positions by the regime of Colonel Maaouiya Ould Sid' Ahmed Taya (q.v.), but varying attitudes among governmental officials and a lack of state economic resources resulted in slow progress toward full emancipation. The persistence of slavery was roundly castigated by the *Forces de Libération Africaine de Mauritanie* (FLAM) (q.v.) in its April 1986 pamphlet, *Le Manifesto du Négro-Mauritanien Opprimé* (q.v.), which also denounced the "racism" of the CMSN in virtually all walks of Mauritanian life. FLAM also sought to cement an alliance between haratines and other free black Mauritanians, a pursuit that yielded few results due to the ex-slaves' near-total acculturation to the way of life of the Beydane Moors, including their use of Hassaniya (q.v.) Arabic as a *lingua franca*. Seizing upon this phenomenon as evidence of the "color-blind" nature of Mauritanian society, the government mounted a strong counterattack against FLAM's allegations, denying that any individuals in the country were still enslaved. Nevertheless, Mauritania soon earned the unenviable distinction in some Western circles of being practically the only country in the world where persons were sometimes considered property. By 1990, stories of horrific punishments allegedly administered to slaves who attempted escape or who were insubordinate began to circulate and were given added publicity in reports issued by Human Rights Watch in 1990 and 1994 (see Bibliography).

By 1996, there is little doubt among most independent observers that slavery is still a fact of life for some Mauritanians, although accurate statistics are nearly impossible to compile and in any event cannot take account of the wide variations in economic status, degree of freedom, and overall conditions for those still enmeshed in Moorish society's least commendable institution. Then, too, any assessment of the dependency situation in Mauritania would need to consider the less tangible, but probably more prevalent psychology of the slaves and ex-slaves themselves, manifested all too often in attitudes (often religiously inculcated) of inferiority and of obligation to the master, which combine with economic adversity to place the prospect of a better life seemingly always beyond the horizon.

SOCIETE ANONYME DES MINES DE FER DE MAURITANIE (MIFERMA). Established in 1952 after a series of geological surveys in the late 1940s had detected enormous quantities of iron ore (q.v.) in the vicinity of Fort Gouraud and Zouerate (qq.v.), MIFERMA's operations evolved into the single most important economic activity in independent Mauritania, by the late 1960s accounting for fully 80 percent of the country's foreign exchange earnings and employing one-fourth of all Mauritanian wage-earners. From the beginning, MIFERMA was controlled by French interests, with the government of France holding 24 percent of the company's stock and private French steel concerns owning 32 percent, and the remainder of the shares split between British, Italian, and West German stockholders. Mauritania's share, acquired in 1962, was only 5 percent. MIFERMA did not confine its activities to the iron mines in Tiris Zemmour (q.v.); the company was responsible also for building and operating the 650-kilometer railway (q.v.) line from Zouerate to the economic center of Nouadhibou (q.v.), where the *Port Minéralier* (q.v.) was constructed along with worker housing and other infrastructure needed for its operations. All told, MIFERMA had by 1966 invested over $200 million in Mauritania.

The presence of MIFERMA, a huge enterprise, was not, however, an unmixed blessing for the government of President Mokhtar Ould Daddah (q.v.). The large number of French and other expatriate technicians in the critical mining sector virtually guaranteed that frictions would develop between them and Mauritanian nationals, who were extremely slow to be recruited into the employ of the company. Those who were on the MIFERMA payroll periodically struck the mines and railway, demanding better pay and conditions. These strikes occasionally turned violent and resulted in Ould Daddah's use of Mauritania's armed forces (q.v.) to restore order, most notably in May 1968 when at least eight workers were killed and twenty-five wounded. Nonetheless, by 1973, MIFERMA's last full year of existence, 10.5 million tons of iron ore were exported by the company, a figure that far exceeded expectations.

MIFERMA continued to act as a focus for Mauritanian nationalist resentment, though, and in 1974 President Ould Daddah, by then firmly embarked on a policy of distancing his regime from Paris as part of an overall restructuring of the country's foreign relations (q.v.), decided to act. On November 28 MIFERMA was nationalized and its ownership assumed by the *Société Nationale Industrielle et Minière* (SNIM) (q.v.), a company set up by the government two years earlier ostensibly to explore for and extract gypsum (q.v.) deposits. With the mining sector now in the hands of the Mauritanian government, the number of expatriate employees was reduced, and loans from Morocco and other Arab financial institutions were secured to compensate the original European MIFERMA shareholders.

SOCIETE DES MINES DE CUIVRE DE MAURITANIE (MICUMA). In 1953, several years before Mauritania's independence, a number of French mining and industrial interests formed MICUMA to exploit the country's deposits of copper (q.v.), which had been discovered near Akjoujt (q.v.). When it was organized, the company was owned jointly by the French *Bureau des Recherches Géologiques et Minières* (25 percent), the *Société Minière et Métallurgique du Pennaroya* (25 percent), the Mauritanian territorial government (25 percent), and the *Banque de Paris et de Pays-Bas* (10 percent), with private stockholders accounting for the remaining 15 percent. Unlike its bigger brother, MIFERMA (q.v.), which soon began intensive extraction of the iron ore (q.v.) deposits near the town of Zouerate (q.v.), the MICUMA consortium never performed any mining operations and was succeeded in April 1963 by the *Société de Cuivre de la Mauritanie* (SOCUMA), also with heavy European as well as North American participation. But this venture also failed, and it was not until 1970 that copper ore began to be mined, under the purview of a new parastatal, the *Société Minière de Mauritanie* (SOMIMA) (q.v.).

SOCIETE MAURITANIENNE DE COMMERCIALISATION DU POISSON (SMCP). Founded in 1984, the Mauritanian Commercial Fish Company functioned as the country's primary purchaser in the substantial fisheries (q.v.) industry. SMCP owned no facilities itself: its task was merely to enforce the state monopoly, which existed until 1993, on fish products landed at Nouadhibou (q.v.), Mauritania's primary port (q.v.) and economic center. After the catch was landed, SMCP would store and market the fish, either selling them to private merchants or exporting them abroad. In the mid-1980s, as much as 60 percent of Mauritania's entire fish exports were made through SMCP.

SOCIETE MINIERE DE MAURITANIE (SOMIMA). The Mining Company of Mauritania was formed by the Nouakchott (q.v.) government in 1967 for the purpose of exploiting the deposits of copper (q.v.) that existed near the town of Akjoujt (q.v.). SOMIMA's establishment followed two unsuccessful attempts to organize a mining operation there, the first being the formation of the French-controlled MICUMA (q.v.) consortium, followed by another foreign-backed company, the *Société de Cuivre de la Mauritanie* (SOCUMA), which folded in 1965. The *Société Minière de Mauritanie,* in common with its predecessors, had heavy European participation, with a plurality of shares (45 percent) held by Charter Consolidated. The Mauritanian government, then headed by President Mokhtar Ould Daddah (q.v.), held a 22 percent stake, and the remainder was the property of French and other foreign interests, including the World Bank. After making preparations, SOMIMA began to extract the estimated 32 million tons of copper ore in 1970, although only 3,000 tons were taken out that year. The company's fortunes were ascendant for a few years, with 28,982 tons extracted in 1973, generating substantial foreign exchange earnings for the Mauritanian regime. After the peak year of 1973, output rapidly declined, due to falling world market prices for copper and the low grade of the Akjoujt ores. In an attempt at reorganization, Ould Daddah shut down SOMIMA's operation in 1975 and nationalized it, making it a part of Mauritania's primary mining parastatal, SNIM (q.v.), whose main activity was the exploitation of iron ore (q.v.) reserves near Zouerate (q.v.). SNIM soon reopened the copper mines and operated them at a loss until 1978. SOMIMA again was made a separate entity, and although copper mining had ceased in 1978 and had not resumed by the mid-1990s, a SNIM subsidiary, *Mines d'Or d'Akjoujt* (MORAK), was extracting gold (q.v.) deposits from the tailings of the old copper mine.

SOCIETE NATIONALE D'EAU ET D'ELECTRICITE (SONELEC). Mauritania's National Water and Electricity Company was established in 1968 as a state-owned enterprise to develop and maintain facilities not only for the supply of electricity, but also to extract and distribute the country's scarce water resources (q.v.). From the beginning of SONELEC's existence, it concentrated on the generation and distribution of electrical power, an effort that soon ran into difficulties, among them managerial inefficiency, lack of finance, the long distances that any electrical distribution network would have to traverse, and the propensity of many Mauritanian enterprises and individuals to generate their own power. A vicious cycle soon developed: as problems presented themselves, more and more power was produced elsewhere, so much so that by the mid-1980s SONELEC accounted for only about 25 percent of Mauritania's total generating capacity of 162 megawatts, and reportedly only half of SONELEC's generators were considered reliable. The country's two largest cities, Nouakchott and Nouadhibou (qq.v.), consumed about 90 percent of the company's production. The giant iron ore (q.v.) parastatal, the

Société Nationale Industrielle et Minière et Société d'Economie Mixte (SNIM-SEM) (q.v.) did not depend on SONELEC and generated all of its own power in both Nouadhibou and at its mining facilities near Zouerate (q.v.).

By the time of the accession to power of Colonel Maaouiya Ould Sid'Ahmed Taya (q.v.) as head of state in December 1984, SON-ELEC's predicament had reached the point of crisis, and so a restructuring of the company was undertaken beginning in 1985 as part of the government's Economic Recovery Program for 1985–88. Prices for electricity were increased (ending heavy subsidization), labor costs were trimmed substantially, and an effort was made to reduce waste and pilferage of the available electrical supply. SONELEC then extended its reach into the Mauritanian hinterland: generating plants were opened in Atar, Kaédi, and Rosso (qq.v.) with an eye to future expansion, and an entirely new water pumping station was constructed approximately fifty kilometers from Nouakchott at Idini with assistance from the People's Republic of China, opening in 1990. A new electrical generating plant in Nouakchott itself was also included in SONELEC's plans, supplementing two other existing plants in the capital. Still, the resources of Mauritania's water and electricity parastatal remained limited, so in 1993 it was announced that the stronger, more experienced mining company, SNIM-SEM, would supervise and provide equipment for the electrification of thirteen Mauritanian towns. Included in this $24 million project (to be operated by SON-ELEC after completion) were twelve new power stations, over thirty generating sets with a capacity between 400 and 800 kilowatts each, and 200 kilometers of new power lines. It was hoped that about 17,000 consumers would use this network. Financing for the project was provided by the Arab Fund for Economic and Social Development (FADES), an international consortium, and completion was scheduled for 1995 or 1996. Mauritanian towns to be included in the new generating and distribution grid included Akjoujt, Ayoun el-Atrouss, Boutilimit, Kiffa, Néma, Tidjikja, and Sélibaby (qq.v.). In addition, the smaller population (q.v.) centers of Aleg, Bogué, Guerou, Maghta Lahjar, M'bout, and Timbédra were scheduled for inclusion. Meanwhile, hydroelectric power generation projects in the Senegal River Valley were under the auspices of the *Organisation pour la Mise en Valeur du Fleuve Sénégal* (OMVS) (q.v.).

SOCIETE NATIONALE D'IMPORTATION ET D'EXPORTA-TION (SONIMEX). The National Import-Export Company of Mauritania was organized in 1966 as a joint venture with certain private interests by the government of President Mokhtar Ould Daddah (q.v.) to regulate imports and exports, with its primary focus on agricultural (q.v.) produce. By the 1970s, SONIMEX possessed a legal monopoly on the importation of such items as sugar, rice, and tea; it would then resell the goods to the private retail trade. However, given the country's tradition of a large informal economy with substantial commerce (q.v.) with neighboring Senegal, SONIMEX's role was always a great deal less significant than it might have at first appeared, since individual trading activities were impossible to control even if it were politically expedient to do so. Moreover, wheat and flour, critical staples, were outside the purview of SONIMEX from the start, as were the economically indispensable activities of the iron ore (q.v.) mining company, the *Société Nationale Industrielle et Minière* (SNIM) (q.v.). In addition, the responsibilities of SONIMEX had by the early 1980s come to overlap with those of the state food supply agency, the *Commissariat à la Sécurité Alimentaire* (CSA) and those of the *Société Nationale pour le Développement Rural* (SONADER) (qq.v.). Like many other Mauritanian parastatals, SONIMEX soon fell prey to a variety of difficulties, and was a focus of corruption allegations during the presidency of Colonel Mohammed Khouna Ould Heydallah (q.v.) from 1980 to 1984. After Ould Heydallah's ouster as head of state in December 1984, SONIMEX underwent a reorganization, part of which involved the raising of consumer prices for basic commodities by approximately 30 percent so as to increase the company's revenues and avoid being undercut by private importers. SONIMEX itself was opened to additional private participation in the late 1980s, and although the Mauritanian government still held 74 percent of its shares in 1992, full privatization had not been ruled out.

SOCIETE NATIONALE INDUSTRIELLE ET MINIERE ET SOCIETE D'ECONOMIE MIXTE (SNIM-SEM). The National Industrial and Mining Company was created as a Mauritanian state enterprise in 1972 by President Mokhtar Ould Daddah (q.v.) as the eventual instrument of his government's takeover of the country's massive iron ore (q.v.) extraction sector, then in the hands of the French-controlled *Société Anonyme des Mines de Fer de Mauritanie* (MIFERMA) (q.v.), a consortium which, beginning in the late 1960s, had become the focus of nationalist resentment due to its slowness in employing Mauritanian staff and its liberal repatriation of profits to the former metropole. Ostensibly, SNIM's role was only to explore for and extract deposits of gypsum (q.v.) in the country, and to build and operate a plant in Nouakchott (q.v.) to produce explosives for mining purposes. But on the fourteenth anniversary of Mauritania's independence from France (November 28, 1974), President Ould Daddah announced that MIFERMA was nationalized and that SNIM would assume ownership and control of not only the iron ore mines near

Zouerate (q.v.), but also of ancillary facilities such as the *Port Minéralier* (q.v.) near the economic center of Nouadhibou (q.v.) and of the vital railway (q.v.) line running between the mine sites and the Atlantic coast. All told, over 80 percent of Mauritania's exports were placed under government control, along with responsibility for thousands of employees. MIFERMA's shareholders were compensated generously, and despite worries that mining operations would be disrupted by the SNIM takeover, the transition process went smoothly. Mauritanian managers and workers were hired in greater numbers, and the Ould Daddah regime was able to press ahead with plans to direct more of the profits from iron ore to the country's development needs.

The next object of SNIM's attentions was the financially shaky copper (q.v.) mine located near the town of Akjoujt (q.v.). Like the iron ore operations, it was partially controlled by France in the form of the *Société Minière de Mauritanie* (SOMIMA) (q.v.), which had been set up in 1967 as a joint-stock corporation. Seeing that SOMIMA was in a parlous state, in April 1975 the Mauritanian government simultaneously nationalized the company and shut down the Akjoujt mine pending a reorganization at the hands of SNIM. From the beginning, therefore, SNIM was primarily concerned with iron ore extraction and allied functions, although it continued its efforts with regard to gypsum and explosives and for a time attempted to operate a steel mill at Nouadhibou, without appreciable success. SNIM's main subsidiary, as a consequence, remained the *Comptoir Minier du Nord* (COMINOR) (q.v.), which had day-to-day managerial authority over the Tiris Zemmour (q.v.) iron mines, and which also operated the railway along with many other services in the Zouerate area.

SNIM was one of the first Mauritanian concerns to feel the impact of the Western Sahara conflict (q.v.), which originated in President Ould Daddah's takeover of the southern one-third of the disputed ex-Spanish colony in late 1975, against the claims of the Polisario Front (q.v.), which demanded full independence for the territory. The iron ore mines and the Zouerate-Nouadhibou railway proved exquisitely vulnerable to Polisario attacks, and soon exports slowed dramatically, tumbling from 9.6 million tons in 1976 to 7.1 million tons in 1978. SNIM's profits suffered accordingly, and so, of course, did the Mauritanian treasury, already in dire straits due to the sharp increase in the size of the armed forces (q.v.) necessitated by the war against Polisario. At times between 1976 and 1978, no dependable rail service was running between the mines and the Port Minéralier, and only the existence of iron ore stockpiles at Nouadhibou kept exports from grinding to a halt. A low point was reached on May 1, 1977, when Polisario troops overran Zouerate itself, destroying great quantities of equipment and capturing several French expatriate workers. SNIM's high exposure to the Western Sahara conflict had considerable psychological consequences for its managers, too: perhaps sooner than other Mauritanians, the mine operators wearied of the seemingly endless hit-and-run conflict against the kindred Saharawi (q.v.) people that was putting SNIM on the brink of oblivion. The chairman of the company, Ismael Ould Amar, therefore, was one of the first to welcome publicly the *coup d'état* of July 10, 1978, which deposed President Ould Daddah and replaced his regime with a military council, the *Comité Militaire de Redressement National* (CMRN) (q.v.). Although the end of the war was over a year away, a cease-fire proclaimed by the Polisario Front against Mauritanian targets a few days after the coup gave SNIM a desperately needed chance to rebuild equipment, obtain foreign financing for improvements, and get exports up to full flow again, a process that only took until 1979, when, confounding skeptics, 9.1 million tons were shipped out of Nouadhibou, roughly equal to the prewar level. The CMRN also took a critical step: in 1978 it opened ownership of SNIM to foreign (mainly Arab) interests, and some time later added *Société d'Economie Mixte* (SEM), or Mixed Economic Company, to SNIM's name as a symbol of what was to become a familiar sight in Mauritania over the next decade—increasing private participation in many hitherto state-run enterprises.

Despite SNIM-SEM's notable successes in restoring the Zouerate (Kediet d'Idjil) mines to full operation and maintaining its reputation as one of the country's better-managed institutions, the 1980s were troubled ones for the company. The new Arab League (q.v.) shareholders brought with them their own demands, and SNIM-SEM was forced to dismiss many employees, jettison its unviable subsidiaries in the industrial development and petroleum (qq.v.) sectors, and allow greater latitude to foreign private capital, a blow to the nationalistic sensibilities of Mauritania's rulers. Another very basic problem was the impending exhaustion of the Kediet d'Idjil open-cast mine sites, which would have meant the end of all SNIM operations if new deposits of iron ore could not be found. Fortunately, after deposits at Guelb el-Rhein had failed to be commercially viable, vast quantities of iron ore (of 60 percent purity) were found farther to the east of Zouerate, at M'Haoudat, a discovery that will probably keep the Mauritanian iron mining industry operational for several more decades, as it is thought that the total deposits there exceed 100 million tons. The extraction and export of these reserves began in the early 1990s, but by this time the iron mining sector had been steadily decreasing in overall importance to Mauritania's economy, its share of total exports falling below 50 percent in 1983, and then under 40 percent by the close of the decade, due in part to a reinvigorated fisheries (q.v.) industry. And as the various directors of SNIM-SEM (the company was headed by Mohammed Salek Ould Heyine in the 1986–1996 period) quickly learned, greatly fluctuating commodity prices in the world market have made any form of fiscal cushion a problematic affair, with profits often showing large variances from year to year and with rising oil prices and personnel costs always an irritant. But SNIM-SEM's days of strictly hand-to-mouth existence seemed to be over, as the M'Haoudat discoveries and fairly generous financial assistance from its Gulf Arab partners guaranteed that it would remain a force to be reckoned with. The company, moreover, again started cautiously to extend its expertise into other areas. With mainly Western financial backing, it created *Mines d'Or d'Akjoujt* (MORAK), a subsidiary, to exploit gold (q.v.) deposits found in the tailings of the former SOMIMA copper mine, a project that yielded Mauritania a steady $5 to $6 million annually by 1995. SNIM-SEM has also been assisting its sister parastatal, the *Société Nationale d'Eau et d'Electricité* (SONELEC) (q.v.) in the mid-1990s on an ambitious project to extend electrical generation and transmission facilities to many unserviced areas of the country. Finally, SNIM-SEM has made additional social contributions beyond the direct benefits its profitable operations yield and the taxes it pays: the company accounts for almost 10 percent of all the jobs in the "modern" sector of the Mauritanian economy, and in the remote areas in which it is situated, it made substantial investments in new educational (q.v.) facilities in Zouerate and in nearby F'Derik (q.v.), constructed housing and water resource (qq.v.) infrastructure in the two settlements, and ensured that about 150,000 people in northern Mauritania had access to adequate sanitary facilities.

SOCIETE NATIONALE POUR LE DEVELOPPEMENT RURAL (SONADER). Mauritania's National Corporation for Rural Development was formed by the government of President Mokhtar Ould Daddah (q.v.) in 1975 and was answerable to the minister of rural development in the Mauritanian cabinet. It is tasked with planning agricultural (q.v.) and irrigation programs as well as serving as an agricultural extension service that communicates to rural residents the techniques of the farming trade. In addition, it provides grants and credits for the acquisition of equipment such as pumps, vehicles, and farm implements, as well as fertilizers. In the first decade of its existence, SONADER also had a more intrusive role in Mauritanian rural life; in various places in the country it had an official monopoly on the milling, transportation, and marketing of most domestically grown produce and maintained a system of warehouses throughout the countryside in conjunction with the food security agency, the *Commis-*

sariat à la Sécurité Alimentaire (CSA) (q.v.), all in an effort to maximize food availability during a period of extremely poor agricultural production caused by severe drought and advancing desertification (q.v.). Beginning in the late 1980s, food output improved somewhat, and this factor, along with a greater emphasis on the private sector by the regime of President Maaouiya Ould Sid'Ahmed Taya (q.v.), led to a curtailment of many of SONADER's functions. In 1987, the rice and cereal mills of SONADER (and the CSA) were privatized, as were other functions such as marketing and transportation. Price controls were relaxed or eliminated, and SONADER's monopoly (never fully realized in practice) was explicitly abolished. But even with all these transfers to private traders and farmers, SONADER retained its responsibilities as an extension service, was engaged in the early 1990s in attempts to form agricultural cooperatives in rural Mauritania, and remained in overall supervision of 30 percent of cereal production in the country.

SONINKE (variant: Sarakolé). A mainly sedentary grouping of black Mauritanian farmers and traders concentrated in the régions of Assaba and Guidimaka (qq.v.), the Soninké are believed to be the descendants of the inhabitants of the Kingdom of Ghana, which existed in parts of what is now Mauritania from about the fifth century A.D. until it was vanquished by the Almoravids (q.v.) in 1076. The political, commercial, and spiritual capital of the Soninké was Koumbi Saleh (q.v.), a city that did not survive the fall of the Ghanaian kingdom and rapidly went to ruin. Most Soninké live outside of Mauritania, in neighboring Gambia, Mali, and Senegal, and form no more than a minority of the total Mauritanian population (q.v.). Of all black Mauritanians, the social organization of the Soninké has historically been the most rigidly stratified, with strongly defined occupational castes and subdivisions within castes as well. Polygyny is recognized, but is not believed to be widespread, and the basic unit of Soninké society is the extended patrilineal family. The Soninké are believed by some historians to have been among the first in Mauritania to convert to the Islamic (q.v.) faith.

SOUS-PREFECTURE. A unit of local government in Mauritania, the *sous-préfectures* (subdivisions) were formally established by the Constitution of May 20, 1961 (q.v.), as administrative bodies one level below the *cercles* (q.v.). Each sous-préfecture encompassed both urban and rural areas of the country, but, like the cercles and all other local and regional organs, had little real power and served instead to execute decisions taken in Nouakchott (q.v.). On July 30, 1968, as part of a restructuring of the government by President Mokhtar Ould Daddah (q.v.), the sous-préfectures were renamed *départements* (q.v.).

However, the territory covered by the newly named units, as well as their subordinate political status, remained almost exactly the same.

STRUCTURES POUR L'EDUCATION DES MASSES (SEM). Established in early 1982 by Mauritania's military leader, Colonel Mohammed Khouna Ould Heydallah (q.v.), the Mass Education Structures were founded, according to a government statement at the time, to "ensure the participation of the Mauritanian people in political life and hence in national construction," to educate all persons on issues as diverse as slavery (q.v.) and reforms to the agricultural (q.v.) system, and to combat illiteracy. In practice they served primarily as an informal vehicle for legitimizing CMSN (q.v.) rule in the country and for keeping the governing armed forces (q.v.) council apprised of developments in the Mauritanian countryside.

In each administrative région (q.v.) of the country, neighborhood "cells" were organized consisting of ten families each, whose leaders (mostly heads of households) would meet once a week to receive news from the CMSN and to air their grievances and suggestions. Twice per month, there would be a meeting of the leaders of ten neighborhoods, and once a month a "departmental" meeting would take place, attended by the designated heads of ten areas. Finally, a "regional" gathering would be held every two months, presided over by a CMSN member who would exercise overall supervision of the SEM in his bailiwick. Some observers saw in this scheme elements of Libya's "Popular Committees" or Niger's "Development Society"—that is, an ostensible political party that would in practice serve as a transmission belt for CMSN decrees and institutionalize military government. On the other hand, a few commentators saw the SEM as holding out the hope of eventually diluting tribal and ethnic/racial loyalties in a still divided country, and even as a means to pave the way to a return to civilian rule. However, the SEM rapidly fell into disrepute, as they were utilized by Ould Heydallah and his supporters to advance their own personal ambitions as well as those of other well-connected Mauritanians inside and outside the army. In addition, they reportedly became a conduit for Libyan influence and propaganda, a phenomenon which may have been caused by Ould Heydallah's periodic flirtations with that country's leader, Colonel Muammar el-Qadaffi. After Ould Heydallah was replaced by Colonel Maaouiya Ould Sid'Ahmed Taya (q.v.) on December 12, 1984, the SEM were purged of pro-Libyan personnel, and a firm hand was applied to those who were using them for personal enrichment. Soon, the Mass Education Structures were scarcely mentioned in discussions of Mauritanian politics, and their informal machinery went into abeyance as the country emphasized more conventional forms of local and municipal governance. The SEM were abolished once and for all in the early 1990s.

TAGANT. A large (95,000 square kilometers) administrative région (q.v.) of Mauritania, Tagant is located roughly in the center of the country's land mass and has a mostly Sahelian climate (q.v.) and physiography. The only substantial town in the province is Tidjikja (q.v.), and although it has been mostly desertified (q.v.) in the late twentieth century, the translation of Tagant ("forest") suggests an earlier, less arid time, as do the presence of carvings and rock paintings of animals, long vanished from the region, at various places in the remote countryside. In independent Mauritania, Tagant has remained a backwater, albeit with some agriculture and livestock (qq.v.) activity. Officially, the province had a population (q.v.) of 75,000 in 1977, declining to 64,508 in 1988, the great majority of the people leading a sedentary way of life. Tagant is notable for having very few reliable roads (q.v.) connecting it to the rest of Mauritania.

TERRITORIAL ASSEMBLY. See Assemblée Territoriale

TIDJIKJA. Founded in 1680 by Moorish (q.v.) exiles from the Adrar (q.v.) area, Tidjikja is the administrative and commercial center of Mauritania's Tagant région (qq.v.) and had a population (q.v.) of only about 4000 in 1977, but which had probably increased by the early 1990s. The town is one of the least accessible in the country, reached only by an unimproved road (q.v.) branching off of the *Route de l'Espoir* (q.v.). Tidjikja is bisected by a *wadi* (q.v.), the historic older portion lying to the northeast and the more modern quarter, which includes a busy market, situated to the southwest. There is also a significant library of Islamic (q.v.) literature. The town was one of the first in Mauritania to be occupied by the French, falling to forces led by Xavier Coppolani (q.v.) in April 1905, although Coppolani was assassinated in Tidjikja a month later by agents of the Saharawi (q.v.) anticolonial leader, Cheikh Ma el-Ainin (q.v.), putting French "pacification" plans for the remainder of the country temporarily in abeyance.

TIRIS EL-GHARBIA. The name given by Mauritania to the southern portion of Western Sahara (q.v.), known to the Spanish as Río de Oro, allotted to Mauritania first by the Madrid Agreement (q.v.) of November 14, 1975, and later in more specific terms by the Moroccan-Mauritanian Conventions of April 14, 1976 (q.v.). Tiris el-Gharbia comprises a total of 96,000 square kilometers of mostly rock and sand, with no resources to speak of except the port city of Dakhla (q.v.) and the small fishing village of La Guera (q.v.). The armed forces (q.v.) of Mauritania first entered the area on December 20, 1975, under the command of Colonel Viah Ould Mayouf, but immediately faced stiff resistance from the armed units of the Polisario

Front (q.v.), who calculated—correctly, as it turned out—that Mauritania was by far the weaker of its two adversaries. Tiris el-Gharbia's long, undefendable borders made it necesary for President Mokhtar Ould Daddah (q.v.) to rely upon Morocco's *Forces Armées Royales* (FAR) from the outset to assist Mauritanian forces in their effort to hold on to the territory. However, from early 1976 until a Polisario cease-fire proclaimed just after the July 10, 1978, military coup that ousted Ould Daddah, attacks by the Saharawi (q.v.) nationalists made even the pretense of effective Mauritanian control difficult to sustain.

For purposes of state civil administration, Tiris el-Gharbia was divided into four parts: regions that included Aoussert, Argoub, Dakhla, and Tichla. La Guera, by contrast, was made an integral part of the Mauritanian province of Dakhlet-Nouadhibou (q.v.). This arrangement remained largely a fiction, though, as it was the Mauritanian and Moroccan military establishments that actually held sway. After the July 1978 coup against Ould Daddah and the Algiers Agreement (q.v.) signed with Polisario by the CMSN (q.v.) military government on August 5, 1979, Mauritanian forces were completely withdrawn except for a small garrison at La Guera. On August 14, 1979, King Hassan II (q.v.) announced that Tiris el-Gharbia was to be formally annexed to the Moroccan kingdom and renamed Oued ed-Dahab.

TIRIS ZEMMOUR. By a substantial margin Mauritania's largest administrative région (q.v.), Tiris Zemmour covers about 253,000 square kilometers in the vast northeastern part of the country. It is one of the most sparsely populated areas, as it is mainly uninhabited desert wasteland. According to official Mauritanian government statistics, Tiris Zemmour had a population (q.v.) of only about 23,000 in 1977, rising to 33,147 in 1988. Despite its small population and inhospitable climate (q.v.), the région was one of the country's most important from an economic viewpoint, as it contains the massive iron ore reserves near F'Derik and Zouerate (qq.v.). F'Derik also serves as the provincial capital. The only readily motorable road (q.v.) in Tiris Zemmour extends from F'Derik and Zouerate northward to Bir Moghrein (q.v.), then turns eastward to the small outpost of Ain Ben Tili near the border with Western Sahara (q.v.), and once again turns north, leaving Mauritanian territory approximately seventy kilometers south of the Algerian town of Tindouf. Tiris Zemmour is also connected to the rest of the country by the railway (q.v.) line from Zouerate to Nouadhibou (q.v.) on the Atlantic coast.

TOUCOULEUR. See Halpulaar

TOURISM. Mauritania's efforts to attract tourists have been severely handicapped by a variety of factors: a lack of good roads (q.v.), long distances separating populated areas with tourist amenities from historical and scenic locations, and shortages of finance for the construction of hotels and other facilities. Nonetheless, the country offers a number of places that are of considerable interest: the *Parc National du Banc d'Arguin* (q.v.), with its beaches and wildlife, ancient cities in the interior such as Aoudaghost, Chinguetti, and Oualata (qq.v.), and the vast Sahara itself. About 13,000 tourists visited Mauritania annually in the 1984–86 period.

TRANS-MAURITANIAN HIGHWAY. See Roads

TRARZA. One of Mauritania's twelve administrative régions (q.v.), Trarza encompasses about 68,000 square kilometers and extends from areas north and east of the country's capital, Nouakchott (q.v.), southward to the border with Senegal. The province is home to most Mauritanian racial and ethnic groupings, with its Moorish (q.v.) inhabitants living in close proximity to Black Africans such as the Wolof (q.v.), who lead sedentary lives and support themselves by trading and agriculture (q.v.). Trarza has been badly affected by droughts and overgrazing of livestock (q.v.), but still contains a substantial amount of cultivable land in the mid-1990s. In 1977, the région had a population (q.v.) of approximately 216,000, which remained stable through 1988, when it had 202,596 people according to government statistics. Of these, fewer than one-eighth were nomadic. Trarza's provincial capital is located at Rosso (q.v.), and the région also includes the town of Boutilimit (q.v.), known as a center of Islamic education (qq.v.) throughout West Africa, and which was the birthplace of Mauritania's first president, Mokhtar Ould Daddah (q.v.).

TREATY OF FRATERNITY AND CONCORD (March 20, 1983). As part of the complex interstate alliance politics played out in North Africa in the early 1980s, Algeria and Tunisia agreed to a close coordination of their political and economic policies with a view toward eventual integration. The Treaty of Fraternity and Concord was open to signature by any Maghreb state (including Algeria's rival, King Hassan II [q.v.] of Morocco), but all parties had to agree to resolve their boundary differences with one another, a requirement that caused the application of Libya to be rejected. Although it was termed the "Tunis axis," it was clear that Algeria would, by reason of its predominant diplomatic and economic position, be the senior member of the grouping. Provisions were made (and partially put into practice) for joint-stock companies to manage the production and distribution of electricity and petroleum (qq.v.) as well as natural gas among the treaty's adherents, as neither Algeria nor Tunisia (nor, as

270 • Treaty of Fraternity and Concord

it transpired, Mauritania) had the funds to complete these projects by themselves.

Mauritania's CMSN (q.v.) military government, then headed by Colonel Mohammed Khouna Ould Heydallah (q.v.), quickly realized that joining the Treaty of Fraternity and Concord could furnish the country with an effective counterweight to King Hassan's Morocco, as well as to the Libyan leader, Colonel Muammar el-Qadaffi, who was moving closer to Rabat to attempt to regain international respectability. Indeed, Ould Heydallah had fought off coup attempts believed to have originated in Rabat (March 1981) and Tripoli (January 1983), and had come to view Algiers, as backer of the pro-independence Polisario Front in Western Sahara (qq.v.) and Morocco's regional rival, as his best insurance against subversion. Therefore, when the treaty was signed on March 20, 1983, Ould Heydallah virtually demanded Mauritania's inclusion. But Algeria and Tunisia initially balked, fearing entanglement in the country's Byzantine internal affairs and shifting foreign relations (q.v.) priorities. A summit conference, held in Algiers on May 30 and June 1, 1983, failed to provide complete reassurance, but Mauritania was able to adhere to the treaty on December 13, 1983, confirming, in the opinion of some observers, Ould Heydallah's leaning toward the so-called "radical" Arab states and in favor of a largely informal Algerian security guarantee.

Mauritania's signing of this "Greater Maghreb" agreement enabled Algeria to assume a predominant influence in several of the country's economic sectors, notably in the areas of fisheries and iron ore (qq.v.) and—in a major development—the oil industry, with a dormant refining and storage facility at Nouadhibou (q.v.) rebuilt with the assistance of the Algerian parastatal, the *Entreprise Nationale de Raffinage et de Distribution des Produits Pétroliers* (NAFTAL). In addition, the relatively short Algerian-Mauritanian border was formally demarcated, and a sugar refinery in Nouakchott (q.v.) was reopened with help from Algiers.

Aside from its economic and (largely intangible) mutual defense aspects, the treaty's utility in stabilizing the alliance structure in North Africa was limited. Libya and Morocco continued to drift toward one another by reason of mutual convenience, and on August 13, 1984, at Oujda, Morocco, the two states signed a treaty establishing an Arab African Union (AAU) as an alternative Maghrebi framework. The AAU only lasted until 1986, though, when it collapsed following a rift between King Hassan and Muammar el-Qadaffi on policies regarding the Arab-Israeli conflict. A greater degree of ostensible harmony was attained in February 1989, when Algeria, Libya, Mauritania, Morocco, and Tunisia agreed to set up a new integrative organization, the *Union du Maghreb Arabe* (UMA) (q.v.).

UNION DES FORCES DEMOCRATIQUES—ERE NOUVELLE

(UFD). The Union of Democratic Forces received formal authorization from the Mauritanian Ministry of the Interior on October 2, 1991, about three months after the formation of multiple political parties in the country was first permitted by the CMSN (q.v.) government of President Maaouiya Ould Sid'Ahmed Taya (q.v.). The UFD was a lineal descendant of the *Front Démocratique Uni des Forces du Changement* (FDUC) (q.v.), an illegal opposition group whose leaders had been placed in detention from June 6 to July 25, 1991. Many FDUC members were found in the UFD: the president of the new group, Hadrami Ould Khattri, was one of those imprisoned, as was its secretary-general, Messaoud Ould Boulkheir, a *hartani* (q.v.) who was a former minister of agriculture and the leader of El-Hor (q.v.), an influential group which in the late 1970s and early 1980s had campaigned against the persistence of slavery (q.v.) in Mauritania. In its first public statement, issued on October 6, 1991, the UFD called for the installation of a government of national unity to supervise free and fair presidential and parliamentary elections, a step which would have entailed President Ould Taya's resignation and which was summarily rejected by the CMSN. Before long, it became apparent that the UFD was the most significant opposition group facing the incumbent Mauritanian president's *Parti Républicain, Démocratique et Social* (PRDS) (q.v.), since no fewer than three former cabinet ministers were affiliated with the party. The UFD also picked up two additional sources of support later in 1991. Ahmed Ould Daddah (q.v.), the brother of the country's first head of state, Mokhtar Ould Daddah (q.v.), returned from his self-imposed exile to express sympathy with the new grouping, and the leadership of the small, underground opposition party, the *Front de la Résistance pour l'Unité, l'Independance et la Démocratie en Mauritanie* (FRUIDEM) (q.v.), voted to dissolve itself and urged its members to join the UFD, although it expressed skepticism about some aspects of its platform.

Thus invigorated, the UFD, by the autumn of 1991, readied itself for participation in the presidential elections (although Ahmed Ould Daddah, the main opposition candidate against Ould Taya, did not officially run under the party's sponsorship), and those for the *Assemblée Nationale* and the Senate (qq.v.), the two branches of the new Mauritanian legislature. UFD partisans mostly voted in Ahmed Ould Daddah's favor when the balloting for president was held on January 17, 1992, and he garnered 180,658 votes of a total of 551,575 cast—nearly 33 percent of the total. This respectable showing, however, was only half the level of support that Ould Taya received, and the CMSN chairman easily remained in office with a six-year mandate. Complaining that its supporters had been prevented from registering to vote, particularly in the country's southern régions (q.v.) where UFD backing was thought to be high, the party announced just after Ould Daddah's defeat that it would boycott the upcoming round of parliamentary elections. The boycott was joined by some (but not all) of the other political parties, and consequently, President Ould Taya's PRDS was awarded sixty-seven of the seventy-nine seats in the National Assembly and thirty-six of the fifty-six places in the Senate, leaving the UFD without a single representative in any of the institutions of Mauritania's Second Republic (q.v.), which was inaugurated on April 18, 1992. Following this series of events, the UFD added the words *Ere Nouvelle* (New Era) to its name on May 25, 1992, as a sign of its thorough reorganization, and Ahmed Ould Daddah assumed effective control of the party on June 15. Before long, though, resentment grew at Ould Daddah's alleged personal domination of the UFD, with many of the party's other leaders apparently believing that the group's abstention from national politics was self-defeating, as it ensured a continued PRDS hammerlock on the state administration.

The developing internecine strife in the UFD came to a head on February 20, 1993, when one of Mauritania's most esteemed politicians, former Foreign Minister Hamdi Ould Mouknass (q.v.), joined with several other prominent UFD supporters and broke with Ahmed Ould Daddah; on June 15 they set up a new party, the *Union pour le Progrès et la Démocratie* (UPD) (q.v.), which styled itself as a "centrist" alternative to the UFD/PRDS bipolarity. The UFD–Ere Nouvelle, in turn, struggled to avoid further defections and splits by announcing at its congress in July 1993 that it would henceforth "struggle within the limits of possibilities offered by the constitution." In other words, it ended its boycott of the electoral process and fielded candidates for the Mauritanian municipal elections set for January 28, 1994. But in those elections, the UFD did poorly, winning control of only seventeen of the country's 208 *arrondissements* (q.v.). Contributing to a bad situation, the UFD was only able to find enough candidates to run in sixty jurisdictions, enabling many PRDS backers to run unopposed. Four months later, in mid-April 1994, the UFD emerged victorious in just one of the seventeen Senate seats up for replacement in biennial elections: of the party's five candidates, only the one from Kaédi (q.v.) managed to outpoll the PRDS. In addition, several more UFD members (along with the El-Hor movement) defected on June 6, 1994, calling the party "too passive" in its political strategy. By the beginning of 1996, consequently, the position of the Union of Democratic Forces appeared weak. Matters were also not helped by the statements made in January and February 1995 by the exiled former President of Mauritania, Mokhtar Ould Daddah, in which he urged greater opposition unity and criticized the Ould Taya regime. These pronouncements (which were made in the French and Moroccan media) had the effect of dimming the appeal of the UFD still further, as more and more opposition members rallied to the side of the ruling PRDS. As a result, further infighting appeared inevitable and the UFD's future seemed in doubt.

UNION DES ORIGINAIRES DE LA VALLEE DU FLEUVE (UOVF). On March 31, 1957, the date of elections to a transitional, pre-independence Mauritanian legislature, the *Assemblée Territoriale* (q.v.), a group of black Mauritanian intellectuals met at Dakar, Senegal, to form a new political organization to protect black interests against perceived Moorish (q.v.) encroachment, which the UOVF's founders saw as coming from Mokhtar Ould Daddah's *Union Progressiste Mauritanienne* (UPM) (qq.v.) and from the *Front National de Libération Mauritanien* (FNLM) (q.v.), which favored a union of Mauritania with Morocco. The UOVF strongly opposed this idea, and favored continued close ties to Black Africa after independence. The party failed to gain any substantial popular support.

UNION DES TRAVAILLEURS MAURITANIENS (UTM). The Mauritanian Worker's Union was established in 1961 as a quasi-governmental federation of all trade unions in the newly independent country, including teachers, workers in the iron ore (q.v.) sector, and the textile and construction fields. Somewhat unusually for trade unions in African states, the UTM remained separate from the single legal political organization in Mauritania, the *Parti du Peuple Mauritanien* (PPM) (q.v.), and its leader, President Mokhtar Ould Daddah (q.v.). As a result, it often took positions contrary to those of the regime, such as was the case in May 1968, when the UTM leadership called a strike at the iron ore mines at Zouerate (q.v.) in order to protest the wide disparity in wages between Mauritanian workers and their French expatriate counterparts. The stoppage ended a short time later, but only after Ould Daddah ordered the Mauritanian armed forces (q.v.) into action against the workers, killing at least eight persons and injuring several dozen more. Apparently stunned by this unprecedented show of opposition to the PPM's hegemony, President Ould Daddah mounted a vigorous campaign to merge the UTM into the governing party's structures to ensure political control, and succeeded in his aim in February 1969. But the UTM suffered several defections as a result of this merger, with a number of the union's constituent organizations denouncing its leaders as no longer representing their interests. After leaving the UTM, the dissidents set up a Directing Committee of Mauritanian Workers (the so-called "progressive" UTM) and requested governmental recognition, which was refused. The new union, however, was well regarded by younger Mauritanians, who joined it in a series of strikes and demonstrations in May 1971, putting the pro-PPM trade unionists on the defensive. It was believed by some observers that the nationalistic pressures brought to bear by the "progressives" in this period played a role in President Ould Daddah's decision, taken in November 1974, to nationalize the French-controlled MIFERMA (q.v.) iron ore mining consortium and replace it with an indigenous company, the *Société Nationale Industrielle et Minière* (SNIM) (q.v.).

Following the military *coup d'état* in Mauritania on July 10, 1978, an event brought about by the country's ruinous involvement in the Western Sahara conflict (q.v.) which began in late 1975, the UTM fell into steep decline, as most forms of independent political activity were prohibited by Mauritania's new rulers and the union's parent, the PPM, was abolished. On the other hand, army leaders, especially the CMSN (q.v.) chairman, Colonel Mohammed Khouna Ould Heydallah (q.v.), who assumed full power in January 1980, saw reinvigorated trade unions as a useful way to cement the loyalties of Mauritanians and harness popular energies. In October 1981, under CMSN sponsorship, an extraordinary UTM congress was held which resulted in the dismissal of many members of the older leadership, whom Ould Heydallah accused of factionalism, corruption, and lack of contact with the rank and file. The government appointed a new UTM secretary-general, Elkhory Ould H'Metty, who was thought to be somewhat further to the left politically than his predecessors. The reorganized trade union also welcomed back into its ranks some of the individual craft and professional organizations that had deserted the UTM in 1969. Finally, the union was permitted, from 1981 onward, to demonstrate in favor of increased wages, better housing and education (qq.v.), and other matters of daily concern to Mauritanians.

The *entente* between the UTM and the CMSN lasted less than two years. In 1983, President Ould Heydallah summarily imprisoned Ould H'Metty, accusing him of unauthorized political activity and of pro-Libyan sympathies, a charge which was possibly related to the recent defeat of a coup plot allegedly masterminded in Tripoli by Libya's leader, Colonel Muammar el-Qadaffi. In place of Ould H'Metty, the UTM's secretary-generalship was assumed by his assistant, Beijel Ould Houmeit, whom Ould Heydallah believed to be more tractable. But in December 1984, after Ould Heydallah was displaced by Colonel Maaouiya Ould Sid'Ahmed Taya (q.v.), Ould H'Metty was freed from jail in a general amnesty, and immediately got his old job back, Ould Houmeit relinquishing the post only reluctantly. Soon, a full-blown power struggle was in progress between the two men, with El-Hor (q.v.) supporters and some black Mauritanians upset over Ould

H'Metty's allegedly "Nasserist," pan-Arab stance. Also, the UTM leader was castigated for his supposedly "collaborationist" attitude toward the Ould Taya government and the private and parastate businesses that were represented by the *Confédération Générale des Employeurs de Mauritanie* (CGEM), the UTM's bargaining opponent. In June 1985 the recriminations largely ceased, as the two factions in the trade union finally agreed to work together. Two months later, in August 1985, Ould H'Metty was again imprisoned for leading illegal, pro-Libyan rallies in the Mauritanian capital, Nouakchott (q.v.). On September 19, he received a one-year suspended prison sentence and was freed, but the UTM to which he returned was in almost complete disarray, with union locals shut down or paralyzed and with the organization's bureaucracy largely divided along ideological, tribal, or regional lines. In this atmosphere, it was not surprising that little or no organizing took place during this time, a task made all the more difficult by layoffs in the economy's "modern" sector carried out by SNIM and other large employers, and the shutdown, for economic reasons, of many of Mauritania's industrial development (q.v.) projects. Although by mid-1987 some union offices began reopening in urban areas, the number of workers represented by the UTM hovered around 45,000, a number that stayed fairly constant into the early 1990s and which comprised about 20 percent of the employed population (q.v.).

Beginning in the first part of 1991, the UTM broke with its customary progovernment positions and began to demand the political liberalization of Mauritania, often before other groups could do the same. In early April, the secretary-general of the union, Mohamed Mahmoud Ould Mohamed Radhy, addressed an open letter to President Ould Taya, demanding better pay and working conditions for Mauritanian workers as well as calling for a national conference to decide upon the country's future course, followed by free elections in a multiparty context. Ould Radhy hinted at "unlimited action" (meaning a general strike) if the UTM's demands were not met. Ould Taya soon announced that some of the union's complaints were well founded and that multipartyism would be enshrined in a new constitution, but the UTM was still not satisfied. In early June, Ould Radhy called for a generalized work stoppage throughout the country to last for forty-eight hours starting on June 19. On that day, many workers (particularly in the private sector) did stay away from their jobs, but most governmental and industrial functions, including the port and airline (qq.v.) services, were undisturbed. Some commentators believed that threats by the regime to dismiss the strikers were persuasive to some, while other observers felt that a split within the UTM itself contributed to the walkout's lack of success, a reference to the fact that just before June 19, a group of seventeen dissident UTM governing committee members urged the union membership to come to work as usual. On June 21, 1991, the schism was formalized by the "suspension" of Ould Radhy from the UTM secretary-generalship. He was replaced by his deputy, Mohamed Ely Ould Brahim, who remained in office in an ostensibly "acting" capacity into 1994. Afterwards, the UTM went once more into relative eclipse and soon faced competition: on January 5, 1994, it was reported that a new independent union, the *Confédération Générale des Travailleurs de Mauritanie* (CGTM) had been recognized by the government.

UNION DU MAGHREB ARABE (UMA). At a summit conference of the heads of state of Algeria, Libya, Mauritania, Morocco, and Tunisia held in Marrakesh, Morocco during February 15–17, 1989, the five countries of the Maghreb issued a declaration stating that they would henceforth attempt to coordinate a wide range of hitherto separate (and often competing) state policies among themselves, including those pertaining to defense, social and cultural affairs, and especially economic matters. To achieve this, several supranational organs were established by the UMA treaty, among which were a Presidential Council and a joint foreign affairs committee. In the economic realm, a framework for joint commercial and industrial ventures was put into place, as were procedures for the eventual abolition of trade barriers between the five member states, a step influenced by Europe's impending 1992 integration. The UMA agreement was an ambitious vehicle for change that had several abortive precursors, most notably the Libya-Morocco Treaty of Oujda signed on August 13, 1984, and a rival axis, the Treaty of Fraternity and Concord (q.v.), adhered to by Algeria and Tunisia on March 20, 1983, and joined by Mauritania on December 13 of that year at the insistence of the country's president, Colonel Mohammed Khouna Ould Heydallah (q.v.).

In the unsettled racial and ethnic climate existing in Mauritania in the late 1980s, its accession to UMA membership led to resentment among some black Mauritanians, as it seemed to confirm the country's orientation toward the Arab north at the expense of Black African states. However, President Maaouiya Ould Sid'Ahmed Taya's (q.v.) decision to sign the UMA treaty was quite consistent with Mauritania's basic foreign relations (q.v.) pattern over the previous twenty years—that is, to cast the state's lot with the Arab League (q.v.) and to deemphasize ties to sub-Saharan Africa, the latter having been a staple only of the earlier years of Mauritanian independence under President Mokhtar Ould Daddah (q.v.).

As with other such ventures, the Arab Maghreb Union soon ran into trouble. Economic integration was a halting process, political differences remained rather sharp, and cultural, social, and defense coordination was still almost nonexistent. In February 1993, the UMA's foreign ministers, meeting in Rabat, agreed to a "pause" in the functioning of the organization, a turn of events which some observers took to be a sign of severe difficulties.

UNION NATIONALE MAURITANIENNE (UNM). A political party born out of a split within the dominant *Parti de Regroupement Mauritanien* (PRM) led by Mokhtar Ould Daddah (qq.v.), the Mauritanian National Union was formed in early May 1959 but was unable to field candidates for the pre-independence elections to the National Assembly (q.v.) held on May 17, allegedly because of interference from Ould Daddah's loyalists. After many difficulties, the UNM was finally chartered on August 4, 1959. The party urged a federation between the newly proclaimed Islamic Republic of Mauritania and neighboring Mali, and it enjoyed considerable backing from black Mauritanians in the Senegal River Valley as well as in eastern Mauritania, in the *cercles* of Hodh ech-Chargui and Hodh el-Gharbi (qq.v.). Additionally, the party sought votes from the country's class of freed black slaves, the *haratines* (q.v.). One year later, however, in May 1960, the UNM ceased independent political activity and rallied behind its former foe, the PRM, in response to a plea for unity by Mokhtar Ould Daddah in the wake of a campaign of violence by the nationalist Nadha (q.v.) party that caused considerable anxiety in the final months before the country's achievement of full independence from France. Thereafter, the UNM was of little political importance, and officially ended its existence at the Congress of Unity (q.v.) held in October 1961 that resulted in the formation of the *Parti du Peuple Mauritanien* (PPM) (q.v.).

UNION POPULAIRE SOCIALISTE ET DEMOCRATIQUE (UPSD). Founded on Sptember 28, 1991 at the beginning of Mauritania's unprecedented political liberalization, the Democratic and Socialist Popular Union was headed by Mohamed Mahmoud Ould Mah, a veteran politician with presidential aspirations who had achieved national prominence in December 1986, when he unexpectedly won election as mayor of Nouakchott (q.v.) in the municipal balloting held by the government of President Maaouiya Ould Sid'Ahmed Taya (q.v.). Ould Mah, who rapidly revealed his intention to run for the Mauritanian presidency against Ould Taya and others, had publicly opposed almost every regime in Mauritania since the country's independence in 1960. The UPSD, once it organized itself, was believed to have constructed a considerable base of support among younger Mauritanians who were often disillusioned by the limited employment opportunities and the poor state of Mauritania's economy under successive armed forces (q.v.) governments. Unlike certain other opposition parties, the UPSD rejected the idea of a national conference to draft a new constitution for the country, an option also firmly ruled out by President Ould Taya himself. Ould Mah characterized a conference as a vehicle for "imposing a dictatorship by those who take to the streets, excluding all others." The party did, however, endorse the concept of a transitional government of national unity, but this idea was also scotched by Ould Taya.

Once the presidential election campaign got under way in late 1991, Ould Mah took pains to describe the UPSD as the only political party in Mauritania that offered a genuine alternative to *"l'hégémonie de Maaouiya,"* as Ould Taya's domination of the country's political life was dubbed by the opposition. Ould Mah also denounced the regime's moves toward privatizing many sectors of the economy, portraying it as a strategy that would cause the state sector to wither without a corresponding increase in private sector activity. More controversially, he urged an end to separate education (q.v.) for black and Moorish (q.v.) Mauritanians at all levels, saying that the policy had exacerbated the country's racial and ethnic divide and had led directly to the Senegal-Mauritania Crisis (q.v.) which erupted in April 1989. Moreover, he advocated accelerated Arabization (q.v.) to correct the situation, advocating the teaching of Hassaniya (q.v.) Arabic to all children from the primary level onward and the abolition of language instruction in Fulani, Sarakolé, and Wolof (qq.v.). Ould Mah did favor the elevation of French to the status of an official second language, however, but though his basically pro-Arab policy prescriptions were popular with some Moors, it did not reassure many black Mauritanians and, in the opinion of some observers, cost the UPSD considerable support. In the elections for President of Mauritania, held on January 17, 1992, Maaouiya Ould Sid'Ahmed Taya, the incumbent, won a lopsided victory, with Ould Mah getting just 7506 votes — only 1.36 percent of the total. The UPSD leader was unable to deliver for himself even a fraction of the voters in his home district of Nouakchott. Along with the main opposition group, Ahmed Ould Daddah's *Union des Forces Démocratiques* (UFD) (qq.v.), Ould Mah alleged that the presidential election was fraudulently conducted and that the UPSD, like the UFD and others, would boycott the elections to the *Assemblée Nationale* and the Senate (qq.v.) to be held in March and April, respectively. As a consequence, President Ould Taya's *Parti Républicain, Démocratique et Social* (PRDS) (q.v.) won a massive majority in the two chambers of the new bicameral Mauritanian legislature. The UPSD found itself in the political wilderness and was not included in any of the institutions of the Second Republic (q.v.) inaugurated on April 18, 1992. Ould Mah's party also boycotted a round of municipal elections held in January 1994, claiming that its participation would only lend credibility to an allegedly preordained outcome; that is, victory for President Ould Taya's PRDS.

UNION POUR LE PROGRES ET LA DEMOCRATIE (UPD). The Union for Progress and Democracy, Mauritania's seventeenth political party to be organized since late 1991, was formed around a nucleus of eight dissidents from the ranks of the dominant Mauritanian opposition party, Ahmed Ould Daddah's *Union des Forces Démocratiques* (UFD) (qq.v.). Among their leaders was the veteran politician and foreign minister during the 1960s and 1970s, Hamdi Ould Mouknass (q.v.). The UPD, which received legal recognition from the government on June 15, 1993, after holding its first meeting in February of that year, styled itself as a "centrist" alternative to both Ahmed Ould Daddah's UFD and the regime of President Maaouiya Ould Sid' Ahmed Taya (q.v.). Indeed, it was a severe split in the UFD's membership concerning the party's strategy in dealing with the Ould Taya government (with Ould Daddah urging total nonrecognition and Ould Mouknass urging a more flexible approach) that led to the UPD's founding. The formation of the UPD also brought into high relief the disarray in the opposition ranks after the UFD boycotted Mauritania's legislative elections held in March and April 1992 and allowed Ould Taya's *Parti Républicain, Démocratique et Social* (PRDS) (q.v.) to win a landslide victory. Hamdi Ould Mouknass and his followers felt that in the year since the elections, Ahmed Ould Daddah's group had failed to achieve anything constructive and that the UFD was becoming a vehicle for realizing Ould Daddah's personal ambitions. Among the UPD's other policy positions, it objected to the sweeping amnesty bill passed by the *Assemblée Nationale* (q.v.) in late May 1993, immunizing from prosecution all those involved in alleged human rights abuses during and after the Senegal-Mauritania crisis (q.v.) of 1989 and 1990. Instead, Ould Mouknass wanted a commission of inquiry to determine guilt and compensate victims. In the municipal elections in Mauritania held in January 1994, the UPD did badly, presenting candidates in only thirty-three districts of the national total of 208 and not winning any of them, with most of the contested seats going to the dominant party, the PRDS. Subsequently, the UPD continued to see an erosion of its base of support, which resulted in the reshuffle of its top officials in 1995 and the reputed beginnings of a more friendly stance toward the Ould Taya government by the party's membership.

UNION PROGRESSISTE MAURITANIENNE (UPM). The Mauritanian Progressive Union was founded more than a decade before Mauritania's independence from France and was designed to oppose the allegedly "socialist" programs of the country's first political party, the *Entente Mauritanienne* (q.v.), a group led by Horma Ould Babana (q.v.) which had triumphed in the 1946 elections to the French National Assembly. Mindful of the fact that Ould Babana was spending much of his time in Paris and was thus isolated from events in Mauritania and that the Entente itself was not efficiently organized and had little grass-roots support, a group of traditional chieftains, both black and Moorish (q.v.), gathered at Rosso (q.v.) in February 1948 with support from the French colonial administration. The monastic *zawiya* (q.v.) tribes were heavily represented, and from the start there was an emphasis placed on the achievement of Mauritanian national unity through the inclusion of both blacks and Moors and the lessening of regional differences, all in close association with France. The UPM set its strategy for the 1951 French National Assembly balloting at a party congress at Kiffa (q.v.), choosing as its candidate Sidi el-Mokhtar N'Diaye, a political unknown who was part Moorish and part Wolof (q.v.), thereby neatly bridging the territory's troublesome racial divide. The first Mauritanian newspaper, *Al-Ittafaq* (qq.v.), founded about the same time as the UPM was reorganized, threw its support to N'Diaye. The UPM's efforts were rewarded: N'Diaye narrowly defeated Horma Ould Babana in the election with 29,323 votes to the latter's 23,649. So well organized (and popular) did the UPM become that about a year later, it won twenty-two of the twenty-four seats to the French-organized *Conseil Général* (q.v.), Mauritania's interim legislature, with the other two going to the representatives of the Entente, which by now was in a rapid state of decline.

Following a period of pronounced political apathy, discontent mounted at the UPM's perceived subservience to French interests, particularly by its younger members, who for various reasons were also dissatisfied with N'Diaye, the party leader. These feelings came to a head in February 1955, when, at a Rosso party congress, the youthful elements broke with the UPM and formed the *Association de la Jeunesse Mauritanienne* (AJM) (q.v.). The AJM, as it turned out, could not hope to match the popularity and financial backing of the UPM; in elections held the following year for the French Assembly, the AJM candidate received only 585 votes, N'Diaye winning by a landslide with 106,603 ballots cast in his favor. The Mauritanian Progressive Union was riding high after this lopsided victory, especially since many Black Africans living in the Senegal River Valley chose to stay with the party rather than transfer their allegiance to the pan-Arabist AJM.

In elections to the newly formed Territorial Assembly (q.v.) held on March 31, 1957, the UPM, by now well under the control of the lawyer Mokhtar Ould Daddah (q.v.), won a stunning victory once again, capturing all but one of the thirty-four seats in the chamber, although the results were questioned by some observers who found the reported vote totals too generous. Ould Daddah was then able to name a new government, dominated by the UPM, on May 21, brushing aside AJM protests at his appointment of two Frenchmen to the cabinet. Even with his party's near-total rout of the opposition, however, Ould Daddah was still disturbed by the presence of the AJM and the remnants of the Entente, as he felt that national cohesion in the progression to independence would best be served by a single party that would present a united front to outsiders but which could still facilitate internal discussion and compromise. As a result, Ould Daddah convened the Congress of Aleg (q.v.) in May 1958, at which time the UPM, the Entente Mauritanienne, and the black-oriented *Bloc Démocratique du Gorgol* (BDG) (q.v.) agreed to merge to form the *Parti de Regroupement Mauritanien* (PRM) (q.v.), with Ould Daddah as the party's powerful secretary-general.

UNION SOCIALISTE DES MUSULMANS MAURITANIENS (USMM). A small political party created on February 25, 1960, the Mauritanian Muslim Socialist Union attempted to reassert the traditional authority of the *hassan* (q.v.) chieftains in the country's far north, particularly in the régions of Adrar and Tiris Zemmour (q.v.), after having been reduced in influence by more secular and nationalist currents, notably the Nadha (q.v.) party. Its founder and leader was Ahmed Ould Kerkoub, a prominent chief from Adrar. The USMM called for close ties to France after Mauritania's independence, opposition to Morocco's claim to the country's territory, and rejection of any federation with Mali. Never of great significance in the Mauritanian political arena, the party ceased to exist at the Congress of Unity (q.v.) held in October 1961, which merged it and several other groupings into a new ruling *Parti du Peuple Mauritanien* (PPM) (q.v.) led by President Mokhtar Ould Daddah (q.v.).

UNITED NATIONS. When Mauritania achieved its independence from France on November 28, 1960, it immediately faced a challenge to its existence from the North African and Middle Eastern members of the Arab League (q.v.), who—with the exception of Tunisia—were supportive of Morocco's territorial claim to the entire country, an outgrowth of the "Greater Morocco" concept advanced in the 1950s by Allal el-Fassi (q.v.) of the Moroccan *Istiqlal* (Independence) Party. These attitudes kept Mauritania out of the United Nations for almost a year, as the Arab position was backed by the Soviet Union, then in the process of aggressively currying favor with Arab states as a counterweight to Western influence. The Soviet veto of Mauritania's membership in the world body was only withdrawn when France and most of Black Africa agreed to allow Mongolia, a Soviet client state, into the UN. Morocco, displeased, brought the issue to the UN General Assembly for a vote, but was defeated, sixty-eight to thirteen, with twenty abstentions. Mauritania was finally admitted to the United Nations on October 27, 1961.

The country's next major engagement with the UN was over the Western Sahara conflict (q.v.), which pitted Morocco against the Polisario Front (q.v.). After exiting the Saharan war in 1979, Mauritania continued to fear the destabilizing effects of the ongoing dispute. As a consequence, the Mauritanian authorities took a strong interest in the UN's efforts to resolve the conflict by means of a referendum of self-determination in the contested territory. These referendum preparations were to include a census of the eligible Saharawi (q.v.) population in and around Western Sahara. By 1994, it was decided that an administrative United Nations presence would be established in the Mauritanian towns of Nouadhibou and Zouerate (qq.v.) for the purpose of voter enrollment.

UNITY, CONGRESS OF (October 4, 1961. Almost a year after Mauritania's achievement of full independence, the country's domestic situation remained unsettled, with the head of state, Mokhtar Ould Daddah (q.v.), in a clearly predominant position but with significant opposition to many of his policies coming from a variety of groups, notably the nationalist Nadha (q.v.) party, the *Union Socialiste des Musulmans Mauritaniens* (USMM) (q.v.), and the *Union Nationale Mauritanienne* (UNM) (q.v.). Elections held in Mauritania in September 1961 saw both Nadha and the UNM included by Ould Daddah in his Council of Ministers (q.v.), but the president wished to consolidate his power further. The following month, he convened a Congress of Unity to consolidate existing political tendencies into a new organization. At the congress, Nadha, the USMM, and Ould Daddah's *Parti de Regroupement Mauritanien* (PRM) (q.v.) agreed to merge and form a new group, the *Parti du Peuple Mauritanien* (PPM) (q.v.), of which Mokhtar Ould Daddah would be the undisputed leader. This arrangement was finalized on December 25, 1961, when the PPM was declared the sole legal political party in Mauritania, realizing Ould Daddah's evident aspirations to institute a one-party, centralized, authoritarian regime. It was not until the Kaédi Conference (q.v.) in January 1964, however, that the country was officially proclaimed a single-party state.

VILLA CISNEROS. See Dakhla

WADI. The Arabic term used to denote a valley or ravine that remains dry except after the onset of rainfall (q.v.). The word is also sometimes used to describe an oasis—an inland area that stays somewhat wetter than the surrounding desert, and which can support limited agricultural (q.v.) activity. Mauritania contains a great many wadis, concentrated mainly in the south of the country, although there are also some in the régions of Adrar and Dakhlet-Nouadhibou (qq.v.).

WALATA. See Oualata

WATER RESOURCES. With the single, major exception of the Senegal River, which accounts for about 650 kilometers of Mauritania's southern border and whose waters are partly managed for the purposes of irrigation and agriculture (q.v.) by the *Organisation pour la Mise en Valeur du Fleuve Sénégal* (OMVS) (q.v.), Mauritania has few permanent rivers or other surface water resources other than several small lakes and many seasonal *wadis* (q.v.). For drinking, agriculture, or domestic uses, Mauritanians, especially those in the arid zones of the country, rely upon wells at various locations to tap into abundant subterranean aquifers. Outside the primary population (q.v.) centers, the gathering of water is almost always done by individuals or family groups, as the country's system of water distribution remains quite rudimentary in the 1990s. Fully one-third of all Mauritanians, it is estimated, have little or no access to clean running water. In Mauritania's capital, Nouakchott (q.v.), as well as in the larger towns, the extraction and distribution of water is the responsibility of the state-owned *Société Nationale d'Eau et d'Electricité* (SONELEC) (q.v.). However, few residences or other buildings are connected with the water system, and most Mauritanians still have either to draw their own water or to use communal taps. Due to the urgent demand for water in Nouakchott, SONELEC operates a major pumping station at Idini, east of the capital, a project which was designed and constructed by the People's Republic of China. But the Idini facility has achieved only partial success, as there are simply too many residents of Nouakchott and its environs to allow residential plumbing connections for everyone. Mauritania's largest industrial corporation, the *Société Nationale Industrielle et Minière et Société d'Economie Mixte* (SNIM-SEM) (q.v.), mostly procures its own water supplies from the Nouadhibou (q.v.) area, with some of it being taken inland to locations such as Zouerate (q.v.) in the tank cars of the country's only railway (q.v.), where it meets the needs of the iron ore (q.v.) mines.

WESTERN SAHARA CONFLICT. Since the late 1950s, the fate of the 266,000–square kilometer territory known as Western Sahara, a Spanish colony from the early 1880s to February 1976, with which Mauritania shares a 435-kilometer border, has been a prime concern of nearly all the country's politicians and administrators. This concern was vastly heightened by the attempted Mauritanian takeover of the southern one-third of the desert land in late 1975, which led to a highly destructive war with the pro-independence Polisario Front (q.v.). The conflict also produced grave economic dislocations and social discontent in the few years that Mauritania was an active participant. The severity of the impact of the Western Sahara conflict upon Mauritania could be measured not only in lives and resources expended, but also in the general realization among the country's citizens that the dispute was continuing to affect Mauritanian domestic policy and foreign relations (q.v.) well into the 1990s.

Mokhtar Ould Daddah (q.v.), Mauritania's foremost political figure and president from 1960 to 1978, had always cast a covetous eye toward Madrid's desert colony, reasoning that the tribal and historical links between the Moorish (q.v.) inhabitants of the two territories would incline the Saharawis (q.v.) of Western Sahara to join the Mauritanian state once the Spanish colonial yoke was thrown off. Even before Mauritania's independence from France on November 28, 1960, therefore, Ould Daddah articulated a formal territorial claim to the thinly populated land. His well-known speech on the subject of Western Sahara, delivered at Atar (q.v.) on July 1, 1957, summarized his feelings:

> An increasingly strong tie of solidarity unites all Mauritanians who are conscious of belonging to a single community from the Atlantic to the Sudan. But the solidarity goes beyond our frontiers; it encompasses the Moorish populations of Spanish Sahara and the borders of Morocco. . . . I cannot help evoking the innumerable ties which unite us [with Spanish Sahara]; we bear the same names, we speak the same language, conserve the same noble traditions, we honor the same religious leaders, graze our herds on the same pastures, give water to them from the same wells. In a word we are referring to that same desert civilization of which we are so justly proud. So I invite our brothers of Spanish Sahara to dream of this great economic and spiritual Mauritania. . . .

Despite the effusive content of what became known as the "Greater Mauritania" speech, however, there was very little that Mokhtar Ould Daddah could have done in the early, difficult years of the country's independence to alter the *status quo* in his favor and "restore" Western Sahara to the Mauritanian fold. The 1960s were the period in which Morocco's King Hassan II (q.v.) pressed a territorial claim to all of Mauritania, and President Ould Daddah's energies in the foreign relations field were thus fully occupied in gaining recognition for his country as a legitimate postcolonial presence in northwest Africa. Ould Daddah also realized that Spain, then under the dictatorship of Francisco Franco, had no intention of giving up its Saharan colony in the foreseeable future, something that the Mauritanian head of state found acceptable and even desirable, since Spain's control of the colony formed a crucial, low-cost buffer between Mauritania and Morocco. In return for Mauritania's acquiescence in practice to Spain's continued occupation, the Franco regime cultivated increasingly close links with President Ould Daddah's government, accrediting a full ambassador to Nouakchott (q.v.), providing some economic aid, and even referring to its dependency as "Spanish Mauritania" on occasion. Mauritania had no fewer than three policies on Western Sahara by this time: a formal territorial claim to the entire colony, official opposition to both the Spanish presence and a parallel Moroccan claim to all of Western Sahara, and diplomatic support for self-determination for the Saharawis, the demand for which was heard with increasing frequency in such bodies as the United Nations (q.v.) from around 1966 onward. But by Ould Daddah's reckoning, any referendum in Western Sahara would result in its citizens' opting to join Mauritania, painlessly satisfying his designs on the territory.

This stable situation began to change rapidly in the early 1970s. Amid the first stirrings of nationalist sentiment among educated Saharawis—a process which began in 1970 with the violent suppression of anti-Spanish demonstrations in the territorial capital of El-Ayoun and the founding of the Polisario Front on May 10, 1973—Mokhtar Ould Daddah soon found himself having to reflect ever more frequently upon his Western Sahara policy line. Looming rather large in his calculations was a continuing fear of Morocco, a feeling that had only been allayed in April 1970 when King Hassan had finally recognized his country's existence and exchanged ambassadors. If Morocco were allowed to occupy all of Western Sahara (and it appeared as though Spain's resolve to remain there was faltering) it would potentially place King Hassan's army within a short distance of the critical railway (q.v.) line connecting the iron ore (q.v.) mining town of Zouerate (q.v.) with the coastal economic center of Nouadhibou (q.v.), over which fully 80 percent of Mauritania's exports moved. With long, hard-to-police borders, Mauritania could be vulnerable to Moroccan pressures. So from around 1973 to the fall of 1975, President Ould Daddah and his ruling *Parti du Peuple Mauritanien* (PPM) (q.v.) stuck to its longstanding position that the future of the colony ought to be decided democratically by the Saharawis, which the leadership still believed would lead to integration with Mauritania. The founding of Polisario was not taken seriously.

It was at an Arab League (q.v.) summit conference held in Rabat on October 26 and 27, 1974, that an embarrassing impasse was broken between Mauritania and Morocco. In return for a Moroccan promise of substantial economic aid, coupled with the abandonment of King

Hassan's claim over the southern one-third of Western Sahara known as Tiris el-Gharbia (q.v.), President Ould Daddah agreed to drop his own claim over the northern part of the Spanish colony and settle for the annexation of Tiris el-Gharbia only. It was apparent that Morocco got the better end of the deal, since it received the most populous and resource-rich portion of the desert, whereas Mauritania was left with a barren swath of land that had little potential for economic development. Despite warnings from both the Polisario Front and Algerian President Houari Boumedienne (q.v.) not to ally himself with what they regarded as an "imperialistic" Moroccan regime, Ould Daddah (with little opposition from either the PPM or the Mauritanian public) went ahead and formalized the partition by signing the Madrid Agreement (q.v.) on November 14, 1975, with Spain and Morocco. The secret treaty made no reference to Saharawi self-determination—an omission which was in defiance of an advisory opinion by the International Court of Justice (ICJ) a fortnight earlier, holding that the historical and legal ties between Western Sahara and Mauritania and Morocco were not of such a nature as to obviate the necessity of consulting the Saharawis as to their wishes. In signing the Madrid Agreement Ould Daddah also disregarded Article 44 of the Constitution of Mauritania of May 20, 1961 (q.v.), which mandated that a popular referendum take place to approve any "exchange or accession of territory." Explicit boundaries between the two zones of occupation were drawn up in the Moroccan-Mauritanian Conventions (q.v.) of April 14, 1976, but by then an intense hit-and-run war was under way between Mauritania's armed forces (q.v.) and the Polisario Front, which was backed to the hilt by Houari Boumedienne's Algeria and which had as its objective the establishment of an independent Saharan Arab Democratic Republic (SADR) (q.v.) in Western Sahara.

Although President Ould Daddah's Saharan strategy was predicated upon a lack of armed opposition to his takeover of Tiris el-Gharbia and the acquiescence of other countries to his policies, events in the following two and one-half years proved him to have been mistaken. Making good on their earlier threats to attack whatever Mauritanian targets they could reach, Polisario's guerrilla fighters ranged far and wide over Mauritania starting in late 1975, deducing (correctly) that they were confronting a foe far weaker than King Hassan's Morocco. Mauritania, with only a 3000-man army and a tiny air force (q.v.), proved incapable of guarding the country's borders or of rapidly responding to Polisario movements. By the beginning of 1976, the Zouerate-Nouadhibou railway had been sabotaged, with rolling stock, track, and locomotives damaged or destroyed. For weeks at a time, exports of iron ore practically ceased, with disastrous economic consequences. Nor did Polisario neglect other targets: cities and towns as far away from Western Sahara as Akjoujt, Tidjikja, and even Néma (qq.v.) were attacked, as were population (q.v.) centers such as Atar, Bir Moghrein, and F'Derik (qq.v.). The tiny settlement of Ain Ben Tili on the Western Saharan border was occupied by Polisario as well. Even Nouakchott itself was not spared: on June 8, 1976, the Polisario Front mounted the first of two audacious raids against the Mauritanian capital, briefly shelling President Ould Daddah's residence before retreating. The second Nouakchott raid (q.v.) was executed on July 3, 1977, and similarly stunned the capital's residents, being timed to humiliate Ould Daddah on the eve of an important summit meeting of the Organization of African Unity (OAU) in Libreville, Gabon. The social effects of the Western Sahara war were almost as decided as the military and financial ones. As the conflict dragged on, fewer and fewer Mauritanians could appreciate the reasons for it, as Ould Daddah had never managed to generate the mass-based, nationalistic enthusiasm on the Western Sahara issue that King Hassan was able to count on in Morocco.

By mid-1977, Mauritania's situation had deteriorated still further. Following a devastating Polisario raid on Zouerate on May 1, 1977, in which the Saharawis succeeded in capturing the town for several hours and taking several French expatriate mine workers prisoner without being menaced by the Mauritanian army, the Ould Daddah government, on May 13, signed an agreement with King Hassan establishing a Moroccan-Mauritanian Defense Committee (q.v.) which essentially merged the two states' military commands and allowed Morocco to station its own soldiers throughout northern Mauritania to try to stem the tide against the Polisario Front. Within a few months, over 9000 troops of Morocco's *Forces Armées Royales* (FAR) were present in almost every city in the country (excluding Nouakchott), and some of the FAR's Northrup F-5E jet fighter aircraft were based at the Nouadhibou airport (q.v.). Given the comparative numbers and capabilities of the Moroccan and Mauritanian armed forces, however, the "joint command" arrangement masked an uncomfortable reality — that Mauritania was becoming Morocco's decidedly junior partner in the Western Sahara conflict. Despite having his country's defenses stiffened by the Moroccan influx, President Ould Daddah felt compelled to go even further: he called upon the French government of Valéry Giscard d'Estaing to assist Mauritania directly. Spurred on by additional Polisario attacks on the Zouerate-Nouadhibou railway line, French Breuguet aircraft, based in Dakar, Senegal, began intensive reconnaissance flights over northern Mauritania on October 25, 1977, and on December 2, Jaguar ground-attack planes went into action, strafing Polisario columns as they withdrew after one of their countless raids. Later in December, at least three more missions were flown against the Saharawis, and on May 4 and 5, further sorties were undertaken by the French, all as part of what Paris code-named Operation Lamantin (q.v.). Costly as these attacks were to the Polisario Front, they did not reverse Mauritania's overall military fortunes.

In January 1978, one of President Ould Daddah's attempts to improve Mauritania's desperate situation inadvertently paved the way for his own downfall. In that month, he appointed Colonel Mustapha Ould Mohammed Salek (q.v.) army chief of staff, a significant move, since Ould Salek, whose personal relations with Ould Daddah were uneven, had only been recalled to active duty the previous year, after he had been relegated by the president to the army reserves in the late 1960s. In spite of this step, carried out in conjunction with almost constant reshuffles of the Council of Ministers (q.v.) and of military commands, the position of Mauritania only got worse, so much so that Colonel Ould Salek and his war-weary officer colleagues began to contemplate replacing President Ould Daddah with a new regime so as to extricate the country from its Western Sahara quagmire. After a few weeks of preparation, the Mauritanian armed forces overthrew and arrested President Ould Daddah in a bloodless coup in the early morning hours of July 10, 1978, replacing him with a military council, the *Comité Militaire de Redressement National* (CMRN) (q.v.), which pledged to restore peace to the battered country. The army takeover was welcomed by the great majority of Mauritanian citizens, and the Polisario Front, pleased by the CMRN's conciliatory stance, proclaimed a unilateral cease-fire regarding Mauritanian targets a few days after the coup.

A lasting peace, however, was to prove extremely difficult to obtain. Over the next nine months, the military committee headed by Colonel Ould Salek bobbed and weaved among competing pressures from Morocco, France, Algeria, and Polisario. The Saharawi nationalists, backed by Algerian President Houari Boumedienne, insisted on a bilateral Mauritania-Polisario treaty, the immediate evacuation of Tiris el-Gharbia, and the CMRN's recognition of the SADR government-in-exile. On the other side of the dispute, Morocco and France were fearful of just such an occurrence. Confronted with these conflicting pressures and agendas, the CMRN temporized, with Ould Salek's preference being to construct a "global," or comprehensive peace treaty among all the parties directly or indirectly involved in Western Sahara, a goal that, if achieved, would spare Mauritania the need to "go it alone" in signing a peace agreement with the Polisario Front and angering King Hassan, who still had 9000 soldiers in the country.

By April 1979 no progress had been reached toward a settlement, and the nearly collapsed state of the Mauritanian economy showed few signs of improvement. As a consequence, on April 6 Colonel Ould Salek was suddenly stripped of all real authority in a bloodless "palace revolution" led by Lieutenant Colonel Ahmed Ould Bouceif (q.v.), another veteran of the Western Sahara war. The CMRN was abolished and replaced the same day with a new *Comité Militaire de Salut National* (CMSN) (q.v.), which immediately embarked on further attempts to reach agreement with Morocco (to remove King Hassan's troops) and Polisario (to extract Mauritania gracefully from Tiris el-Gharbia). But Ould Bouceif made no further progress than his predecessor before he was killed in a plane crash near Dakar on May 27. This threw the CMSN into further disarray, but strengthened the position of those who were more willing to reach a unilateral deal with the Polisario Front. Prominent among these was the skilled desert commander, Lieutenant Colonel Mohammed Khouna Ould Heydallah (q.v.), who managed on June 3 to gain the key post of prime minister. In spite of his reputed sympathy with the Saharawi nationalists, Ould Heydallah, too, tested the diplomatic waters cautiously at first, and was ill-disposed to antagonize Morocco. But the Polisario Front would tolerate no more hesitations, and on July 12, 1979, it resumed military attacks on the country, breaking their yearlong truce. After this, events moved quickly, as Ould Heydallah agreed to vacate Tiris el-Gharbia and formally make peace with Polisario. On August 5, the CMSN's representative, Lieutenant Colonel Ahmed Salem Ould Sidi (q.v.), signed the Algiers Agreement (q.v.) with the Saharawi organization, by which Mauritania permanently relinquished all claim to Western Sahara. A secret addendum to the treaty provided that Mauritania would convey Tiris el-Gharbia directly to the Polisario Front, but this proved impossible to effectuate as Moroccan forces swiftly occupied it as soon as Mauritanian troops and administrators departed. Ould Heydallah, however, did keep a garrison in the small fishing settlement of La Guera (q.v.) opposite Nouadhibou to prevent it from being overrun in similar fashion.

After August 1979, Mauritania was to remain clear of direct involement in Western Sahara. But the conflict and the anxieties it had generated were never far from the surface. President Ould Heydallah still suspected that King Hassan resented his leanings toward the Polisario Front and feared reprisals from Rabat. He did not have long to wait: just as Ould Heydallah was preparing to normalize Mauritanian political life by promulgating a Provisional Constitution (q.v.) in December 1980, his regime was shaken to its foundations by a violent coup attempt on March 16, 1981, spearheaded by the allegedly Moroccan-backed *Alliance pour une Mauritanie Démocratique* (AMD) (q.v.), among whose leaders were Ahmed Salem Ould Sidi and ex–air force commander Lieutenant Colonel Mohammed Ould Bah Ould Abdel Kader (q.v.). Both were executed, along with two other junior officers, a few days after the coup was put down by loyal army units.

Diplomatic relations with Morocco were severed a few days afterwards, heating up an already tense relationship and giving rise to persistent accusations by King Hassan that Mauritania was allowing the Polisario Front's guerrillas to transit its territory to attack Moroccan forces in Western Sahara. Ould Heydallah denied these charges, and relied ever more on guarantees of assistance from Algeria's new President, Chadli Benjedid. Yet the Western Sahara problem would still not go away, a situation brought forcefully home on January 20, 1983, when a Moroccan warship briefly shelled La Guera. Although no casualties resulted and no damage was done, the CMSN moved closer to Algeria, adhering to the implicitly anti-Moroccan Treaty of Fraternity and Concord (q.v.) in December of that year. Another bone of contention concerned the status of the SADR, Polisario's government-in-exile. President Ould Heydallah had long threatened to recognize the Saharawi state formally if no progress were made by the OAU to hold a referendum of self-determination in Western Sahara, and finally carried it out on February 27, 1984—though he apparently did not inform his CMSN colleagues about his impending move and acted alone. This alienated many on the ruling committee, who felt it was a precipitous step that could result in Moroccan military retaliation and plunge Mauritania into renewed involvement in the conflict. Two CMSN members who felt this way were Lieutenant Colonel Anne Ahmadou Babaly (q.v.), and the army chief of staff (and until March 1984 minister of defense) Colonel Maaouiya Ould Sid'Ahmed Taya (q.v.), who were believed to be less favorably inclined toward the Polisario cause. For this as well as other domestic political reasons, Ould Taya and his like-minded officers mounted an efficient, bloodless putsch against Ould Heydallah on December 12, 1984, that was intended to restore the CMSN's tradition of collegial decision making and to maintain a more neutral stance on Western Sahara.

Mauritanian-Moroccan relations underwent a rapid improvement after the December coup. Diplomatic relations, broken in March 1981, were soon restored. Ould Taya also distanced himself from his predecessor's recognition of the SADR, although he did not try to retract it. But no Mauritanian government, whatever its leanings, could by itself resolve what was still the country's single most persistent threat to its security: the continued unsettled status of Western Sahara and the possibility that the dispute could once again involve Mauritania. A reminder of the country's vulnerability came in April 1987 when, following a strategy it had pursued since the early 1980s, Morocco extended a series of "defensive walls" or "berms" (meant to seal Polisario forces out of the territory) far into Río de Oro (q.v.) and adjacent to the Mauritanian border. Reportedly, the new Moroccan wall, essentially an earthen ridge several meters high and studded with mines and other obstacles, came to within about 400 meters of Mauritania's frontier at the tiny settlement of Inal in a remote part of the administrative région of Dakhlet-Nouadhibou (qq.v.). The Ould Taya regime filed a stiff protest with Rabat, the army went on alert for a time, and recourse was once more had to Algerian defense assurances, although the CMSN declined an offer to station Algerian troops in Nouadhibou for fear that it would be too provocative.

In subsequent years, Mauritania has kept a careful watch on developments in the ex–Spanish colony, and has been included as an "interested party" in United Nations efforts to organize a referendum of self-determination for the Saharawis. UN officials have often visited Nouakchott for consultations with President Ould Taya and his ministers, and Mauritanian towns with substantial numbers of Saharawis living in them, such as Nouadhibou and Zouerate, have hosted voter registration facilities in an attempt to ascertain which Western Saharans are eligible to take part in the plebiscite. Overall, Mauritania still observes a studied neutrality on the merits of the dispute, and the official government position is that it would be satisfied no matter what the outcome of the referendum; that is, it could live peacefully next to either Morocco or an independent Saharawi Republic.

WILAYA (pl. Wilayaat). See Région.

WOLOF. Although the Wolof are the most numerous ethnic group in Senegal, they rank well behind in numbers in Mauritania to the Halpulaaren and the Soninké (qq.v.). The Wolof are concentrated in the administrative région of Trarza (qq.v.), and they exert a significant influence in the border town of Rosso (q.v.). The Wolof share many characteristics with their fellow black Mauritanians: their adherence to the Islamic (q.v.) faith, the recognition of a historically rigid occupational caste system with little intermarriage outside the caste group, and the practices of polygyny and slavery (q.v.), though the latter was found only vestigially among black Mauritanians by the 1990s. The Wolof earn their livelihood through agriculture, livestock herding, and commerce (qq.v.). The Wolof are unique among Mauritanians, however, in that they do not subject their young women (q.v.) to the often-condemned practice of female genital excision, or clitoridectomy.

WOMEN. As in nearly all Middle Eastern and North African countries, women have occupied a disadvantaged position relative to males in Mauritania both before and after independence. However, female Mauritanians, depending to some extent on where they live and to which of the country's major ethnic groups they belong, possess several advantages compared to men, and often have shown a remarkable degree of adaptability to severe economic hardships. At the same time, traditional practices and beliefs, often underpinned by Islamic (q.v.) teachings, coupled with poor access to education (q.v.), have conspired to make progress for women a halting, uncertain affair well into the 1990s. If a history of effective exclusion from Mauritanian politics is added to this clouded situation, the character of the overall social structure of the country assumes decidedly patriarchal dimensions.

A pair of studies conducted by Barbara Abeillé and Melinda Smale of the United States Agency for International Development (USAID) in 1979 and 1980 respectively (see Bibliography) which extensively analyzed the economic and social conditions of women in the administrative régions of Assaba and Guidimaka (qq.v.), as well as in the Mauritanian capital of Nouakchott (q.v.), found great disparities between Beydane Moorish (qq.v.) women, their *haratine* (q.v.) or "Black Moor" counterparts, and the free black groups such as the Halpulaaren and the Soninké (qq.v.) living in the Senegal River Valley. In general, Beydane women, especially those from nomadic backgrounds, were found to have the least mobility (both physical and social), the lowest level of motivation, and the highest level of dependence on men, all caused, in the opinion of the researchers, by a long tradition of letting slaves (q.v.) do most of the work, a religious factor that impeded emergence from seclusion, and a barrier composed of male misunderstandings of women and distrust of men by women in a nomadic environment. As a consequence, many women who were forced along with their families and husbands to move into urban areas such as Nouakchott because of drought and desertification (q.v.) in the countryside had few if any skills with which to sustain themselves. This dependence on men was especially unfortunate since male Mauritanians also found themselves confronted by a glaring lack of employment prospects and training opportunities, and were also greatly affected by the anonymity and fragmented social structure of the city. Over time, though, many Beydane women adapted to their new condition, showing a particular aptitude for commerce (q.v.) in handicrafts, foodstuffs, and yard goods, a trade conducted almost entirely with other women behind closed doors and which sometimes yields relatively handsome monetary returns despite a critical shortage of start-up capital for such small-scale businesses. Moreover, women settled more readily into domestically based trades, since traditional social stigmas on work in the agricultural and livestock (qq.v.) herding sectors remained strong, as did informal prohibitions on taking work as housekeepers in the homes of wealthier Mauritanians. Generational differences exist too; younger Beydane women have shown little inclination to emulate the isolated, conservative mores of their mothers, and so have acclimated themselves to a more active way of life even in a small city such as Kiffa (q.v.), where opportunities are more limited than in Nouakchott or Nouadhibou (q.v.). But overall, the ancient reliance upon slave labor (even in childrearing), the traditional lack of education beyond the learning of the Koran at a very young age, and the physically debilitating practice of force-feeding young women (*gavage*) to make them obese and hence highly prized in male Moorish society, continue to be negative factors standing in the way of future development. Finally, as with men, female Moorish life is highly stratified, with the lowest caste, the *znaga* (q.v.), enjoying perhaps the fewest prospects.

Among haratine women the situation is quite different. Because of the greater burdens placed on their shoulders while they were in a servile condition, the female hartani entered the 1990s with more skills, fewer inhibitions about engaging in certain kinds of work, and a greater adaptability to changing and adverse circumstances. Like their ex-masters, the Beydanes, haratine women were quick to form cooperatives and set up informal trading networks in handicrafts, clothing, and the like. In addition, agricultural and livestock-related endeavors were not shunned as they were by "white" Moors, increasing haratine economic viability. Against this optimistic description, however, there have been a lack of capital, uncooperative men who wanted women to stay at home, continued dependency—both actual and psychological—on Beydane Moors, and the same difficulties that beset the rest of Mauritania—poor climatic (q.v.) conditions, an underdeveloped national infrastructure, and lack of access to education. There has also been an abundance of unstable personal relationships caused by the flood of migrants to the cities as well as by the presence of polygyny, a practice which, although on the decline in post-independence Mauritania, was actively encouraged by the head of state from 1980 to 1984, Colonel Mohammed Khouna Ould Heydallah (q.v.). In the opinion of many observers, the "servant mentality" of the ex-slaves, more than anything else, kept the hartani woman from achieving her full potential insofar as the country's straitened economic condition permitted.

While still disadvantaged in relation to men, the free black Mauritanian female, concentrated in and near the Senegal River Valley, has apparently been the least handicapped and tradition-bound. As a result of forced out-migrations of Halpulaaren and other black men to Nouakchott, Dakar, Paris, or other cities to earn a better living, women found themselves the *de facto* heads of households, with a lower degree of earning power than males but with fewer problems of adaptation. By some accounts, women in the Senegal River Valley comprise the backbone of the agricultural workforce, and their commercial efforts have thus been directed toward the distribution and marketing of foodstuffs, a state of affairs that eventually forced the country's rural extension agency, the *Société Nationale pour le Développement Rural* (SONADER) (q.v.) to take note and provide assistance to this crucial sector. Other forms of business, such as shops or teahouses, are still frowned upon by men (and older women) in the small towns and villages, but a good many Halpulaar women have such enterprises up and running in Nouakchott and other urban locations, their profits serving as a much-needed source of support for relatives in the hinterland. Black Mauritanian women also take a much more active role physically and emotionally in the day-to-day operation of the household than do many Moors, although Soninké women, from the available evidence, are more constrained by tradition.

Politically, the position of women in Mauritania has followed a worldwide pattern from independence onward—entry into the mainstream of the country's decision making and power centers has been agonizingly slow and incomplete. Under the government headed by President Mokhtar Ould Daddah (q.v.) between 1960 and 1978, educated women were able to take part in national affairs in an advisory capacity by affiliating themselves with the *Mouvement National Féminin* (MNF), a group that was under the domination of Ould Daddah's ruling political organization, the *Parti du Peuple Mauritanien* (PPM) (q.v.). In 1971, two women were elected as deputies to the PPM-controlled *Assemblée Nationale* (q.v.) and a woman, Aissatou Kane, was named minister of health, both events the first of their kind. The two female members of parliament, as well as Mme. Kane, continued to serve in the government until July 10, 1978, when President Ould Daddah was overthrown by a military coup and replaced by a new ruling body, the *Comité Militaire de Redressement National* (CMRN) (q.v.). As could be expected, this armed forces (q.v.) group was wholly male, and the CMRN-appointed Council of Ministers (q.v.), like those chosen by the later *Comité Militaire de Salut National* (CMSN) (q.v.) army council, consisted entirely of men. This situation did not change until 1987, when, on the heels of expanding educational and employment opportunities for Mauritanian women, the head of state, President Maaouiya Ould Sid'Ahmed Taya (q.v.), appointed three women to his cabinet to rectify, in his words, "countless managerial mistakes committed in the past." At the inauguration of the Mauritanian Second Republic (q.v.) on April 18, 1992, President Ould Taya created a new cabinet post, that of minister of women's affairs, whose occupant, Mariam Mint Ahmed Aiche, served in that position until late 1994. As women continue to find their voice in Mauritania's affairs, more attention to their sisters' plight seems assured, including efforts to eliminate the intensely controversial practice of clitoridectomy, or female genital circumcision, performed upon young Halpulaar and Moorish girls (but not at all by the Wolof [q.v.] and very little by the Soninké) and which had drawn strong international condemnation by the late 1980s.

ZAWIYA. In Mauritania's social hierarchy, *zawiya* denotes a Moorish (q.v.) tribe which is respected for its members' knowledge of Islam (q.v.) and for their monastic, peaceable character. The zawiya rank just below the *hassan* (q.v.), or warrior, tribes.

ZNAGA (Variant: Zenaga). *Znaga* is the term for vassals or tributaries, assigned to those of mainly Sanhadja Berber (qq.v.) extraction who had been compelled, by virtue of their defeat at the hands of the *Beni Hassan* (q.v.) in the 1644–1674 Char Bobha (q.v.) to accept a low social status. Their inferior position in traditional Mauritanian society was constantly driven home by their obligation to pay tribute (*horma*) and perform various services.

ZOUERATE. A settlement that owes its existence to the nearby iron ore (q.v.) extraction operations conducted by the *Société Nationale Industrielle et Minière et Société d'Economie Mixte* (SNIM-SEM) (q.v.) and its predecessor, MIFERMA (q.v.), since 1963, Zouerate is one of the most economically vital population (q.v.) centers of Mauritania. Located near the older town of F'Derik (q.v.) in the administrative région of Tiris Zemmour (q.v.) and a short distance from Western Sahara (q.v.), the town and its facilities came under heavy attack during the war over Western Sahara by the Polisario Front (q.v.) against the Mauritanian armed forces (q.v.). One particularly embarrassing and destructive raid took place on May 1, 1977, when Polisario units fought their way into the center of the town and held it for several hours, the Saharawi (q.v.) guerrillas encountering no resistance from Mauritania's army. This attack made it virtually impossible for French and other expatriate iron ore and railway (q.v.) workers to remain, thereby helping to cripple a mainstay of the Mauritanian economy, exactly as Polisario intended. Following Mauritania's exit from the Western Sahara conflict, life at Zouerate slowly returned to normal, with foreign assistance helping reactivate SNIM's mines. In later years, the town benefited from the discovery of new iron ore reserves at el-Rhein and M'Haoudat between fifteen and thirty kilometers to the east. The population of Zouerate grew from 17,500 in 1976 to upwards of 50,000 by the mid-1980s, many of the new arrivals formerly nomadic livestock (q.v.) herders forced by droughts to settle in one place permanently. As primarily an industrial community, Zouerate has little to offer the tourist (q.v.), although there are a few basic amenities operated by SNIM-SEM. The town is linked to the larger city of Atar (q.v.) by an improved road (q.v.), and has an airport (q.v.) with scheduled service.

Bibliography

Introduction

As a whole, the body of scholarly and other literature on Mauritania deals primarily with historical, sociological, or anthropological matters either during the long precolonial period or the years during which the French "pacified" the region and subjected the territory to their rule. Beyond 1960, books and articles (at least in English) steadily become less common, often declining to the vanishing point in some years. This bibliography makes no pretense to being fully comprehensive, as it covers, like the dictionary itself, mainly the colonial and postcolonial period in Mauritanian history, and is restricted almost entirely to works in English and French. Readers seeking a bibliography with somewhat broader coverage are directed to volume 141 of the Clio Press's World Bibliographical Series, devoted to Mauritania, compiled by Simonetta Calderini and others, published in 1992.

Two works in particular stand out among English-language books on the subject of modern Mauritania. Alfred Gerteiny's *Mauritania,* published in 1967, is still of great value for the breadth of its treatment and historical insights despite its age, and *Mauritania: A Country Study,* issued by the United States Government in 1990 and current as of 1987, contains an extensive and impartial survey of the country from a broad perspective. Among the articles written on post-1960 Mauritanian history, society, and politics in specialized journals and books, the works of Mark Doyle, Howard Schissel, and Charles C. Stewart are recommended, as are the lengthy chapters on Mauritania contained in *Africa Contemporary Record: Annual Survey and Documents,* edited by Colin Legum.

Newspaper and media coverage of Mauritania is nearly nonexistent in the United States and Great Britain, making it necessary for researchers to cast their nets all the wider for regular, reliable information on the country and its people. Some helpful sources include *Africa Confidential, Africa Research Bulletin,* and *West Africa,* as well as the *Country Reports* published quarterly by the Economist Intelligence Unit. Lastly, *Africa South of the Sahara,* an annual volume comprising part of the Europa World Yearbook series, contains up-to-date political and especially economic analysis and statistics.

To simplify the contents of this bibliography, it has been divided into subject categories. Consult the Table of Contents below.

Contents

1. General

Bibliographies and Dictionaries

Calderini, Simonetta, Delia Cortese, and James L. A. Webb, Jr. *Mauritania*. World Bibliographical Series, no. 141. Oxford and Santa Barbara: Clio Press, 1992.

Gerteiny, Alfred G. *Historical Dictionary of Mauritania*. Metuchen, N.J. and London: Scarecrow Press, 1981.

Hodges, Tony. *Historical Dictionary of Western Sahara*. Metuchen, N.J. and London: Scarecrow Press, 1982.

Joucla, E. *Bibliographie de l'Afrique occidentale française*. Paris: Société d'Editions Géographiques Maritimes et Coloniales, 1937.

Mohamed Said Ould Hamody. *Bibliographie générale de la Mauritanie*. Paris: Editions Sepia, 1995.

Pazzanita, Anthony G., and Tony Hodges. *Historical Dictionary of Western Sahara*, 2d ed. Metuchen, N.J. and London: Scarecrow Press, 1994.

Richard-Mollar, J. "Bibliographie de l'AOF." *Information géographique* (Paris) (November/December 1948).

Toupet, Charles. "Orientation Bibliographique sur la Mauritanie." *Bulletin de l'Institut Français d'Afrique Noir* (IFAN) (Dakar) (1959): 201–39.

———. "Orientation Bibliographique sur la Mauritanie." *Bulletin de l'Institut Français d'Afrique Noir* (IFAN) (Dakar) (1962): 594–613.

General Information

Arnaud, Jean. *La Mauritanie*. Paris: Le Livre Africain, 1972.

Belvaude, Catherine. *La Mauritanie*. Paris: Editions Karthala, 1989.

Captot-Rey, Robert. *La Sahara français*. Paris: Presses Universitaires de France, 1953.

Centre de Recherches et d'Etudes sur Sociétés Méditerranéennes et Centre d'Etudes d'Afrique Noir. *Introduction à la Mauritanie*. Paris: Editions Centre National de la Recherche Scientifique, 1979.

Chartrand. P., ed. *La Mauritanie en mutation*. Nouakchott: Ecole Nationale d'Administration, 1976.

Curran, Brian Dean, and Joann Schrock. *Area Handbook for Mauritania*. Washington, D.C.: U.S. Government Printing Office, 1972.

Daure-Serfaty, Christine. *La Mauritanie*. Paris: Editions Harmattan, 1993.

Du Puigaudeau, Odette. "Mauritanie: république des sables." *Esprit* (February 1961): 230–48.

Europe France Outremer. *Mauritanie: un an d'indépendance*. ITS (Paris), no. 384 (February 1962): 1–60.

Gaudio, Attilio. *Le Sahara des Africains*. Paris: Editions Julliard, 1960.

Gerteiny, Albert G. *Mauritania*. New York: Praeger Publishers, 1967.

Handloff, Robert E., ed. *Mauritania: A Country Study,* 2d ed. Washington, D.C.: U.S. Government Printing Office, 1990.

Knapp, Wilfrid. *North West Africa: A Political and Economic Survey*. London and New York: Oxford University Press, 1977.

Legum, Colin (ed.). *Africa Contemporary Record: Annual Survey and Documents*. Vols. 1–22. New York: Africana Publishing Company, 1968–95.

Mokhtar Ould Daddah. *Mauritania: A Land of People*. Nouakchott: Centre d'Information et Formation, 1973.

Reichold, Walter. *Islamiche Republik Mauritanien*. Bonn: Kurt Schroeder, 1964.

Toupet, Charles, and Jean-Robert Pitte. *La Mauritanie*. Paris: Presses Universitaries de France, 1977.

United States Department of State. *Mauritania: Background Notes*. Washington, D.C.: U.S. Government Printing Office, August 1981.

———. *Mauritania: Background Notes.* Washington, D.C.: U.S. Government Printing Office, October 1987.
———. *Mauritania: Background Notes.* Washington, D.C.: U.S. Government Printing Office, July 1992.

Travel and Description

Du Puigaudeau, Odette. *Barefoot Through Mauritania.* London: George Routledge and Sons, 1937.
Ellis, William S. "Africa's Sahel: The Stricken Land." *National Geographic* 172, no. 2 (August 1987): 140–79.
Fischer, Rudolf. *Drei Glaschen Tee: Reisenotizen aus Maureitanien.* Bern: Vyss Druck + Verlag A.G., 1983.
Fondation Internationale de Banc d'Arguin. *Banc d'Arguin National Park: A Haven for Life.* Nouadhibou, 1988.
Frérot, Anne-Marie. *Découverte de l'Espace Mauritanien.* Nouakchott: Centre Cultural Français/Antoine de St. Exupéry, June 1991.
Hansen, Jan. *Tichitt 1971: Le Vie d'un Village Isolé du Sahara Mauritanien.* Nouakchott: Centre Culturel Antoine de St. Exupéry/Imprimère Nationale, 1971.
Hemp, Paul. "Mauritania: Traveling to the End of the World." *The Boston Globe* (Travel Section), 29 April 1991.
Hudson, Peter. *Travels in Mauritania.* London: Virgin Books, 1990.
Klotchkoff, Jean-Claude. *La Mauritanie aujourd'hui.* Paris: Les Editions du Jaguar/Les Editions Jeune Afrique, 1990.
Langewiesche, William. "The World in its Extreme: A Sahara Journal." *The Atlantic* 268, no. 5 (November 1991): 105–40.
Moorhouse, Geoffrey. *The Fearful Void.* 2d ed. Harmondsworth, England: Penguin Books, 1986.
Sleigh, Adderly W. (Capt.). *Preliminary Treatise on the Resources of Ancient Mauritania, or the Territory of Zarara-Zuz, Describing Its Rich Productions, Healthful Climate, Fertile Soil, Valuable Mines, Commercial Advantages; Inhabitants—Their Ancient Descent, Laws, Manners, Habits, Form of Government and Independence, with Observations on the Introduction of Christianity, the Promotion of Civilisation, and the Suppression of Slavery.* London: Aylott and Jones, 1851.

2. Economic

Amin, Samir. *Neo-Colonialism in West Africa.* Harmondsworth, England: Penguin Books, 1973.
Bennoune, Mahfoud. "Mauritania: Formation of a Neo-Colonial Society." *MERIP Reports* 54 (Washington, D.C.: Middle East Research and Information Project), February 1977.
Bonte, Pierre. "Multinational Companies and National Development: MIFERMA and Mauritania." *Review of African Political Economy* 2 (1975): 89–109.

Brierly, Tim. "Mauritania: An Islamic Republic with a Mountain of Iron Ore." *Geographical Magazine* 37, no. 10 (February 1965): 754–65.

Bureau d'Etude d'Information et de Marketing. *Guide de l'Opérateur Economique en République Islamique de Mauritanie.* Nouakchott, November 1993.

Carr, David. W. "Difficulties of Restoring Economic Viability with Lopsided Development: The Mauritanian Case." *Journal of Developing Areas* 18, no. 3 (April 1984): 373–86.

Centre Culturel Antoine de St. Exupéry and Ministère de l'Industrialisation et des Mines. *Richesses & Promesses du Sous-Sol Mauritanien.* Nouakchott: Centre Culturel Antoine de St. Exupéry (Panorama Special no. 14), February 1969.

Gibbs, David. "The Politics of Economic Development: The Case of the Mauritanian Fishing Industry." *African Studies Review* 27, no. 4 (December 1984): 79–93.

Gillet, Jean-Noel. "La 'Transmauritanienne,' Route de l'Espoir." *Balafon* 35 (April 1977): 15–21.

"Mauritania: Hope in the Desert." *Africa Confidential* (London), vol. 12, no. 7 (2 April 1971).

"Mauritania: The Chinese Factor." *Africa Confidential* (London), vol. 12, no. 20 (1 October 1971).

"Mauritania: Outposts of the Desert." *The Courier* (Brussels) no. 98 (July/August 1986): 40–56.

"Mauritania: A Delicate Balancing Act." *The Courier* (Brussels) no. 137 (January/February 1993): 17–42.

Mauritanian Ministry of Information. *La Mauritanie 15 ans après l'independance, n. 3: l'économie nationale enfin libérée.* Paris: L'Avenir Graphique, 1978.

Mohameden Ould-Mey. *Global Restructuring and Peripheral States: The Carrot and the Stick in Mauritania.* Lanham, MD: Littlefield Adams Books, 1996.

Rogers, Glenn Roy. *The Theory of Output-Income Multipliers with Consumption Linkages: An Application to Mauritania.* Ph.D. diss., University of Wisconsin at Madison, 1986.

Sonko, Karamo N. M. "Export Diversification in the West African Sahel: The Problems and Prospects in Mauritania and Niger." *Stanford Journal of International Affairs,* vol. 2, no. 2 (Summer 1993).

"Special Mauritanie," in *Afrique, Industrie, Infrastructures* 143 (July 1977): 28–78. (Contains interviews with Ahmed Ould Daddah and Mokhtar Ould Daddah.)

Toupet, Charles. "Nouadhibou (Port Etienne) and the Economic Development of Mauritania." In *Ports and Development in Tropical Africa,* ed. B. S. Hoyle and D. Hilling. London: Macmillan, 1970.

Tymowsky, Michal. "La Saline d'Idjil en Mauritanie." *Africana Bulletin* 30 (1981): 1–38.

United Nations. *Country Presentation: Mauritania 1990.* Geneva: Second United Nations Conference on the Least Developed Countries, UNCLDC II/CP.25 (1990).

————. *Mauritania: Industrial Reorientation and Rejuvenation.* Vienna: United Nations Industrial Development Organization, Regional and Country Studies Branch, Industrial Development Review Series, PPD.115 (27 April 1989).

————. *Report of Mission on Needs Assessment for Population Assistance.* New York: United Nations Fund for Population Activities, no. 17, 1979.

Westebbe, Richard M. *The Economy of Mauritania.* London and New York: Praeger Publishers, 1971.

————. *Mauritania: Guidelines for a Four-Year Development Program; Report of a Mission Organized by the International Bank for Reconstruction and Development at the Request of the Islamic Republic of Mauritania.* Washington, D.C.: International Bank for Reconstruction and Development (World Bank), 1968.

3. Historical

The Precolonial Period

Ahmed Baba Miské. *Al-Wasit: Tableau de la Mauritanie au début du XXé siècle.* Paris: Librairie C. Klinchsieck, 1970.

Amilhat, P. "Les Almoravides au Sahara." *Revue Militaire de l'Afrique Occidentale Française* (15 July 1937): 1–31.

————. *Petite chronique des Idou Aich, heritiers guerriers des almoravides sahariens.* Paris: Revue des Etudes Islamiques, cahier 1, 1937, 41–130.

Basset, R. *Mission au Sénégal: Etude sur le dialecte zénaga; Notes sur le hassania; Recherches historiques sur les Maures.* Paris, 1909.

Baudel, Pierre Robert, ed. *Mauritanie: entre arabité et Africanité.* Revue du Monde Musulman et de la Méditerranée, no. 54. Aix-en-Provence: Editions Edisud, 1990.

Bovill, Edward William. *The Golden Trade of the Moors.* London and New York: Oxford University Press, 1958.

Garnier, Christine and Philippe Ermont. *Désert fertile: un nouvel état La Mauritanie.* Paris: Librairie Hachette, 1960.

Gerteiny, Alfred G. "On the History, Ethnology, and Political Philosophy of Mauritania." *Maghreb Review* (London) 3, nos. 7 and 8 (May/August 1978): 1–6.

Jacques-Meunié, O. *Cités Anciennes de Mauritanie.* Paris: Librairie C. Klinchsieck, 1961.

Mauny, Raymond. "Koumbi-Saleh, capitale du pays de l'or." *Le Courrier de l'UNESCO* (Geneva), October 1959: 24–25.

———. "Les liaisons transsahariennes avant l'arrivée des arabes." *A.O.F. Magazine* 17 (December 1956): 38–39.

The Period of "Pacification" and French Colonial Rule

Bonte, Pierre. "L'émirat de l'Adrar après sa conquête coloniale et la dissidence de l'Emir Sidi Ahmed." *Journal des Africanistes* (Paris) 54, no. 2 (1984): 5–30.

Coppolani, Xavier. "Rapport à M. le Gouverneur général de l'A.O.F.: Mission d'organisation des Territoires du Tagant." *Archives de Mauritanie* (St. Louis, Senegal), 1 July 1904.

Desiré-Vuillemin, Geneviève. *Contribution à l'Histoire de la Mauritanie de 1900 à 1934*. Dakar: Editions Clairafrique, 1962.

———. "Coppolani en Mauritanie." *Revue d'Histoire des Colonies,* 40 (1955): 291–343.

———. *Les rapports de la Mauritanie et du Maroc*. St. Louis, Senegal, 1960.

Duboc, Général. *Mauritanie*. Paris: Librairie Fournier, 1935.

Du Puigaudeau, Odette. "La Ziara de Cheikh Mohammed Fadel (Adrar)." *Bulletin de l'Institut Français d'Afrique Noir* (IFAN) (Dakar) (October 1961): 1218–26.

Faidherbe, Louis. *Notice sur la colonie du Sénégal et sur les pays en relation avec elle*. St. Louis, Senegal, 1856.

El-Fassi, Allal. "Documentaires joints au livre rouge." *Perspectives Sahariennes,* nos. 18–22 (1950): 149–340.

Féral, Gabriel. *Le tambour des sables*. Paris: Editions France-Empire, 1983.

Garnier, Christine. "Opération Ecouvillon." *La Revue des deux mondes* (Paris) (1 November 1960): 93–102.

Gillier, L. (commandant brévete). *La pénétration en Mauritanie*. Paris: P. Geuthner, 1926.

Gouraud, Henri. *La pacification de la Mauritanie*. Paris, 1910.

———. *Mauritanie, Adrar: Souvenirs d'un Africain*. Paris: Librairie Plon, 1945.

Mamadou Hamidou Bâ. "L'émirat de l'Adrar Mauritanien de 1872 à 1908." *Bulletin de la Société de Géographie et d'Archéologie de la Province d'Oran* (Oran, Algeria) (March 1932): 85–119; June 1932: 263–98.

The Post-Independence Period

Adloff, Richard. *West Africa: The French-Speaking Nations*. New York: Holt, Rinehart and Winston, 1964.

Balans, Jean Louis. "La Mauritanie entre deux mondes." *Revue Française d'Etudes Politiques Africaines* 13 (May 1975): 54–64.

Balans, Jean Louis, and Mireille Duteil. "Chronique Mauritanienne." *Annuaire de l'Afrique du Nord* 14 (1975): 637–69.

Duteil, Mireille. "Chronique Mauritanienne." *Annuaire de l'Afrique du Nord* 23 (1984): 943–55.

French Government. "Accord avec la République de Mauritanie." *Journal officiel, République française: Debâts parlementaires* (16 November 1960): 3865–72.

Hargreaves, John D. *West Africa: The Former French States.* Englewood Cliffs, N.J.: Prentice-Hall, 1967.

Laigret, Christian. *La naissance d'une nation: Contribution à l'histoire de la République Islamique de Mauritanie.* Nouakchott: Imprimêrie Nationale, 1969.

4. Political

General

de Chassey, Francis. *Mauritanie, 1900–1975.* Paris: Editions Harmattan, 1984.

Decraene, Philippe. "La poursuite des mutations de la République Islamique de Mauritanie." *L'Afrique et l'Asie Modernes* 160 (1989): 78–86.

Du Puigaudeau, Odette. *Le passé maghrebin de la Mauritanie.* Rabat: Moroccan Government, 1962.

S'ad, Jamal. *The Problem of Mauritania.* New York: Arab Information Center (Information Paper No. 14), 1960.

Soudan, François. *Le Marabout et le Colonel: La Mauritanie de Ould Daddah à Ould Taya.* Paris: Editions Jalivres, 1992.

Zartman, I. William. *Ripe for Resolution: Conflict and Intervention in Africa.* Oxford and New York: Oxford University Press, 1989.

Domestic Politics, 1960–1978

Assemblée Nationale (of Mauritania). *Liste des Parlementaires: Texte de la Constitution,* November 1960. (Contains text of the Constitution of Mauritania of March 22, 1959.)

Bennoune, Mahfoud. "The Political Economy of Mauritania: Imperialism and Class Struggle." *Review of African Political Economy* 12 (1978): 31–52.

de Focault, Bertrand Fessard. "Le Parti du Peuple Mauritanien." Parts 1 and 2. *Revue Française d'Etudes Politiques Africaines* (Paris) 94 (October 1973): 33–60; 95 (November 1973): 72–98.

"Dry Times in Mauritania." *Swiss Review of World Affairs* (Zurich) 22, no. 10 (January 1973): 15–17.

Eagleton, William, Jr. "The Islamic Republic of Mauritania." *Middle East Journal* 19, no. 1 (Winter 1965): 45–53.

Gerteiny, Alfred G. "The Racial Factor and Politics in the Islamic Republic of Mauritania." *Race* (Journal of the Institute of Race Relations) 8, no. 1 (January 1967): pp. 263–75.

"Mauritania: Land of Nomads." *Swiss Review of World Affairs* (Zurich) 21, no. 10 (January 1972): 9–11.

Moore, Clement Henry. "One-Partyism in Mauritania." *Journal of Modern African Studies* (Chagford, Devon) 3, no. 3 (October 1965): 409–20.

Peaslee, Amos J., ed. *Constitutions of Nations,* 3d ed., vol. 1, pp. 546–57. The Hague: Martinius Nijhoff, 1965. (Contains text of the Constitution of Mauritania of May 20, 1961.)

Watson, J. H. A. "Mauritania: Problems and Prospects." *Africa Report* 8, no. 2 (February 1963): 3–6.

Willcox, S. "President Ould Daddah Consolidates His Position." *Africa Report* 7, no. 2 (February 1962): 7.

Wolfers, Michael. "Letter from Nouakchott." Parts 1 and 2. *West Africa* (London), 6 January 1975.

Domestic Politics, 1978 and After

Abo, Klevor. "Future Collaborators?" *West Africa* (London), 6–12 February 1995: 181–83. (Contains interviews with Ahmed Ould Daddah and Dieng Boubou Farba.)

Baudel, Pierre Robert. "La difficile sortie d'un régime authoritaire: Mauritanie 1990–1992." *Revue du Monde Musulman et de la Méditerrannée* (Paris), vols. 63 and 64 (1992): 225–43.

Blaustein, Albert P., and Gisbert H. Flanz, eds. *Constitutions of the Countries of the World: Islamic Republic of Mauritania* (Release 93–5, translated by Norman S. Ellman). Dobbs Ferry, N.Y.: Oceana Publications, August 1993. (Contains text of the Constitution of Mauritania of July 20, 1991.)

Bourgi, Robert, and Pierre Weiss. "Mauritanie: Nation Inachevée," *Jeune Afrique Plus* (Paris) 3 (November/December 1989): 36–43.

da Costa, Peter. "Democracy in Doubt." *Africa Report* 37, no. 3 (May/June 1992): 58–60.

Dahmani, Abdelaziz. "La Chute de Haidalla." *Jeune Afrique* (Paris) 1271 (15 May 1985): 11–15.

———. "Les secrets d'un putsch manqué." *Jeune Afrique* (Paris) 1401 (11 November 1987): 20–21.

Doucet, Lyse. "Mauritania: Fragile Politics." *West Africa* (London), 17 January 1987.

Doyle, Mark. "One Foot in Black Africa." *West Africa* (London), 24–30 July 1989.

Forces de Libération Africaine de Mauritanie. *Un Apartheid Méconnu: Livre Blanc sur la Situation des Noirs en Mauritanie.* Paris: Forces de Libération Africaine de Mauritanie, Section Europe-Nord, January 1991. (Contains the French text of *Le Manifesto du Négro-Mauritanien Opprimé.*)

Garba Diallo. *Mauritania: The Other Apartheid?* Current African Issues, No. 16. Uppsala, Sweden: The Scandinavian Institute of African Studies, February 1993.

"Heydallah Consolidates." *Africa Confidential* (London), vol. 21, no. 5 (27 February 1980).

Hodges, Tony. "Mauritania After the Coup." *Africa Report* 23, no. 6 (November/December 1978): 13–18.

International Commission of Jurists. "Mauritania." *The Review* 33 (December 1984): 13–17.

———. "Mauritania." *The Review* 37 (December 1986): 13–15.

Kpatindé, Francis. "Mauritanie: Délicate cohabitation." *Jeune Afrique* (Paris) 1439 (3 August 1988): 30–31.

M'Barek Ould Beyrouk. "Le Dilemme des Harattines." *Jeune Afrique* (Paris) 1807 (24–30 August 1995): 38–39.

Maaouiya Ould Sid'Ahmed Taya. " 'Je gagnerai, dans la transparence.' " *Jeune Afrique* (Paris) 1619 (16–23 January 1992): 24–27. (Contains interview with President Maaouiya Ould Sid'Ahmed Taya by François Soudan.)

———. " 'La Mauritanie ne sera pas le Liberia!' " *Jeune Afrique* (Paris) 1605 (2–8 October 1991): 28–31. (Contains interview with President Maaouiya Ould Sid'Ahmed Taya by François Soudan.)

———. " 'Le Sénégal nous veut du mal.' " *Jeune Afrique* (Paris) 1513 (1 January 1990): 34–37. (Contains interview with President Maaouiya Ould Sid'Ahmed Taya by François Soudan.)

———. " 'L'opposition, quelle opposition?' " *Jeune Afrique* (Paris) 1672 (21–27 January 1993): 56–59. (Contains interview with President Maaouiya Ould Sid'Ahmed Taya by François Soudan.)

"Mauritania: After Bouceif?" *Africa Confidential* (London), vol. 20, no. 14 (4 July 1979).

"Mauritania and Its New Leader." *West Africa* (London), 14 January 1980.

"Mauritania: Behind the Coup." *Africa Confidential* (London), vol. 19, no. 16 (4 August 1978).

"Mauritania: Ethnic Tension." *Africa Confidential* (London), vol. 20, no. 5 (28 February 1979).

"Mauritania: Facing Up to Realities." *Africa Confidential* (London), vol. 23, no. 8 (14 April 1982).

"Mauritania: Haidalla Hangs On." *Africa Confidential* (London), vol. 22, no. 8 (8 April 1981).

"Mauritania Loses a Strongman." *West Africa* (London), 4 June 1979.

"Mauritania: Maintaining the Balance." *Africa Confidential* (London), vol. 24, no. 6 (16 March 1983).

"Mauritania: More Plots." *Africa Confidential* (London), vol. 29, no. 9 (29 April 1988).

"Mauritania: Opposition Stirs." *Africa Confidential* (London), vol. 21, no. 18 (3 September 1980).

"Mauritania: Ould Taya Lashes Out." *Africa Confidential* (London), vol. 29, no. 20 (7 October 1988).

"Mauritania: Palace Coup No Solution." *Africa Confidential* (London), vol. 20, no. 10 (9 May 1979).

"Mauritania: Political Merry-Go-Round." *Africa Confidential* (London), vol. 26, no. 6 (13 March 1985).

"Mauritania: The Politics of a Pogrom." *Africa Confidential* (London), vol. 31, no. 13 (June 29, 1990).

"Mauritania: Pressure for Peace." *Africa Confidential* (London), vol. 19, no. 19 (22 September 1978).

"Mauritania: Problems of Peace." *Africa Confidential* (London), vol. 21, no. 10 (7 May 1980).

"Mauritania: Staying Out of Trouble." *Africa Confidential* (London), vol. 23, no. 2 (20 January 1982).

"Mauritania: The Oppressed." *Africa Confidential* (London), vol. 27, no. 23 (2 November 1986).

"Mauritania: Tricky Alliances." *Africa Confidential* (London), vol. 22, no. 3 (28 January 1981).

"Mauritania: Unconvincing Democrats," *Africa Confidential* (London), Vol. 35 No. 19 (23 September 1994).

"Mauritania: Whiffs of the End." *Africa Confidential* (London), vol. 25, no. 6 (14 March 1984).

Mauritanian Government. *Projet de Constitution: Soumis au Référendum de 12 Juillet 1991*. Nouakchott: Imprimêrie Nationale, 1991 (contains French text of the Constitution of Mauritania of July 20, 1991.)

"Mauritanie: un tournant Démocratique?" *Politique Africaine* (Paris) 55 (October 1994).

Mohammad-Mahmoud Mohamedou. "Mauritania at the Crossroads." *Civil Society* (March 1995): 14–16.

———. "Opposition in Trouble." *Civil Society* (August 1994): 7.

———. *Societal Transition to Democracy in Mauritania*. Cairo: Ibn Khaldoun Center for Development Studies/Dar Al-Ameen Publishing, 1995.

Onwordi, Ike. "A Question of Race." *West Africa* (London), 24–30 October 1988.

Owona, Joseph. "Les institutions du nouveau régime Mauritanien." *Revue Française d'Etudes Politiques Africaines* 159 (March 1979): 28–39.

Schissel, Howard. "The Haratine Question." *West Africa* (London), 12 July 1982.

———. "Praying for Rain." *West Africa* (London), 12 March 1984.

———. "Road to Recovery." *West Africa* (London), 5 July 1982.

———. "Saharan Sandstorm Blows On." *Africa Report* 18, no. 3 (May/June 1983): 55–56, 58.

————. "Stability for the Time Being." *West Africa* (London), 28 June 1982.

————. "Taya at the Helm". *Africa Report* 31, no. 4 (July/August 1986): 85–88.

Simon, Catherine. "God Beckons for Mauritania's Dispossessed." *Manchester Guardian Weekly,* 16 April 1995: 15.

Soudan, François. "Crise: L'Etat ne s'est pas effondré." *Jeune Afrique* (Paris) 1531 (7 May 1990): 35–38.

————. "Diplomatie: Quand le fleuve est une déchirure." *Jeune Afrique* (Paris) 1531 (7 May 1990): 43–44.

————. "L'affaire Ould Daddah." *Jeune Afrique* (Paris) 1787 (6–12 April 1995): 16–18.

————. "La république, une et divisible." *Jeune Afrique* (Paris) 1729 (24 February–4 March 1994): 32–34.

————. "Pourquoi Ould Taya a limogé Gabriel Cimper." *Jeune Afrique* (Paris) 1520 (19 February 1990): 28–29.

————. "Profil: L'obsession de la modernité."*Jeune Afrique* (Paris) 1531 (7 May 1990): 39–40.

————. "Saddamania à Nouakchott." *Jeune Afrique* (Paris) 1554 (10–16 October 1991): 40–41.

Soudan, François, and Mohamed Selhami. "Vents de sable sur l'unité nationale." *Jeune Afrique* (Paris) 1350 (19 November 1986): 34–38. (Includes interview with President Maaouiya Ould Sid'Ahmed Taya by François Soudan.)

Stewart, Charles C. "North-South Dialectic in Mauritania: An Update." *Maghreb Review* (London) 2, no. 1 (1986): 40–45.

Foreign Policy: General

Adeleye Ojo, M. "The Foreign Policy of Mauritania." *A Current Bibliography of African Affairs* 17, no. 4 (1984–1985): 347–61.

Ahmed Baba Miské. "Mauritanie: la délicate synthése de l'Afrique et de l'arabité." In *Maghreb: les Années de Transition,* ed. Bassma Kodami-Darwish and May Chartouni-Dubarry. Paris: Institut Française des Relations Internationales/Masson, 1990.

Ashford, Douglas E. "The Irredentist Appeal in Morocco and Mauritania." *Western Political Quarterly* 15, no. 4 (December 1962): 641–51.

Burgat, François. "Qadhafi's 'Unitary' Doctrine: Theory and Practice." In *The Green and the Black: Qadhafi's Policies in Africa,* ed. René Lemarchand. Bloomington: Indiana University Press, 1988.

Du Bois, Victor D. *The Search for Unity in French-Speaking Black Africa, Part III: Mauritania's Disengagement from Black Africa.* New York: American Universities Field Staff Reports Service, vol. 8, no. 5 (July 1965).

Gallagher, Charles F. *Morocco and its Neighbors, Part III: Morocco and Mauritania.* New York: American Universities Field Staff Reports Service, vol. 13, no. 4 (April 1967).

La République Islamique de Mauritanie et le Royaume du Maroc. Paris: Islamic Republic of Mauritania, 1960.

Limagne, Joseph. "La politique étrangère de la République Islamique de Mauritanie." *Revue Française d'Etudes Politiques Africaines* (Paris) 75 (March 1972): 34–46.

Moroccan Ministry of Information and Tourism. *La Libération de la Province Mauritanienne et l'Opinion Internationale.* Rabat: Moroccan Government, 1961.

Pazzanita, Anthony G. "Mauritania's Foreign Policy: The Search for Protection." *Journal of Modern African Studies* (Chagford, Devon) 30, no. 2 (1992): 281–304.

Zartman, I. William. "A Disputed Frontier Is Settled." *Africa Report* 8, no. 8 (August 1963): 13–14.

———. "Foreign Relations of North Africa." *Annals of the American Academy of Political and Social Science* 489 (January 1987): 13–27.

———. "Mauritania's Stand on Regionalism." *Africa Report* 11, no. 1 (January 1966): 19–20, 37.

The Western Sahara Conflict, 1975–1979

Ahmed Baba Miské. *Front Polisario: l'âme d'un peuple.* Paris: Editions Rupture, 1977.

Hodges, Tony. "After the Treaty of Oujda." *Africa Report* 29, no. 6 (November–December 1984): 26–31.

———. *Western Sahara: The Roots of a Desert War.* Westport, Conn.: Lawrence Hill Publishers, 1983.

Morgan, Susan. "Crisis Time in Mauritania." *West Africa* (London), 30 May 1977.

"Ould Daddah's Dilemma." *West Africa* (London), 9 February 1976.

Stewart, Charles C. "Much Ado About Nothing." Parts 1 and 2. *West Africa* (London), 3 November; 10 November 1975.

Thompson, Virginia, and Richard Adloff. *The Western Saharans: Background to Conflict.* London and Totowa, N.J.: Croom Helm and Barnes and Noble Books, 1980.

The Senegal-Mauritania Crisis, 1989–1990

Alabi, Niyi. "When the Going Gets Rough." *Africa Events* (London), June 1989.

Blunt, Elisibeth. "In the Midst of the Madding Crowd." *Africa Events* (London), June 1989.

Diallo, Siradou, Abdelaziz Dahmani, and Elemane Fall, "Mauritanie-

Sénégal: après le cauchemar." *Jeune Afrique* (Paris) 1480 (17 May 1989): 6–33.

Doyle, Mark. "Blood Brothers." *Africa Report* 34, no. 4 (July/August 1989): 13–16.

———. "Nouakchott's New Nationalism." *Africa Report* 34, no. 5 (September/October 1989): 37–40.

———. "The Tragic Aftermath." *West Africa* (London), 15–21 May 1989.

———. "Troubled Waters." *West Africa* (London), 19–25 June 1989.

Fritscher, Frédéric. "Flight of Senegalese Drains Mauritania of its Life-Blood." *Manchester Guardian Weekly,* 4 June 1989.

"Mauritania: On the War-Path." *Africa Confidential* (London), vol. 30, no. 19 (22 September 1989).

"Mauritania: War on Black Citizens." *Africa Confidential* (London), vol. 30, no. 17 (7 July 1989).

Mauritanian Government. *Book of Facts: Conflict with Senegal.* Nouakchott, 31 August 1989.

Nyang, Sulayman S. "Fighting Cousins." *Africa Events* (London), June 1989.

Parker, Ron. "The Senegal-Mauritania Conflict of 1989: A Fragile Equilibrium." *Journal of Modern African Studies* (Chagford, Devon) 29, no. 1 (1991): 155–71.

"Toughing it Out." *Africa Events* (London), June 1989.

Slavery and Human Rights

Africa Watch. *Mauritania: Slavery Alive and Well, Ten Years After It Was Last Abolished.* New York and London: Africa Watch, 29 June 1990.

Amnesty International. *Mauritania, 1986–1989: Background to a Crisis: Three Years of Political Imprisonment, Torture, and Unfair Trials.* London and New York: Amnesty International, November 1989.

———. *Mauritania: Human Rights Violations in the Senegal River Valley.* London and New York: Amnesty International, October 1990.

Bossyut, Marc. *Slavery and Slavery-Like Practices: Question of Slavery and the Slave Trade in All Their Practices and Manifestations, Including the Slavery-Like Practices of Apartheid and Colonialism: Report of the Mission to Mauritania.* Geneva: United Nations Economic and Social Council, Commission on Human Rights, 37th Session, Agenda Item 12(a), E/CN./Sub.2/1984/23 (2 July 1984).

Derrick, Jonathan. "Slavery and Mauritanian Society." *West Africa* (London), 21 July 1980.

Fleischman, Janet. "Ethnic Cleansing." *Africa Report* 39, no. 1 (January/February 1994): 45–46.

Human Rights Watch/Africa. *Mauritania's Campaign of Terror: State-*

Sponsored Repression of Black Africans. New York: Human Rights Watch/Africa, April 1994.

————. *Mauritania: More than Two Hundred Black Political Detainees Executed or Tortured to Death.* New York: Human Rights Watch/Africa, 31 May 1991.

Mercer, John. *Slavery in Mauritania Today.* Edinburgh: Human Rights Group, 1982.

Omaar, Rakiya, and Janet Fleischman. "Arab vs. African." *Africa Report* 36, no. 4 (July/August 1991): 34–38.

Paringaux, Roland-Pierre. "The Desert of the Slaves." *The Reporter* (Journal of the Anti-Slavery Society, London), December 1990: 38–44.

United States Department of State. *Country Reports on Human Rights Practices.* Chapter on Mauritania in each annual volume from 1979 to 1994. Washington, D.C.: U.S. Government Printing Office.

The Politics of Agriculture and Land Reform

Bonte, Pierre. "L'herbe ou le sol? L'évolution du système foncier pastoral en Mauritanie du sud-ouest." In *Heritier en pays musulman, hubus, lait-vivant, Manyahuli,* ed. M. Gast. Marseilles: Editions du Centre National de la Recherche Scientifique, 1987.

————. "Une agriculture saharienne: Les grayr de l'Adrar Mauritanien." *Revue de l'Occident Musulman et de la Méditerranée,* nos. 41 and 42 (1986): 378–96.

Bradley, Philip, Claude Raynaut, and Jorge Torrealba. *The Guidimaka Region of Mauritania: A Critical Analysis Leading to a Development Project.* London: War on Want, 1977.

Cheikh Saad Bouh Kamara. "Le Foncier rural et le développement en Mauritanie: Perspective historique. L'Aftût de Mbûd à l'heure du barrage de Fum-Lägläytä." Ph.D. diss., Leval University (Québec, Canada), 1993.

Crousse, Bernard. "Les relations entre l'agriculture et l'industrie en Mauritanie. Situation présente et perspectives de développement." *Mondes en Développement,* nos. 31 and 32 (1980): 516–46.

Crousse, Bernard, Paul Mathieu, and Sidi M. Seck. *La vallée du fleuve Sénégal. Evaluations et perspectives d'une décennie d'aménagements (1980–1990).* Paris: Editions Karthala, 1991.

Grayzel, John. *Modernizing Land Tenure in Mauritania: The Role of Law in Development.* Boston: Boston University, African Studies Center, 1986.

Mohamed Fall Ould Ahmed. "La réforme mauritanienne en droit foncier." *Revue Juridique et Politique, Indépendance et Coopération* (Paris) 24, no. 4 (1970): 735–40.

Park, Thomas K., ed. *Risk and Tenure in Arid Lands: The Political Ecol-*

ogy of Development in the Senegal River Basin. Tuscon: University of Arizona Press, 1993.

Park, Thomas K., Mamadou Barro, and Tidiane Ngaido. *Conflicts Over Land and the Crisis of Nationalism in Mauritania.* Madison: University of Wisconsin Land Tenure Center (LTC Series No. 142), February 1991.

5. Social

Sociology, Archeology, and Religion

Abeillé, Barbara. *A Study of Female Life in Mauritania.* Washington, D.C.: United States Agency for International Development, Office of Women in Development, July 1979.

Bâ Oumar Moussa. *Noirs et Beydanes mauritaniens: L'école, creuset de la nation?* Paris: Editions Harmattan, 1992.

Briggs, Lloyd Cabot. *The Living Races of the Sahara.* Cambridge: Harvard University Press, 1958.

————. *Tribes of the Sahara.* Cambridge: Harvard University Press, 1960.

Centre d'Etudes Démographiques et Sociales. *Femmes et développement en Mauritanie: Actes du séminaire national organisé par le Centre d'Etudes Démographiques et Sociales (CEDS) à Nouakchott du 25 au 31 Janvier 1988.* Nouakchott: Centre d'Etudes Démographiques et Sociales (Les Séminaires du CEDS, No. 2), 1988.

Daddah, Amel. "State-Society Exchange in Modern Sahelian Africa: Cultural Representation, Political Mobilization, and State Rule (Senegal, Mauritania, Chad, Sudan)." Ph.D. Dissertation, University of Arizona, 1993.

Gerteiny, Alfred G. "Islamic Influences on Politics in Mauritania." In *Aspects of West African Islam,* ed. Daniel F. McCall and Norman R. Bennett. Boston: Boston University, African Studies Center, 1971.

————. "Mauritania." In *Islam in Africa,* ed. James Kritzeck and William H. Lewis. New York: Van Nostrand, 1969.

————. "Moors," "Soninké," and "Tukulor." In *Muslim Peoples: A World Ethnographic Survey,* ed. Richard V. Weekes. Westport, Conn. Greenwood Publishers, 1978.

Goodsmith, Lauren. *The Children of Mauritania: Days in the Desert and by the River Shore.* Minneapolis: Carolrhoda Books, 1993.

Ignegongba, Keymaye. *Fécondité et Ethnie en Mauritanie.* Bamako, Mali: Centre d'Etudes et de Recherche sur la Population pour de Développement, and Centre d'Etudes et de Recherches sur les Populations Africaines et Asiatiques, October 1992.

Laborie, Jean-Pierre, Jeaen-François Langumier, and Cheikh Saad Bouh Kamara. *L'urbanisation de la Mauritanie: enquête dans trois villes secondaires: Rosso, Kiffa, et Aioun el-Atrouss.* Paris: Documentation Française, 1988.

Lefort, François, and Carmen Bader. *Mauritanie: la vie reconcilée.*

Paris: Fayard (Collections "les Enfants du Fleuve"), 1990.

Lespés, Jean-Louis, ed. *Les Practiques Juridiques, Economiques et Sociales Informelles*. (Actes du Colloque International de Nouakchott, 8–11 December 1988). Orleans: Université d'Orleans et Université de Nouakchott, 1991.

"Littérature Mauritanienne." *Notre Libraire* (Paris, CLEF), nos. 120–121, January/March 1995.

Mamadou Hamidou Bâ. "Les tribus secondaires du Sahel Mauritanien." *Bulletin de la Société de Géographie et d'Archéologie de la Province d'Oran* (Oran, Algeria) (June 1933): 163–82.

Marchessin, Philippe. *Tribus, ethnies, et pouvoir en Mauritanie*. Paris: Editions Karthala, 1992.

Marty, Paul. *Etudes sur l'Islam et les tribus maures: les Brakna*. Paris: Editions Ernest Leroux, 1921.

———. *Les Tribus de la Haute Mauritanie*. Paris: Comité de l'Afrique Française, 1915.

Mauny, Raymond. "Les fouilles de l'Université de Dakar en Mauritanie." *Tropiques* (August/September 1961): 19–21.

———. "Notes d'Histoire et d'Archéologie sur Azougui, Chinguetti, et Ouadane." *Bulletin de l'Institut Français d'Afrique Noire* (IFAN) (Dakar) 17, nos. 1 and 2 (January/April 1955): 141–62.

Mohamed El-Mokhtar Ould Bah. *La littérature juridique et l'evolution du malikisme en Mauritanie*. Tunis: Faculté des Lettres et Sciences Humaines de Tunis (Publications de l'Université de Tunis, Faculté des Lettres et Sciences Humaines de Tunis, Sixième série, XIX), 1981.

Smale, Melinda. *Women in Mauritania: The Effects of Drought and Migration on Their Economic Status and Implications for Development Programs*. Washington, D.C.: Agency for International Development, Office of Women in Development, October 1980.

Wolff, Ursula. "Mauritania's Nomadic Society Preserves Its Lifestyle." *Africa Report* 17, no. 8 (September/October 1972): 11–16.

Geography and Urbanization

Arnaud, Jean. "Profils démographiques des villes de Mauritanie, d'après l'enquête urbaine de 1975." *Bulletin de l'Institut Fondamental d'Afrique Noir,* series B, vol. 38, no. 3 (July 1976): 619–35.

Brownlie, Ian. *African Boundaries: A Legal and Diplomatic Encyclopedia*. Berkeley and Los Angeles, University of California Press, 1979.

Caruba, Raoul, and René Dars. *Géologie de la Mauritanie*. (Institut Supérieur Scientifique de Nouakchott). Nice: CRDP/Sophia Antipolis, 1991.

Devisse, Jean, Abdourahmane Bâ, Claire Bernard, and Brigitte Bougerol. "Fleuve Sénégal: la question frontalière." *Afrique Contemporaine* (Paris) 154, (1990): 65–69.

D'Hont, Olivier. "Les kébé (bidonvilles) de Nouakchott." *Afrique Contemporaine* (Paris) 139, (1986): 36–55.

Furon, R. *Le Sahara: Géologie; Ressources minérales, mise en valeur.* Paris, 1958.

Greene, Mark. "Impact of the Sahelian Drought in Mauritania." *African Environment* (Dakar) 1, no. 2 (1975): 11–21.

Perta, Joseph, Roger Fourcade, Sonia Hammam, and Denis Light. *Mauritania: Shelter Sector Assessment.* Washington, D.C.: National Savings and Loan League, 1979.

Pitte, Jean-Robert. *Nouakchott: Capitale de la Mauritanie.* Paris: Département de Géographie de l'Université de Paris—Sorbonne, 1977.

Schissel, Howard. "Capital or Cancer?" *West Africa* (London), 19 March 1984.

Toupet, Charles, ed. *Atlas de la République Islamique de Mauritanie.* Paris: Editions Jeune Afrique, 1977.

————. "Les grand traits de la République Islamique de Mauritanie." *L'Information Géographique* (Paris) (1962): 47–56.

United States Agency for International Development. *Mauritania: A Country Profile.* Washington, D.C.: United States Agency for International Development, Bureau for Private and Development Cooperation, Office of Foreign Disaster Assistance, 1978.

United States Department of State. *Mali-Mauritania Boundary.* Office of the Geographer (International Boundary Study no. 23). Washington, D.C.: U.S. Government Printing Office, 1963.

United States Government. *Mauritania: Official Standard Names Approved by the United States Board on Geographic Names.* Washington, D.C.: Office of Geography, Board of Geographic Names (Gazetteer no. 100), 1966.

About the Author

Anthony G. Pazzanita is a writer and lawyer who holds an M.A. degree in political science and international relations from the University of Pennsylvania. Specializing in North Africa, he has published numerous articles on Mauritania, Algeria, and Western Sahara in various professional journals, and in 1995 visited Mauritania at the invitation of the University of Nouakchott. He is also the co-author (with Tony Hodges) of the second edition of the *Historical Dictionary of Western Sahara* (Scarecrow Press, 1994).